From Divided Pasts to Cohesive Futures

Today, the cohesion of multi-ethnic societies is at risk across the globe. Throughout history, to the present day, African countries have been facing this challenge. Historical inequalities and social division undermine cohesion and sow seeds of instability. How can Africa build a future where ethnic and other differences are a strength, a driver of growth and development, rather than sources of division and instability? Drawing together historians, economists and political scientists, each an authority on Africa, this book delivers a comprehensive study of that question through an exploration of the continent's divided histories, to understand where Africans stand now, and to reflect on how they might now work towards a more trusting society. Numerous case studies, statistical expositions and theoretical reflections bring conceptual clarity to the often poorly understood processes and contexts of social cohesion, not only in Africa, but across the developing and developed world.

Hiroyuki Hino is DUCIGS Fellow at Duke University and Visiting Professor at the University of Cape Town, where his field specialities are African economic development, social cohesion and poverty in Africa, and economic policies in Africa. He is a co-editor of Youth and Employment in Sub-Sahara Africa: Working But Poor (2013) and Ethnic Diversity and Economic Instability in Africa: Inter-Disciplinary Perspectives (Cambridge, 2012).

Arnim Langer is Director of the Centre for Research on Peace and Development (CRPD), Chair Holder of the UNESCO Chair in Sustainable Peacebuilding and Professor of International Politics at KU Leuven, Belgium. In addition, he is currently holding an Alexander von Humboldt Fellowship for experienced researchers at Ruprecht-Karls-Universität Heidelberg. He has published numerous articles and book chapters on matters of ethnicity, inequality and conflict.

John Lonsdale is a fellow of Trinity College, University of Cambridge where he retired as Professor of Modern African History. He was co-winner of the Trevor Reece prize in Commonwealth history (1992) with co-author Bruce Berman, for Unhappy Valley: Conflict in Kenya and Africa (1992), he has co-edited and contributed to Mau Mau and Nationhood (2003); Writing for Kenya: The Life and Works of Henry Muoria (2009); Ethnic Diversity and Economic Instability in Africa (Cambridge, 2012); and S. H. Fazan's memoir, Colonial Kenya Observed (2015).

Frances Stewart is Emeritus Professor of Development Economics, University of Oxford. Her previous publications include Advancing Human Development: Theory and Practice (2018) with Gustav Ranis and Emma Samman; Horizontal Inequalities and Conflict: Understanding Group Violence in Multiethnic Societies (2008); and War and Underdevelopment, with E. V. K. Fitzerald and others (2001).

From Divided Pasts to Cohesive Futures

Reflections on Africa

Edited by

HIROYUKI HINO
Duke University and University of Cape Town

ARNIM LANGER
KU Leuven, Belgium

JOHN LONSDALE
University of Cambridge

FRANCES STEWART
University of Oxford

CAMBRIDGE
UNIVERSITY PRESS

University Printing House, Cambridge CB2 8BS, United Kingdom

One Liberty Plaza, 20th Floor, New York, NY 10006, USA

477 Williamstown Road, Port Melbourne, VIC 3207, Australia

314–321, 3rd Floor, Plot 3, Splendor Forum, Jasola District Centre, New Delhi – 110025, India

79 Anson Road, #06–04/06, Singapore 079906

Cambridge University Press is part of the University of Cambridge.

It furthers the University's mission by disseminating knowledge in the pursuit of education, learning, and research at the highest international levels of excellence.

www.cambridge.org
Information on this title: www.cambridge.org/9781108476607
DOI: 10.1017/9781108645195

First published 2019

Printed and bound in Great Britain by Clays Ltd, Elcograf S.p.A.

A catalogue record for this publication is available from the British Library.

Library of Congress Cataloging-in-Publication Data
Names: Hino, Hiroyuki, 1945- editor. | Langer, Arnim, editor. | Lonsdale, John, editor. | Stewart, Frances, 1940- editor.
Title: From divided pasts to cohesive futures : reflections on Africa / edited by Hiroyuki Hino, Arnim Langer, John Lonsdale, Frances Stewart.
Description: New York, NY : Cambridge University Press, 2019. | Includes bibliographical references and index.
Identifiers: LCCN 2019005633 | ISBN 9781108476607 (hardback : alk. paper) | ISBN 9781108701136 (pbk. : alk. paper)
Subjects: LCSH: Cultural pluralism–Political aspects–Africa. | Ethnic conflict–Africa. | Africa–Ethnic relations–Political aspects.
Classification: LCC HN780.Z9 S623 2019 | DDC 305.80096–dc23
LC record available at https://lccn.loc.gov/2019005633

ISBN 978-1-108-47660-7 Hardback

Contents

Figures

Tables

Contributors

Ama de-Graft Aikins
Ama de-Graft Aikins is Dean of International Programmes and Professor of Social Psychology at the Regional Institute for Population Studies, University of Ghana (UG). She received her PhD in Social Psychology from the London School of Economics and Political Science (LSE) and completed postdoctoral training at the University of Cambridge. Her research focuses on experiences and representations of chronic physical and mental illnesses and on Africa's chronic noncommunicable disease (NCD) burden.

Kojo Sebastian Amanor
Kojo Amanor is a research professor at the Institute of African Studies, University of Ghana, with a background in political economy and anthropology. He mainly researches on land relations, agribusiness, smallholder agriculture, environmental and natural resource management issues, and south–south cooperation in Africa. He is currently working on agricultural mechanisation, long-term agrarian change within the cocoa industry, and the political economy of charcoal production, and is involved in a project on mitigating climate change for smallholders through tree management and planting.

Ernest Aryeetey
Ernest Aryeetey is a former Vice-Chancellor of the University of Ghana. Before his appointment as Vice-Chancellor, he was a Senior Fellow and Director of the Africa Growth Initiative at the Brookings Institution, Washington, D.C. He was also Director of the Institute of Statistical, Social and Economic Research (ISSER) of the University of Ghana, Legon for the period from February 2003 to January 2010. His research work focuses on the economics of development with interest in institutions and their role in development, regional integration,

economic reforms, financial systems in support of development, and small enterprise development.

Bruce J. Berman

Bruce Berman is professor emeritus of politics and history at Queens University, Canada. He was the Director and Principal Investigator of the Ethnicity and Democratic Governance Project from 2006 to 2012, and Smuts University Research Fellow at Cambridge in 2012 and 2013, and a recurrent visiting Fellow of Wolfson College since 2012.

Hiroyuki Hino

Hiroyuki Hino is a Visiting Research Scholar at Duke University and Visiting Professor at the University of Cape Town. He was Professor at Kobe University (2007–2015) and Visiting Professor at Yale University (2014–2015); Economic Advisor to the Prime Minister of Kenya (2009–2013); and Director of the Regional Office for Asia and the Pacific, Senior Advisor of the African Department, and others at the International Monetary Fund (IMF). Hino is an editor/author of several books on Africa's challenges, including youth employment and ethnic diversity.

Emma Hunter

Emma Hunter is Senior Lecturer in History at the University of Edinburgh. She holds a PhD in History from the University of Cambridge (2008). Her research focuses on the intellectual history of twentieth-century Africa. She is the author of *Political Thought and the Public Sphere in Tanzania: Freedom, Democracy and Citizenship in the Era of Decolonization*, published by Cambridge University Press in 2015.

Eric Kramon

Eric Kramon is an Assistant Professor of Political Science and International Affairs at George Washington University. His research focuses on clientelism, ethnic politics, and electoral accountability in new democracies, with a regional focus on Sub-Saharan Africa. His book, Money for Votes: The Causes and Consequences of Electoral Clientelism in Africa, was published by Cambridge University Press in 2018.

Line Kuppens

Line Kuppens is a Senior Education Advisor Primary and Secondary Education at VVOB – education for development; a Belgian-based

NGO which aims to improve the quality of education in developing countries. She is also post-doctoral research fellow at the Centre for Research on Peace and Development (CRPD) at KU Leuven.

Arnim Langer
Arnim Langer is Director of the Centre for Research on Peace and Development (CRPD), Chair Holder of the UNESCO Chair in Sustainable Peacebuilding and Professor of International Politics at KU Leuven. He is also associate researcher at the Oxford Department of International Development, Honorary Researcher at the University of Western Australia (Perth) and Alexander von Humboldt Fellow at the University of Heidelberg in Germany. He has published widely on matters of ethnicity, inequality, and conflict.

Murray Leibbrandt
Murray Leibbrandt holds the NRF/DST Research Chair in Poverty and Inequality Research in the Southern Africa Labour and Development Research Unit at the University of Cape Town. He is the Director of the African Centre of Excellence for Inequality Research. From 2007 to the present, he has served as a Principal Investigator on the National Income Dynamics Study, South Africa's national panel study. His research uses these and other longitudinal survey data to analyse South Africa's poverty, inequality, and labour market dynamics.

John Lonsdale
John Lonsdale is emeritus professor of modern African history and fellow of Trinity College Cambridge. Among his books are (as co-author) Unhappy Valley: conflict in Kenya and Africa (James Currey, 1992); (as co-editor) Mau Mau and Nationhood; (as co-editor) Writing for Kenya: The Life and Works of Henry Muoria (2019); and (as co-editor) Trinity: a Portrait (2011).

Ratjomose Machema
Ratjomose Machema holds an M.Phil. in Economics from University of Ghana and is pursuing a PhD in Economics from the University of Cape Town (UCT). He is also a lecturer at the National University of Lesotho (NUL). He has extensive background in strategic planning,

scenario building, and programme coordination. His research focuses on economics of inequality, impact evaluations, and health care.

Wilfred E. Mbowe

Wilfred E. Mbowe is currently a manager and researcher at the Bank of Tanzania. His research interest is on macroeconomic policies, international trade, regional integration, and the public sector. He holds a PhD degree in economics.

Abdul Raufu Mustapha

Raufu Mustapha was associate professor at the Oxford Department of International Development from 1996 to 2017. Before his appointment in Oxford, he held positions at Bayero, Kano, and Ahmadu Bello Universities in Nigeria. He was one of the foremost Nigerian scholars of politics, both making substantive contributions of his own and supporting young scholars in Oxford and Nigeria. His interests encompassed environmental management and agrarian transformations, ethnicity, religion, federalism, conflict and conflict resolution, and democratisation. He edited three major books on these topics and many articles, book chapters, reports, working papers and newspaper contributions. He was a member of the scientific committee of CODESIRIA, and the Board of Trustees of the Kano-based Development Research and Projects Centre (DRPC).

Benno Ndulu

Benno Ndulu currently holds the Mwalimu Nyerere Professorial Chair in Development at the University of Dar es Salaam. He has served as Governor of the Bank of Tanzania for the last 10 years. Previously, he served as the Executive Director of the AERC, Research Manager and Adviser at the World Bank, and Professor of Economics before that at UDSM. He has published widely on growth, macroeconomic policy, and governance.

Daniel N. Posner

Daniel N. Posner is the James S. Coleman Professor of International Development in the Department of Political Science at UCLA. He has written widely on ethnic politics, research design, distributive politics, and the political economy of development in Africa.

Gustav Ranis

Gustav Ranis was the Frank Altschul Professor Emeritus of International Economics at Yale University. He was Director of the Yale Center for International and Area Studies from 1995 to 2003, a Carnegie Corporation Scholar from 2004 to 2006, Director of the Economic Growth Center at Yale from 1967 to 1975, Assistant Administrator for Programme and Policy at USAID from 1965 to 1967, and Director of the Pakistan Institute of Development Economics from 1958 to 1961. Professor Ranis was author, co-author, or editor of more than twenty books and 300 articles on theoretical and policy-related issues of development to his credit.

Ciraj Rassool

Ciraj Rassool is professor of history at the University of the Western Cape, where he also directs the African Programme in Museum and Heritage Studies. He was a board member and chairperson of the District Six Museum in Cape Town and of Iziko Museums of South Africa. He serves on the board of the activist archive, South African History Archive. Among his co-authored and co-edited books are Museum Frictions: Public Cultures/Global Transformations (2006); The Politics of Heritage in Africa: Economies, Histories, and Infrastructures (2015); and Unsettled History: Making South African Public Pasts (2017).

Muna Shifa

Muna Shifa is a Post-doctoral research fellow, Southern Africa Labour and Development Research Unit, University of Cape Town. Her research is in development economics, with a particular focus on land tenure systems and rural livelihoods, subjective well-being and relative income, inequality and social cohesion, and urbanisation and development.

Crain Soudien

Crain Soudien is the Chief Executive Officer of the Human Sciences Research Council and formerly a Deputy Vice-Chancellor at the University of Cape Town, where he remains an emeritus professor in Education and African Studies. His publications in the areas of social difference, culture, education policy, comparative education, educational change, public history, and popular culture include three books, three edited collections, and more than 190 articles, reviews, reports, and book chapters. He was educated at the Universities of Cape Town and Unisa and holds a PhD from the State University of New York at Buffalo.

Frances Stewart

Frances Stewart is emeritus professor of Development Economics, University of Oxford. She has an honorary doctorate from the University of Sussex and received the Leontief Prize for Advancing the Frontiers of Economic Thought in 2013. Among many publications, she is leading author of Horizontal Inequalities and Conflict: Understanding Group Violence in Multiethnic Societies; and Advancing Human Development: Theory and Practice.

Motoki Takahashi

Motoki Takahashi is a Professor in the Graduate School of Asian and African Studies at Kyoto University; Professor Emeritus, Kobe University; and a member of Science Council of Japan. Takahashi has been the president of Japan Society for International Development and the Editor-in-Chief of the *Journal of African Studies and African Study Monographs*. He has authored and edited numerous books and articles on African political economy, socioeconomic development, and international aid.

Foreword

Divisions in a society – by ethnicity, race, and religion – have once again come to the forefront of the challenges that confront the international community. We now see greater incidence of conflict or tension, of differing scales and intensities, among people of different ethnic, religious, or traditional backgrounds in regions, villages, and communities in much of the world. Blaming globalisation for such divisions is short sighted. Religious extremism is deplorable and should be deplored. However, causes of social divisions are more complex and deep rooted.

How can we move forward to a cohesive society where diversity is not a cause of division, but rather a source of social enrichment and growth? It may be surprising to some, but the world has a lot to learn from Africa. In that continent, ethnicity evolved over centuries and diverse ethnic communities emerged to foster trade and commerce and as people migrated in response to climatic changes and in search of more fertile lands. The colonial regimes drew artificial ethnic boundaries solely to create their own administrative structures. With land having become more scarce and economic adversity severe, division among ethnic communities has become part of the social fabric in many parts of Africa. However, Africans have institutions and customs to manage conflicts that may arise from such divisions; there have been few major wars in the history of the continent. In contrast, in Europe, it took brutal wars that spanned decades to forge a more cohesive society. Indeed, African communities are naturally more multiethnic, multilingual, and multicultural than on any other continent.

This book draws together scholars of several disciplines, each an authority on Africa, to look back at history to see where we are now, to reflect on what the continent needs to make a transformation to where citizens live more peacefully with each other, and to conjecture what the future holds for its citizens. It reflects on what the world can learn from Africa to achieve cohesive futures. This book presents an exceptionally holistic and yet cohesive multidisciplinary exposition on managing diversity in Africa.

Contributing to peace and stability is one of the core principles that guide development assistance of the Japan International Cooperation Agency (JICA). Indeed, Japan's Constitution states in its preamble that 'We recognize that all people of the world have the right to live in peace, free of fear and want.' Thus, Japan has been a strong advocate of the protection of human security since the late 1990s, and it is now widely recognised that the international community has a responsibility to look after security of individuals, not national security alone. I strongly support this principle and will lead JICA to continue to make important contributions to peace and stability in the developing world.

It must now be evident to our readers that this book is a product of JICA's quest for peace and stability in the world. In October 2008, JICA Research Institute launched the research project 'Ethnic Diversity and Economic Instability in Africa' as one of its early initiatives. Recognising that the nature and consequences of interactions between ethnicity and economy critically depend on historical contingencies, political structures, constitutional designs, and economic circumstances, JICA drew together internationally renowned scholars in economics, history, political science, anthropology, and constitutional law from Africa, Japan, Europe and North America, to carry out this research. It was organised in collaboration with the Research Institute for Economics and Business Administration of Kobe University, and was led by Professor Hiroyuki Hino, former Consulting Fellow of the JICA Research Institute, Research Fellow of Kobe University, and now Visiting Research Scholar at Duke University and Visiting Professor at the University of Cape Town. The research was conducted under the guidance of the late Gustav Ranis of Yale University, Professor John Lonsdale of Cambridge University, and Professor Frances Stewart of the University of Oxford. This book is a sequel to the first publication of this project, *Ethnic Diversity and Economic Instability in Africa: Interdisciplinary Perspectives*, published by Cambridge University Press in 2012. I am grateful to Professors Hino, Lonsdale, Ranis, Stewart for their invaluable contribution to the project.

I believe that this book offers insightful reflections on and from Africa. It is my sincere hope that African governments and civil societies as well as international development institutions and indeed the international community will draw on the findings of this book in their respective efforts to enhance social cohesion in Africa and the world. On my part, I pledge that JICA will continue to make its contributions to peace and stability through development projects and research, in particular on poverty in disadvantaged areas and villages in sub-Saharan Africa.

Shinichi Kitaoka

President
Japan International Cooperation Agency

Acknowledgments

This book is the latest of several products from the research project, 'Ethnic Diversity and Economic Instability in Africa: Policies for Harmonious Development', which the Japan International Cooperation Agency Research Institute (JICA-RI) launched in October 2008 in collaboration with Kobe University Research Institute for Economics & Business Administration (RIEB). The project director was Hiroyuki Hino. In this project, JICA assembled a team of economists, historians, political scientists, and anthropologists from Africa, Japan, Europe, and North America, and organised a series of workshops in which members of the team contributed papers and deliberated on key issues. This book is a collection of the updated papers from those presented in the workshops, with a few papers added to make the coverage more complete. A first set of papers from the workshops was published in 2012 as *Ethnic Diversity and Economic Instability in Africa: Interdisciplinary Perspectives* (Cambridge University Press, 2012) .

We are most grateful to our colleagues in our team for remaining committed to the project for such a long time. We thank especially Professor Gustav Ranis, a leader and mentor of the team, who passed away in 2013. Sadly, another dear colleague and key driver of this project, Dr Raufu Mustapha, died earlier this year. Together they inspired many of the ideas discussed in this book – their contributions going well beyond the specific chapters they authored. We devote this book to their memory.

We are most grateful to JICA-RI for funding this project and taking care of its administrative and logistical arrangements. The project was also partly funded by a Grant-in-Aid for Scientific Research of Ministry of Education, Culture, Sports, Science and Technology, Japan (Grant number: 22330085). The views and opinions expressed in the book are those of the authors and do not necessarily reflect those of JICA or Kobe University.

We would like to express our sincere gratitude to Dr Keiichi Tsune-kawa, former Director of JICA-RI, and his successor, Dr Akio Hosono, both of whom provided strong support to this project during their tenure at JICA-RI. We are also deeply indebted to Professor Nobuaki Hamaguchi, Director of RIEB, for encouragement and guidance. In addition, we thank especially Mr Philip Good, Commissioning Editor of the Cambridge University Press, Economics and Finance, for his encouragement, guidance, and patience during the preparation of this book. Our thanks also go to the anonymous readers for their most helpful comments. Finally, we wish to thank Line Kuppens and Simon Saldner for their editorial assistance, and Ms Asaka Miyamoto of RIEB for her assistance in the overall management of this research project.

Introduction: Understanding Processes of Change in Social Cohesion: Learning from Comparative History

HIROYUKI HINO, ARNIM LANGER,
JOHN LONSDALE, AND FRANCES STEWART

The social cohesion of multiethnic states is today at risk across the globe. African states have been facing that risk since their independence from colonial rule more than half a century ago. As elsewhere in the world, Africa's histories of division and contest have sown seeds of political, social, and economic instability. However, Africa is not a place; it is a large continent. There are nearly 40 states south of the Sahara. A few are constantly wracked by instability, while the rest of the continent is experiencing considerable economic transformation. Ethnic conflict is not universal in Africa.

This book enquires into the historical roots of sub-Saharan Africa's internal divisions and, with insights from a number of scholarly disciplines, discusses the future prospects for building greater social cohesion. Africa's rich histories of varied social, political, and economic diversity and a brief review of comparative history give us our foundation for arguing that it is possible, but not easy, to grow cohesive futures out of the continent's divided pasts.

We do not ignore the natural temptation of ruling classes to cultivate their core votes in historically constructed fields of ethnic, religious, or regional difference. Our reviews of some of these histories and our case studies of the contemporary relationships between development and social cohesion nonetheless encourage us to look ahead towards more cohesive outcomes. On the basis of these case studies and our interdisciplinary research, we offer modest recommendations for policies and institutions that could foster more cohesive societies in future. We recognise the difficulties that stand in the way of their implementation. Nevertheless, we do not believe it is sufficient simply to try to manage the frictions caused by ethnic diversity, regional inequality, and social conflict.

1

While this book is primarily about sub-Saharan Africa, the continent is not alone in having to cope with the challenge of building social cohesion within multicultural nations. Even Europe's seemingly cohesive nationhood, products of centuries of warfare, face serious tests from a tide of migrants and refugees, driven by instability and hardship in western Asia and Africa and, more generally, by globalization. Africa has long known the pushes and pulls of globalization. We believe, therefore, that the rest of the world has something to learn from Africa. In more parts and periods of the continent's history than is often realized, one can discern deep traditions and pragmatic social practices that embraced multicultural, multilingual, and multiethnic yet neighbourly living. How far that wide experience of an often flourishing plurality has been compromised by colonial and postcolonial oppression is one of our questions. A brief excursion into comparative history also suggests that, to build socially cohesive societies in Africa, such as can be seen in Tanzania in particular, has little instructive precedent elsewhere in the world. First, however, we must clarify what we mean by social cohesion.

I.1 The Concept of Social Cohesion

"Social cohesion" is a complex concept, variously understood from different perspectives. However, we believe that at its heart lies the notion of a society that is greater than and therefore protective of its various parts. Such a society allows its individual members and their several smaller communities of cultural, regional, gendered, or religious belonging to pursue mutually fruitful relationships with confidence. When differences develop in a cohesive society, as is only to be expected, they can also be expected to be resolved openly, amicably and peacefully. Further, "social cohesion", it has been said, "is not only good in itself, as it improves the quality of the societies in which people live, but also because it is likely to help avoid violent conflict with all its attendant ills" (Langer et al., 2017). Despite an increased recognition of the importance of social cohesion for political stability and development, the concept remains poorly researched and understood. This point, we believe, is where this book has something to contribute by separating out the social attributes that, in our understanding, are constitutive of social cohesion.

Following Langer et al. (2017), we argue that social cohesion is founded on the connections between three major elements, each being largely determined by historical and political forces. These elements are identity, equality, and trust, variably linked in different chains of causation. Identity can take many forms and is adaptable to different contexts. Inclusive or plural senses of identity foster social cohesion; conversely, in the absence of such cohesion, identities of exclusion can be exaggerated. Exclusive identities place prime, or even sole, value on their specific, often ethnic, communities, especially in contexts of threat. Where ethnicity is politicized and people see themselves, whether defensively or triumphally, as belonging primarily to a particular group rather than to the nation as a whole, then the cohesion of a society is clearly at risk.

It follows that policies conducive to social cohesion must aim to weaken exclusive identities and strengthen inclusive ones. This point is where our second element, equality, comes in. While the presence of severe income and wealth inequalities is generally bad for the cohesiveness of a society, social cohesion is particularly under threat where there are marked disparities between identity-based groups or so-called horizontal inequalities (Stewart, 2008). Severe horizontal inequalities are almost bound to sharpen ethnic consciousness, and grievances are likely to fester among members of disadvantaged groups, creating resentment against not only those who are better off but also, very probably, against the incumbent government or indeed the state itself. At the same time, the richer communities will use all the means at their disposal to preserve, or even increase, their privilege. Inequality is, therefore, not only damaging in itself, but may also contribute towards destroying the third element, trust – whether between individuals or between identity groups and, in consequence, between large sections of the population and their government. The more widely and deeply people trust other persons, people from other ethnic groups and their common public institutions, the more cohesive their society is likely to be.

All this may seem rather obvious, but it is a useful framework to think about social cohesion, not least because these strong interconnections suggest that, where social cohesion is lacking, the politics of creating it will not be easy. Each of these three elements will react against the other elements. For example, building trust between groups

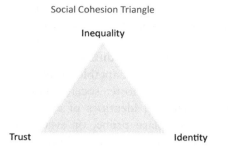

Social Cohesion Triangle

Inequality

Trust   Identity

Figure I.1 Social cohesion and its building blocks
Source: Langer et al. (2017: 327).

will be difficult when their history has made group identities inward-looking and strong. Africa's economic history, in particular, has generated severe horizontal inequalities that tend to sharpen resentful perceptions of more successful regions, generally the territory of some other, often proudly different, ethnic group (Chapter 1). There is no simple causal chain here but, rather, a mutually reinforcing set of factors that increase or decrease social cohesion and that are, therefore, difficult to break by political intervention. We can think of the elements of social cohesion as a triangle of mutually dependent building blocks, and triangles are notoriously resilient figures, resistant to reconfiguration.[1]

I.2 Social Cohesion in Comparative History

How, then, can history's triangles of social division, lacking in sufficiently inclusive identities and mutual trust, or tolerable inequalities, be reconfigured? Outside observers have too often regretted that African nations fall short of the democratic standards and economic productivity that encourage social cohesion in most European nations and a few Asian and Latin American states. It is true that some countries enjoy enviable levels of social cohesion based on democratic practice and a high regard for human rights reliably protected in law. But, whether one looks at Europe, Asia, or the Americas, these relatively cohesive societies are the products of violently divisive pasts – of dynastic wars, civil wars, revolutions, or class conflict between owners

---

[1] This is elaborated in Langer et al. (2017).

and workers. For many of them, too, any experience of colonial subjection is in their distant past, quite unlike Africa's more recent ordeal. If, then, one looks at comparative history, one can only conclude that, if Africans so wish, they will have to build social cohesion in their own more deliberate way, as some African countries are already doing.

Not so long ago, in May 2000, the cover story of London's influential weekly *The Economist* called Africa a "hopeless continent" on which the rest of the world "might just give up", It did not accuse Africans of racial incompetence but blamed, instead, a triple alliance of tribalism, dictatorship, and corruption – all being the fruit of Africa's divided histories (Lonsdale, 2002). In 2000, there seemed to be much truth in that generalisation. There is much less now. Many Africans have long tried to tackle their problems, as *The Economist* has acknowledged in a more recent issue with its cover entitled "A Hopeful Continent", African societies, after all, are not normally at war with each other. What Africans have been learning in how to foster social cohesion from their divided pasts may, therefore, help others to resolve the tensions in what more and more Westerners feel is their own dangerously diverse present. It has often been argued in the West that Africans should learn more of the political arts as practised in the West. It seems to us that it is time to ask what the West – because so many of its peoples see multilingual, multicultural diversity as an entirely new threat – might, to the contrary, learn from Africa.

To ask that question productively it is as well to remember that popular memory can be short and that the West, no less than Africa, has in fact always faced conflicts of cultural and religious diversity as well as social and regional inequality. Politically destabilising migrations, conquests, culture conflicts, and regional disparities are nothing new in Europe. In the past, European kingdoms and their republican successors had to reach (always provisional) solutions to the challenges that human and geographical diversity presented for the creation and maintenance of relatively cohesive societies, to recall our triangular model, that can solve differences by constructive argument rather than disruptive violence. The Kikuyu of Kenya, and doubtless other African peoples, have an apt proverb to illustrate the virtues of such openly argumentative cohesion: "He who is defeated by a club can always return to an argument; he who is defeated by argument never returns."

It has taken centuries of warfare, with weapons more deadly than clubs, for Europe to accept the wisdom of this African proverb. To appreciate this point, one needs to think more about the historical construction of modern European states, for in our triangular model of social cohesion – of trust, identity, and equality – the role of state-building is central. Without trustworthy public institutions, whether legislative, judicial, or executive, social trust is impossible. If the law is corrupted, self-help, the ultimate expression of exclusive identity, becomes the first recourse in settling disputes. In the same way, arbitrary rule, reliant on surveillance rather than consent, inevitably creates a fearful mistrust between neighbours. Confidence in the same shared public institutions, on the other hand, may well generate a sense of common identity, equality of citizenship under an impartial law, mutual trust, and, in sum, what we have called social cohesion.

But how was the West's relatively high degree of trust, inclusive identity, and equality before the law – none perfect and all dependent on constant vigilance – achieved in the struggles of Europe's past? The answer is not one that anybody would wish on Africa. For in the past half millennium, Europe's political foundations were dug in blood by religious and dynastic warfare. By the eighteenth century CE the military–fiscal state was a common phenomenon, demanding ever more from its subjects in blood and treasure. This forced them, in reaction, to struggle to be recognised as citizens, with a voice to which governments must respond. They were helped by a parallel process in which print capitalism and growing literacy gave access to mass-produced vernacular bibles that told how a prototype nation, the children of Israel, could overcome conquest and unjust rule. An often-turbulent dialectic between state-building for the purpose of external military competition and the emergence of discursive, potentially subversive, internal public spheres saw a growing identity between state and nation. Central to this process for the stronger European states in the nineteenth century was compulsory education in a standardised national language and conscription into a national army, both in the name of national defence and international competitiveness.

So, peoples were educated for war, for industrial efficiency, and, through their own struggles, for political participation. The almost inevitable consequence, so our hindsight suggests, was the ghastly carnage of the twentieth century's two intra-European civil wars that became world wars, thanks to the geographical range of Europe's empires. They produced blood and destruction across the world, not least in Africa. But they also produced, in Europe, alert citizenries, all – including rich and poor, women and men — now equipped with the franchise, a tool of peaceful social argument, of more inclusive identity and wider trust, even an increase in material equality. Some identity struggles persisted even then, and violently, as in Northern Ireland or the Basque region of Spain. But how terrible was the price that this relative national cohesion had cost, including not only the carnage of world wars, but also the loss of historically rich group identities, languages, and cultures as the price of national integration?

One can find other global examples of large-scale state-making by warfare in the history of successive Chinese dynasties, the Mughals in India, or the several Muslim caliphates of West Asia (the Middle East from another perspective) and Mediterranean Africa. In a historical contrast of great importance for national integration and social cohesion, sub-Saharan Africa's past saw few such state-building histories, and its longest-lived state, Ethiopia, was more of a confederation of regional baronies than a unified monarchy. The nineteenth-century *jihadi* cavalry states of the Western Sudan, the forest kingdom of Asante, lakeside Buganda, and the pastoral Zulu kingdom were all relatively short lived, owing to the coming of European colonial conquest. They have nonetheless shown a remarkable afterlife in their sense of cultural identity in the larger postcolonial states of Nigeria, Ghana, Uganda, or South Africa within which they are now enclosed. But nobody would propose further war as the way to future social cohesion in Africa.

Industrialisation, to turn to a related argument drawn from comparative history, accompanied and intensified the wars of the West. Naval dockyards were the first large-scale factories, and the officers who commanded navies and armies were among the first technically qualified professionals. Britain's industrial revolution gave it a strategic advantage, accordingly; steamships and trains were good at transporting troops. Other nations industrialised to compete. But industry – and this is another point of contrast with Africa – also created new, centralised, forms of social belonging, as regionally dispersed peasantries came to town and discarded their provincial dialects and customs to join in the urban, socially cohesive possibilities of collective action as a working class.

The modern Western state, born in war, prepared for war, and for that reason all the more fearful of the internal social conflicts bred by inequality, had to protect its legitimacy and internal peace by increasing expenditure on social protection for the poor. This aimed to recreate that sense of a moral economy of reciprocal responsibility, of social trust, however unequal, between capitalist owner and worker, rich and poor that had once existed, at least in folk memory, between master and servant, farmer and tenant, in the pre-industrial age that had gone (Polanyi, 1944). The nationally connected economies that were created by industry also gave people, even the poor, an incentive to be a part of the national society, their only hope for social mobility out of misery. But this long European dialectic of increasing social cohesion through successive attempts by ever stronger states to mitigate class conflict has little relevance for Africa, with its limited industrialization and lack of historically strong states.

Africa in the late twentieth and early twenty-first centuries has certainly experienced the urbanisation of nineteenth-century Europe, but not the industrialisation that might create both a national economy and a national argument about the unequal social entitlements associated with class difference that Europe has known. Most Africans remain largely self-employed primary producers; many others are self-employed in the informal sector in the growing cities. The infrastructure connecting people across a country is also often weak. Within many countries, their regions' specialised primary producers supply external markets at least as often as they promote national unity by trading with each other. Ethnic identities are often built on regional identities that thrive on whatever economic specialisation is encouraged by their natural environment. Cocoa, cotton, or coffee all need different ecological conditions and produce different social and market relations; regions too dry for such crops or too distant from a railway may have only migrant labour to export, an experience that can produce its own tight-knit identities of survival.

If European history, with its growing national arguments about the socially divisive costs of war and industry, is therefore irrelevant to Africa, what about more recent East Asian history? Might this offer to Africa's future a model of state-led industrialisation for export, with its parallel potential for enlarging more inclusive national identities? Again, the model seems scarcely relevant. East Asia's industrialisation, from Japan's in the past to China's in the present, was achieved on the shoulders of often long histories of monarchical state-building and its social disciplines, together with national education systems and intensive agricultures able to feed rapidly growing towns. Africa's past has by contrast been largely one of ecologically rather than politically efficient productive systems, based on local peasant freedoms and shifting cultivation. African states, therefore, with their very different pasts, and as even later industrialisers than East Asia, would find it difficult to initiate and sustain a similar economic revolution. Even the continent's existing extractive industries will not be easily detached from global supply chains, particularly those linked to China, for the purpose of building, downstream, a manufacturing industry of their own. Globalization makes new industrial start-ups ever more difficult.

We conclude, therefore, that sub-Saharan African countries must chart and make their own path towards greater social cohesion. Comparative history, we suggest, offers no useful models for either state-sponsored or class-contested social cohesion. True, the continent's present states were also created by wars. But those were colonial conquests, small wars apart from the Italian conquest of Ethiopia in 1935 or the earlier Anglo–South African wars, and with few Africans trained in new solidarities to fight them. Although some still-independent African kingdoms imported large quantities of firearms in the late nineteenth century, their wars of resistance to conquest were soon over; they created few new loyalties from below. From above, the new colonial conquest states were alien, not national; they ruled over division and, unlike their own European imperial powers at home, had no interest in national integration before their final years. Nor, in general, apart from white-settled southern Africa, did national liberation require more than brief mobilisations of political solidarity. Neither colonial states nor, therefore, their postcolonial successors, depended for survival on the creation of the social and economic sinews that dynastic or international competition had previously demanded of states elsewhere in the world.

Therefore, given sub-Saharan Africa's historic singularity– with its lack of a long history of state-building, the absence of integrated national economies, its religious plurality, its many ethnic communities, and, today, the fastest population growth in world history – the continent's statesmen and women face extraordinary demands on their political imagination, authority, and integrity. They have no useful leaders to follow, neither a Cromwell, Washington, nor Robespierre; neither a Stalin nor Mao Dzedong; nor even the more attractive figure of Pandit Nehru, given his political assets in India's relatively sophisticated industry and large middle classes in 1947.

Africa's leaders, now and in the future, are and will be, pioneers, setting out from very particular pasts and building on what are often quite substantial achievements since independence, for what can only be unexplored futures.

I.3 The Argument of this Book

Africa is a continent where, according to opinion surveys, interpersonal and political trust is more limited than elsewhere; its ethnic identities can seem to be exclusive, often touched only lightly by the more inclusive, plural, or situational identities that are more commonplace elsewhere; and its gendered, regional, and social inequalities can be stark. Of course, none of these generalisations is universally true. If they were, then Africa might indeed approximate the *Economist*'s hopeless continent. It is not – and the three sections into which this book is divided in their several ways show why this is so.

The five case studies of past and present that set the scene in Section I, are studies, above all, of changes in identity, trust, and inequalities, not of rigid and unyielding division. The seven chapters in Section II offer reasoned ideas for policies and institutions that are designed to encourage social cohesion. However, because they are in conflict with the political interest of incumbent elites whose power has been built on division, these ideas will be hard to put into sustained political practice. In Section III, which ties the book together, the first chapter shows how urgent and varied are the various areas of social and economic policy that can build on cross-cutting, inclusive, identities – of gender, class, and age – that animate all civil relations throughout Africa. Whether the policies and institutions discussed in Section II are introduced and sustained depends in large part on whether these nonsectarian identities can be persuaded to become active, inclusive and powerful political constituencies.

To turn then to Section I, Lonsdale's chapter on Kenya (Chapter 1) and Mustapha's on Nigeria (Chapter 2) well illustrate the political contingency of ethnic loyalties and their historical variability. No imaginable future can, therefore, be declared impossible, a conclusion that is reinforced by the reading of the common citizenship that has emerged in Tanzania, as analysed by Ndulu, Mbowe, and Hunter (Chapter 3). The post-Apartheid South African story, as told by Hino, Leibbrandt, Ratimose, Shifa, and Soudien (Chapter 4), further reinforces this theme. The identities of race and ethnic groups became more mutually inclusive with the birth of a democratic nation, but have turned more exclusive again, partly because of an increase in inequality between racial and ethnic groups whose relations are historically difficult and partly because of growing social inequality within them. The first chapters rely, implicitly, on the understanding that all group identities are to some extent fluid and mixed, not easily classified or measurable. The last chapter in Section I, by Berman and Takahashi, thus dismisses the Ethnolinguistic Fractionalisation Index as a basis for an analysis of Africa's situation. Berman and Takahashi place ethnic conflict in Africa in a global context and argue that such conflict is not the source of the crisis, "but a response to the impact of globalization on historic vertical and horizontal cleavages and a growing threat to social cohesion" (Chapter 5). The solution to ethnic conflict must therefore be found in part of "a global approach to achieving greater equity and security for the populations of all nations".

Section II explores different aspects of our approach to those futures. Stewart starts us off by showing that there is no necessary conflict between individual, social, or regional equality and economic growth because a more equal distribution will tend to improve public services more widely and, with them, social cohesion and political peace (Chapter 6). Ranis makes a similar case for the deconcentration and devolution of executive state power, the competition for the exclusive enjoyment of which is often held responsible for many of Africa's interethnic conflicts (Chapter 7). Amanor then discusses sub-Saharan Africa's perhaps most fundamental challenge: the reform of its many intricate systems of land tenure. If property rights are rationalised for greater productivity, many relations of trust stand to be destroyed, and many identities threatened (Chapter 8). Educational reform would be equally complex and controversial. Kramon and Posner show how closely unequal access to education can be related to the regional partisanship of power (Chapter 9); and Kuppens and Langer's proposals for multicultural education would challenge some current patterns of power. Given past histories of inequality and its conflicts, the teaching of history must be a matter of deep controversy (Chapter 10). But Rassool shows us just how vital the rememorialisation of past injustice is if subjected people are to recover their trust in the state and emerge from a hurt and resentful identity (Chapter 11). Mustapha's second contribution to the book is unblinking in its discussion of how difficult greater social cohesion will be to build, even where the political will exists (Chapter 12).

Section III nonetheless rounds the discussion up on a cautiously hopeful note. Aryeetey and de-Graft Aikins remind us just how varied Africa's many interest groups and identities can be, how rapidly urban and religious contexts are creating new and possibly less manipulable, more critical, publics (Chapter 13). In the last chapter, Langer and Lonsdale draw out the main conclusions emerging from the different contributions to this book and reflect on the way forward in terms of policy and reforms to establish more cohesive futures in Africa.

References

Langer, A., Stewart, F., Smedts, K. and Demarest, L. 2017. Conceptualising and measuring social cohesion in Africa: Towards a perceptions-based index. *Social Indicators Research*. 131(1): 321–343.

Lonsdale, J. 2002. Globalization, ethnicity and democracy: A view from "The hopeless continent", In Hopkins, A. G. (ed.), *Globalization in World History*. London: Pimlico, pp. 194–219.

Polanyi, K. (1944) *The Great Transformation: The Political and Economic Origins of our Time*. Boston: Beacon Press.

Stewart, F. (Ed.). 2008. *Horizontal Inequalities and Conflict: Understanding Group Violence in Multiethnic Societies*. London: Palgrave.

PART I

Social Cohesion in Africa: Case Studies of Past and Present

1 | Kenya's Four Ages of Ethnicity

JOHN LONSDALE[1]

1.1 Argument: From Moral Ethnicity to Political Tribalism

Our various human civilities are taught and disputed within circles of belonging; most of us have a couple or more of these communities that in different contexts we can call our own. These situational identities differ in their existential importance; the fellowship we feel most deeply is likely to be our ethnicity. This imagined community – "imagined" because we cannot know all its members (Anderson, 1983) – is not easy to define. Its supposedly shared history will nonetheless shape our "overall fabric of ideas" (Anderson & Broch-Due, 1999, p. 10). Its cultural disciplines, taught from childhood, stimulate argument about our self-conduct, rights, and duties (Waller, 2013). The Kikuyu people sum up these tensions of belonging in the proverb: "those without previous dealings with each other have no cause to quarrel" (Lonsdale, 1992, p.463). Our ethnicities encourage this competitive thought and behaviour in two dimensions, internal and external. Within our groups, we try to attain the civic virtues that, in defining "us", also generate mutual trust, so that the poor, who cannot meet certain obligations, are often despised (Tilly, 2005). As an imagined community we also compete, rhetorically at least, with "others", a flexible category that can enable "them" to become "us". The French and English, for instance, see each other as cultural opposites but in some contexts become fellow Europeans, "sweet enemies" (Tombs & Tombs, 2006). These various "levels of intimacy" (Spear, 1978, p. 5) differ in size and intensity, from close kin and region to common language, religion, or nationality, and even humanity. We are formed, as well, by gender, generation, class, and profession, identities that are to varying degrees transethnic. Ethnicity itself comes in many shapes and sizes, able to expand or split. Some groups are loose knit, others

---

[1] I thank David Anderson, Ian Parker, Richard Waller, and Tom Wolf for wise comments.

hierarchical, some unreflective majorities, others prickly minorities. But, whatever the case, in Kenya and all over the world, it seems that formerly fluid ethnicities with fuzzy, neighbourly, frontiers are becoming more "tribal", with harder borders, endangering the cohesion of citizenship. This chapter explores possible reasons why.

To portray ethnicity as a fluid, layered, category frustrates precise analysis, but social historians welcome inexactitude because, unlike clean models of rational conduct or authentic culture, it makes the historian's chief interest, change, easier to explain. The "creative imprecision" (Waller, 1993b, p. 297) of social imaginations permitted change in precolonial times, and change is what many Kenyans hope for today. But we need a minimal definition of ethnicity if the term is to have any use. In brief it is, in general, an imagined moral community of any size between several thousand to many millions of people, very like nationhood, but also, like nationhood, with historical reasons for unease. Felt by its members to be united by history and language, its singular myth of origin will almost certainly mask a complex, uneasy, past. This history has the potential to break in on the present, to divide what seems to be whole (Geschiere, 2009). Some Britons, for instance, feel they are an "island race"; some French believe their ancestors were all Gauls: both are misled by historically constructed myth. Simple narratives of political destiny have to forget past hybridity and conflict (Renan, 1882). Moreover, nations or ethnicities have always entwined with neighbours in restless "ethnoscapes" created by cultural and religious diaspora or expanding empires (Appadurai, 2000, in Bayly, 2004, p. 44). Pure, unalloyed cultures are illusory (Bayart, 2005; Chabal & Daloz, 2006) – as, for example, Sikh and Catholic Britons or Luo and Muslim Kenyans well know. But illusions are what people live by and what Kenya's parents are not alone in teaching their children, telling of ethnic purity and difference rather than of the reality, plural nationality (Ngarachu, 2015).

Our cultures, however mixed or shared, rest on moral economies – realms of mutual obligation, historically negotiated to legitimise, for the moment, the always unequal social relations within and between ethnic groups (Siméant, 2015). When times change, as they do, moral economies become articulate public spheres of anxiety; people ask how far relations must be reinterpreted – in households, between patrons and clients, men and women, first and later comers, rulers and ruled. When drought decimates herds or commercial capitalism enters a precapitalist economy of reputation, when literacy appears in the arms of a new religion, or kinship is stretched by migrant labour, when rich and poor begin to live separately, appeals to moral economy animate patriotic debate – if by patriotism, "left" or "right", one means a concern for the social justice that a community deserves. People will ask: who still owes what to whom? Do social climbers have a duty to those they leave behind, or are the new poor themselves to blame, undeserving of patronage, no longer "us" (Anderson & Broch-Due, 1999)? Domestic debate arouses ethnic awareness as much as external threat. "There is nothing so inflammatory as a call for the return of an imagined realm of virtue and justice" (Schama, 2009, p. 89). A sense that one's moral ethnicity, as I have called it (Lonsdale, 1992, pp. 461–468, 2012, pp. 25–32), is being betrayed can stimulate the angriest of public spheres. In Kenya, this intimate unease has varied in regional intensity, so that some groups have pursued with more determination than others the state power with which to heal communal wounds. This competition for the state, over which Africans had no control before independence in 1963, has at election times required of each ethnic group a previously unknown degree of solidarity while also exposing them to the risk of opportunist secession. This combination of ambition and anxiety generates what Kenyans call negative ethnicity, a euphemism for what I call "political tribalism" (Lonsdale, 2003).

The idea of different intensities of belonging helps us to think about our multilayered ethnoscapes: global, national, and what used to be called "tribal". A growing appearance of pan-national belonging may, for instance, seems to sustain international capitalists or the migrant workers they employ around the world. But do such global class relations warrant an ethnic label of belonging (Cohen, 1974)? Surely not unless, that is, bosses come to imagine Alexander the Great, Tamerlane, or other world-bestriders as ancestors and believe neoliberalism to be their moral economy. Migrant workers might also "belong" together globally if, improbably, they recognised as their forebears past pilgrims to Rome or Jerusalem, Mecca or Bodh Gaya (Bayly, 2002, p. 43, pp. 351–357). But, and here's the point, however much these shallow, transactional identities at present lack the sense of historical continuity characteristic of ethnicity, they can still attract ethnic hostility. Less mobile people resent both the globally privileged and the migrant masses, rootless citizens of nowhere or unfair competitors in the labour market, disruptive of local loyalties. Moreover, similar transactional beginnings in dynastic war, commercial or sectarian competition, class struggle, and so on, have been the anvil on which nation states have been forged, the least worst guarantors of political legitimacy, with rulers supposedly accountable to a rights-bearing citizenry. Just as global oligarchs share no ethnicity, historians know there is nothing natural about nation states, as shown in this book's concern for their cohesion. And the Western nation state – the model against which Africa is wrongly measured – is, as our Introduction reminds us, the product of a blood-stained past in which statesmen tried, at the cost of pogroms, Holocaust, and two world wars, to construct monoglot, quasi-ethnic, communities. Who is to say that global ethnicities cannot be imagined in the future? The notion of single European nations has needed centuries of story telling, forgetful of sedimented immigrant strata, religious dissidence, and civil or industrial conflict. Many-stranded histories are now more than ever needed, inclusive of minorities sensitive to the insult of oblivion, whose diverse numbers will only increase in future (Eisenberg & Kymlicka, 2011).

Like others at the time, Mugo Gatheru underestimated the risks of single-stranded nationhood when at independence he dedicated his autobiography, *Child of Two Worlds*, to "a future Kenya nation in which tribalism has become only a historic memory and tribes' mere ceremonial units" (Gatheru, 1964, p. v). He failed to see that African nation-builders, like Europe's nationalist historians, would have to choose whom to embrace and whom to exclude, or that ethnicity would still flourish as a readily constructed pressure group, to command state favour or to combat its neglect. "Constructed" is the right word – not to imply that any old ethnicity can be invented, but that in its historical malleability the ethnic idea possesses different potential uses and harms (Spear, 2003). Just as historians deconstruct national myths, therefore, we have dropped the term "tribe", to combat the common illusion that African tribes are primordial, natural lineages of kin descended from particular ancestors lost in the mists of time. Africans can certainly hold such ideologies of linear descent, like European national myths, for they mask past disruption and pain; more positively, too, they authorise the household discipline, reciprocal obligation, and patron–client negotiations that constitute moral ethnicity, an African portfolio of insurance premiums (Lonsdale, 1977b). Gatheru ignored these benefits of belonging, perhaps because he was also blind to its underlying anxieties. For Kenya's academic historians agree – against popular belief – that none of the country's current ethnic groups is unchangingly primordial. Like all nationalities, they have diverse immigrant pasts, potential animators of secession today (Ayot, 1979; Fadiman, 1993; Iliffe 2007, pp. 10–12; Makila, 1978; Muriuki, 1974; Mwaniki, 1973; Ochieng', 1974; Ogot, 1967; Spear, 1981; Were, 1967). They have also been stretched by migration to Kenya's towns or in global diasporas, while preserving rural homelands that still reclaim their dead (Cohen & Atieno Odhiambo, 1992; Maupeu, 2003a, 2003b). There are contrary loyalties to call on here. Politicians in search of vote banks can choose among layers of laminated identity, whether an historically immigrant clan or the larger community that for the moment calls itself a tribe, or the urban workers for whom interethnicity makes daily sense, the last being the threat behind two political assassinations – of Pio Gama Pinto in 1965 and Tom Mboya in 1969.

The premise of hybrid or situational layers of ethnicity, then, is as important as the concept of moral economy in understanding historical change and its limits. East Africa's regional culture has always, as elsewhere in the world, traded ideas and institutions of social action between its ethnic categories. We know of three phases of cross-border adaptation in Kenya's history. Different peoples long ago learned from their neighbours the social disciplines encouraged by age and generation sets, and exchanged the seeds of new food crops or cross-bred livestock. In the colonial era, local religious entrepreneurs adapted world religions, Islam and Christianity, to their own beliefs; literate elites translated imperial doctrines of progress into ethnic patriotisms. Templates of trusting conduct are still more varied today. Kenya's elites play golf in multiethnic clubs (Connan, 2013), intermarry, and deploy their graduate children across the world. The poor get along with each other in multiethnic slums. Nongovernmental organisations offer advice to both. Kenyans can, therefore, look to find trust in three dimensions: within their ethnic moral community, in instrumental electoral coalition with other such groups, or even among people they see as fellow middle class or slum-dwelling citizens, regardless of ethnicity (Bratton & Kimenyi, 2008; but see Chapter 13). This choice helps to make change thinkable. In a lively press, Kenyans criticise the horizontal inequalities between regions that generate interethnic hostility, and the social differentiation – vertical inequality – within them that ethnic solidarity hides (Brown & Stewart, 2012). As this chapter suggests, this lively public sphere could well find helpful precedents in the ancestral past.

There is nothing peculiarly Kenyan in the way that its layered loyalties might stimulate cohesive action. Knowing scripture as they do, Kenyans might ponder a precedent 2,000 years old. In religious shock, Saul of Tarsus took a new name, Paul, and, like many Kenyans, changed his ritual allegiance. Born a Pharisee, he became a Nazarene or Christian, but kept his Hebrew nationality and his tribe of Benjamin. As a Roman citizen, he nonetheless felt bound to criticise his people's contempt for "others": Jews should not call all Cretans liars nor should they value their distinctive initiation ritual, circumcision, above their common humanity – a notoriously divisive issue in Kenya. Plural, situational identities may well, on this evidence, fortify self-confidence and, with it, the power to change history.[2]

Eighty-year-old Perus Angaya Abura of western Kenya, interviewed in 2009, took the same inclusive, Pauline view of cultural diversity. A census enumerator, had he been able to find her, would have offered her a choice of three identities under which to register: national, ethnic, or subethnic. Perus had been born into the Kisa section of the Luhya people; her husband was from next door, Isukha. She would have liked to choose a fourth option, "all of the above", had it been available: "'Kenyan,' 'Luhya,' 'Isukha,' 'Kisa,' how can I choose? I am all of these" (MacArthur, 2016, pp. 1–3). She was not alone in this view, especially after conflict between one of the identities on offer, ethnicity, had proved so lethal in a general election only two years before .

1.2 Four Ages of Ethnicity

Since 1900, Kenya's ethnic self-awareness and interethnic relations have been transformed in response to new contexts of economy, power, population, and communication. Argumentative ecological ethnicities have become more obedient political tribes. Their external relations, formerly a kaleidoscope of livestock theft, marriage, trade, and contracts of survival between famine refugees and their more

---

[2] Acts 21:39, 23:6 and 27, 24:5 and 14, 28:17; Philippians 3:5; Titus 1:12–14; for circumcision, Romans 2:25–29, Corinthians 7:19, and Galatians 5:6.

fortunate neighbours, have been scarred by violent electoral contests for state power.

Before 1900, groups were defined by the expertise they needed – as hunters, herders, or farmers – to master specific environments. Their moral economies celebrated the skilled household or herd management that attracted industrious clients and affinal allies who, without much concern for their origin, were expected to strengthen the social resilience needed to survive recurrent natural disaster. Authority was dispersed. Interethnic relations were largely complementary, bartered between comparative ecological advantages enjoyed in producing skins, livestock, legumes, and grains. Conflict was fiercest when pastoralists had to compete for sweet pasture, *ntoror* to the Maasai, when it withered in recurrent dry seasons or became scarcer still when, less frequently if just as predictably, successive rainy seasons failed.

Colonial conquest set the context for a second ethnic age. Kenyans were quick to realise that the most creative resistance to subjection was to be of use to the new state. Argument about this alignment helped an ethnic group to define itself, as elders came to reluctant terms with their young, the mission-taught "readers", so called, moral innovators (Hutchinson, 2013), with offensive new ways. This sharper imagination of ethnic community also owed much to the print with which readers could convene a wider vernacular audience than the little neighbourhoods that gave ear to elders. Readers also claimed citizenship of the imperial world for their newly conceived people, not to compete with neighbours but to win a civic equality with the white settlers, whose needs the British rulers met largely at African expense.

Interethnic competition, the third age, had, however, emerged by the 1940s, thanks to the structural differentiation created by new markets in produce and labour, rather than by either British or African intent. Inequalities developed within and between ethnic regions, beneath the privileged white settlers. In an agricultural–educational revolution, pastoral peoples lost out to peasant farmers whose young took more eagerly to school (see Chapter 9). The gap between them widened further when social differentiation threatened the moral economy of the agrarian Kikuyu, one-fifth of Kenya's population. A few of these had done well out of colonial rule, but many more had suffered. In the 1950s their "Mau Mau" insurgency gave Kikuyu a two-fold political advantage: it showed that they harboured more dangerous discontents than others; it also taught their "loyalists", so called, how to suppress even dangerous rebels. Here were the roots of the current, fourth, age of Kenyan ethnicity that, to flourish, needed only the addition of full African access to state power.

Independence in 1963 gave Africans that power – to choose between claimants, to welcome some and deny others (see Chapter 5). Ethnic competition has intensified accordingly. For nearly sixty years (almost as long as the colonial era) ethnic coalitions have alternately allied with or opposed a dynastic Kikuyu class, to control the state. The main policy question has been how far power should be concentrated or devolved. To centralise power rewards the ethnic, regional winners of the agrieducational revolution. The losers have sought protection, especially against the winners' colonisation of their land, by demanding a devolution of power, formerly to a few large regions and now, under a new constitution, to many small counties. It is not yet clear how far this reform will disarm the conflicts of political tribalism, to usher in a fifth age of ethnicity more comparable with the first (see Chapter 7).

To sum up this potted history: ecological ethnicities with divided counsels and relatively peaceful relations have become political tribes, obedient to dynastic patrons who trade on fears of exclusion from state power. Many of today's leaders have generations of privilege behind them, with grandfathers who were colonial chiefs or mission teachers (Kipkorir, 1969). Population growth has decreased the price of clients and increased the cost of household self-mastery beyond the reach of many. New forms of communication have hardened ethnic division by reaching wider audiences. Changing attitudes to immigrant strangers best reveal the difference. In the thinly populated, stateless, past, economic migrants from famine were welcome as scarce labour and, for lack of other options, were willing to be adopted as dependants into another ethnic group. In colonial times, migrants became resented as "infiltrators", unwilling to take a new identity when already protected by a church or employer. In recent decades, finally, many thousands who lived outside their "home" districts have been ethnically cleansed, even killed, as "foreign colonies" on the land of indigenous others, electoral rivals for state favour (quote from Sang, 2015, p. 359; see also Jenkins, 2012).

This chronology has less to do with ancient tribal rivalry than with changing contexts of survival. Personal security requires trustworthy relations. In precolonial times, people negotiated oral contracts of horizontal solidarity, lopsided clientage, and marriage, face to face, within pedestrian circles smaller than their ethnic culture. Ethnic groups have since become communities of trust and interethnic conflict has grown in parallel. In a national arena ruled by ethnic prejudice and adjudicated by mistrusted public institutions (Mueller, 2008), people have to trust in linguistic kin too numerous to know in person, but with whom a common history can be imagined in print, on the buses, and in social media. This segmented enlargement of the moral horizon is Africa's equivalent to European nationalisms (Berman & Lonsdale, 2013). Political tribes are not anachronisms, but creative responses to a modern world filled with anxiety, putting trust in leaders who know how to exploit it.

1.3 Uncertain Times

Kenya's past two centuries, less than one-third of them under colonial rule, have been anxious times. Disquiet has grown in step with the increasing population and greater state power, wider communication, the tension between pastoral decline and agrarian development, and, underneath all, the erosion of household disciplines.

The colonial, now postcolonial, conquest state, able to allocate assets to some and not to others, has enlarged the scale of mistrust (see Chapter 5). As power has widened its reach, so personal self-mastery has diminished. In former times, one could negotiate access to grazing, arable land, or water face to face; by the later colonial period, differential human possibilities were decided by expert estimates of which regions would best grow marketable crops, especially coffee or tea, among Kenya's most profitable exports. This differential trend in opportunity has since accelerated with a logic of its own: public investment in schools, clinics, roads, and energy tends to flow to already wealthy regions, with leaders well-practised in the exercise, and enjoyment, of power.

As divisive state power has grown, so too has the distance between patrons and clients, previously householders and their dependants, today politicians and electors (Ogot, 1999). Demography has reinforced this trend. Since 1900, Kenya's population has increased twenty-fold, from around 2 million to more than 40 million. In line with Africa as a whole, this is the most rapid demographic increase in world history – a classic recipe for political instability (Iliffe, 2007, pp. 250–252). Human needs have also increased, together with a reliance on strangers to supply them. Before 1900, one's rights to life's essentials, land, livestock, and useful labour, were embedded in reciprocal social relations. With population scarce and natural resources abundant, clients had some, if little, room to bargain the price of their support between potential patrons. Today, resources are scarce, or owned by the few, and populations large. This reversal of relations between resources and people, land and labour, is modern Africa's most fundamental social change, causing a crash in the value of people, especially the poor (Lonsdale, 2012, p. 25). Patrons once had to be privately generous to attract clients; today's politicians must be publicly astute. They no longer offer competitive rights in the use of their own land or livestock in return for loyalty and labour; they deal, instead, and profit in, the supply of scarce public assets to a community – roads, schools, hospitals, building contracts, and so on. This gives them a power unimaginable to precolonial "big men". Their ability to mediate between the only available state and their own section of a clamant citizenry rests on their reputation within whichever turns out to be the ruling coalition. Their constituents hesitate to vote for any candidate other than the one favoured by the probable winning side. Political tribalism's fear of exclusion from state largesse is stronger than any patriotic concern for an ethnic champion's character or policy (Burbidge, 2014), a situation leaders are not slow to exploit for private gain.

The growth of power and population are the more menacing when set against the shrinkage of time and space. In the 1890s, it took three months to walk, at 15 kilometres per day with porters each carrying 30 kilograms of goods, from the Indian Ocean to the Victoria Nyanza, from Mombasa to Kisumu. After 1901, it took two days by rail at 10 per cent of the cost; after 1920, 24 hours by car in the dry seasons when roads were not "black seas" of mud, as white settlers called them. Now one can fly. The space of opportunity has shrunk accordingly. This cuts the more deeply because of its contrast with the experience of an earlier generation, for whom, contrary to common belief, colonial rule enlarged domestic space. Pax Britannica allowed downhill migration from stockaded villages into their surrounds, formerly left empty at night for fear of strangers. White settlers also opened up what had been thinly peopled Maasai pasture to farm "squatters", labour tenants, before mechanisation in the 1940s allowed them to throw these largely Kikuyu families back into their "native reserves". Today, Kenyans crowd together in some of Africa's largest slums where more than one-half the population is under twenty years old, underemployed, and with little hope of respectable adulthood (Van Stapele, 2015). Language has also become more threatening. Before 1900, it needed half a dozen languages, audible only within earshot, to talk one's way across "Kenya"; now only two – Swahili and English – serve to negotiate or intimidate, on air, in the press, or by cell phone. Conflicts used to evaporate in small cockpits of oral debate; now, they fester in the national arena, in print, on air, on-line.

Regional inequality reflects another revolution. In colonial times, agriculture trumped pastoralism and created an unequal political economy. Herders whose capital is in livestock do not need a state; seasonally indebted commercial farmers do. States, in turn, dislike mobile pastoralists but need taxable peasants, workers, and clerks. Kenya's white settlers needed a state to build a railway, seize land, create a labour market, guarantee loans, and so on. Today's ethnic relations reflect this revolution; the Rift Valley is its battleground. In the nineteenth century, Maasai fought Maasai for control of rainy season pastures on the valley floor and the dry season plateaux on either side (Waller, 1973). Both the nature of the Rift's competition and its contestants have changed – from seasonal grazing to national elections, from scores of spearmen to millions of voters. Rift Valley constituencies, one-quarter of the total, are among the most marginal, thanks to their two layers of colonisation. Maasai and Kalenjin pastoralists used to rule the Rift. The British expelled both from many of their best lands, to make room for settlers (Hughes, 2006; Waller, 1976), who, in turn, recruited largely Kikuyu labour tenants, only to expel most of them after 1945. These groups have returned in ever larger numbers since independence. The Rift's former pastoral autonomies have twice given way, first to a vanished white colonisation and now to a largely Kikuyu agrarian occupation, late-comers whose growing numbers can contest with the first-comers who will rule Kenya.

This power transfer, from cow and spear to hoe and pen, has created a partisan politics. Maasai were once called the "Lords of East Africa". The new aristocracy are facilitators for global capital, allied with local tea or coffee tycoons, maize magnates, or cut-flower kings. In the past, barefoot warriors controlled grazing, water, and salt licks; farm exports help to pay police and bureaucrats. The state sees sedentarisation as the solution to pastoral poverty, but pastoralists are humiliated when forced to become the cultivators they once despised (Anderson, 2002). The graduate grandsons of peasant farmers run this state. Agricultural growth among western Kenya's Luo and Luhya, together with Kikuyu and their highland neighbours, financed missionary schooling. Pastoralists and the coast's Muslims were left behind (Cruise O'Brien, 1995, p. 202). Tax registers, censuses, and maps completed their undoing: the 1948 census revealed that pastoralists who occupied three-quarters of the land were fewer than one-fifth of the population. It is no surprise that these peoples, educated later than the cultivators, have often called for a decentralised state. But the three-quarters of the population, peasants, artisans, and townspeople, who live on 12 per cent of the land, mostly within three hours' drive from the capital, Nairobi, have an equal interest in centralised government (Branch et al., 2010, p. 4).

Change has been even more brutal in intimate relations, what matter most. Ben Kipkorir's autobiography (2009) illustrates the tension between his seniors' sense of order and the new freedoms enjoyed by the educated minority of his own generation. His story raises two questions for social historians, central to the self-examination of moral ethnicity. Was his father's house liberated by its Christian literacy or enslaved to new domestic disciplines that clearly alienated his mother? How painful was what we blandly call social change? Second, if Kipkorir gained personally from his education, did the unlettered majority of his Marakwet people thereby lose? In changing times, those who alter least may lose the most in unseen opportunities.

Households used to be the dutiful nexus of labour relations before colonial capitalism enlarged labour's sphere, to cause domestic conflict and ethnic anxiety. Young men and women worked for seniors who controlled the assets one invested in marriage, to start a household, their culture's prize. Generational conflict over this reward for labour was endemic; a father might acquire a new wife before allocating the livestock of bridewealth to an unmarried son. But these conflicts were fragmented, household by household. Labour became mobile only when, in lethal famines, big men abandoned their clients or juniors in the selfishness of survival, leaving them to seek a new dependence elsewhere – as servants, pawns, or cut-price brides (Waller, 1985; 1988). Kenya's languages have long lexicons of social inequality, poverty, and shame (Iliffe, 1987, pp. 68–70). But refugees only changed households, adopted as fictive kin. They were not a labour pool, nor was there an employer class, only a mosaic of domestic enterprise. Colonial rule changed all this, first with the push of conscription and taxation, and then with the pull of market demand for farm or railway labour, domestic service, or clerical office. Young men could now follow their own route to adulthood, no longer reliant on parental largesse; women also evaded rural patriarchy to become urban traders (Kanogo, 2005; Robertson, 1997; Thomas, 2003; White, 1990). Labour became more "free" in Marx's terms, escaping household control. Elders complained that young people who "absconded" to town were "lost" to decent society. The range of moral anxiety expanded, linking rural and urban households (Weisner et al., 1997). Ethnic patriots felt unprecedented collective shame when rural households learned of the sexual laxity of their urban young (Peterson, 2012). Coastal Muslims, townsfolk for centuries, were similarly scandalised when upcountry Christians, drinkers, footballers, English-speakers, captured the local labour market (Strobel, 1979, pp. 34–36).

Anxiety, then, has been the crucible for ethnic self-consciousness and conflict. The youthful freedom of the early twentieth century has become for many the pauper shame of unachieved adulthood in Kenya's slums. But for their ancestors, the early nineteenth century could be a still more terrible time.

1.4 Ecological Ethnicity: Age One

Most of Kenya's modern peoples arrived within the past millennium (Ehret, 1998; Sutton, 1973, 1993). A triple theme of plural origins, growing specialisation, and interethnic exchange is the best guide to understanding centuries of change, governed by a dramatic topography of forested highlands, savannah plateaux, green valleys, and arid plains. Ecological diversity supported distinctive modes of production: hunting, fishing, farming, mixed agropastoralism, or herding alone. Different skills fostered systems of knowledge and trust, the cultures of ecological ethnicity (Feierman, 1990; Lonsdale, 2012, pp. 29–30; Spear, 1981, pp. 74–75). Environmental difference also stimulated exchange. Before 1900, "Kenya" existed primarily as a regional market – in goods, marriage, fashion, armaments, ritual, concepts of divinity, and social institutions (compare: von Oppen,

1993). Tiny populations hospitable to strangers had to work at ways of living that, each in their own ecosystem, encouraged growth in good seasons and resilience when times were bad. In displacing earlier Khoisan-speaking hunters, Kenya's immigrants brought with them Africa's three great language families, Afroasiatic or Cushitic from northern and northeast Africa, Nilo-Saharan or Nilotic from the Nile basin, and Bantu from the Niger-Congo region, the language group that has colonised most of tropical and southern Africa (Iliffe, 2007, pp. 10–12).

Productive specialisations had to be learned. Ethnic cultures taught local knowledge by celebrating the steps in life that led to wealth and wisdom. In tribute to their reproductive power, heads of polygynous households shaped values and hierarchies (Kenyatta, 1938, p. 9, p. 76, pp. 174–175, pp. 315–316). Wealth came from and in turn attracted the service of scarce people. Argument about this household honour (Lonsdale, 2005, pp. 110–112) is centuries old. In the ancestral language of the Luhya-speaking group, now of western Kenya, it seems that, although some believed wealth was honourable, others condemned it as selfish, acquired at others' expense (Stephens, 2016). Precolonial moral economy is egalitarian only in rose-tinted retrospect. The elders' calls of *atiriri aGikuyu* or *kalenjin*, and in other languages – "I say to you" – invited discussion on legal issues more often than they summoned to war. Ties of trust and obligation were to small platoons: to shallow lineages around three generations deep, to affinal kin, age sets, trading partners, or clustered clients. The marriage alliances of the wealthy, insurances taken out against the drought or disease that killed the poor, could give birth to clans that straddled ethnic borders. Ethnic origin myths – when told to the earliest colonial enquirers – told of polyglot migration from different directions (Ambler, 1988; Muriuki, 1974; Were, 1967).

Oral tradition is tight-lipped about past disaster; "famine" is rarely found in the index of local histories. But it is now clear that much of central Kenya suffered catastrophic drought, possibly thirty years long, in the early nineteenth century. The Rift Valley's lakes almost dried out; one of them, Baringo, was completely desiccated for perhaps twenty years. Pastoralists were hardest hit, but Kikuyu also recall a killer famine, *kirika*, "destruction", of the 1830s. Mortality rates can only be guessed. When the rains returned, societies were recreated as if at the beginning of time: age sets and ritual generations are rarely remembered earlier than the 1840s. But demographic and economic recovery was swift, spurred by social and economic innovation in which some peoples took up laboriously irrigated agriculture and others concentrated still more on their herds (Anderson & Bollig, 2017; Kershaw, 1997, pp. 13–46).

Interethnic marriage protected the trade that specialisation promoted (Marris & Somerset, 1971, pp. 23–54; Spear, 1993, p. 120). Grain and livestock had seasonally varied barter rates; women exchanged seeds across linguistic borders (Hay, 1971). Ethnic neighbours came to dress alike: wire and beads decorated head, ears, neck, and arms in a common "East African silhouette". Ethnic styles differed within a shared aesthetic (Klumpp & Kratz, 1993). Warrior fashion was catching, too, the fearsome Maasai setting the standard (Muriuki & Sobania, 2007). Yet "Kenya" scarcely appears in the only history of East African warfare; its peoples were raiders, not campaigners. They lacked the stamina of state power, with its military elites and tributary peasants – unlike Ethiopia or the Ugandan kingdoms (Fadiman, 1982; Reid, 2007). Colonising groups could displace or absorb others; young men also had a predatory need for livestock to invest in marriage and reproduction. But sustained "tribal rivalry" was rare, except in the dry north, where seasonal grazing orbits were vast and reliable water holes far apart. No ethnic group had the sort of authority that could determine what one could call "foreign policy". The most destructive war occurred within an ethnic group, as Maasai competed for the pasture of recovery after the early nineteenth-century drought. They had no use for the lands of others, too wet in the hills, too dry in the northern plains (Spear, 1993; Waller, 1985).

Armed clashes stirred an interethnic market in shared disciplines that made fighting more efficient. Different peoples borrowed and adapted a stock of institutions that created the solidarities of age and generation. Youths were initiated into age sets that climbed age grades of growing self-mastery – held in tension with generation classes of judicial authority that men paid to enter when, as mature household heads, they became eligible. These balanced constitutions set warrior spirit against elders' caution. In the nineteenth century, they seem to have been reinterpreted in favour of warriorhood, thanks – speculatively – to the rise of a transethnic school of prophecy, wandering intellectuals who supplied a market demand for prediction, explanation, and social solidarity, possibly to aid recovery after the drought decades. Maasai *laibons,* Nandi *orkoiik,* the *abbu boku* of the Boran, Meru *agwe,* and other seers aroused a sceptical awe; Nandi went so far as to kill a failed prophet. All saw them as "others", without kinship. Emollient elders resented their charisma. But the dreamers protected warriors from sorcery and purified them before a raid; some instigated a new intensity of combat (Bernardi, 1959, 1985; Berntsen, 1979; Lamphear, 1992, pp. 27–32; Peatrik, 1999, p. 336, pp. 353–354, p. 367, pp. 377–379; Waller, 1995). But not invariably. Among the lakeside Luo – with neither age nor generation classes – their prophetic *jabilo* won occult knowledge by visiting Maasailand, land of the *laibons,* but their influence was more civil than martial. They were said to be able to restore social order whenever mediation was needed (Whisson, 1962, pp. 12–14).

Prosperity seems to have rewarded the specialisation that followed the dry decades. Growing populations had to be fed (Spear, 1981, p. 66); the spread of the hardy zebu cow raised pastoral productivity; maize did the same for farming; ivory exports benefited hunters (Lamphear, 1970). Imported beads allowed greater ethnic variety in adornment (Klumpp & Kratz, 1993, p. 197). Busier markets seem to have prompted more ethnic stereotyping, perhaps only because European travellers were now on hand to record it. To herders and farmers, hunters were paupers, *il-torobo;* farmers thought herders idle; herders despised sweaty farmers (Lonsdale, 2002a, pp. 305–314, 2008a; Spear & Waller, 1993, p. 7, p. 50; Waller, 1999, p. 26). Luo, disliked as market "hagglers" (Bienda, 1973, p. 37), feared the Nandi as *jolango,* possessed by the excitable spirit of battle; Maasai disparaged Kipsigis as herders who had taken up the hoe. In the arid north, Boran distinguished full members with rights to core pastures from lesser herders in border areas, "the land of fools" (Oba, 2013, p. 12). Stockaded villages in southern Kikuyu protected against Maasai raids and coastal slavers (Leakey, 1977, pp. 128–130). This insecurity had a long history, seen in the fortified *kayas* of the Mijikenda people inland from the coast (Spear, 1978), and the care with which ancestral Kalenjin hid their cattle in "Sirikwa holes" (Sutton, 1973).

The 1890s offer grim evidence of how natural disaster could raise antagonism. In a terrible decade, drought and cattle plague exposed huddled refugees to epidemic smallpox, so that it became rational to fear rather than welcome strangers (Ambler, 1988, pp. 122–157; Fadiman, 1993, pp. 108–120; Waller, 1988). It was during this episode of a doubtless recurrent pattern of interethnic suspicion that the British extended control over Kenya with a splatter of small wars (Lonsdale, 1989). So a "polyglot collection of communities" became a colony through a mix of "force, diplomacy, *and epidemics*" (Ndege, 2001, p. 159, my emphasis; Waller, 1993a, p. 227). Kikuyu were among those who tried to cleanse their land of evil, but famine and disease clung on (Lonsdale, 1992, pp. 344–346); southern Kikuyu pioneers retreated north, vacating their fertile frontier, what became the colonial district of Kiambu. To the British, it cried out for productive white settlement, casting a racial shadow over Kenya's future (Sorrenson, 1968). But Kiambu also led the way in creative African resistance.

1.5 Patriotic Ethnicity: Age Two

One might expect that the conquest that initiated my second age of ethnicity would have two consequences. Resistance to invasion might infuse mundane ethnic practice with tribal sentiment, as in southern Africa (Mahoney, 2012; Ranger, 1967). And "collaborators", so-called, who helped the British to enter might be remembered as traitors. Neither assumption is true of Kenya. African communities did not reform to fight and there were too many British allies for any to be subsequently condemned.

Apart from the Turkana in the north, no ethnic group united to resist conquest (Lamphear, 1992). Not all Nandi, the next most resistant people, supported their embattled *orkoiyot* (arap Ng'eny, 1970; Matson, 1972a). Elsewhere, it was not ethnic solidarity but lineage and locality, the lowest levels of intimacy, that inspired defiance (Anderson 2004; Lonsdale, 1977a, 1989). The British found allies everywhere, opportunists who got the red strangers to crush local rivals and then sponsored missionary schooling: a history of interethnic borrowing had taught them to learn the secrets of another's strength. Many dynastic fortunes among Kenya's political class stem from early decisions to ally with the new power.

The Maasai exception to this generalisation is instructive. The warriors who initiated the *il Dwati* age set in the disastrous 1890s needed to rebuild their herds. So they volunteered to act as "native auxiliaries" in British "punitive expeditions" against others. After what were, in effect, cattle raids, the British paid the Maasai in much of the confiscated stock. The *il Dwati* became wealthy elders and, holding sway for an unusually long time, helped the British to frustrate the dreams of their warrior successors (Waller, 1976, 1988, pp. 110–111). Maasai as a whole lost rather than gained. The British twice moved these picturesque but periodically famished pastoralists from their best Rift Valley pastures before 1914, to allow whites to occupy the colony's strategic core (Cashmore, 1965, pp. 137–165; Hughes, 2006). Of all Kenya's peoples, Maasai lost the most land to the colonists. This British betrayal may explain why their "collaboration" has been forgotten. Moreover, many who suffered from Anglo-Maasai raids then profited more lastingly by taking to the schooling that the pastoralists spurned. The agricultural–educational revolution was soon under way.

The politics of memory (compare with Chapter 11) has, in consequence, erased all but patriotic heroes from early colonial history by changing the definition of heroism over time. Between the wars, the first literate historians to look for reputable ethnic pasts focused on leaders who had helped rather than opposed the British; they were not traitors, but enlightened innovators or, at worst, innocent dupes of deceitful imperialists (Kenyatta, 1938, pp. 44–52; Lonsdale, 1995). More recently, the search for a unifying national story has focused on their opposites, local resistance leaders. To remember only these as heroes, forgetting the modernisers, has silenced divisive questions about who, the cultivators, profited by the British conquest at whose, the pastoralists', expense.

Resistance to conquest had failed to unify ethnic categories into more coherent "tribes". In due course, this creative process was stimulated by the way in which Africans explored colonialism's possibilities as the better way to resist its threats. Here we enter into what used to be a heated controversy over the origins of modern political tribalism, once supposed to be an embarrassingly antique survival. The baleful inventiveness of colonial "divide and rule" used to be blamed (Ranger, 1983; Vail, 1988), so denying Africans any moral imagination of their own. Historians today tend to credit Africans with the common desire to look again at their moral ethnicities to live as well as possible with colonialism's constraints and opportunities (Iliffe, 1979, pp. 318–341; Hastings, 1997, pp. 148–150; Ranger, 1993; Reid, 2011).

Alien rule and social change did indeed divide, but within ethnic groups before it did so between them. The community-building arguments of moral ethnicity preceded the divisive competitions of political tribalism. How reciprocal obligations could survive the emergence of private interests forged by alliance with alien power, literacy, produce markets, and migrant labour soon exercised elders' councils. This next creative age of the ethnic imagination also turned to issues of external policy. After their sacrifices for the empire in the First World War, Africans were angered by postwar oppressions. Fresh demands for land and labour were poor reward for the blood and treasure they had spent in helping to drive the Germans from "German East", now Tanzania. But they also received a helpful tutorial in politics from a noisy competition for local supremacy between white colonists and the more numerous Indian immigrants, each exercising their rights as imperial citizens. Some Africans dared to hope they too might attain that citizenship and so challenge colonial subjection. Throughout history ethnic patriots have looked to the world for the defence of local interests (Geschiere, 2009).

Africans faced three levels of British power – imperial, colonial, and local. Kenya's white racial supremacy denied them a voice at the middle, colonial, level. After a little more than a decade of missionary schooling in "upcountry" agricultural districts some "readers" tried to outflank the white settlers with progressive ethnic culture, not to compete with other ethnicities, but to attract imperial favour, a strategy that exploited the concessions with which the British tried to silence them. After the police dispersed a Nairobi mass meeting in 1922, killing some twenty-five, the British offered imperial citizenship in theory and local responsibility in practice. They rushed out a KiSwahili official newspaper, *Habari*, or *News*, in which they assured Africans that Kenya's recent change in status, from protectorate to colony, constituted a promise, not a threat. In the East African Protectorate (as Kenya was before 1920), Africans were *wageni*, foreigners. In a colony they became *raia*, British subjects equal in status to the settlers (*Habari*, 1 July 1922, p. 13). Africans took this assurance more seriously than the British must have intended, but did so initially at the local, district level, which had been designed for them by the colony's administrative framework.

As elsewhere in colonial Africa, the British imagined an internal ethnic coherence and interethnic separation that Kenya's peoples had never known. New administrative districts supposedly enclosed "tribes" or sections of larger ones. This political grid hardened ethnic frontiers; it made it easier to count taxpayers and set "native authorities" over them, where such authority had rarely existed before

(Berman, 1990, pp. 199–255). Plural identities that had previously ensured survival now looked like tax evasion or, on the northern frontier, mutiny (Oba, 2013, pp. 59–88). The British were trying to create identifiable subjects, a status humiliatingly inscribed after 1918 with an identity tag, the *kipande*, for male migrant workers, who were filed under chief *and tribe*. But officials were also committed to a "progress" that created personal ambition and careers inherently subversive of any supposed tribal order. In 1925 the British tried to square this circle by instituting Local Native Councils. Chiefs were councillors ex officio, but in "advanced" – that is, agricultural – districts there were elected majorities from the start, drawn from the mission churches (Omusule, 1974, p. 195). Local Native Councils, among the most progressive local governments in British Africa, levied a local rate to fund schools, clinics, roads, and so on, under the chairmanship of British district commissioners.

One can understand why such a process, paralleled elsewhere, gave rise to the thesis that colonial rulers knowingly created modern tribalism as an alliance between white officials and African elders. Because each sought social control in the face of change, they were said to have invented an unprecedented degree of ethnic cohesion by codifying for each imagined tribe the procedures and penalties of its "customary law", contrary to the contextual flexibility of past judgments. Few now support this thesis; it neglected two sets of evidence. The first is the local tradition of institutional, social, and economic innovation of the first ethnic age in which African thought was set, to ignore which is to credit colonialism with an unlikely degree of transformative power over credulous natives (Reid, 2011). Second, while the British might preside over vernacular debates on who had which rights over what resources, they could scarcely participate in them; moreover, in many cases their codification of law stirred up dispute rather than resolved it (Beidelman, 2012; Berry, 1993; Phillips, 1945). Africans pursued these arguments within colonial administrative structures, certainly, but based them on their own usefully reimagined histories (Heald, 1999, pp. 147–149; Lonsdale, 1992; Osborne, 2014; Ranger, 1993; Spear, 2003). Only Africans could resolve the contradiction with which the British had complicated their lives, between "tribal order" and new identities – teacher, midwife, clerk, nurse, police inspector, and so on.

There is good evidence, in the cases of the Luo, Luhya, Kikuyu, and Kamba, that unlettered senior elders (with nearly adult children) did indeed argue out the issues with literate, junior elders (with young children). Seniors complained of household disorder. In their large new world of print, readers tried to reconcile them by building, in a wider household idiom, the reputable ethnicities that would earn imperial citizenship (Lonsdale, 2009b; Peterson, 2012). This creative imagination of a purposeful, coherent, community, reconciled to modernity, could only be African, never British, the fruit of an intergenerational argument about moral ethnicity. The British were more sympathetic to the elders, for social order was the basis of rule (Morris & Read, 1972, pp. 167–212). The household patriarchs of the major agrarian peoples, Kikuyu, Luhya, and Luo, complained of sons who came home "spoilt" and selfish after working elsewhere (Beech, 1912; East Africa Protectorate, 1913, pp. 149–163, pp. 201–241). Young women were still more of a worry, especially if self-willed enough to become Christian and marry one. British law made them legal adults, able to choose whom to remarry if widowed (Kanogo, 2005, pp. 150–154). This breach of parental rights scandalised southern Kikuyu elders, who demanded that all Kikuyuland's best elders be summoned to decide what to do (Northcote, 1912). When household authority, the core of moral ethnicity, was threatened, it was Africans who called for an ethnic forum, not the British. Elders were equally concerned for the safety of the land. Before the Kenya Land Commission (CPK, 1933), Kikuyu put forward the best defence of their land they could imagine. They denied they had ever been the complex mix of immigrants they had earlier admitted to being by telling of their laborious agrarian progress as a purely indigenous people. In their case, as in others, to invent tradition was to try (in vain) to thwart the British, not to ally with them.

Younger readers, moral innovators like the prophets of the past, had to enter this politics of local knowledge. Elders initially regarded their Christianity as cultural treachery. Readers had to reassure them of their obedience if fathers were ever to release to them the bridewealth that made Christian marriage respectable. Readers not only felt a duty to those who had paid for their schooling (Kipkorir, 1972), but also felt better able than elders to combat the modern disorder of cultural amnesia. They had acquired a purposeful, biblical model of history that showed that the children of Israel had repeatedly saved themselves from slavery by recalling who they were. Kikuyu readers founded the first African-owned newspaper, *Muigwithania, The Reconciler*, in

1928, to acquire a convening power independent of the British, a print public sphere wider than an elder's voice could carry (Lonsdale, 2005; Peterson, 2003, pp. 93–99). The pen, a modern spear, could also set down the customs that memory forgot. Minutes of meetings, membership lists, and correspondence files kept order; tea parties open to all taught etiquette better than the beer drinks only elders could enjoy. Christian knowledge, in short, was not the enemy, but rather the renovator of tradition, able to persuade the British to listen without betraying their people.

Young Luo agreed. The modern Luo nation was repeatedly born in Nairobi's railway station when the night train took migrant workers back to their regional capital, Kisumu (personal observation). Paulo Mboya, knowing that nations needed a memory, set down Luo traditions in a book often reprinted, *Luo Kitgi gi Timbegi* (Mboya, 1938, p. 9), so that they were not "lost to our children". Christianity and custom, again, were complementary; people could not "develop well with imported traditions if they discard their own practices and counsels". He thought, like the Gisu along the Uganda border, that the value of "tradition" lay in the authority with which fresh knowledge was transmitted, not in unchanging rules (Heald, 1999, p. 153). If a community forgot its laws it would fall apart, unable to win "a good reputation before other nations in which people are ruled by their own customs". Mboya, like Kenyatta, felt that the British, progressive rulers who valued tradition would respect a patriotic ethnicity built on adapted custom and adopted progress. Among Kenya's three largest peoples, the Luhya of western Kenya argued differently, but to the same effect, that one of their local leaders, Mumia, Kenya's nearest approximation to a constitutional (rather than colonial) chief, had proved his sovereign equality by his treaty relations with Queen Victoria (MacArthur, 2016, pp. 101–102).

Less favoured regions tried to attract imperial notice by other means. The pastoral Pokot proudly paid more tax than their farmer neighbours while dancing before the tax collector, flaunting ostrich feathers, twirling spears (Hennings, 1951, p. 117, pp. 129–130, pp. 133–16); Somali went further, with the racial rather than ethnic argument that, as descendants of the Prophet, they should be taxed as "Asiatics" more highly than mere "natives" (Turton, 1972). A minority of Maasai proposed giving up cattle for the plough (Waller, 1993a, p. 244). In the north, the Boran reputation for truth telling got the British to take their side against Ethiopians in border disputes (Oba, 2013, p. 308). But the Kamba, trading on their loyalty as a "martial race" who served in police and army, were the people the British were most careful not to offend (Osborne, 2014).

These ethnic patriotisms, like all patriotisms, were comparative in mood (Smith, 1981, pp. 87–93). There were successful peoples to emulate and, as yet, no fear of transethnic cooperation. Kenyans were envious of the Baganda in Uganda; the British respected their king, the *kabaka*, and allowed them much local autonomy. In the 1920s, it seemed for a time that a respectable ethnicity required the office of paramount chief, a replica *kabaka* (MacArthur, 2016, pp. 101–105; Spencer, 1983, p. 14). The Baganda made their own comparisons and aimed still higher (Rowe, 1969, 1977). More widely felt than envy was men's shame when "their" women consorted with strangers in town. Between the two world wars male clerks and artisans all over East Africa shouldered the role of outraged ethnic fatherhood and organised "tribal welfare associations" to send such women "home". This patriarchal concern could be at odds with progressive claims to citizenship. The British deplored the rough treatment of alleged prostitutes and in 1929 Kikuyu leaders seemed to regret the anger they had stirred in defence of clitoridectomy, "female circumcision", that bodily discipline that defended rural property from urban disorder (Fazan, 1930; Lonsdale, 1992, pp. 386–395; Peterson, 2012; White, 1990, pp. 190–194).

African hopes of imperial citizenship had by the late 1930s failed to dislodge white racial supremacy. Some readers turned to the more experienced Kikuyu for help in getting the British to listen (Bravman, 1998, pp. 239–245; MacArthur, 2016, pp. 89–90, pp. 107–108; Osborne, 2014, pp. 109–111, p. 129; Rosberg & Nottingham, 1966, pp. 163–164, p. 170, p. 174, pp. 177–178, pp. 185–187; Spencer, 1985, pp. 88–91, pp. 94–96). Scarcely any pastoralists were involved, less tightly governed as they were, and as largely unlettered losers in the emerging agrarian revolution. Ethnic patriots among the larger agrarian peoples, however, were prepared to ally against the common enemy, colonial rule. They were ready to learn from each other; there was as yet no great gulf of unequal political militancy to deter them. In interethnic relations, as in other politics, context is all.

1.6 The Mau Mau Rupture: Age Three

Regional inequality and, with it, divergent ethnic militancy, soon became more marked, caused, like patriotic ethnicity before it, in a dialectic between African unrest and British reform. The Second World War transformed Kenya (Lonsdale, 1986). White farmers, formerly the state's dependants, became its business managers. Officials, following new imperial priorities (Hyam, 2006, pp. 94–167) and nervous of black veterans returning from what had been called a war for freedom, tried to match white advantage with African concessions. The first black member of the legislature, Eliud Mathu, Kikuyu, was nominated in 1944. Local leaders were also spending more public money. In 1948/ 1949, when Kenya's central tax revenue stood at £8 million its African local governments raised more than £645,000. In 1955, the North Nyanza district budget of £250,000 was larger than all the white rural district councils put together (Hicks, 1961, p. 320; Kipkorir, 2009, p. 181; Low & Smith, 1976, p. 604; Omusule, 1974, p. 209). Some Africans renewed their hopes that, as loyal citizens of the empire at war, they might begin to share legislative power with Kenya's whites and South Asians. In 1944 they formed a Kenya African Union (KAU; Spencer, 1985, p. 116). It was then that others realised how advanced Kikuyuland had become, a regional superiority that internal social conflict made all the more menacing. This double inequality crippled what would always have been difficult to imagine, a unified African nationalism.

Regional inequality was driven by differences in numbers, education, markets, and new forms of social differentiation. Three agrarian peoples constituted one-half the colony's population, with Kikuyu around 20 per cent of the total and the Luo and Luhya around 15 per cent each. Kikuyu market farming had funded an educational lead over the two Nyanza peoples by the 1930s (see Chapter 9). Of the 900 boys who attended the premier African secondary school, "Alliance", before 1940, nearly 70 per cent were Kikuyu; only 11 per cent came from Nyanza – where, admittedly, Maseno school was second only to Alliance in excellence (Kipkorir, 1969, p. 147). At a higher level Kikuyu provided one third of the Kenyans at Uganda's Makerere College in the 1930s and 1940s, increasing to 45 per cent in the early 1950s, after Makerere attained university status (Goldthorpe, 1965, p. 28). There was a more startling disparity in access to higher education overseas. Black undergraduate numbers outwith East Africa increased from around 80 in 1949 to 225 in 1957. From 1946 to 1952, 45 per cent were Kikuyu and 33 per cent from Nyanza. In 1945, one Omino argued that, as "Britishers", the Luo had "a right to claim the best that the Empire can afford for the progress of her peoples" (Charton, 2002a, p. 182). Hopes for imperial citizenship were still alive. Luo and Luhya relied on British bursaries, mainly for teacher training, but increasing numbers of Kikuyu could afford to go privately, to South Africa, to India, and, increasingly, the United States. In 1948, a single lorry owner, Louis Weciuma, paid for the young Julius Kiano to go to America (Charton, 2002a, pp. 213–214, pp. 271–273).

Higher education linked self-interest with patriotic ethnicity by imparting imperial qualifications. Farm enterprise was different; it set self-interest against moral ethnicity, turning patrons into landowners. As early as 1925, Kikuyu chiefs, budding rural capitalists, warned that most Kikuyu were only tenants, belittling the clients who, in less populous, less commercial, times had enlarged a patron's support (Lonsdale, 1992, p. 362). Luo elders did not similarly question the rights of the poor until after 1945 (Peterson, 2012, pp. 136–141; Shipton, 2009, pp. 109–136; Wilson & Malo, 1961, pp. 56–57). This difference in class consciousness (a not inappropriate term) reflected three other contrasts between central and western Kenya. First, Kikuyu landowners enjoyed greater opportunity for profit (Bates, 1989, pp. 11–72). Nairobi was their local market town; no other region could compete in feeding the city or supplying its charcoal fuel, burned from Kikuyu wattle trees (Cowen, 1978). Second, Kikuyu had lost good land; Luo had not. Kikuyu elders, finally, were unusually disturbed by their former dependants, thanks to a regional contrast in patterns of migration.

The Nyanza peoples did as well as Kikuyu in the skilled labour market; where they differed was in colonising land. By 1940, around one in five Kikuyu were in "squatter" families, labour tenants on the "white highlands", the new Kikuyu frontier; but at the end of the war they learned the bitter truth that they had no security of tenure. When wartime profits enabled settlers to farm more intensively, they reduced their squatters' domestic entitlements to pasture and cultivation. Any who tried to reclaim their rights in Kikuyuland found that rural capitalism and population growth at 2.5 per cent per annum stood in their way (Furedi, 1989, pp. 53–55, pp. 90–92; Kanogo, 1987, pp. 54–55,

p. 67, p. 103, p. 106). Some tried their luck in other "tribal reserves". Many, as in earlier centuries, must have adopted a new identity as their hosts' quasi-kin. But some, often with an independent church to give them confidence, now claimed a colonist's right to settle. Kikuyu "infiltrators" (a British term) stirred argument about land rights all over highland Kenya (Parsons, 2011, 2012; Waller, 1993a). No other people caused such intruder unease, a fear of "immigrants" that has only grown over time (Oucho, 2002, pp. 12–13, p. 58; Jenkins, 2012).

Luo had no similar cause for intimate enmity, nor did they attract much antagonism from others. Their land was relatively poor and distant from markets. Their diaspora (as distinct from temporary migrant workers), amounted to only 10 per cent of their 800,000 population by the 1950s, and they colonised the relatively empty lands of northern Tanganyika, not Kenya's "white highlands". Not only did they run no risk of eviction, but it was on this new frontier that some Luo became rural capitalists, maize magnates. Luckier than their Kikuyu counterparts, they could introduce the plough without challenging the land entitlements of relatives or clients back in a crowded Nyanza (Iliffe, 1979, p. 294, p. 316; Perrin Jassy, 1973, pp. 43–47). No Kenyans other than along the Luhya border then complained of Luo infiltration.

This case study of regional difference helps to explain more recent antagonisms. A few Kikuyu had done sufficiently well out of colonial rule to threaten the expectations of the many. Nyanza's contrasts were not so stark. Kikuyu became divided between hope and despair; other peoples had less cause for mutual mistrust. Divided by quarrels over their rights in land (see Chapter 8), Kikuyu differed over political strategy too: if propertied progress might, just conceivably, earn the right to self-rule, the landless would clearly need direct action (Lonsdale, 1992, pp. 410–416, pp. 431–432, 2002a, pp. 239–246, 2009a, pp. 3–56; Peterson, 2003, 2012, pp. 195–248; Pugliese, 2003). No other of Kenya's peoples knew such conflict between personal ambition and moral ethnicity; neither did they experience such anguished political debate (Lonsdale, 2003, pp. 52–55). For non-Kikuyu, the increasing revenue and competent expenditure of their local councils offered satisfaction enough (Kipkorir, 2009, pp. 171–189).

Africans, therefore, brought very different energies and hopes to KAU ("cow"; Lonsdale, 2000). Nationalisms tend to be led by subjects who have prospered under and are most useful to an alien ruler; their frustrations are keenest and their opportunity greatest. Kikuyu had more money for politics and more traders frustrated by racial discrimination. Their political energy was difficult for others to bear, it looked like superiority; some groups withdrew their earlier cooperation (Bravman, 1998, p. 245, pp. 250–251). Eliud Mathu, the legislator for whom KAU was his constituency party, was notoriously sarcastic. In 1945 he visited Kisumu, the Luo "capital", to meet Oginga Odinga, political apprentice, in "a poky little room". Looking around with disdain, he asked "Where are your Luo people? You don't even have a building of your own." Odinga was stung into community action, thinking commerce would prove political virtue (Odinga, 1967, p. 81; see also Atieno Odhiambo, 1975; Carotenuto, 2006). Other activists pursued similar local ambitions in the belief that a pan-ethnic nationalism, led by Kikuyu, would deny their own people the moral responsibility of self-help. In this belief, Nandi speakers, some inspired by frontline comradeship in the Second World War, combined as a composite new people, the Kalenjin: greater size might make up for poor education (Lynch, 2011, pp. 33–34; Matson, 1972b, p. 20; Omusule, 1974, pp. 368–370). Luhya and Kamba peoples pursued similar self-consolidation through modern local government (MacArthur, 2016; Osborne, 2014).

Wealthy Kikuyu were investing in land and education, assets that increased in value, no longer in clients who increased only in number. This crisis in patronage pitted moderates against radicals, with KAU as their polemical arena. Other ethnic groups, not so divided, tended to desert the party. The core issue between Kikuyu was the conflict between authority and action (Anderson, 2005a, pp. 9–53; Branch, 2009, pp. 16–19; Kershaw, 1997; Lonsdale, 1992). Land elders possessed a patchwork authority incapable of coordinated action; their influence was dissipated over the hundreds of lineage "houses" or *mbari*, which held on to the autonomies they had known in the prepolitical nineteenth century. Their young, lacking authority, were driven by the anger of despair. Denied the help once offered by Kikuyu patronage or labour tenancy on white farms, their poverty prevented marriage and, with it, their adult self-mastery, *wiathi* (Hobson, 2008). Women resisted the compulsory labour of soil conservation, workers became unionised, entrepreneurs joined trade associations, beleaguered squatters swore solidarity farm by farm, and the underemployed of outcast Nairobi joined in ruffianly rackets (Throup, 1987a). All these had the solidarity to act. As the politics of petition pursued by Kenyatta and other landed elders yet again failed to unseat white supremacy, their disjointed authority was "greedily eaten", *mau-mau*'d, by their juniors (Lonsdale, 2003, pp. 56–60). A moral ethnicity of patrimonial obligation had collapsed. Class conflict begins in this way at home, in claims for effective rights to an ethnic culture of belonging that, in Kenya, had been written into existence by a generation of patriots, Jomo Kenyatta and Paulo Mboya among them.

The Mau Mau war lasted for 4 years until late 1956; the state of emergency, that abrogated many human rights, did not end until early 1960, when Britain finally set Kenya on the road to independence under African rule. The conduct of the war, heroic, brutal, and vindictive in equal measure on both sides (Anderson, 2005a; Bennett, 2013; Elkins, 2005; French, 2011), warned Kenyans, senior Kikuyu above all, of the dangers inherent in any politics that subverted ethnic hierarchies of property, lineage, and age. The British had respected these in an effort to turn their alien force into local authority. Postcolonial rulers would find that alchemy equally difficult.

1.7 Political Tribalism: Age Four

Kenya's fourth age of ethnicity began with the first African elections to legislative council in March 1957 and the glimmerings, therefore, of a future share in power. In the 6 years before independence, an increasing number of ethnic districts, ecological zones, became electoral constituencies. Some representatives looked forward to the prospect of power with misgiving: Kenya's history told them it would be inherently unequal. Any disparity between Africans could only grow when some acquired coercive authority over others. The Mau Mau war had restated this truth in blood; 50,000 Kikuyu had died, half of them children, owing to famine and disease (Blacker, 2007). Questions gathered like storm clouds: had this dreadful price been paid by all Kenyans or by Kikuyu alone? If the latter, were they more entitled to power than others (Wrong, 2009)? But what of the panethnic ranks of constitutional nationalists, whose weapons had been print and persuasion, not secret oaths and the gun (Ogot, 2003)? Were Perus Abura's many layers of belonging to be denied an equal citizenship? Independence posed these questions, it did not answer them.

Mau Mau continues to divide Kenya's memory. Its partisans argue that, even when militarily defeated, it broke the British will and so accelerated African rule, very different from London's vision of a "multiracial" successor state shared with specially represented white and South Asian minorities. Others ask, why then was Kenya the last of East Africa's territories to be free, while a peaceful and undivided Tanganyika was first (Iliffe, 2005)? The politics of memory are delicate (MacArthur, 2017), since to ask if the forest fighters were national heroes or tribal thugs is to miss the point, which is that Mau Mau – against which non-Kikuyu police and soldiers fought under British command – was defeated largely by Kikuyu themselves. Its own generals mistrusted each other (Lonsdale, 2003, pp. 60–70, 2017) and Kikuyu "loyalists" were the most effective units to fight on the British side – in their own interest, as in the small wars of conquest fifty years before (Branch, 2009; CPK, 1961; Parker, 2009, pp. 169–173, pp. 315–334). Mau Mau's clearest consequence, therefore, was the rise of a successor ruling elite, recruited largely from "loyalists". These made it safe for the British to decolonise. But it was a divided elite: on one side, battle-hardened loyalists had learned how to use the state's repressive power. For their own safety – and some slept out in the bush on independence night for fear of being murdered in their beds – they were determined to hold on to it. In transforming Kenya, therefore, Mau Mau consolidated a Kikuyu ascendancy (Atieno Odhiambo, 2004; Muigai, 2004). But another educated leadership had also emerged, largely among the Luo and Luhya of Nyanza. These had made brilliant use of constitutional pressure to thwart "multiracialism". Elite political culture was, then, divided between executive ruthlessness and democratic manoeuvre. Echoing the reservations that local leaders had held of a Kikuyu-dominated KAU, some now looked to a regionally devolved constitution, *majimbo*, to protect them from what they feared would be an ethnocratic state, unheeding of less assertive citizens (Anderson, 2005b, 2010; Lynch, 2016).

These divided views shaped the politics of the last hectic years before independence in 1963. British officials, African leaders, white settlers, and Asians were all divided in their visions of the future, indecisions that were finally resolved by recourse to the man more hated and feared than most, Jomo Kenyatta (Angelo, 2016; Kyle, 1999; Ogot, 1995). It remains to be discussed how he and his successors have ruled over the divisive afterlife of the agrieducational revolution with which, unknowingly, colonialism had rigged the race for postcolonial power.

Three threads of argument may clear a way through this most recent period of Kenya's history, its era of political tribalism. These are the political ideology and social formation of Kenya's rulers, the legacy of the colonial revolution, and a chronology that hinges on the end of the Cold War in 1989. Largely single-party rule kept political violence personal or ideological before that date, multiparty democracy has been blamed for its interethnic excesses thereafter.

Jomo Kenyatta and his successors are not counted among Africa's political thinkers. They have not emulated Julius Nyerere (see Chapter 3) or Léopold Senghor, fathers of African socialism or *négritude*. More profitably, they have practised rather than published their ideology. Kenyatta (like the British) had long argued that ethnic tradition was the tutor of self-discipline and social order. It was the ethnographic theme of his book, *Facing Mount Kenya* (1938). Called *Mzee*, the elder, he aimed, if not in so many words, to restore a moral ethnicity that respected senior elders with their prosperous, hospitable, households, founts of civic virtue. This core value was embodied in his "ethnic feudalism" (Prunier, 1998), a pyramid of patronage justified only insofar as it fostered self-mastery in its clients. Kenyatta welcomed a Kenya that was not a nation so much as a community of communities, "a kind of United Nations in miniature" (Kenyatta, 1968, p. 247). Its proper constituents were political tribes, not parties. In return for a cut of what the state offered, a kind of management fee, their representatives, elders of a democratic age, would shoulder their household duty: to obtain from the state the largesse that sustained client voters with schools, roads, and clinics. This was the new moral ethnicity, adapted to the context of state power under the slogan *harambee*! – let us go in for self-help – (Blunt, 2019; Lonsdale, 2002b; Lynch, 2016; Ocobock, 2017, pp. 226–246).

From 1961, 2 years before independence, until 1968, Kenya knew multiparty competition. Ethnic elites became local champions in the central national arena. It is hard to know how far their rivalry affected the daily lives of the common people, *wananchi*. For most of the time the poor seem to have maintained a neighbourly ethnicity of survival (Branch, 2011, pp. 292–294, quoting Kinuthia Macharia, 1988; van Stapele, 2015; Wamai, 2016). Public meetings, *barazas*, exhibited both the ethnically divisive performance of elite power on the podium and disrespectful criticism from among the common crowd (Haugerud, 1995). But competitive political tribalism has clearly been the easiest rallying cry at election times, with truly lethal consequences in the 1990s and in 2007–2008.

Observers saw these "one-party tribes" from the start (Bennett, 1963, p. 154), but that was not always true. Had ethnic solidarity been an entirely reliable vote-bank, Kenya's rulers might have felt more secure, less nervously determined to retain power. But class fraternity has on occasion questioned ethnic solidarity, falsifying strategic calculation. The classic case is Tom Mboya's long tenure of Nairobi East's constituency. Famously, he won 90 per cent of the vote in the 1961 "Kenyatta election", 2 years before independence. Yet 60 per cent of his electorate was Kikuyu; his own Luo people numbered little over 10 per cent. As migrant workers, they also had sturdy rural reasons to mistrust his urban guile (Parkin, 1978, pp. 217–241). But he won by a landslide. His effective trade unionism and astonishing student airlift to America overwhelmed his Kikuyu opponent's promise of solidarity with his fellow Kikuyu *kamwene*, "the little person who belongs" (Bennett & Rosberg, 1961, pp. 176–181; Goldsworthy, 1982, p. 177; Sanger & Nottingham, 1964, p. 6). Many little Kikuyu had lost trust in ethnic belonging, a failing for which Mboya himself would later pay.

At independence, Kenyans were nonetheless divided between two parties that were defined by ethnicity more than by any other of Perus Abura's layers of identity. There were no other Mboyas to upset the ethnic reckoning. "Little persons", most of them illiterate at the time, voted with their one-party tribes. The difference between the two parties, the Kenyan African National and Democratic Unions (KANU & KADU), historically created, underlies all later history. Understanding starts with a reminder that all of Kenya's ethnic groups are minorities; with only 20 per cent of the population, Kikuyu are the largest. In 1963, barely 8 per cent of Kenyans were mixed together in towns. Because ethnic identities and rural constituencies were territorially matched, ethnic coalitions that gathered enough minorities into a parliamentary majority were the key to legitimate power. KANU and KADU represented, respectively, the winners and losers in the agrie-ducational revolution (Lynch, 2011, p. 64). The only agrarian people not to give KANU majority support were the Luhya, electoral jokers thanks to their divisions, familiar to Perus Abura (MacArthur, 2008,

2016). The clearest winners, leaders on the schooling ladder since before 1914, were Luo and Kikuyu, uneasily allied in KANU: the Luo Oginga Odinga, the small man's friend, was increasingly critical of Kenyatta's dynastic leanings. KADU represented, mainly, the pastoralists of the dry north and, more vitally, the better watered Rift Valley, home to Maasai and Kalenjin – whose most prominent leader was Daniel arap Moi.

Muslims, possibly 15 per cent of the population, were politically marginal; both coastal Swahili and pastoral Somali imagined different sovereignties: the renewal of historic links to Zanzibar (Brennan, 2008) or secession to an already independent Somalia (Whittaker, 2015). Somali had taken little part in colonial Kenya's politics; Muslims in a nominally Christian country, nonpartisanship also protected their interethnic trades in cattle and, more recently, *khat*, a leafy stimulant grown on Mount Kenya and chewed around the world (Aguilar, 1996; Carrier, 2007; Carrier & Lochery, 2013; Dalleo, 1975; Turton, 1972). In the event, after 4 brutal years of war, their secessionist guerrillas were contained by astute manipulation of their clan rivalries; the coast, by contrast, was for a long time largely ignored.

The electoral struggle for Kenya, therefore, centred – as it does still – on the swing constituencies of the Rift Valley. At independence, its vacant white farms beckoned to both their former pastoralists and to immigrant peasants, mostly Kikuyu. Landless in their "native reserves", both poor loyalists (Branch, 2009, pp. 127–130) and ex-Mau Mau detainees were determined to acquire the self-mastery through property, *ithaka na wiathi*, for which each had fought, if against each other. The state absorbed many into settlement schemes, funded by western loans, to pre-empt peasant land seizures (Angelo, 2016; Furedi, 1989, pp. 172–224; Kanogo, 1987, pp. 162–178; Leo, 1984; Vianni, 2016). Others joined land-buying companies, one of which, called "Pipeline", recalled the pipeline of detention camps down which British counter-insurgency had pushed them (Wamai, 2016). For these the struggle continued. Their laborious sweat was also a civilising successor to the indigenous pastoralism that had lost the Rift to white settlement (Lonsdale, 1992, pp. 333–338). The Rift was indeed a "historical text" (Diepeveen, 2010, p. 239) in which two histories collided. Kenyatta's KANU backed the recent history of the colonising hoe that had, in squatter hands, subsidised white farming, Moi's KADU sponsored the first-comers' cow, an *ancien régime* that the agrarian revolution had pushed aside and for whom the Kikuyu incomers were invaders. This immigration, converting Kalenjin lands into electorally volatile, multiethnic, territory, was not the only issue in the *majimbo* debate between central power and regional autonomy, but it was, and remains, fundamental (Boone, 2014, pp. 139–157).

It may seem, given the interethnic violence that has disfigured recent years, that this divided past put a curse on any hope of a cohesive future. But it was not an inevitable tragedy: choices were made, a particular political culture has grown. Ruling coalitions, lacking other sources of trust, have attracted allies with offers of complicit investment in the private percentages of power, not least when measuring out land for resettlement (Berman, 1998; Branch, 2011, pp. 161–244; Hornsby, 2013, pp. 398–617). These collusions gave power its retentive logic: a first defence, when challenged, is to raise the ethnic alarm among supporters. Deliberate neglect of intraparty democracy has eroded that other potential cradle of trust. Murder was thinkable as part of the defensive repertoire from the start – another legacy of a colonial regime so lately engaged in counter-insurgency. In 1952, the killing of a Kikuyu chief was the trigger for the Mau Mau war. Kenyatta's own life had been threatened three times: by rebel leaders before the emergency, during the detention he shared with the same hard men, and, before independence, by those wanting to colonise the Rift as their Mau Mau reward. An army unit mutinied weeks after independence, followed by rumours of coups – in Africa's era of coups. British special forces protected Kenyatta for a time (Parsons, 2003, pp. 151–155, pp. 169–170, pp. 190–193; Percox, 2012, p. 171). African elders were supposed to grow out of the warrior's hot-blooded desire to kill; Kenyatta was an elder with cold, deniable, state violence available over the phone. His vulnerability also made him insist that his inner cabinet speak only Kikuyu: a cabal at the core of his community of communities (Atieno Odhiambo, 2004, p. 180; Leys, 1975, p. 246).

This is not the place for a history of postcolonial Kenya (see Branch, 2011; Githuku, 2016; Hornsby, 2013). Three narratives in miniature will have to serve to illustrate the dialectic between political culture and ethnic relations: Kenyatta's presidency from 1963 until his death in 1978; Moi's presidency from 1978 to 2002, disrupted by the end of the Cold War; and the years of constitution making since then in search of a less divisive, less centralised power over a more cohesive people.

Kenyatta's regime seemed to be successful, for many an era of social mobility created by Africanising the state bureaucracy, land ownership, and business (Hornsby, 2013, pp. 123–135). Few could match the spectacular rise of Dr. Njoroge Mungai, an American-trained doctor and cabinet minister, at one time a possible presidential successor, who bought the farm that his father had served as houseboy and turned it into a cut-flower plantation (Charton, 2002b). But Swahili, already full of loan-words, borrowed a French make of car to picture the rapid promotion possible for university graduates: *ku-pujo*; some even joined the *wabenzi* (Hornsby, 2013, pp. 124–125). But underneath there was growing mass poverty, especially after the oil crises of the 1970s. Thirty years after independence, many Kikuyu peasants, settled unsuitably on former white ranches, could barely keep their families from starving (Droz, 1999).

This gross inequality explains why a presidency that began with a Kikuyu alliance with fellow "revolutionaries", the Luo migrant workers of western Kenya, ended as a Kikuyu alliance with former "aristocrats", the Rift's Kalenjin and Maasai pastoralists. Agile ethnic manoeuvre did not mask class conflict, because "class" was not yet a collective imagination, so much as defeat an antipoverty strategy that challenged the elders. At a time of public protest at freedom's miseries, a president's office flooded with beggarly petitions (Branch, 2011, pp. 35–55; Githuku, 2016, pp. 232–258), rumours of Russian arms imports, and Somali border war, the ruling party KANU was rent by argument. Kenyatta the elder insisted on disciplined self-help, lifted by property ownership bought with loan finance. His vice president Odinga supported the Kikuyu *kamwene*, the little belongers who argued that the land for which they had fought should now be free, allocated by the state, not patronage. Land should go to the pioneer tiller, neither to the indigenous pastoralist nor a foreign corporation, nor yet to well-connected politicians – Kenyatta's family being a prime example.

After Mboya, Kenyatta's manager, had eased these populists (scarcely socialists) out of KANU, Odinga formed the Kenya Peoples Union, raising the spectre of disaffected Kikuyu splitting Kenyatta's ethnic base by supporting an opposition party. The KPU took a lot of ruthless beating, an early loss of innocence for Kenya's political culture that taught the wisdom of ethnic loyalty and the cost of forfeiting presidential favour. By the time, in 1969, that Kenyatta the elder had defeated Odinga and his little men – both Kikuyu and Luo – the retentive logic of power saw the return of political detention, restrictions on basic freedoms, and the presidential bodyguard's killing of one hundred, some say, among a Luo crowd at whom Kenyatta himself hurled obscenities (Ogot, 2012, pp. 114–116). There were also two assassinations – of the Goan Pio Gama Pinto, Odinga's socialist thinker, and of Tom Mboya, far from socialist but still the seducer of the capital city's Kikuyu. What shook opinion still more was the taking of "tea at Gatundu", Kenyatta's home. Up to 300,000 people were forced to take oaths similar to the Mau Mau rituals Kenyatta had once condemned, as they swore to keep Kenya's flag in Kikuyu hands, out of the grasp of the uncircumcised Luo (Branch, 2011, pp. 35–88; Hornsby, 2013, pp. 156–319; Knighton, 2010; Mueller, 1972, pp. 200–210, 2010; Ogot, 2012, pp. 110–116). Autocratic eldership was suffocating the self-mastery that Kenyatta used to praise. It seemed his presidency had only an intimidated people on which to rely.

Kenyatta's attack on the KPU was possible only because he had organised a two-fold rearguard: a tacit understanding with leading Kalenjin and a strengthened provincial administration. Kenyatta secured the dissolution of KADU and an end to *majimbo*'s regionalism in 1964 by bringing Moi into government and granting him a silent Rift Valley concordat that could at times protect the indigenous Kalenjin against Kikuyu colonists (Throup, 1987b, pp. 44–45). In this patched-up elders' peace, fearful of the landless left, Kenya's ethnically calculated future was foretold. It was safe to dispense with the Luo, if that was what the Luo wanted. Kenyatta also used his rapprochement with Moi to concentrate more power in his presidency, a centralised regime that has only begun to be dismantled. He strangled county councils, colonial legacies, ostensibly because of financial failings (Hornsby, 2013, p. 112), but more to strengthen control (Kipkorir, 2009, p. 204). Here his instrument was the provincial administration, another legacy. For field administrators, the councils complicated the presidential chain of command that led down, through provincial and district commissioners, to chiefs, another colonial inheritance, but now the president's eyes on the ground. The only wall-chart in Moi's office, Kenyatta's successor, showed the administration as a family tree, rooted in the president, with officials' names easily changed from slot to slot along its provincial branches (personal observation). This centralisation and the decay of other institutions to which a citizen might appeal (Mueller, 2008) politicised ethnicity still more. Its sense of belonging, the cradle of reciprocal responsibility, was reduced to dependence on the presidential will. That is why Kenyatta's presidency, or at least its legitimacy, ended not with his death in 1978, but 3 years earlier, with the murder of the former Mau Mau detainee, Kikuyu member of parliament and racehorse owner, "J. M." Kariuki. His appeals on behalf of the poor and exposure of high-level corruption were too close to home for the Kikuyu establishment to bear (Branch, 2011, pp. 110–120; Githuku, 2016, pp. 271–284; Hornsby, 2013, pp. 281–290). Political tribalism could not stand too much moral ethnicity.

Yet Kenyatta was a lucky president, able to allow most ethnic localities to "eat" from the national cake. Single-party or no-party rule enabled him to ring the changes among his ethnic vassals and for voters to express displeasure – as they did – without more ethnic conflict than he himself imposed. Africa's terms of trade also remained favourable and the Africanisation of opportunity continued for several years. Smallholder coffee and tea flourished. Although there was little to choose between the two regimes in terms of economic growth (Jerven, 2011), Kenyatta's successor, arap Moi, was less fortunate. Even as he inherited power (as Kenyatta intended), the 1970s oil shocks hit Africa hard; drought was just as damaging. The best opportunities in state and business were already filled. Yet Moi's Kalenjin clients had decades of disadvantage to catch up by unseating others, to undo the agri-educational revolution.

By the 1980s, the extractive political morality of carving ethnic benefit out of state largesse began to face its limits (Throup & Hornsby, 1998, pp. 26–50). Competition for power became fiercer – as the population grew, the fertilising rain of Africanisation dried up, and Africa's terms of trade turned down. Moi's regime, shocked by a real, largely Luo, coup attempt in August 1982, became more brutally fearful, especially of intellectual dissent in the universities and the arts, largely from Luo and Kikuyu students, lecturers, and writers. Torture became a political instrument, causing a costly brain drain (Atieno Odhiambo, 2004). There was rising anger, even from otherwise compromised churches (Lonsdale, 2009c), but it was the end of the Cold War and, with it, the end of Western toleration of African dictatorship, that ended Moi's management of dissent by exemplary repression. The 1990s have been called the decade of Africa's "second liberation". It did not seem so in Kenya. True, Moi was forced to end his one-party regime and allow an exhilarating renewal of civil society initiatives (Branch, 2011, pp. 183–190), but the neoliberal Washington consensus also forced the state out of much of its economic management, at the expense of medical and educational services to the poor. It was then, to a divided Kenya, as before, that Moi reluctantly restored multiparty democracy for the 1992 elections.

Until then, there had been sporadic interethnic violence over rights to land but no political campaign to change the manner of its allocation. One-party rule had offered no popular leverage. This perception now changed, especially in the Rift. Kalenjin or Maasai awoke to the fact that party politics – with ethnicity soon re-established as the basis for partisanship – could decide whether to confirm their ownership rights or overturn them in favour of "foreigners", who could now vote for a party dominant in their homeland (as regions began to be called), but opposed to that of their "hosts". Kikuyu and other "guests", Luo, Luhya, and Gusii, no longer members of the one party, KANU, had the same, if opposite, fear: their "hosts" called them *madoadoa*, "stains", treacherous agents of a potentially renewed Kikuyu ascendancy. Before and after the elections of 1992 and 1997, in what could well be called pogroms (Boone, 2014, p. 265), thousands were killed and hundreds of thousands ethnically cleansed from the Rift. Their properties, often of uncertain title, were available for "native" repossession. Many suffered sexual violence, including forcible circumcision of Luo (Ogot, 2010, pp. 153–154). Refugees remained in camps, told only to "return home", but to which home was unclear, whether historically indigenous or recently settled (Klopp & Sheekh, 2008). Elsewhere, Maasai who tried to regain former pastures were forcibly restrained (Kantai, 2007). Nobody has been held to blame: elite political manipulation coincided too well with popular fears (Anderson & Lochery, 2008; Jenkins, 2012; Oucho, 2002; Throup & Hornsby, 1998, pp. 173–237). It was the revoltingly logical conclusion of a collusive political culture that relied on the factional support of political tribalism, reinforced by ethnic militias – "elders' armies" or *majeshi ya wazee* (Ocobock, 2017, p. 245) – by electoral largesse looted from the public treasury (Branch, 2011, pp. 218–222; Hornsby, 2013, pp. 506–509, pp. 559–560), and by the complicity of the police and judiciary (compare with Chapter 2).

The years since 2002, when newly introduced term limits obliged Moi to step down, have seen a return to Kikuyu presidencies and, in a repeat of the first years of independence, a shift in the core of the ruling coalition from a Kikuyu-Luo to a Kikuyu-Kalenjin alliance, thanks to all-too familiar arguments about regional inequality, poverty, the conflicts of land in the Rift, all in the context of a constitutional struggle between popular dismay at the corrupting arrogance of power and a political establishment reluctant to shed its privileges and submit to a rule of law, safeguarded by a separation of powers (Diepeveen, 2010; Ghai, 2012; Chapter 12). Even the personalities are familiar, with the most recent election, in 2017, fought between a Kenyatta and an Odinga, sons of the first president and vice president – Jomo Kenyatta's dynastic ideology in the life.

All ask if the bloody mayhem of Moi's last years has really been laid to rest, for it returned with renewed horror after the elections of 2007, with Kalenjin "warriors", under elders' orders, fighting for their land. More than 1,000 were killed and 500,000 were made homeless; Kikuyu suffered most, fighting back against their ethnic cleansing with their own elder's army, *Mungiki* – temporarily forgiven for its entrepreneurial criminality (Cheeseman & Branch, 2008; Schuberth, 2018). This disaster brought in international mediation and, in 2010, finally secured an agreement to a new constitution that, when fully implemented, takes important powers from the presidency and devolves much responsibility, not on six or seven regions, as in the former, aborted, *majimbo*, constitution but on 47 counties. There have been two almost peaceful elections since, with that of 2017, in what seems to have been an encouraging separation of powers, being rerun after a supreme court ruling.

Has, therefore, devolution and the deconcentration of power (Chapter 7), disarmed political tribalism? It is early days. Kenya's ruling class – as it has become – is resistant to change and has found no political principles to dispute, in substitution for ethnic championship. The common people, *wananchi*, especially the women, *Wanjiku*, may in this be wiser than their rulers. After the bloody 1990s, women with mixed marriages and multiethnic sons were the local peace-makers in parts of the Rift (Achieng', 2005). More recently, the domestic realities of survival for the Rift's mixed population has taught Kikuyu and Kalenjin neighbours how to live and let live – a plebeian understanding that has not allowed their ethnic champions to pull them apart (Wamai, 2016). The negotiation of horizontal trust with citizen others, it seems, has in some places and in some contexts, qualified the more common reliance on a vertical tie of clientage with ethnic political patrons. But caution is needed: it is still all too easy for the Islamicist Somali militias of *al-Shabaab* to exploit the factional and ethnic frictions that still exist between fellow Kenyans, not yet a cohesive citizenry (Anderson & McKnight, 2015; Lochery, 2012).

1.8 Conclusion

There is no original sin in ethnicity. Diversity is a danger only when it is a profitable instrument of power (compare with Chapter 3). Kenya's ethnicities have come a long way from the hybrid vigour of their thinly populated, stateless, past. The negotiation of trustworthy relations, however unequal, that once mastered specific environments used to be pursued within moral ethnicities, communities of disciplined belonging. These communities welcomed and assimilated newcomers prepared to serve and maintained interethnic relations of marriage and trade that spasmodic warfare did not disrupt. In the twenty-first century, immigrants are a danger, potential electoral traitors. Wealth and authority no longer lie in managing a household of wives, juniors, and clients, but in controlling public office; moral disapproval has to bite its tongue as the price of electoral solidarity (Jenkins, 2012, p. 592; Lynch, 2010, pp. 184–186; 2011, pp. 27–29). Dealing with such unknowable power in the past would have been called sorcery, punishable by fire. Kenyans often, and with reason, have seen politicians as similar self-seekers, but find it difficult to call them to account.

If that were the whole story, then Kenyans could have little hope of further change. But it is not: just as some Nairobi Kikuyu once voted for the Luo Tom Mboya, so some Kikuyu intellectuals have braved accusations of treachery, like "J. M." Kariuki before them, by denouncing the deferential "one voice" demanded by "the Kikuyu oligarchy, ... old men sipping malt whisky after a game of golf" (Kiai & Muite, 2009). Many Luo too, consider loyalty to their version of social democracy, as exemplified by Oginga Odinga, is worth the cost of exclusion from power (Morrison, 2007). Civil society organisations vigorously debate alternative paths to justice and peace (Kanyinga, 2011). In 1998 and in 2013, when many died in acts of jihadist terror, many volunteered to donate blood to fellow Kenyans, ethnic strangers but common citizens. And there are the local armistice agreements, some cemented by intermarriage, between the mixed populations of the Rift. It remains to be seen if the new constitution will so demobilise political tribalism as to usher in a fifth age of decorative, noncompetitive, ethnicity, as imagined by Mugo Gatheru. A precolonial past of complementary diversity is always there, whenever the time is ripe, ready to be imagined as the myth of a hybrid, shared, national genesis more friendly to the plural but cohesive citizenship that Perus Abura so longed to be able to express.

References

Achieng', R. 2005. *"Home away from home"? Internally displaced women and their trans-local ethnic and gender co-operation in reconstructing the meaning of places (Burnt Forest and Langas, Uasin Gishu, Kenya).* PhD thesis. University of Bielefeld.

Aguilar, M. 1996. Writing biographies of Boorana: Social histories at the time of Kenya's independence. *History in Africa*, 23, pp. 351–367.

Ambler, C. H. 1988. *Kenyan Communities in the Age of Imperialism: The Central Region in the Late Nineteenth Century.* New Haven, CT: Yale University Press.

Anderson, B. 1983. *Imagined Communities: Reflections on the Origins and Spread of Nationalism.* New York & London: Verso.

Anderson, D. M. 2002. *Eroding the Commons: The Politics of Ecology in Baringo, Kenya 1890–1963.* Oxford: James Currey.

   2004. Massacre at Ribo Post: Expansion and Expediency on the Colonial Frontier in East Africa. *International Journal of African Historical Studies.* 37(1): 33–54.

   2005a. *Histories of the Hanged: Britain's Dirty War in Kenya and the End of the Empire.* London: Weidenfeld & Nicolson.

   2005b. "Yours in the struggle for Majimbo": Nationalism and party politics of decolonization in Kenya, 1955–64. *Journal of Contemporary History.* 40(3): 547–564.

   2010. Majimboism: The Troubled History of an Idea. In Branch, D., Cheeseman, N., and Gardners, L. (eds.), *Our Turn to Eat: Politics in Kenya.* Berlin: LIT Verlag, pp. 23–52.

Anderson, D. M., and McKnight, J. 2015. Understanding al-Shabaab: Clans, Islam, and insurgency in Kenya. *Journal of Eastern African Studies.* 9(3), pp. 536–557.

Anderson, D. M., and Broch-Due, V. (eds.). 1999. *The Poor Are Not Us: Poverty & Pastoralism in Eastern Africa.* Oxford: James Currey.

Anderson, D. M., and Lochery, E. 2008. Violence and exodus in Kenya's Rift Valley, 2008: Predictable and preventable? *Journal of Eastern African Studies.* 2(2): 328–343.

Anderson, D. M., and Bollig, M. (eds.). 2017. *Resilience and Collapse in African Savannahs*. Abingdon: Routledge.

Angelo, A. 2016. *Becoming President: A Political Biography of Jomo Kenyatta (1958–1969)*. PhD thesis. European University Institute (Florence).

arap Ng'eny, S. K. 1970. Nandi resistance to the establishment of British administration 1883–1906. In Ogot, B. A. (ed.), *Hadith 2*. Nairobi: East African Publishing House, pp. 104–126.

Atieno Odhiambo, E. S. 1975. "Seek ye first the economic kingdom": A history of the Luo Thrift and Trading Corporation (LUTATCO) 1945–1956. In Ogot, B. A. (ed.), *Hadith 5: Economic and Social History of East Africa*. Nairobi: East African Literature Bureau, pp. 218–256.

    2004. Hegemonic enterprises & instrumentalities of survival. In Berman, B., Dickson, E., and Kymlicka, W. (eds.), *Ethnicity and Democracy in Africa*. Oxford: James Currey, pp. 167–182.

Ayot, H. O. 1979. *A History of the Luo-Abasuba of Western Kenya from AD 1770 to 1940*. Nairobi: Kenya Literature Bureau.

Bates, R. H. 1989. *Beyond the Miracle of the Market: The Political Economy of Agrarian Development in Kenya*. Cambridge: Cambridge University Press.

Bayart, J.-F. 2005. *The Illusion of Cultural Identity*. London: Hurst.

Bayly, C. A. 2002. "Archaic" and "modern" globalization in the Eurasian and African arena, c. 1750–1850. In Hopkins, A. G. (ed.), *Globalization in World History* London: Pimlico, pp. 47–73.

    2004. *The Birth of the Modern World, 1780–1914*. Oxford: Blackwell.

Beech, M. W. 12 December 1912. *The Kikuyu Point of View*. Kenya National Archives, PC/CP. 1/4/2.

Beidelman, T. O. 2012. *The Culture of Colonialism: The Cultural Subjection of Ukaguru*. Bloomington: Indiana University Press.

Bennett, G. 1963. *Kenya: A Political History*. London: Oxford University Press.

Bennett, G., and Rosenberg, C. G. 1961. *The Kenyatta Election: Kenya 1960–1961*. Oxford: Oxford University Press.

Bennett, H. 2013. *Fighting the Mau Mau: The British Army and Counterinsurgency in the Kenya Emergency*. Cambridge: Cambridge University Press.

Berman, B. J. 1990. *Control and Crisis in Colonial Kenya: The Dialectic of Domination*. London: James Currey.

    1998. Ethnicity, patronage and the African state: The politics of uncivil nationalism. *African Affairs*. 97(388): 305–341.

Berman, B. J., and Lonsdale, J. 2013. Nationalism in colonial and postcolonial Africa. In Breuilly, J. (ed.), *The Oxford Handbook of the History of Nationalism*. Oxford: Oxford University Press, pp. 308–317.

Bernardi, B. 1959. *The Mugwe, a Failing Prophet: A Study of a Religious and Public Dignitary of the Meru of Kenya*. London: Oxford University Press.

1985. *Age Class Systems: Social Institutions and Polities Based on Age.* Cambridge: Cambridge University Press.

Berntsen, J. L. 1979. Maasai age-sets and prophetic leadership 1850–1912. *Africa.* 49, pp. 134–146.

Berry, S. 1993. *No Condition Is Permanent: The Social Dynamics of Agrarian Change in Sub-Saharan Africa*. Madison: University of Wisconsin Press.

Bienda, G. N. 1973. *The Evolution of the African District Council in South Nyanza up to 1961*. University of Nairobi: BA dissertation in History.

Blacker, J. 2007. The demography of Mau Mau: Fertility and mortality in Kenya in the 1950s – A demographer's viewpoint. *African Affairs.* 106(423): 205–227.

Blunt, R. W. (2019) *For Money and Elders: Ritual, Sovereignty, and the Sacred in Kenya*. Chicago: Chicago University Press.

Boone, C. 2014. *Property and Political Order in Africa: Land Rights and the Structure of Politics*. Cambridge: Cambridge University Press.

Branch, D. 2009. *Defeating Mau Mau, Creating Kenya: Counterinsurgency, Civil War, and Decolonization*. Cambridge: Cambridge University Press.

2011. *Kenya, Between Hope and Despair, 1963–2011*. New Haven, CT: Yale University Press.

Branch, D., Cheeseman, N., and Gardner, L. (eds.). 2010. *Our Turn to Eat: Politics in Kenya Since 1950*. Berlin: LIT Verlag.

Bratton, M., and Kimenyi, M. S. 2008. Voting in Kenya: Putting ethnicity into perspective. *Journal of Eastern African Studies.* 2(2): 272–289.

Bravman, B. 1998. *Making Ethnic Ways: Communities and Their Transformations in Taita, Kenya, 1800–1950*. Portsmouth, NH: Heinemann.

Brennan, J. 2008. Lowering the Sultan's flag: Sovereignty and decolonization in coastal Kenya. *Comparative Studies in Society and History.* 50(4): 831–861.

Brown, G. K., and Stewart, F. 2012. Horizontal inequalities and market instability in Africa. In Hino, H., Lonsdale, J., Ranis, G., and Stewart, F. (eds.), *Ethnic Diversity and Economic Instability in Africa: Interdisciplinary Perspectives*. Cambridge: Cambridge University Press, pp. 254–285.

Burbidge, D. 2014. "Can someone get me outta this middle-class zone?" Pressures on middle-class Kikuyu in Kenya's 2013 election. *Journal of Modern African Studies.* 52(2): 205–225.

Carotenuto, M. 2006. *Cultivating an African community: The Luo Union in 20th century East Africa*. PhD thesis. Indiana University.

Carrier, N. C .M. 2007. *Kenyan Khat: The Social Life of a Stimulant.* Leiden, the Netherlands: Brill.

Carrier, N. C. M., and Lochery, E. 2013. Missing states? Somali trade networks and the Eastleigh transformation. *Journal of Eastern African Studies.* 7(2): 334–352.

Cashmore, T. H. R. 1965. *Studies in district administration in the East Africa Protectorate (1895–1918).* PhD thesis. University of Cambridge.

Chabal, P., and Daloz, J. P. 2006. *Culture Troubles: Politics and the Interpretation of Meaning.* London: Hurst.

Charton, H. 2002a. *La genèse ambiguë de l'élite kenyane: Origines, formations et intégration de 1945 à l'indépendance.* PhD thesis. Université Paris 7.

2002b. Conversation with author, 16 December 2002.

Cheeseman, N., and Branch, D. (eds.). 2008. Special issue on Kenya's election crisis. *Journal of Eastern African Studies,* 2(2).

Cohen, A. 1974. *Two-Dimensional Man.* London: Tavistock.

Cohen, D., and Atieno Odhiambo, E. S. 1992. *Burying SM: The Politics of Knowledge and the Sociology of Power in Africa.* London: James Currey.

Connan, D. 2013. *La décolonisation des clubs kényans: Sociabilité exclusive et constitution morale des élites africains dans le Kenya contemporain.* PhD thesis. Université Paris 1.

Colony & Protectorate of Kenya (CPK). 1933. *Kenya Land Commission Evidence,* 3 vols. Nairobi: Government Printer (CPK).

1957. *Statistical Abstract 1955.* Nairobi: Government Printer (CPK).

1961. *History of the Loyalists.* Nairobi: Government Printer (CPK).

Cowen, M. P. 1978. *Capital and household production: The case of wattle in Kenya's Central Province, 1903–1964.* PhD thesis. Cambridge University.

Cruise O'Brien, D. B. 1995. Coping with the Christians: The Muslim predicament in Kenya. In Hansen, H. B., and Twaddle, M. (eds.), *Religion and Politics in East Africa.* London: James Currey, pp. 200–219.

Dalleo, P. T. 1975. *Trade and pastoralism: Economic factors in the history of the Somali of northeastern Kenya 1892–1948.* PhD thesis. Syracuse University.

Diepeveen, S. 2010. "The Kenyas we don't want": Popular thought over constitutional review in Kenya, 2002. *Journal of Modern African Studies.* 48(2): 231–258.

Droz, Y. 1999. *Migrations Kikuyus: Des pratiques sociales à l'imaginaire.* Neuchâtel, Switzerland: l'Institut d'ethnologie.

East Africa Protectorate (EAP). 1913. *Native Labour Commission, 1912–13: Evidence and Report.* Nairobi: Government Printer (EAP).

Ehret, C. 1998. *An African Classical Age: Eastern and Southern Africa in World History 1000 B.C. to A.D. 400*. Charlottesville: University Press of Virginia.

Eisenberg, A., and Kymlicka, W. (eds.). 2011. *Identity Politics in the Public Realm: Bringing Institutions Back In*. Vancouver, Canada: UBC Press.

Elkins, C. 2005. *Britain's Gulag: The Brutal End of Empire in Kenya*. London: Pimlico.

Fadiman, J. A. 1982. *An Oral History of Tribal Warfare: The Meru of Mt. Kenya*. Athens: Ohio University Press.

1993. *When We Began There Were Witchmen: An Oral History from Mount Kenya*. Berkeley: University of California Press.

Fazan, S. H. 12 Jan 1930. *Political Situation Report by District Commissioner Kiambu*. Kenya National Archives: DC/MKS.10B/12/1.

Feierman, S. 1990. *Peasant Intellectuals: Anthropology and History in Tanzania*. Madison: University of Wisconsin Press.

French, D. 2011. *The British Way in Counter-Insurgency 1945–1967*. Oxford: Oxford University Press.

Furedi, F. 1989. *The Mau Mau War in Perspective*. London: James Currey.

Gatheru, M. 1964. *Child of Two Worlds: A Kikuyu's Story*. London: Routledge & Kegan Paul.

Geschiere, P. 2009. *The Perils of Belonging: Autochthony, Citizenship, and Exclusion in Africa and Europe*. Chicago: University of Chicago Press.

Ghai, Y. P. 2012. State, ethnicity and economy in Africa. In Hino, H., Lonsdale, J., Ranis, G., and Stewart, F. (eds.), *Ethnic Diversity and Economic Instability in Africa: Interdisciplinary Perspectives*. Cambridge: Cambridge University Press, pp. 129–168.

Githuku, N. K. 2016. *Mau Mau, Crucible of War: Statehood, National Identity, and Politics of Postcolonial Kenya*. Lanham, MD: Lexington Books.

Goldsworthy, D. 1982. *Tom Mboya, the Man Kenya Wanted to Forget*. Nairobi: Heinemann.

Goldthorpe, J. E. 1965. *An African Elite: Makerere College Students 1922–1960*. Nairobi: Oxford University Press.

Habari. 1 July 1922. Enclosure in Despatch 1922/963: UK National Archives, CO533/280.

Hastings, A. 1997. *The Construction of Nationhood: Ethnicity, Religion and Nationalism*. Cambridge: Cambridge University Press.

Haugerud, A. 1995. *The Culture of Politics in Modern Kenya*. Cambridge: Cambridge University Press.

Hay, M. J. 1971. *Economic change in Luoland: Kowe, 1890–1945*. PhD thesis. University of Wisconsin.

Heald, S. 1999. *Manhood and Morality: Sex, Violence and Ritual in Gisu Society.* London: Routledge.

Hennings, R. O. 1951. *African Morning.* London: Chatto & Windus.

Hicks, U. K. 1961. *Development from Below: Local Government and Finance in Developing Countries of the Commonwealth.* Oxford: Clarendon.

Hobson, F. 2008. Freedom as moral agency: *Wiathi* and Mau Mau in colonial Kenya. *Journal of Eastern African Studies.* 2(3): 456–470.

Hornsby, C. 2013. *Kenya: A History Since Independence.* London: I.B. Tauris.

Hughes, L. 2006. *Moving the Maasai: A Colonial Misadventure.* Basingstoke: Palgrave Macmillan.

Hutchinson, J. 2013. Cultural nationalism. In Breuilly, J. (ed.), *The Oxford Handbook of the History of Nationalism.* Oxford: Oxford University Press, pp. 75–94.

Hyam, R. 2006. *Britain's Declining Empire: The Road to Decolonisation 1918–1968.* Cambridge: Cambridge University Press.

Iliffe, J. 1979. *A Modern History of Tanganyika.* Cambridge: Cambridge University Press.

1987. *The African Poor, a History.* Cambridge: Cambridge University Press.

2005. Breaking the chain at its weakest link: TANU and the Colonial Office. In Maddox, G., and Giblin, J. (eds.), *In Search of a Nation: Histories of Authority and Dissidence in Tanzania.* Oxford: Currey, pp. 168–197.

2007. *Africans, the History of a Continent,* 2nd edn. Cambridge: Cambridge University Press.

Jenkins, S. 2012. Ethnicity, violence, and the immigrant-guest metaphor in Kenya. *African Affairs.* 111(445): 576–596.

Jerven, M. 2011. Revisiting the consensus on Kenyan economic growth, 1964–95. *Journal of Eastern African Studies.* 5(1): 2–23.

Kanogo, T. 1987. *Squatters and the Roots of Mau Mau, 1905–63.* London: James Currey.

2005. *African Womanhood in Colonial Kenya 1900–1950.* Oxford: James Currey.

Kantai, P. 2007. In the grip of the vampire state: Maasai land struggles in Kenyan politics. *Journal of Eastern African Studies.* 1(1): 107–122.

Kanyinga, K. 2011. Stopping a conflagration: The response of Kenyan civil society to the post-2007 election violence. *Politikon: South African Journal of Political Studies.* 38 (1): 83–107.

Kenyatta, J. 1938. *Facing Mount Kenya.* London: Secker & Warburg.

1968. *Suffering without Bitterness: The Founding of the Kenya Nation.* Nairobi: East African Publishing House.

Kershaw, G. 1997. *Mau Mau from Below.* Oxford: James Currey.

Kiai, M., and Muite, P. 2009. Challenging the Kikuyu oligarchy. *Daily Nation,* Friday 17th April—and their critics. Retrieved from www.kikuyus forchange.com

Kipkorir, B. E. 1969. *The Alliance High School and the origins of the Kenya African elite 1926–1962.* PhD thesis. Cambridge University.

1972. The educated elite and local society: The basis for mass representation. In Ogot, B. A. (ed.), *Hadith 4: Politics and Nationalism in Colonial Kenya.* Nairobi: East African Publishing House, pp. 250–269.

2009. *Descent from the Cherang'any Hills: Memoirs of a Reluctant Academic.* Nairobi: Macmillan Kenya.

Klopp, J., and Sheekh, N. M. 2008. Can the Guiding Principles make a difference in Kenya? *Forced Migration Review (Guiding Principles 10).* pp. 19–20.

Klumpp, D., and Kratz, C. 1993. Aesthetics, expertise, & ethnicity. In Spear, T. T., and Waller, R. (eds.), *Being Maasai: Ethnicity and Identity in East Africa.* London: James Currey, pp. 195–221.

Knighton, B. 2010. Going for *cai* at Gatundu: Reversion to a Kikuyu ethnic past or building a Kenyan national future? In Branch D., Cheeseman N., and Gardners, L. (eds.), *Our Turn to Eat: Politics in Kenya.* Berlin: LIT Verlag, pp. 107–128.

Kyle, K. 1999. *The Politics of the Independence of Kenya.* Basingstoke: Macmillan.

Lamphear, J. 1970. The Kamba and the northern Mrima coast. In Gray, R., and Birmingham, D. (eds.), *Pre-Colonial African Trade: Essays on Trade in Central and Eastern Africa before 1900.* London: Oxford University Press, pp. 75–118.

1992. *The Scattering Time: Turkana Responses to Colonial Rule.* Oxford: Clarendon Press.

Leo, C. 1984. *Land and Class in Kenya.* Toronto: University of Toronto Press.

Leakey, L. S. B. 1977. *The Southern Kikuyu before 1903.* London: Academic Press.

Leys, C. 1975. *Underdevelopment in Kenya: The Political Economy of Neo-Colonialism.* London: Heinemann.

Lochery, E. 2012. Rendering difference visible: The Kenyan state and its Somali citizens. *African Affairs.* 111(445): 615–639.

Lonsdale, J. 1977a. The politics of conquest: The British in western Kenya, 1894–1908. *Historical Journal.* 20(4): 841–870.

1977b. When did the Gusii (or any other group) become a "tribe"? A review essay. *Kenya Historical Journal*. 5, pp. 123–133.

1986. The depression and the second world war in the transformation of Kenya. In Killingray, D., and Rathbone, R. (eds.), *Africa and the Second World War*. Basingstoke: Macmillan, pp. 97–142.

1989. The conquest state of Kenya. In Moor, J. A., and Wesseling, H. L. (eds.), *Imperialism and War: Essays on Colonial Wars in Asia and Africa*. Leiden, the Netherlands: Brill, pp. 87–120.

1992. The moral economy of Mau Mau. In Berman, B. J., and Lonsdale, J. (eds.), *Unhappy Valley: Conflict in Kenya and Africa*. London: James Currey, pp. 265–504.

1995. The prayers of Waiyaki: Political uses of the Kikuyu past. In Anderson, D. M., and Johnson, D. H. (eds.), *Revealing Prophets: Prophecy in Eastern African History*. London: James Currey, pp. 240–291.

2000. KAU's cultures: Imaginations of community and constructions of leadership in Kenya after the Second World War. *Journal of African Cultural Studies*. 13(1): 107–124.

2002a. Contests of Time: Kikuyu historiographies, old and new. In Harneit-Sievers, A. (ed.), *A Place in the World: New Local Historiographies from Africa and South Asia*. Leiden, the Netherlands: Brill, pp. 201–254.

2002b. Jomo Kenyatta, God, and the modern world. In Deutsch, J. G., Probst, P., and Schmidt, H. (eds.), *African Modernities: Entangled Meanings in Current Debate*. Portsmouth, NH: Heinemann, pp. 31–66.

2003. Authority, gender & violence: The war within Mau Mau's fight for land and freedom. In Atieno Odhiambo, E. S., and Lonsdale, J. (eds.), *Mau Mau and Nationhood*. Oxford: James Currey, pp. 46–75.

2005. "Listen while I read". Patriotic Christianity among the Young Kikuyu. In Falola, T. (ed.), *Christianity and Social Change in Africa: Essays in Honor of J.D.Y. Peel*. Durham, NC: Carolina Academic Press, pp. 563–593.

2008a. Soil, work, civilization and citizenship in Kenya. *Journal of Eastern African Studies* 2(2): 305–314.

2009a. Henry Muoria, public moralist. In Muoria-Sal, W., Frederiksen, B. F., Lonsdale, J., and Peterson, D. R. (eds.), *Writing for Kenya: The Life and Works of Henry Muoria*. Leiden, the Netherlands: Brill, pp. 1–58.

2009b. Writing competitive patriotisms in eastern Africa. In Peterson, D. R., and Macola, G. (eds.), *Recasting the Past: History Writing and Political Work in Modern Africa*. Athens: Ohio University Press, pp. 251–267.

2009c. Compromised critics: Religion in Kenya's politics. In Knighton, B. (ed.), *Religion and Politics in Kenya: Essays in Honor of a Meddlesome Priest*. New York: Palgrave Macmillan, pp. 57–94.

2012. Ethnic patriotism and markets in African history. In Hino, H., Lonsdale, J., Ranis, G., and Stewart, F. (eds.), *Ethnic Diversity and Economic Instability in Africa: Interdisciplinary Perspectives*. Cambridge: Cambridge University Press, pp. 19–55.

2017. Mau Mau's debates on trial. In MacArthur, J. (ed.), *Dedan Kimathi on Trial*. Athens: Ohio University Press, pp. 258–283.

Low, D. A., and Smith, A. (eds.). 1976. *History of East Africa III*. Oxford: Clarendon.

Lynch, G. 2006. Negotiating ethnicity: Identity politics in contemporary Kenya. *Review of African Political Economy*. 33(107): 49–65.

2010. Histories of association and difference: The construction and negotiation of difference. In Branch D., Cheeseman N., and Gardners, L. (eds.), *Our Turn to Eat: Politics in Kenya*. Berlin: LIT Verlag, pp. 177–197.

2011) *I Say to You: Ethnic Politics and the Kalenjin in Kenya*. Chicago: University of Chicago Press.

2016. *Majimboism* and Kenya's moral economy of ethnic territoriality. In Berman, B. J., Laliberté, A., and Larin, S. J. (eds.), *The Moral Economies of Ethnic and Nationalist Claims*. Vancouver: UBC Press, pp. 49–69.

MacArthur, J. 2008. How the West Was Won: Regional Politics and Prophetic Promises in the 2007 Kenya Elections. *Journal of Eastern African Studies*. 2(2): 227–241.

2016. *Cartography and the Political Imagination: Mapping Community in Colonial Kenya*. Athens: Ohio University Press.

MacArthur, J. (ed.). 2017. *Dedan Kimathi on Trial*. Athens: Ohio University Press.

Macharia, K. 1988. *Social networks: Ethnicity and the informal sector in Nairobi. Working paper n. 463*. University of Nairobi: Institute of Development Studies.

Mahoney, M. 2012. *The Other Zulus: The Spread of Zulu Ethnicity in Colonial South Africa*. Durham, NC: Duke University Press.

Makila, F. E. 1978. *An Outline History of the Babukusu of Western Kenya*. Nairobi: Kenya Literature Bureau.

Marris, P., and Somerset, A. 1971. *African Businessmen: A Study of Entrepreneurship and Development in Kenya*. London: Routledge & Kegan Paul.

Matson, A. T. 1972a. *Nandi Resistance to British Rule*. Nairobi: East African Publishing House.

1972b. Reflections on the growth of political consciousness in Nandi. In Ogot, B. A. (ed.), *Hadith 4: Politics and Nationalism in Colonial Kenya.* Nairobi: East African Publishing House, pp. 18–45.

Maupeu, H. 2003a. Enterrement des *big men* et nation kenyane. In Droz, Y., and Muapeu, H. (eds.), *Les figure de la mort à Nairobi: Une capitale sans cimetières.* Paris: L'Harmattan, pp. 231–263.

2003b. La mort dans le Kenya contemporain. In Droz, Y. (ed.), *La Violence et les Morts: Eclairage anthropologique sur les rites funéraires.* Genève: Georg Editeur, pp. 122–135.

Mboya, P. 1938. *Luo Kitgi gi Timbegi.* Internet translation (2002) by Jane Achieng' & Jim Harries as *The Luo, Their Cultures and Traditions* from the 8th edn (1983). Kisumu, Kenya: Anyange Press.

Morris, H. F., and Read, J. S. 1972. *Indirect Rule and the Search for Justice: Essays in East African Legal History.* Oxford: Clarendon.

Morrison, L. B. 2007. The nature of decline: Distinguishing myth from reality in the case of the Luo of Kenya. *Journal of Modern African Studies.* 45(1): 117–142.

Mueller, S. 1972. *Political parties in Kenya: Patterns of opposition and dissent 1919–1969.* PhD thesis. Princeton University.

2008. The political economy of Kenya's crisis. *Journal of Eastern African Studies.* 2(2): 185–210.

2010. Government and opposition in Kenya, 1966–69. In Branch, D., Cheeseman, N., and Gardners, L. (eds.), *Our Turn to Eat: Politics in Kenya.* Berlin: LIT Verlag, pp. 77–105.

Muigai, G. 2004. Jomo Kenyatta & the rise of the ethno-nationalist state in Kenya. In Berman, B., Dickson, E., and Kymlicka, W. (eds.), *Ethnicity and Democracy in Africa.* Oxford: James Currey, pp. 200–217.

Muriuki, G. 1974. *A History of the Kikuyu 1500–1900.* Nairobi: Oxford University Press.

Muriuki, G., and Sobania, N. 2007. The truth be told: Stereoscopic photographs, interviews and oral tradition from Mount Kenya. *Journal of Eastern African Studies.* 1(1): 1–15.

Mwaniki, H. S. K. 1973. *The Living History of Embu and Mbeere.* Nairobi: East African Literature Bureau.

Ndege, G. 2001. *Health, State, and Society in Kenya.* Rochester, NY: University of Rochester Press.

Ngarachu, F. 2015. *Why not ask the children? Understanding young people's perspectives on ethnicity and politics in Kenya.* PhD thesis. University of Southampton.

Northcote, G. A. S. 21 June 1912. *Letter to PC Kenia Province.* Kenya National Archives: PC/Coast 64/252A

Oba, G. 2013. *Nomads in the Shadows of Empires: Contests, Conflicts and Legacies on the Southern Ethiopian-Northern Kenyan frontier*. Leiden, the Netherlands: Brill.

Ochieng', W. R. 1974. *A Pre-Colonial History of the Gusii of Western Kenya c. A.D. 1500–1914*. Nairobi: East African Literature Bureau.

Ocobock, P. 2017. *An Uncertain Age: The Politics of Manhood in Kenya*. Athens: Ohio University Press.

Odinga, O. 1967. *Not yet Uhuru*. London: Heinemann.

Ogot, B. A. 1967. *History of the Southern Luo: Volume I, Migration and Settlement, 1500–1900*. Nairobi: East African Publishing House.

1995. The decisive years. In Ogot, B. A., and Ochieng', W. R. (eds.), *Decolonization & Independence in Kenya 1940–93*. London: James Currey, pp. 48–79.

1999. The siege of Ramogi: From national coalitions to ethnic coalitions, 1960–1998. In Ogot, B. A. (ed.), *Building on the Indigenous: Selected Essays 1981–1998*. Kisumu, Kenya: Anyange Press, pp. 277–288.

2003. Mau Mau and nationhood: The untold story. In Atieno Odhiambo, E. S., and Lonsdale, J. (eds.), *Mau Mau and Nationhood*. Oxford: James Currey, pp. 8–36.

2010. *Who, if Anyone, Owns the Past? Reflections on the Meaning of 'Public History*. Kisumu, Kenya: Anyange Press.

2012. Essence of ethnicity: An African perspective. In Hino, H., Lonsdale, J., Ranis, G., and Stewart, F. (eds.), *Ethnic Diversity and Economic Instability in Africa: Interdisciplinary Perspectives*. Cambridge: Cambridge University Press, pp. 91–126.

Omusule, M. 1974. *Political and constitutional aspects of the origins and development of local government in Kenya 1895–1963*. PhD thesis. Syracuse University.

Osborne, M. G. 2014. *Ethnicity and Empire in Kenya: Loyalty and Martial Race among the Kamba, c. 1800 to the Present*. New York: Cambridge University Press.

Oucho, J. O. 2002. *Undercurrents of Ethnic Conflict in Kenya*. Leiden, the Netherlands: Brill.

Parker, I. 2009. *The Last Colonial Regiment: The History of the Kenya Regiment (T.F.)*. Milton Brodie, UK: Librario.

Parkin, D. 1978. *The Cultural Definition of Political Response: Lineal Destiny among the Luo*. London: Academic Press.

Parsons, T. H. 2003. *The 1964 Army Mutinies and the Making of Modern East Africa*. Westport, CT: Praeger.

2011. Local responses to the ethnic geography of colonialism in the Gusii highlands of British-ruled Kenya. *Ethnohistory*. 58(3): 491–523.

2012. Being Kikuyu in Meru: Challenging the tribal geography of colonial Kenya. *Journal of African History.* 53(1): 65–86.

Peatrik, A.-M. 1999. *La vie à pas contés: Génération, âge et société dans les hautes terres du Kénya (Meru-Tigania-Igembe).* Nanterre, France: Société d'Ethnologie.

Percox, D. 2012. *Britain, Kenya and the Cold War: Imperial Defence, Colonial Security and Decolonisation.* London: I.B. Tauris.

Perrin Jassy, M.-F. 1973. *Basic Community in the African Churches.* Maryknoll, NY: Orbis Books.

Peterson, D. R. 2003. Writing in revolution: Independent schooling and Mau Mau in Nyeri. In Atieno Odhiambo, E. S., and Lonsdale, J. (eds.), *Mau Mau and Nationhood.* Oxford: James Currey, pp. 76–96.

2012. *Ethnic Patriotism and the East African Revival: A History of Dissent, c. 1935–1972.* Cambridge: Cambridge University Press.

Phillips, A. 1945. *Report on Native Tribunals.* Nairobi: Government Printer.

Prunier, G. 1998. Jomo Kenyatta et son temps. In Grignon, F., and Prunier, G. (eds.), *Le Kenya contemporain.* Nairobi: IFRA, pp. 113–139.

Pugliese, C. 2003. Complementary or contending nationhoods? Kikuyu pamphlets and songs, 1945–52. In Atieno Odhiambo, E. S., and Lonsdale, J. (eds.), *Mau Mau and Nationhood.* Oxford: James Currey, pp. 97–120.

Ranger, T. O. 1967. *Revolt in Southern Rhodesia 1896–7: A Study in African Resistance.* London: Heinemann.

1983. The invention of tradition in colonial Africa. In Hobsbawm, E., and Ranger, T. (eds.), *The Invention of Tradition.* Cambridge: Cambridge University Press, pp. 211–262.

1993. The invention of tradition revisited: The case of colonial Africa. In Ranger, T., and Vaughan, O. (eds.), *The Legitimacy of the State in Twentieth Century Africa.* London: Macmillan, pp. 62–111.

Reid, R. 2007. *War in Pre-Colonial Eastern Africa: The Patterns & Meanings of State-Level Conflict in the Nineteenth Century.* Oxford: James Currey.

2011. Past and presentism: The "precolonial" and the foreshortening of African history. *Journal of African History.* 52(2): 135–155.

Renan, E. 1882. *Qu'est-ce qu'une nation?* Lecture at the Sorbonne, 11 March.

Robertson, C. C. 1997. *Trouble Showed the Way: Women, Men, and Trade in the Nairobi Area, 1890–1980.* Bloomington: Indiana University Press.

Rosberg, C. G., and Nottingham, J. 1966. *The Myth of 'Mau Mau': Nationalism in Kenya.* London: Pall Mall.

Rowe, J. A. 1969. Myth, memoir and moral admonition: Luganda historical writing 1893–1969. *Uganda Journal*. 33, pp. 17–40.

  1977. "Progress and a sense of identity": African historiography in East Africa. *Kenya Historical Journal*. 5, pp. 23–34.

Sang, G. K. 2015. *Just for Today': The Life and Times of Jean-Marie Seroney*. Thatcham, UK: Dolman Scott.

Sanger, C., and Nottingham, J. 1964. The Kenya general election of 1963. *Journal of Modern African Studies*. 2(1): 1–40.

Schama, S. 2009. *A History of Britain II: The British Wars 1603–1776*. London: Bodley Head.

Schuberth, M. 2018. Hybrid security governance, post-election violence and the legitimacy of community-based armed groups in urban Kenya. *Journal of Eastern African Studies*. 12(2): 386–404.

Shipton, P. 2009. *Mortgaging the Ancestors: Ideologies of Attachment in Africa*. New Haven, CT: Yale University Press.

Siméant, J. 2015. Three bodies of moral economy: The diffusion of a concept. *Journal of Global Ethics*. 11(2): 163–175.

Smith, A. D. 1981. *The Ethnic Revival in the Modern World*. Cambridge: Cambridge University Press.

Sorrenson, M. P. K. 1968. *Origins of European Settlement in Kenya*. Nairobi: Oxford University Press.

Spear, T. T. 1978. *The Kaya Complex: A History of the Mijikenda Peoples of the Kenya Coast to 1900*. Nairobi: Kenya Literature Bureau.

  1981. *Kenya's Past: An Introduction to Historical Method in Africa*. Harlow, UK: Longman.

  1993. Being "Maasai" but not "people of cattle": Arusha agricultural Maasai in the nineteenth century. In Spear, T. T., and Waller, R. (eds.), *Being Maasai: Ethnicity and Identity in East Africa*. London: James Currey, pp. 120–136.

  2003. Neo-traditionalism and the limits of invention in British colonial Africa. *Journal of African History*. 44(1): 3–27.

Spear, T. T., and Waller, R. (eds.). 1993. *Being Maasai: Ethnicity and Identity in East Africa*. London: James Currey.

Spencer, J. 1983. *James Beauttah, Freedom Fighter*. Nairobi: Stellascope.

  1985. *The Kenya African Union*. London: KPI.

Stephens, R. 2016. Who is a person of wealth? Greater Luyia concepts of wealth in precolonial East Africa. Presentation at 59th Annual Meeting of the African Studies Association, Washington DC.

Strobel, M. 1979. *Muslim Women in Mombasa 1890–1975*. New Haven, CT: Yale University Press.

Sutton, J. E. G. 1973. *The Archaeology of the Western Highlands of Kenya*. Nairobi: British Institute in Eastern Africa.

1993. Becoming Maasailand. In Spear, T. T., and Waller, R. (eds.), *Being Maasai: Ethnicity and identity in East Africa*. London: James Currey, pp. 38–60.

Thomas, L. M. 2003. *Politics of the Womb: Women, Reproduction, and the State in Kenya*. Berkeley: University of California Press.

Throup. D. W. 1987a. *Economic and Social Origins of Mau Mau 1945–53.* London: James Currey.

1987b. The construction and destruction of the Kenyatta state. In Schatzberg, M. G. (ed.), *The Political Economy of Kenya*. New York: Westport, pp. 33–74.

Throup. D. W., and Hornsby, C. 1998. *Multi-Party Politics in Kenya: The Kenyatta & Moi States & the Triumph of the System in the 1992 Election*. Oxford: James Currey.

Tilly, C. 2005. *Trust and Rule*. Cambridge: Cambridge University Press.

Tombs, R., and Tombs, I. 2006. *That Sweet Enemy: The British and the French from the Sun King to the Present*. London: Pimlico.

Turton, E. R. 1972. Somali resistance to colonial rule and the development of Somali political activity in Kenya 1893–1960. *Journal of African History*. 13(1): 119–143.

Vail, L. (ed.). 1988. *The Creation of Tribalism in Southern Africa*. Berkeley: University of California Press.

Van Stapele, N. 2015. Respectable *"Illegality"*: Gangs, masculinities and belonging in a Nairobi ghetto. PhD thesis: Universiteit van Amsterdam.

Vianni, W. 2016. Jomo Kenyatta: War, land and politics in Kenya. In Obadare, E., and Abdeanwi, W. (eds.), *Governance and the Crisis of Rule in Contemporary Africa: Leadership in Transformation*. New York: Palgrave Macmillan, pp. 97–117.

Von Oppen, A. 1993. *Terms of Trade and Terms of Trust: The History and Context of Pre-Colonial Market Production around the Upper Zambezi and Kasai*. Münster: LIT Verlag.

Waller, R. D. 1973. *"The Lords of East Africa"*: The Maasai in the mid-nineteenth century. PhD thesis. Cambridge University.

1976. The Maasai and the British 1895–1905: The origins of an alliance. *Journal of African History*. 17(4): 529–553.

1985. Ecology, migration and expansion in East Africa. *African Affairs*. 84(336): 347–370.

1988. Emutai: Crisis and response in Maasailand 1883–1902. In Johnson, D., and Anderson, D. (eds.), *The Ecology of Survival: Case Studies from Northeast African History*. London: Lester Crook, pp. 73–112.

1993a. Acceptees and aliens: Kikuyu settlement in Maasailand. In Spear, T. T., and Waller, R. (eds.), *Being Maasai: Ethnicity and Identity in East Africa*. London: James Currey, pp. 226–257.

1993b. Conclusions. In Spear, T. T., and Waller, R. (eds.), *Being Maasai: Ethnicity and Identity in East Africa*. London: James Currey, pp. 290–302.

1995. Kidongoi's Kin: Prophecy and power in Maasailand. In Anderson, D. M., and Johnson, D. H. (eds.), *Revealing Prophets: Prophecy in eastern African History*. London: James Currey, pp. 28–64.

1999. Pastoral poverty in historical perspective. In Anderson, D. M., and Broch-Due, V. (eds.), *The Poor Are Not Us: Poverty & Pastoralism in Eastern Africa*. Oxford: James Currey, pp. 20–49.

2013. Ethnicity and identity. In Reid, R. (ed.), *The Oxford Handbook of African History*. Oxford: Oxford University Press, pp. 94–109.

Wamai, E. N. 2016. *Peace, justice, and "moving on": Local political contestation of the International Criminal Court in Kenya*. PhD thesis. University of Cambridge.

Whisson, M. G. 1962. *The will of God and the wiles of men*. Limuru: East African Institute of Social Research conference paper.

White, L. 1990. *The Comforts of Home: Prostitution in Colonial Nairobi*. Chicago: University of Chicago Press.

Whittaker, H. 2015. *Insurgency and Counterinsurgency in Kenya: A Social History of the Shifta Conflict, c. 1963–1968*. Leiden, the Netherlands: Brill.

Weisner, T. S., Bradley, C., and Kilbride, P. L. (eds.). 1997. *African Families and the Crisis of Social Change*. Westport, CT: Bergin & Garvey.

Were, G. S. 1967. *A History of the Abaluyia of Western Kenya c.1500–1930*. Nairobi: East African Publishing House.

Wilson, G., and Malo, S. 1961. *Luo Customary Law and Marriage Laws [and] Customs*. Nairobi: Government Printer.

Wrong, M. 2009. *It's Our Turn to Eat: The Story of a Kenyan Whistle Blower*. London: Fourth Estate.

2 | Better Elections, More Deaths
Nigeria

ABDUL RAUFU MUSTAPHA[1]

2.1 Introduction

In 2007, Nigeria held one of the most farcical elections ever conducted in the history of electoral competition on the African continent (Omotoshio, 2009; Zasha, Mustapha, and Meyer 2007). These elections were greeted with such levels of domestic and international condemnation and derision that even the winner of the presidential election, the late President Yar Adua, announced that electoral reform was one of his top priorities. Yet, despite all its glaring short comings, only 300 people were killed in election related violence in 2007 (Amnesty International, 2007; Improving Institutions for Pro-Poor Growth, 2009). By contrast, the elections that took place in April 2011 'were heralded as among the fairest in Nigeria's history, but they also were among the bloodiest' (Human Rights Watch, 2011). There were 800 people killed in a wave of postelection violence in April; in the 4 months before the elections proper, another 50–90 people were reported killed and 209 injured in political violence during the campaigns (Abubakar et al., 2011; Wisdom, 2011). Some observers like Human Rights Watch have noted the paradox of 'Improved Elections but a New Cycle of Violence' in 2011. Why have better elections led to more electoral deaths when, by definition, improved electoral choice and voter efficacy should lead to the opposite effect?

There is no doubt that a section of public and official opinion in Nigeria holds the opposition Congress for Progressive Change (CPC) and its presidential candidate, General Muhammadu Buhari, responsible for the violence. Some, like Nobel Laureate Wole Soyinka, argue that the violence was deliberately stoked, whereas others suggest indirect culpability, arguing that Buhari should have more strenuously

---

[1] Sadly, Abdul Raufu Mustapha passed away before the completion of the book. To the extent possible, the reference list has been checked and completed by the editors.

condemned the violence at the very onset if he was indeed opposed to it. It is true that the fighting started when polling trends were beginning to suggest that Buhari was losing the election to the incumbent president, Goodluck Jonathan, from the Peoples' Democratic Party (PDP). It is equally true that many rioters were chanting slogans in support of the CPC. However, on closer analysis, explanations that the CPC 'caused' the violence fail to explain important aspects of the violence. How was it possible to organise, coordinate, and orchestrate violence across five states of the federation, covering vast distances without these activities and arms build-up being detected in the tense atmosphere surrounding the elections? How do we explain the fact that General Buhari's convoy was attacked by the rioters? Finally, how do we explain the different patterns of violence in different states? Why was the violence targeted largely against leading PDP members and traditional authorities within the same ethnic community as the rioters in some states, and against other ethnic and religious communities in others? Significantly, a former PDP minister, Femi Fani-Kayode observed shortly after the rioting:

As regards the unfortunate and sad events that took place in the core north immediately after the just concluded presidential elections, during the course of my research and consultations with various groups and stakeholders in the last few days, I have established the following facts . . . (a) That Muhammadu Buhari, the CPC flag bearer, was deeply pained and actually wept as the massacres were going on, and he tried his best to stop them . . . (b) That even a convoy of his own vehicles was attacked during the riots . . . (c) That even though the rioters, murderers and arsonists were championing his cause, carrying his posters and calling his name, once the barbarism and pogroms actually started, he had absolutely no control over it or any way of stopping it. (Fani-Kayode, 2011)

In this chapter, I seek to explain the postelectoral violence of 2011 in the context of long-term trends within Nigerian society and short-term political manoeuvres immediately before the elections. Although the long-term trends in ethnic and regional inequalities created the latent conditions for ethnic conflict, the short-term manoeuvres surrounding the elections provided the immediate trigger that ignited the conflict. The combination of both tendencies created a volatile and combustible climate which continues to threaten the stability of Nigeria's fragile democracy. The paradox of better elections leading to more deaths can therefore best be explained by the converging consequences of: (1) the long-run structural horizontal inequalities and tensions that divide Nigerian society along ethnoregional lines – and this also substantially overlaps with religion and (2) the short-term pursuit of narrow political advantage by politicians in the 2011 elections which ended up exacerbating the tensions arising from the long-term inequalities. The combined effect of both tendencies was that despite an improved electoral system, violence resulted from the alienation and discontent that had become rife in those communities in which the violence took place. The CPC defeat was the justification for, rather than the cause of, the violence. Those targeted by the rioters varied across the states, depending on how deeply ingrained the long-term and short-term grievances were, and depending on how 'culpable' the targets of the violence were held to be.

In Section 2, I outline the key features of the long-run horizontal inequalities, showing their destabilising impacts at both the societal and the individual levels. In Section 3, I outline the short-term political manoeuvres that complicated the tensions arising from the horizontal inequalities. Section 4 provides a conclusion, drawing particular attention to what scholars of the management of ethnic diversity in Nigeria call the 'boomerang effect'.

2.2 Long-Run Horizontal Inequalities

Inequalities between and within Nigerian communities have a long history, dating back to precolonial times in the nineteenth century. Some precolonial entities developed extensive state systems with elements of class stratification, whereas others were organised in simple clan polities. Some precolonial states were multi-ethnic in composition, and others were based on ethnic homogeneity. Precolonial Nigerian entities were, therefore, unequal in their levels of political and economic sophistication. Bringing these diverse entities together under one state was one of the major achievements of colonial occupation. However, colonial cultural geography also tended to reinforce existing differences between these groups through the reification of the unity of the trinity of chief, people, and territory. In the colonial context, some old patterns of inequalities between communities and entities were reinforced and new ones evolved. The net result was a conception of society built on discreet ethnic communities operating within a system of colonial hierarchies held together by the superintending presence of the colonial administration.

These hierarchies ranked ethnic groups according to perceived characteristics. Some ethnic groups were regarded as 'warlike' and 'loyal', and their members were encouraged to join the colonial military forces. Others were considered as 'intelligent' and encouraged to be clerks within the administration, while some others were regarded as 'natural leaders' and were accordingly given the control of local chieftaincies, even over other ethnicities. Those categorised as 'truculent' or 'lazy' found themselves at a serious disadvantage within the colonial order. These colonial ethnic hierarchies, working in conjunction with the variable natural resource endowments of different ethnic territories, their demographic dynamics, and their cultural and religious tendencies, led to a situation in which ethnic groups were increasingly differentiated in terms of their control over socioeconomic, political, bureaucratic, and cultural resources in the country. Colonialism not only brought diverse Nigerian groups together, it also fundamentally divided them.

Since 1900, therefore, the policies and prejudices of colonial administrations have combined with the political economies of native communities to produce discernible patterns of ethnic inequalities and hierarchies that continue to affect Nigerian society today. These horizontal inequalities often became entrenched and cumulative over time, threatening both the cohesion and stability of the country. This long-drawn process has in recent times led to a concentric pattern of seven ethnic and political cleavages in Nigeria: (a) between the north and the south, (b) between the three majority ethnic groups (Hausa, Igbo, and Yoruba), (c) between these majority ethnic groups on the one hand and the 300-odd minority ethnic groups on the other, (d) interstate rivalry between states, sometimes within and sometimes between ethnic groups, (e) interethnic rivalry in a mixed state composed of minority groups of different strengths or a segment of a majority ethnicity surrounded by minority groups, (f) intraethnic or subethnic rivalry within each majority ethnic group, sometimes also corresponding with state boundaries and sometimes within a single state, (g) and finally, interclan and intraclan rivalries, particularly in the southeast and the northcentral parts of the country.

The most politically significant cleavages are, however, the first three: between the northern and southern halves of the country, between the three majority ethnic groups, and between the majority groups, on the one hand, and the 'minorities', on the other. The majority groups are the composite Hausa–Fulani of the northwest, the Yoruba of the southwest, and the Igbo of the southeast. These three constituted 57.8 per cent of the population in 1963.[2] The Hausa (without the Fulani) were 20.9 per cent, the Yoruba, 20.3 per cent, and the Igbo, 16.6 per cent (Munzali, 1991, p. 111). Eleven of the largest ethnic minorities together constituted 27.9 per cent (Afolayan, 1983, p. 155). Since the 1970s, ethnoregional cleavages have been joined by the increasing polarisation of society along religious lines between Muslims and Christians (see Mustapha, Diprose, and Ehrhardt, 2012).

Although Nigeria is divided into thirty-six states, the key overlapping cleavages of ethnicity, regionalism, and religion are well-captured in the division of the thirty-six states into six geopolitical zones: northwest, northeast, northcentral, southwest, southeast, and southsouth. Each geopolitical zone can be given a broad ethnic/regional/religious identification, based on the majority of the indigenous population in that zone. In this regard, the northwest zone is the core Hausa–Fulani area, whereas the northeast zone contains a mixture of Hausa–Fulani, Kanuri, and many northern ethnic minorities. Both zones are heavily Muslim and are regarded as constituting the 'far north', sharing overlapping cultural and Islamic attributes. However, Kanuri ethnonationalism is an important factor in the northeast. The northcentral is traditionally regarded as the zone of the non-Islamic northern ethnic minorities. It is also regarded as the 'lower north'. Many of the ethnic minorities here are Christians, although others follow traditional African religions. Although this zone was equally involved in the political construction of a monolithic pan-Northern regional identity against the South in the 1950s (Kwanashie, 2002), it is nevertheless a zone of cultural/religious resistance against alleged Hausa–Fulani Muslim domination and oppression in the colonial and immediate postcolonial periods. The culture of this 'lower north' is very different from that of the 'far north'.

The southwest zone is made up of the old Western region, the heartland of the Yoruba. The Yoruba are divided between Islam and Christianity, with ethnic identity often taking precedence over religious. The southeast is made up of the Igbo heartlands of the old

---

[2] Ethnicity and religion were omitted in the 2005 census.

Table 2.1 *Post–primary educational institutions in Nigeria by Zones, 1989*

Zone	Population in 1991 (Per Cent of National Total)	Number of Institutions (Per Cent of National Total)
Northwest	22,910,412 (25.8)	567 (9.7)
Northeast	11,900,913 (13.4)	343 (5.9)
Northcentral	12,133,696 (13.6)	1,022 (17.5)
Southwest	17,455,138 (19.6)	1,575 (27.0)
Southeast	10,774,977 (12.1)	1,208 (20.7)
Southsouth	13,392,963 (15.1)	1,114 (19.1)

Sources: Adapted from the Federal Republic of Nigeria, 2001; Tell, November 14, 1994, p. 15.

Eastern region. The Igbo are predominantly Christians, the major religious schism within them being the sectarian divisions between Catholics, Protestants, and Pentecostals. The last zone, the southsouth, is the zone of southern ethnic minorities, from the peripheries of the Igbo core of the old Eastern region, and the whole of the old Mid-West region. The majority here are also Christians and followers of traditional religions.

2.2.1 Socioeconomic Inequalities

From the colonial period, patterns of socioeconomic inequalities have developed between the various ethnic communities in Nigeria. As in 1989, the persisting educational inequality is indicated in Table 2.1.

Table 2.1 shows the number of post–primary institutions in each zone, relative to their share of the population. The general trend is that the northern zones have a low share of the educational institutions, relative to their share of the national population. Second, although precise figures are not available to establish this fact, many of the students in the educational institutions in the northern zones are likely to come from the southern zones. In short, there is a serious north–south educational imbalance amongst Nigeria's ethnic and regional groups. The educational gap between the Muslim north and the rest of the country is partly because of cultural resistance against alien Christian, Western culture. But it is also as a result of deliberate colonial policy, which held back education in the north (Barnes, 1997).

Table 2.2 *Admissions to Nigerian Universities by zone of origin, 2000/2001*

Zone	Number of Admitted Candidates	Per Cent of Total Admissions	Per Cent of Total Population (1991 Census)
Northwest	2,341	4.7	25.8
Northeast	1,979	3.9	13.4
Northcentral	5,597	11.1	13.6
Southwest	8,763	17.4	19.6
Southeast	19,820	39.4	12.1
Southsouth	11,734	23.3	15.1

Source: Adapted from the Joint Admissions and Matriculation Board (JAMB) website: www.jamb.gov.ng.

Because these educational institutions are responsible for preparing candidates for bureaucratic recruitment, the inequalities in educational access are also reflected in the patterns of bureaucratic recruitment. The influence of the educational system on the process of elite formation is further demonstrated when we look at the number of candidates from each state/zone, seeking admission into the universities. In 2000 and 2001, in the thirty-six states of the federation, the six states with the largest number of candidates for admission were all from the south – two from each southern zone. They presented a total of 218,475 candidates for admission. In contrast, the six states with the least number of candidates were all from the north – three each from the northwest and northeast. They presented a total of 6,729 candidates, a mere 3.1 per cent of the candidates from the six southern states that also happen to have a lower share of the national population, compared with the six northern states (Joint Admissions and Matriculation Board, n.d.).

Figures for actual admissions into the universities, by zone of origin, are shown in Table 2.2. What these tables make clear is that the original educational gap between the northern and southern parts of the country, established in the early colonial period, is persisting, with serious implications for the process of elite formation and recruitment; 80.1 per cent of young people going into the universities in 2000 were from the south, which has only 46.8 per cent of the national population.

Furthermore, a 2010 survey of educational opportunities across the country showed that educational inequalities across Nigeria are persisting. The Nigeria Educational Data Survey 2010 conducted by the National Population Commission revealed that of all children between 6 and 16 years of age, the highest percentages who have never attended any school are to be found in the northeast and northwest: northeast – Borno 72 per cent, Yobe 58 per cent, Bauchi 52 per cent; and northwest – Zamfara 68 per cent, Sokoto 66 per cent, and Kebbi 60 per cent. By contrast, all the southsouth states have less than 3 per cent of children out of school, while the southeastern states ranged from 1 to 10 per cent: Ebonyi 10 per cent; Enugu 2 per cent; Abia 1 per cent. For the southwest states, the figures are: Oyo 8 per cent; Ogun 6 per cent; and Lagos 2 per cent. Furthermore, 'On average, less than N5,000 [US $32] is spent per pupil on primary schooling by households in the North-east and North-west zones compares with over N20,000 [US $129] in Lagos and Rivers states' (Edet, 2011).

The persistent and cumulative educational inequalities across Nigeria are further reflected in the level of professional and manpower development in different parts of the country. In 1990, of the 6,407 engineers registered with the Council of Registered Engineers, only 129 or 2.0 per cent are from the northern zones. Similarly, of the 1,344 lawyers called to the Nigerian bar in that year, only 196 or 14.6 per cent are from the northern zones. Of the 669 registered estate surveyors, only 5 or 0.7 per cent are from the northern zones. Only 160 (14.2 per cent) of the 1,125 registered architects are from the northern states. And out of the 522 registered firms of accountants, only 14 (2.7 per cent) are thought to be established by people of northern origins (Tell, 1994).

The overlapping educational and professional inequalities also coincide with wider economic and social inequalities. Of the total number of registered businesses between 1986 and 1990, 57 per cent are in Lagos, located in the southwest; 16 per cent in the north; 14 per cent in the east; and 13 per cent in the core southwest (Hamalai, 1994). By 1997, things had improved slightly, with the northern zones being responsible for 34 per cent of all registered establishments; but this is still well short of the 64 per cent share of the southern zones (Federal Office of Statistics, 1997, p. 188).

Inequalities in the social sector also mirror the inequalities in the educational and economic spheres. As Table 2.3 illustrates, the northern zones are disadvantaged in most indicators of social well-being.

Table 2.3 *Social indicators by zone (in percentages): 1995–1996*

	North-west	North-east	North Central	South-west	South-east	South-south
Households using stream or pond	13.6	26.4	44.4	22.6	61.4	50.4
Households without electricity	79.8	78.3	61.2	30.4	47.7	55.7
Adult literacy (≥15 years of age)	20.7	25	44.7	68.9	75.8	77.2
Women using family planning	2.6	1.4	4.5	12.1	14.9	9.1
Pregnant women using clinics	25.3	39.4	66.8	74.7	84.8	60.7
Newborns not immunised	65.9	60.7	54	29.1	29	56.9

Source: Adapted from Federal Office of Statistics (FOS), 1995/1996, General Household Survey 1995/96, National Report, 1995/1996.

They have more households without electricity, a higher percentage of illiterate adults, and a lower proportion of their women and children with access to basic health care. Another indicator of overlapping patterns of inequalities is the level of poverty in each zone. Amidst generally high levels of poverty, there is a higher concentration of the poor in the northern zones, as Table 2.4 suggests. One-third of Nigeria's poor are concentrated in the three northwest states of Sokoto, Kaduna, and Kano (Canagarajah, 1995, p. 9). Poverty in Nigeria has a very northern face.

Consistent with this poverty trend, a 2011 study by the Lagos Business School showed that the difference in gross domestic product (GDP) per capita between the northern and southern zones of Nigeria has widened with time, with the current GDP per capita in the southern zones being twice that of the northern zones. The GDP per capita in the three northern zones is US$718, while that of the southwest is US$1,436. Those of the southsouth and southeast are US$2,010 and US$933, respectively (Akanbi, 2011). These persisting socioeconomic inequalities, seen in the politicised context of the north–south cleavage, are summarised in Table 2.5.

Table 2.4 *Poverty trends 1980–2004 by zone (in percentages)*

Zone	1980	1985	1992	1996	2004
Northwest	37.7	52.1	36.5	77.2	71.2
Northeast	35.6	54.9	54.0	70.1	72.2
Northcentral	32.2	50.8	46.0	64.7	67.0
Southwest	13.4	38.6	43.1	60.9	43.0
Southeast	12.9	30.4	41.0	53.5	26.7
Southsouth	13.2	45.7	40.8	58.2	35.1
All Nigeria	28.1	46.3	42.7	65.6	54.4

Source: Federal Office of Statistics (FOS), 1999; National Bureau of Statistics (NBS), 2005.

Table 2.5 *Regional socioeconomic inequalities in Nigeria*

Factor	North (%)	South (%)
Population (1991)	53	47
Tertiary educational institutions (1989)	34	66
University admissions (2000)	21	79
Households with immunisation coverage (2006)	22	51
Household heads with formal education (2006)	35	71
Households with floor other than mud (2004)	53	74
Share of population in poverty (2004)	70	36
GDP per capita (USD)	$718	$1,491

Abbreviation: GDP, gross domestic product.
Source: Mustapha, 2012.

2.2.2 *Political Inequalities*

As can be expected, the long-term and entrenched patterns of overlapping socioeconomic inequalities have come to shape peoples' life chances and their political perceptions. They have also had a tremendous impact on the electoral politics of the country and the composition of different governments. Under conditions of scarcity, inequalities and uneven access to economic and political resources, ethnicity (plus regionalism and increasingly religion) has provided a convenient platform for political mobilisation (see Melson and Wolpe, 1971). From the late colonial period, northern Muslim elites became increasingly fearful of the domination of the country by the better educated southern Christian ethnic groups. For example, the influential Northern newspaper, *Gaskiya*, warned against the precipitous granting of self-government to Nigeria by the British in the late 1950s because:

Southerners will take the places of the Europeans in the North ... it is the Southerner who has the power in the north. They have control of the railway stations; of the Post Offices; of Government Hospitals; of the canteens; ...; in all the different departments of Government it is the Southerner who has the power. (Gaskiye, in Agbaje, 1989, p. 105).

Accordingly, the northern elites mobilised around a programme of 'northernisation' (Kwanashie, 2002) with a two-pronged strategy. First, they sought to prevent a southern takeover of the northern regional bureaucracy. Second, through the conversion of the northern population numerical superiority into a parliamentary majority, they sought to gain control of the federal government. The aim of the combined strategies was the entrenchment of northern interests in the political system and the protection of wider northern interests against the better educated southerners. The patterns of political inequalities that emerged from this process, favouring the northern majority, were therefore often the inverse of the socioeconomic inequalities that, as we have shown, favour the southern groups.

The political inequalities in the country are often reflected in the composition of the federal cabinets. Those groups favoured politically tended to be more prominent within the cabinet, relative to the less favoured groups. As Table 2.6 shows, we can see that in quantitative terms, the high periods of Hausa–Fulani domination of the cabinet were the Balewa years of the early 1960s and the Shagari years of the early 1980s. Only under the Gowon and Murtala regimes were the Hausa–Fulani under-represented in the cabinet. The northern ethnic minorities from the northcentral zone, in contrast, were largely excluded at Independence in 1960, but did well after 1967, mainly because this period was dominated by military regimes and northern ethnic minority elites were prominent within the army.

Except for the Balewa and Murtala cabinets, the ethnic minorities from the southsouth have been well represented. With the exception of the Shagari and Obasanjo's (2004) cabinets, the Yoruba from the southwest have also had a fairly proportionate representation in the

Table 2.6 *Ethnic composition of various Nigerian cabinets, 1960–2004, in per cent*

Regime	Hausa–Fulani	Igbo	Northern Minorities	Yoruba	Southern Minorities
Balewa 1960	60	13	0	20	6.7
Gowon 1967	21	0	21	36	21
Murtala 1975	25	0	35	35	5
Shagari 1983	38	8.8	20.5	14.7	17.6
Buhari 1984	35	10	25	20	10
Obasanjo 2004	30	15	18	18	18

Sources: Osaghae (1989, p. 158); Nigerian Army Education Corp & School, 1994, 330–349; list of Obasanjo's ministers in 2004.

cabinets, despite the fact that the dominant political group in that area has often been in opposition to the government at the centre. Indeed, the Yoruba were over-represented in the Gowon and Murtala cabinets. However, the one group that has been consistently under-represented are the Igbo from the southeast.

In summary therefore, although there have been periods of Hausa–Fulani domination of the cabinet, the Igbo have been, by and large, under-represented. The minorities discriminated against in the 1950s and early 1960s have found some representation since 1967. The Yoruba have been adequately represented for most of the period.

Qualitatively, however, the distribution of actual governmental powers might seem to be different from the quantitative distribution of cabinet portfolios described in Table 2.6. It has been pointed out that, of the fourteen heads of government Nigeria has had between 1960 and 2013, nine have been of northern origins, three of Yoruba extraction, with only one each coming from the Igbo ethnicity and the southern minority. Of the fourteen leaders, only two can seriously be said to be of ethnic minority origins. The ethnic majorities have dominated the leadership of the country and, within that context, the north – and more particularly the ethnic Hausa–Fulani – have been at the helm of affairs for a disproportionately long period.

A second qualitative argument often made is that northern politicians have tended to dominate ministries and departments with the greater power of patronage and political sensitivity, leaving the lesser

Table 2.7 *Ethnic distribution of very important and less important portfolios, 1960–2004*

	Hausa–Fulani	Northern Minorities	Igbo	Yoruba	Southern Minorities	Total
Very important portfolios	49 (33%)	37 (25%)	17 (11.6%)	24 (16%)	20 (13.6%)	147
Less important portfolios	6 (13%)	5 (11%)	10 (22%)	13 (28.9%)	11 (24%)	45

Very important portfolios are Finance, Agriculture, Internal Affairs, External Affairs, Education, Federal Capital Territory, Defence, Works, Transport, Communications, Petroleum, and Mines and Power. The less important portfolios are Labour, Employment and Productivity, Information, Science and Technology, Sports and Social Development, Women's Affairs, and Culture and Tourism.

Due to incomplete data, the second Abacha cabinet, the Abdusalami cabinet and the first (1999) Obasanjo cabinet have not been included. Their inclusion is unlikely to change the picture fundamentally.

ministries to others. The ethnic distribution of twelve very important and six less important portfolios between 1960 and 2004 is shown in Table 2.7. In the very important portfolios, there is an over-representation of northern ethnic groups in general and the Hausa–Fulani in particular. Conversely, these northern ethnicities are under-represented in the less important portfolios. In contrast, the southern ethnic groups, but particularly the Igbo, and to a lesser extent, the Yoruba, seem to be under-represented in the very important portfolios and over-represented in the less important portfolios. Southern minorities are over-represented in both categories, particularly in the less important cabinet portfolios.

In effect, for most of postcolonial Nigerian history, northern political elites sought to use their ethnoregional numerical majority to gain political ascendancy and thereby balance out the long-term socioeconomic disadvantages faced by the north. The high instability of immediate postcolonial Nigerian government was because the southern ethnic groups were not content to acquiesce to 'perpetual' northern political domination, while the north remained painfully aware of its socioeconomic deficits and saw political power as the main guarantor of its relevance. Political power was increasingly seen in a zero-sum context.

Table 2.8 *Ethnoregional tendencies in the staffing of Federal Bureaucracies*

	North-west	North-east	North Central	South-west	South-east	South-south
Percentage in the bureaucracy	10.4	8.6	18.4	24.9	16.0	20.17
Percentage in the directorate	16.8	12.7	16.4	24.4	13.4	15.8
Percentage in the technocracy	7.9	5.3	12.8	30.5	21.5	21.6
Percentage in the police	12.0	12.7	22.0	14.0	12.4	26.1

Sources: Adapted from Federal Character Commission, 2000, Consolidated Manpower Statistics – Federal Civil Service, Abuja, p. 2; Official list of all Directors in the Federal Civil Service as of 1998; Federal Character Commission advertorial in Weekly Trust, 1–7 October 1999, p. 23; Federal Character Commission, 1999, Federal Civil Service, 1999 Manpower Statistics, Abuja p. 25.

2.2.3 Bureaucratic Inequalities

If the ethnicities from the northern zones have used their demographic advantage to gain political advantages, the southern ethnicities have tended to convert their higher educational skills into a stranglehold on the bureaucratic institutions of the state. The imbalances in the different bureaucratic arms of the state around 1999 are reflected in Table 2.8.

Despite northern domination of the political system, the shares of the northern zones in the different arms of the bureaucracy are invariably lower than their share of the population, and the inverse is true for the southern zones. The northern zones are particularly under-represented in the technocracies of the state that require high levels of specialist education. It should, however, be noted that northern representation in the political directorate arm of the bureaucracy is relatively high because of the implementation of affirmative action programmes referred to in Nigeria as the 'federal character' principle.

2.2.4 Cultural Status Inequalities

Cultural status inequalities are the least problematic in Nigeria. But this is not to suggest that they are not an issue. The ability of different

Nigerian ethnoregional groups to imprint their cultural symbols, language, and norms on the national psyche is dictated partly by the cultural preferences of the state, and secondarily by the cultural resources available to members of the different groups. The cultural dominance of the three majority ethnic groups – Hausa–Fulani, Igbo, and Yoruba – is captured by the term *wazobia*, which refers to the three groups combined, especially in language matters. National news is in English, but translated into just these three languages; the minority languages are used at the subnational levels. Similarly, the implicit 'respectable' dress code of the Nigerian state borrows heavily from Hausa–Fulani and Yoruba cultural attire, although this has invariably forced elites from other ethnic groups to resuscitate or even invent their own ethnic regalia for public use and symbolic attachment.

State bias has also been alleged – in favour of the Hausa–Fulani Muslims – in the way in which the federal capital, Abuja, has been designed. It is often claimed that the National Assembly complex resembles a mosque, and that statues representing the human form are not used on Abuja streets out of deference to Islamic objections to representing the human form in artistic production. In contrast, when a Christian Igbo Governor of the Central Bank decided to replace the Arabic inscriptions on the Nigerian currency used since colonial times with Roman letters (in the *wazobia* languages, of course!), he was promptly accused of waging a campaign against Muslims and northerners.

Cultural status inequality is also manifested through the differential control of cultural resources by the different ethnic groups outside of the immediate reach of the state. The Hausa–Fulani and Yoruba, in particular, have private newspapers in the vernacular languages, and artists and entrepreneurs whose prodigious production of news, music, and nollywood films incessantly projects their language and norms onto the national scene and psyche. Most minority ethnic groups either lack this nonstate capacity entirely or are in no position to challenge the dominance of the majority ethnic groups. The Igbo are in a somewhat anomalous position; they have a thriving private movie industry, but its production is largely in English. And the development of Igbo vernacular literature is stymied by a poorly developed orthography. Although cultural status inequalities might not be a burning issue, there is no doubt a tendency for the cultures of the ethnic majorities, particularly of the Hausa–Fulani and the Yoruba, to be disproportionately imprinted on national life. But this discrepancy cannot be entirely blamed on state policy.

2.2.5 Consequences of Horizontal Inequalities

Ethnic diversity in itself need not lead to violent conflict, but:

[G]overnance is more likely to be affected when ethnic differences overlap with income differences or, in other words, what really matters for government quality are ethnic group inequalities… Ethnic group inequality is always … statistically significantly associated with worse governance. (Kyriacou, 2013)

In Nigeria, the persisting and pervasive horizontal inequalities outlined here have predictably had a destabilising impact on Nigerian society and the state. Not only does the actual maldistribution lead to ethnic agitation and sometimes conflict, even the mere fear of possible disadvantage can often lead to the same system-threatening effects. And because the inequalities touch on both individual and group life chances in a very real sense, they constitute a fertile ground for political or religious entrepreneurs wishing to mobilise a sectarian following. For example, in the old Western Region in 1964, a much-hated regional government sought to protect itself by fanning anti-Igbo sentiments within its Yoruba constituency. In a White Paper, the government detailed alleged Igbo domination of many federal establishments, ostensibly at the expense of the Yoruba. The composition of various bureaucracies thereby became a major lightening rod for ethnoregional conflict. Alleging nepotism and 'tribalism' in the Nigerian Railway Corporation under an Igbo chairman, the White Paper claimed that:

Out of a grand total of 431 names on the current staff list of our Railway Corporation, 270 are Ibos and 161 belong to other tribes. Of fifty-seven direct senior appointments made by the Nigerian Railway Corporation during the tenure of office of the present chairman, Dr Ikejiani (an Igbo), twenty-seven were Ibos, eight other tribes and twenty two expatriates. (Agbaje, 1989, pp. 111–112)

On its part, the northern elite's position was expressed by Dr Iya Abubakar, who called for a probe of the federal statutory corporations in the hope that northerners will get 'their fair share of office in the federation' (in Agbaje, 1989, p. 113). The northern regional mouthpiece, the *Nigerian Citizen*, referred to the corporations as rotten, scandalous, and treacherous (Agbaje, 1989, p. 113). It is this level of political vitriol, especially between the majority ethnicities, that led to the collapse of the First Republic in 1966.

In contemporary Nigeria, the persisting horizontal inequalities continue to undermine the stability of the society and the cohesion of the state. Commenting on the pattern of northern educational disadvantage in 1994, the former Minister of Education, Professor Jubril Aminu stated:

Certain sections of this country will be highly disturbed about their future in a united Nigeria if they study the pattern of higher educational opportunities in the country. It is this kind of disturbance which promotes among the people some actions and counteractions, mutual suspicion, nepotism and loss of confidence in the concept of fair play. (In Tell, 1994, p. 15)

In a similar vein, another northern politician, then Vice President Abubakar Atiku lamented to northern leaders in 2002:

It is painful, I must say, how we continue to pay lip service to education while our teeming youth who represent our future rot away, without education, skills or moral guidance of any kind. It is tormenting to see how young children, especially girls, are left hawking or leading beggars on our streets at a crucial point in their lives when their peers in sensible societies are busy learning and building their future. It is disturbing to see how illiteracy is gaining the better of our society while others are competing in computer literacy and surfing the Internet. With this depressing profile, what role do we expect to play in the future of our country? Hewers of wood and carriers of water? Unfortunately, these frightening possibilities are not far-fetched. (In The Guardian, 19 May 2002)

Along the same lines, while presenting the Lagos Business School's study of the regional distribution of GDP in 2011, Mr Bismark Rewane, pointed out that 'the high poverty level in the north as well as growing economic inequality should be blamed for the recurring orgy of violence' (Akanbi, 2011).

Since the coup of 1966, which ended the acrimonious First Republic and the civil war of 1967–1970 in which more than one million lives were lost, Nigeria has been experimenting with different ways of managing the tensions deriving from its ethnoregional diversity and its associated inequalities. Some policies, such as the Federal Character Principle, introduced affirmative action in bureaucratic recruitment. Other reforms, like the fixing of uniform prices across the country for vital economic commodities like petroleum and fertiliser, sought to ameliorate regional/geographical economic disparities and opportunities. Another set of reforms targeted the political party system, banning the formation of regional and ethnic parties, and making it more difficult to form sectarian parties. These reforms also introduced a majoritarian electoral system with minimum vote thresholds across the country for winning elections, thereby forcing politicians aspiring to the presidency or the governorships to canvass for support outside of their immediate ethnoregional constituencies. Finally, there is the building of the city of Abuja, right in the geographical middle of the country, as a 'centre of unity'.

Considerable institutional imagination has clearly gone into the design of the Nigerian state since the crisis of 1966. These policies are far from perfect, either in conception or in their execution, but collectively they have managed to keep the lid on the acrimonious tensions that continue to emerge from the persisting inequalities. In fact, the argument can even be made that, despite all its current problems, Nigeria is far more integrated today than it was in 1966. And these reform policies played critical roles in this positive transformation.

However, the closer integration of the country itself has also meant that the level of acrimonious dispute has intensified in some instances. That sectarian violence broke out after the 2011 elections shows the limits of the efficacy of the stabilising reforms. Specifically, how did the damping effects of the reforms breakdown in 2011? One of the reforms, albeit limited to within the ruling PDP, is the policy of zoning critical offices of state and party to different ethnoregional constituencies, such that all key sectors of Nigerian society have a place at the high table when national affairs are being discussed. If the persisting horizontal inequalities continued to fuel northern fears and alienation, it was the tampering with the zoning principle of the PDP that set the stage for the postelection violence. The opposition CPC electoral loss in 2011 only provided a trigger event for a tinder-dry situation already primed to explode.

2.3 Short-Term Political Manoeuvres

As part of the post–civil war reforms aimed at dousing ethnoregional competition through power sharing, the National Party of Nigeria introduced a 'zoning' system aimed at cementing the alliance of regional elites from across the country by sharing the most important offices of state between different ethnoregional constituencies. The aim was to ensure that no single ethnic constituency dominated the state. Article 21 of the National Party of Nigeria constitution stated:

Zoning shall be understood ... 'as a Convention in recognition of the need for adequate geographical spread' ... At the national level, the following offices shall be zoned: namely the office of the National Chairman, the President, the Vice-President, President and Deputy President of the Senate, National Secretary, Speaker of the House of Representatives, Senate Leader, and the Majority Leader of the House of Representatives. (Okpu, 1984, p. 115)

It is this zoning arrangement that the PDP also incorporated into its own constitution (Section 7.2.c) when it was formed in 1998. From the beginning, some ambitious politicians did try to undermine the PDP zoning arrangement, but the party was always able to impose its will. In 2002, as President Obasanjo's first term in office was coming to an end, conflict arose within the party as to who should be the presidential candidate in the 2003 elections. The agreed policy of zoning faced a problem of which rotational pattern to adopt for maintaining zoning. Some southern members of the PDP, claiming that the north had had its fair share of executive authority over the years, demanded rotation by geopolitical zones, so that Obasanjo from the Yoruba southwest could be succeeded by a candidate from one of the two other southern zones. Some northern members insisted that rotation be from one southern zone to a northern zone, thereby putting a regional constraint on the zonal rotation. In December 2002, PDP leaders met and signed an agreement that (1) allowed Obasanjo to run again in 2003, and (2) agreed that, after Obasanjo's second term in 2007, a northern zone would produce the party candidate for the next election. Just as Obasanjo was being allowed to run for two terms, it was understood that this northern candidate would also run for two terms.

At the end of Obasanjo's second term in 2007, a candidate from the northwest zone, Umaru Yar Adua, became the PDP candidate with Goodluck Jonathan from the southsouth zone as his running mate. When President Yar Adua died in office in May 2010, his southern deputy, Goodluck Jonathan took over, leading to an unanticipated switch of leadership from north to south. Many, particularly in the north, expected Jonathan to serve out Yar Adua's first term, but then allow another northern candidate to run in 2011 in fulfilment of the agreement of 2002. Instead, both Obasanjo and Jonathan claimed first that Jonathan had a right to run so as to 'complete' Yar Adua's two terms. Furthermore, they also claimed that there was no agreement on zoning and rotation in 2002. This repudiation of one of the key institutional foundations of the ruling party amounted to changing the rules of the game midway through a match and precipitated an unprecedented crisis of confidence within the PDP.

Northern PDP leaders, led by former minister of finance, Adamu Ciroma, mobilised under the Northern Political Leaders Forum to enforce the rotational agreement of 2002. The Northern Political Leaders Forum was able to get the leading northern presidential aspirants – former Head of State General Babangida, General Aliyu Gusau, and Governor Bukola Saraki – to step down for former Vice President Atiku Abubakar. At the PDP national convention in January 2011, which was called for the selection of the party's presidential candidate, Atiku made a speech that reflected the depth of northern anger over Jonathan's manipulation of the party's position on zoning. He said:

> *I am the candidate that you can trust. Anyone who cannot be trusted to stand by his word should not be entrusted with the leadership of this country. . . .If rules can be thrown away by just anyone who feels that he is powerful enough to do so, then it is an invitation to lawlessness and anarchy. . . . The founders of this party, in their wisdom, devised rules for the rotation of power between North and South in response to cries of marginalization and domination. We wanted peace and justice to reign. And we put it in our Constitution (Section 7.2.c) . . . That provision has not been altered. In 2002, an expanded caucus of our great party met and reaffirmed that policy. . . . My main opponent [Jonathan] was at that meeting and voted in favour of that resolution. He signed as no. 35 on the list. Today he pretends that that meeting never took place and that the resolution never happened. . . . In fact on October 27, 2010, he publicly declared that zoning does not exist in our party. Talk about throwing away the ladder that got you up there! That is not the kind of person you would entrust the fate of this country. Our word must be our bond.* (Atiku, 2011)

From this point, the political atmosphere in the country was soured by sectarian mobilisation on both sides. Expecting the numerical dominance of northern delegates at the PDP convention to lead to Atiku's victory, many in the north were shocked when Jonathan won 77 per cent of the votes cast at the convention. Long accustomed to thinking that their demographic majority could always be converted to political victory, many in the north had expected the northern majority at the

PDP convention in January 2011 to deliver an Atiku Abubakar victory over the incumbent Jonathan. In this expectation, they failed to factor in the powers of patronage wielded by Jonathan as the incumbent president and his ability to sway important northern governors and traditional leaders to his side. Jonathan's victory led to street protests in some northern cities like Katsina and Bauchi. One of the demonstrating youths argued that 'they were disappointed with some of the governors in the north that compelled delegates to vote for Jonathan' (*This Day*, 2011). The idea began to gain ground in the north that some political and traditional leaders from the region were prepared to sell out their constituencies in return for favours from Jonathan's federal government. The postelection riots in April 2011 started precisely when such leaders were attacked by irate members of their own communities.

Between the convention and the election proper, the political atmosphere went from bad to worse. In the important northern city of Sokoto, the Imam of the influential Farfaru Juma'at Mosque was arrested along with two of his sons, allegedly for 'using black paint to deface the posters of President Goodluck Jonathan and Alhaji Namadi Sambo [his northern running mate]' (*Vanguard*, 2011). Some members of the Northern Political Leaders Forum were also arrested in Abuja allegedly for plotting to poison Jonathan (Okocha and Ogbu, 2011). The crisis over zoning and rotation therefore generated a profound sense of injustice and unfairness that was deeply felt in northern society, well beyond the narrow confines of the political elite.

After the convention, many turned their hopes to the election proper, during which they expected the voices of the 'real people' to be heard. By this time, northern hopes rested on a victory by the opposition CPC candidate, General Buhari, and the large turnout at his rallies gave the impression that he stood a chance. But again, these hopes were dashed by a combination of factors, not least of which was the effective use of presidential patronage in the north to buy electoral support and the ability of PDP political operatives to indirectly influence the electoral system.

2.3.1 'I Assure You of Fresh Air': Incumbency and the 2011 Elections

Using his powers of incumbency, President Jonathan had forced the resignation of the PDP Chairman, Vincent Ogbuluafor, who sought to enforce the zoning rules. Second, he struck deals with incumbent PDP governors and legislators, ensuring them an automatic ticket for re-election if they supported his bid. To consolidate his deal with the governors, an unscheduled meeting of the Federal Accounts Allocation Committee was called on December 31, 'on the eve of electioneering and primaries of the ruling People's Democratic Party' to share out US $1 billion, or 25 per cent of the country's Excess Crude Account, an important component of the national foreign currency reserve. Even newspapers sympathetic to him complained of the unscheduled disbursement of funds so close to the PDP primaries (*The Guardian*, 2011). Third, the considerable powers of the presidency and the party were then used to undermine his opponent at the parties National Convention in Abuja on January 13, 2011 (Ezea, 2011). It was hardly surprising that Jonathan won the nomination with a landslide.

Having secured the PDP nomination, Jonathan also used his powers of incumbency to ensure that he won the election. Specifically, he used a number of instruments: (1) the merging of official and campaign activities so as to evade the ban on incumbents using state funds and equipment for campaigns, (2) complete domination of the publicly owned media, contrary to the electoral rules, and (3) the use of 'shadowy' organisations like 'Neighbour to Neighbour' campaigning for him to dominate the private media, and the use of these same shadowy organisations to spread negative campaigns against his opponents. Merging official and campaign functions made it possible for Jonathan to criss-cross the country at public expense. The publicly funded Nigerian Television Authority gave 80 per cent of its coverage to the ruling PDP and 75 per cent of the direct speech reported was that of Jonathan. The privately owned television networks with a national coverage tended to follow the NTA pattern (European Union Election Observation Mission, 2011). In the print media, Jonathan had about 55 per cent of the total space dedicated to the campaigns. In some instances, Jonathan's shadowy organisations placed more negative campaign adverts about their opponents than the positive adverts placed by the campaign offices of the opponents!

According to one public commentator, about US$ 1.5 billion was allegedly spent to prosecute Jonathan's campaign (Momodu, 2013). According to a leading national newspaper, 'Jonathan has shown that while he may be an accidental president, he is certainly not a reluctant presidential candidate'. The newspaper then went on to point out a catalogue of specific instances of the abuse of incumbency: (1) the brazen tampering with the Electoral Act in a way designed to suit the incumbent, by flooding the primaries with his acolytes and associates, (2) the reported tinkering with the PDP website when it seemed to show his major opponent within the party, Atiku Abubakar, winning more hearts than he, (3) outdoor advertising companies initially refused to take on presidential campaign billboards at the airports because they wanted to stay neutral, until Jonathan's billboards, and only his, appeared from nowhere, and (4) a cable television network that insisted that it would not take political ads, until again His Excellency's – and only His Excellency's – ads appeared. Riding on the powers of incumbency, Jonathan made extravagant promises to different constituencies, including promising the Nigerian public 'fresh air'!

Another avenue for the exercise of incumbency was in the election process itself. In the April 2011 elections, some suspicious figures were produced for constituencies in the Southsouth and Southeast of the country won by Jonathan, leading to charges of suspicious conduct of vote collation in those constituencies. The election results from the Imo State can be used to illustrate these improbable results. With a total registered voter population of 1,687,293, turnout for the presidential election in Imo was said to be 83.6 per cent, with Jonathan getting more than 90 per cent of the votes. Yet, in the same state, turnout for the National Assembly elections was put at 32.9 per cent, and turnout for the governorship election was put at just 44.5 per cent (Ibrahim, 2011). In the first place, the trend in Nigerian elections is that more people tend to vote in governorship elections because the governors are seen as having a direct impact on local lives. Furthermore, governors also exert a more direct mobilising effect on the electorate. It is therefore improbable that the turnout for the presidential election should be so much higher than the turnout for the governorship election. In short, the election numbers released for the southeast and southsouth defy logic in some important respects, leading to suspicions of the manipulation of the vote collation process in those two zones. Accordingly, the senior constitutional lawyer, Professor Itse Sagay:

...dismissed reports that the 2011 elections were credible, free and fair...He also rejected the reports of both local and foreign electoral observers, declaring that there were no real elections in the South East and South-South geopolitical zones of the country. (In Saharareporters, 2011)

Given the blatant impact of incumbency on the elections, many
people in the northern parts of the country felt that they had been
systematically cheated out of their democratic right to choose their
leaders. The inability to defeat Jonathan in the election, coupled with a
deeply held view that his victory was tainted by injustice, led to the
built-up frustration over the zoning debacle boiling over into electoral
violence. The first targets were the northern political and traditional
leaders, seen as 'letting the side down' through opportunistic collaboration with the presidency. Their houses and properties were set alight
by rampaging mobs. For the first time in the history of northern
Nigeria, highly influential traditional and religious leaders were ver-
bally and physically assaulted by their subjects. General Buhari's
motorcade was attacked because he must have been mistaken for one
of the 'unreliable' elite by the mob.

However, the patterns of violence varied from place to place. In
those parts of the north with pre-existing high levels of communal
and religious conflict, such as Kaduna, Bauchi, and to a lesser extent,
Kano, the intra–Hausa-Fulani nature of the violence was quickly
superseded by an intercommunal dynamic that pitted Muslims against
Christians and northerners against southerners. Many analysts have
tended to highlight the intercommunal violence, while ignoring or
downplaying the equally important intracommunal dimension.

2.4 Conclusion: The Boomerang Effect

Foreign observers were effusive in their praise of the 2011 elections.
According to the Commonwealth Observer Group:

*The 2011 elections in Nigeria, by and large, met the national, regional and
international standards for democratic elections. Indeed, they marked a
genuine celebration of democracy in Nigeria, helped to redeem the image
of Nigeria as a country that was known only for flawed elections and served
to restore the faith of the Nigerian people in democracy.* (Commonwealth
Observer Group, 2011)

However, arguing from a contrary position, a leading social commentator, Okey Ndibe, suggested that many Nigerians are living a lie
when they make great claims for the elections. Instead, he saw the
elections as:

*...a season, alas, when Nigeria's manifold contradictions have bubbled to
the surface all at once. Instead of revealing the promise of cohesion, Nigeria*

has never looked more like a map of two or more irreconcilable nations, two mutually antagonistic sectarian tents... The astonishment is how a large swathe of the nation's youth and elite have embraced and propagated a lie. (Ndibe, 2011)

The 2011 elections were certainly better than the electoral farce of 2007. There was no doubt that the electoral management body tried all within its power to carry out a clean election. But, as we have seen, the run up to the elections were also characterised by the deliberate breaking of existing rules of the game and the deployment of the powers of incumbency. The ultimate outcome was the higher level of electoral violence, despite the best efforts of the electoral management body at cleaning up the electoral system.

Regarding the acrimony over zoning in 2011, some have emphasised Jonathan's unquestioned constitutional right to run for the presidency, while ignoring the political context of both his rise to high office – he benefitted from zoning – and his attempts to retain that office by breaking the same rules he had benefitted from. Given the highly disruptive influence of entrenched ethnic inequalities, since 1967, Nigeria has experimented with formal and informal rules to manage the tensions resulting from ethnoregional inequalities. These formal and informal rules matter in fragile institutional and political contexts like Nigeria. The self-serving abandonment of the semiformal rules governing zoning and rotation within the PDP was bound to have a destabilising consequence. Once the rules of the game within the PDP were controversially set aside, and patronage used to buttress Jonathan's presidential claims, even some northern elites long opposed to General Buhari's 'inflexible' style of politics turned to him for ethnoregional salvation. To ascribe the causation of the violence to General Buhari and the CPC in this context is to sweep aside the historical, social, and immediately political roots of the violence.

The 2011 election has also thrown open an important question regarding the management of ethnic diversity in Nigeria. The series of affirmative action programmes and other reforms discussed here set out to create ethnically inclusive institutions. However, this process has also had the unanticipated consequence of consolidating ethnic group boundaries and stimulating the activities of ethnic political entrepreneurs. In many places, the primordial claims of 'indigenes' are set against the civic rights of resident 'settlers', leading to new forms of conflict. This 'boomerang effect' has led some to suggest that affirmative action programmes like Federal Character and zoning are not effective or useful instruments for managing an ethnically diverse society like Nigeria (see Bach, 1989; Ehrhardt, 2011). The renunciation of zoning by both Obasanjo and Jonathan in 2010, therefore, created a new scenario in which we could begin to imagine new ways of managing ethnic diversity in Nigeria.

However, the result of this new approach has been underwhelming to say the least. Once Jonathan's presidential candidature was secured, Obasanjo shifted back to a pro zoning stance, claiming that:

I am an apostle of federal character ... and I cannot now preach anything different. The accident of history of the recent past [President Yar Adua's death and Jonathan 'completing' his tenure] must be understood once again that it was an unexpected situation. (In Owete & Ogala, 2011)

This attempt to have his cake and eat it further infuriated many in the north. By June 2011, the PDP as a party was once again fully behind zoning, having assigned key posts in the legislature, the executive, and the government to major ethnoregional constituencies in the country. However, to the shock of the party leadership, rebel party members in the House of Representatives rejected the new attempt to reimpose zoning, claiming that zoning was no longer party policy. They voted for a speaker and deputy speaker of their choice, totally up-turning the party's carefully calibrated ethnoregional balancing act. Since then, not only have two important sections of the country – the northeast and the southwest – been completely absent from PDP's highest deliberation bodies, a civil war of sorts has also broken out within the party as each ethnoregional group seeks to secure its own position in a chaotic free-for-all (Kolawole, 2011; Okocha, 2011). Despite the 'boomerang effects', therefore, plural societies like Nigeria still have the important need for affirmative action principles, if they are to overcome the inherent handicaps bequeathed to them by their ethnic plurality and sociopolitical inequalities.

References

Abubakar, I., Ayegba, I. E., Isa, G., Yushau, I., and Hamza, I. 2011. Bloody cost of violent power struggle – at least 90 killed – 209 injured weeks to elections. *The Daily Trust*, 13 March.

Afolayan, A. A. 1983. Population. In Oguntoyinbo, J. S., Areola, O. O., and Filani, M. (eds.), *A Geography of Nigerian Development*, 2nd edn. Ibadan: Heinemann, pp. 147–157.

Agbaje, A. 1989. Mass media and the shaping of federal character: A content analysis of four decades of Nigerian newspapers (1950–1984). In Ekeh, P. P., and Osaghae, E. E. (eds.), *Federal Character and Federalism in Nigeria*. Ibadan, Nigeria: Heinemann, pp. 98–127.

Akanbi, F. 2011. *Income disparity between north and south widens.* Retrieved from: www.thisdayonline.com/. Accessed 15 May 2011.

Amnesty International. 2007. *Nigeria: Impunity for Political Violence in the Run-up to the 2007 Elections*. London: Amnesty International Publications.

Atiku, A. A. 2011. *Speech to the PDP Convention. Abuja*, 14 January.

Bach, D. 1989. Managing a plural-society – The boomerang effects on Nigerian federalism. *Journal of Commonwealth & Comparative Politics*. 27(2):218–245.

Barnes, A. E. 1997. Some fire behind the smoke: The Fraser Report and Its aftermath in Colonial Northern Nigeria. *Canadian Journal of African Studies*. 31(2):197–228.

Canagarajah, S. 1995. *Poverty and Welfare in Nigeria*. Washington, DC: World Bank.

Commonwealth Observer Group 2011. *Nigeria National Assembly and Presidential Elections 9 & 16 April 2011*. London: Commonwealth Secretariat.

Edet, B. 2011. N/East, N/West have highest illiteracy rates – Survey. *The Daily Trust*, 17 May.

Ehrhardt, D. 2011. *Struggling to belong: Nativism, identities, and urban social relations in Kano and Amsterdam*. PhD thesis. Oxford University.

European Union Election Observation Mission. 2011. *Preliminary statement: Important step towards strengthening democratic elections, but challenges remain*. Retrieved from: http://eeas.europa.eu/eueom/pdf/missions/preliminary-statement-nigeria2011_en.pdf. Accessed 18 April 2011.

Ezea, S. 2011. Atiku Alleges Fraud in PDP Presidential Primary Election. *The Guardian*, 29 January.

Fani-Kayode, F. 2011. *The killings in the north: The facts and the slippery slope*. Retrieved from: http://234next.com/ Accessed 2 May 2011.

Federal Office of Statistics (FOS). 1995/1996. *General Household Survey 1995/96*.

1997. *Report of the National Listing of Establishments*. Abuja: FOS.

1999. *Poverty Profile for Nigeria 1980–96*. Abuja: FOS.

Hamalai, L. 1994. Distribution of Industrial Enterprises in Nigeria and National Unity. In Mahadi, A., Kwanashie, G., and Yakubu, M. (eds.), *Nigeria: The State of the Nation and the Way Forward*. Kaduna: Arewa House, Ahmadu Bello University.

Human Rights Watch. 2011. *Nigeria: Post-election violence killed 800.* Retrieved from: www.hrw.org/en/news/2011/05/16/nigeria-post-election-violence-killed-800 Accessed 18 September 2018.

Ibrahim, J. 2011. Deepening Democracy: An anthropology of the Imo election. X, 14 May.

Improving Institutions for Pro-Poor Growth. 2009. *Votes and Violence in Nigeria (Briefing paper 06).* Oxford: University of Oxford.

Joint Admissions and Matriculation Board (JAMB). (n.d.). Homepage on the Internet. Retrieved from: www.jamb.gov.ng.

Kolawole, Y. 2011. PDP zoning crisis deepens as South-west demands chairmanship. *This Day*, 6 July.

Kwanashie, G. A. 2002. *The Making of the North in Nigeria: 1900–1965.* Kaduna: Arewa House, Ahmadu Bello University.

Kyriacou, A. P. 2013. Ethnic group inequalities and governance: Evidence from developing countries. *KYKLOS.* 66(1):78–101.

Melson, R., and Wolpe, H. 1971. *Nigeria: Modernization and the Politics of Communalism.* East Lansing: Michigan State University Press.

Momodu, D. 2013. Why I'm Not President Jonathan's Fan. *This Day*, 9 March.

Munzali, J. 1990. Minority-languages and Lingua Francas in Nigerian education. In Emenanjo, E. N. (ed.), *Multilingualism, Minority Languages and Language Policy in Nigeria.* Agbor: Central Books, pp. 109–117.

Mustapha, A. R. 2012. Boko Haram: God and governance in Nigeria. Retrieved from: http://gga.org/analysis/boko-haram-god-and-governance-in-nigeria (No longer available).

Mustapha, A. R., Diprose, R., and Ehrhardt, D. 2012. *Coping with Religious Pluralism: Muslims, Christians, and Others in Northern Nigeria (NRN Working Paper No. 4).* Oxford: Nigeria Research Network.

National Bureau of Statistics (NBS). 2005. *Poverty Profile for Nigeria.* Abuja: NBS.

Ndibe, O. 2011. The Burden of a Lie. *Saharareporters*, 26 April.

Nigerian Army Education Corp & School (1994). pp. 330–349.

Okocha, C. 2011. Don't be greedy, N'East cautions S'East. *This Day*, 7 July.

Okocha, C., and Ogbu, A. 2011. Ciroma's men quizzed over alleged plot to poison Jonathan. *This Day*, 14 March.

Okpu, U. 1984. Nigerian Political Parties and the "Federal Character". *Journal of Ethnic Studies.* 12(1):106–121.

Omotoshio, M. 2009. Electoral violence and conflict in Nigeria: The 2007 elections and the challenges of democratisation. *Africa Workshop American Political Science Association.* Accra, Ghana, 22 June–10 July.

Osaghae, E. 1989. The federal cabinet, 1951–1984. In Ekeh, P. P., and Osaghae, E. E. (eds.), *Federal Character and Federalism in Nigeria*. Ibadan, Nigeria: Heinemann, 128–163.

Owete, F., and Ogala, E. 2011. Zoning is alive and kicking in PDP says Obasanjo. *X*, 26 March.

Saharareporters. 2011. No election took place in south east and south-south, Prof. Sagay Says. 12 May.

Tell. 1994. Title unknown. 14 November, pp. 16–20.

The Guardian. 2002. Title unknown. 19 May.

2011. Posers over sharing of $1b by govt on New Year Eve. 1 January.

This Day. 2011. Anti-Jonathan protests in Katsina, Bauchi. 18 January.

Vanguard. 2011. Title unknown. 1 March.

Wisdom, P. 2011. Party primaries claimed 50 lives. Retrieved from: www.leadership.ng/nga/ Accessed 14 March 2011.

Zasha, J., Mustapha, A. R., and Meyer, R. 2007. *A Lessons Learning Exercise Following the April 2007 Elections in Nigeria (UNDP Report)*. Abuja: United Nations Development Programme (UNDP).

3 | Ethnicity, Citizenry, and Nation-Building in Tanzania

BENNO J. NDULU, WILFRED E. MBOWE, AND EMMA HUNTER

3.1 Introduction

This chapter offers an account of the interplay between ethnicity and social norms in the context of nation-building in Tanzania, a dialogue that began well before independence in 1961. In contrast with Kenya, South Africa, and Nigeria, Tanzania is commonly cited as a success story, where a cohesive society has been built in tandem with its nationhood, led by the country's founding father and leader, Mwalimu Julius Kambarage Nyerere. This chapter offers a more nuanced analysis. It highlights the transformation of localised, ethnic-based, trust networks of self-protection into a national framework for trust enhancement and conflict resolution at local levels; this transformation has been the key reason why Tanzanians have accepted that national identity can be protective, so offering a bridge from divided pasts to a cohesive future. Our combination of this bottom-up perspective with the more usual top-down narrative helps to capture the cohesiveness of Tanzanian society. We end on a hopeful note, arguing that the current government's emphasis on social justice has secured popular trust in programmes of national social cohesion.

There has been increasing interest in examining the consequences of ethnic diversity for social cohesion in Africa. In explaining Africa's growth tragedy of the period to the 1990s, for example, Easterly and Levine (1997) associated it with Africa's high ethnic fragmentation. Their basis for quantitative analysis, particularly the Ethnolinguistic Fractionalisation (ELF) index, has been strongly criticised by many historians (see the Introduction). Nonetheless, Easterly and Levine (1997) lent support to theories that interest group polarisation leads to rent-seeking behaviour and decreases the consensus for investment in public goods. Ethnic diversity has been associated with lower levels of growth, less public goods provision, and higher risks of violent

98

conflict (Langer, 2013), ethnic favouritism and lower public goods (Burgess et al., 2015; Miguel, 2004), a vehicle for political competition (Posner, 2004a), and source of conflicts within states (Gurr, 2000; Horowitz, 2001; Lake & Rothchild, 1998) and between them (Huntington, 1996). However, these findings were correlations, not causalities, and were observed largely in the historical context of economic stagnation in Africa in the 1980s and 1990s.

This chapter argues, echoing statements elsewhere in this book, that there is nothing inherently wrong or negative about ethnicity. Diversity is like a rainbow, made of different colours that coexist without conflict. However, it becomes a liability when exploited for political gain. This chapter shows, equally, that it was not Tanzania's unusually great degree of ethnic fragmentation that of itself deterred the damaging ethnicisation of the country's politics. The path dependence of its national unity moulding process provides a better explanation. Nation-building is generally considered to be a means to avoid the negative outcomes of ethnic diversity (Greenfeld, 2003; Langer, 2013; Miguel, 2004). The Tanzanian case certainly seems to bear this out, thanks to a determined political elite (Green, 2009; Kessler, 2006; Nyang'oro, 2006; Therkildsen, 2009). Ethnic toleration, which has been associated with social stability and harmony in Tanzania, is no accident, but the result of deliberate initiatives under Mwalimu Nyerere's regime that were designed to make ethnicity irrelevant to politics and economic progress.

Although the relevant literature emphasises other unifying interventions in Tanzania, as will be seen, Nyerere's insistence on the egalitarian distribution of development expenditure across the country, together with a centralised mechanism to solve local problems, played a vital role in nationalising older, ethnic-based trust networks of conflict avoidance and resolution. Tanzania is not the first case of successful state creation of harmony and social stability. Crepaz and Damron (2009) have argued that the early welfare states in Europe, for example, were not only built to bridge class divisions but also to "mollify ethnic divisions in the vast multi-ethnic empires of nineteenth-century Germany and Austria". They also show that natives are more ready to tolerate immigrants where welfare states are more comprehensive (Crepaz & Damron, 2009). In this chapter, we show how nation-building in Tanzania has played a pivotal role in transforming an ethnically very diverse country into one where most citizens consider themselves primarily as Tanzanians. Tolerance of ethnic diversity has been extended to hosting large refugee populations and granting citizenship to large numbers of them. Political leadership matters (compare Chapter 1).

The chapter is organised as follows: Section 2 provides an account of the extent and nature of ethnic diversity and its impact on public goods production and delivery, public employment, as well as social and political stability in Tanzania. Section 3 traces the evolution of nation-building in the country's history from well before its independence and suggests some reasons for the distinctiveness of the Tanzanian experience. Section 4 assesses its sustainability. Section 5 concludes.

3.2 Ethnic Diversity in Tanzania

With more than 126 ethnic groups, one might assume great political instability in Tanzania. Those who use the ELF index would expect that. The validity of the ELF index, which measures the likelihood that two people chosen randomly will be from different ethnic groups, has been challenged by Lonsdale and others (e.g., see Lonsdale, 2012), but nonetheless provides a broad impression of a country's ethnic diversity. Table 3.1 shows the ELF index and other measures of ethnic diversity. Various studies suggest values of greater than 0.15, signifying high ethnic diversity. The index value ranges from Posner (2004a)'s 0.53 to 0.95 proposed by Fearon (2003), even after controlling for "politically relevant ethnic groups" as proposed by Posner (2004b). With an ELF index of 0.93 and the politically relevant ethnic groups value of 0.59, Tanzania is clearly one of the most ethnically fractionalised countries in Africa, a home to many ethnic groups with small or relatively equal percentages of the population.

Characteristics of ethnic fractionalisation summarised in Table 3.2 suggest further that there are no dominant ethnic groups in Tanzania. Barkan (2012) notes that the largest group in the country accounts for only 12 per cent of the total population, and that the three and five largest groups account for only 23 per cent and 31 per cent of the total population, respectively. Nor does the geography of economic development reinforce their position (contrast with Chapter 1). The largest group of people, the Sukuma, live more than 350 miles from the capital and port city of Dar es Salaam, in one of the poorest and least

Table 3.1 *Tanzania's ethnolinguistic fractionalisation index*

Selected Studies	Index Value
Easterly and Levine (1997)	0.93
Scarrit and Mozaffar (1999)	0.86
Roeder (2001)	0.91
Alesina et al. (2003)	0.74
Fearon (2003)	0.95
Posner (2004a)	0.53
Posner (2004b) – politically relevant ethnic group	0.59

Note: Alesina et al. (2003) and Posner (2004a) take into account whether or not the ethnic group engages in political or policy competition, while Posner's (2004b) politically relevant ethnic group index is computed based on politically relevant ethnic groups. Other findings are the Ethnolinguistic Fractionalisation Index.
Source: Authors' compilation from different sources.

Table 3.2 *Characteristics of ethnic fractionalisation in Tanzania*

Item	Characteristics
No. of ethnic groups	126
Per cent of population in largest group	12
Per cent of population in three largest groups	23
Per cent of population in largest five groups	31
Per cent of population in ten largest groups	41
Extent of uneven development	Low
Largest group privileged by uneven Development	No
History of ethnic conflict	Very low (peace)

Source: Cited from Barkan (2012).

developed regions of the country. According to Barkan (2012), while Haya and Chagga have historically enjoyed the greatest concentration of primary and secondary schools in their areas, their share of total population is very small, at 4 per cent and 3 per cent, respectively. Both groups are far apart from each other, and are very far (more than 250 miles) from the capital city. This geographical dispersion of size and educational advantage has made it relatively unattractive for politicians to try to mobilise the electorate on the basis of ethnic constituencies; this deterrence has been reinforced by the relatively equitable distribution of factors of production, particularly labour and land (Green, 2009).

This relative lack of ethnic mobilisation supports Posner's argument (2004b) that "politically relevant ethnic groups" have to be taken into account in any analysis of ethnicity and politics. Tanzania's largest or educationally most advanced groups would be more "politically relevant" if Tanzania's demographic and economic geography were more centralised. According to Posner (2004a), the political salience of a cultural cleavage depends not on the nature of the cleavage itself, but on the sizes of the groups it defines and whether or not they are useful vehicles for political competition. But this chapter argues that this important observation is not enough in itself. One cannot ignore the charismatic leader, in our case Mwalimu Julius K. Nyerere, whose vision from the beginning of Tanzania's independent history was to build a unified nation.

The key pillars of the nation-building project are taken up elsewhere in this chapter, but before that we present some evidence on whether ethnic diversity has had an adverse effect on government's provision of public goods and employment in the public sector.

3.3 Ethnic Diversity, Public Employment, and the Production of Public Goods in Tanzania

Ethnic diversity can affect an economy and society in a number of ways. According to Mozaffar and Scarrit (2005), these factors include macroeconomic policy distortions thanks to ethnically based interest group polarisation that generates such uneconomic policies as rent seeking, overspending, and poor provision of public goods; violent conflicts that undermine social cohesion, destroy capital, and block growth; and political instability, seen in electoral and legislative volatility. According to Collier and Hoeffler (1998), the existence of multiple ethnic groups can even hinder the creation of a coherent opposition; tensions then fester, a situation in which violence can emerge (Langer, 2013). Rent-seeking models suggest that the resources spent by groups in trying to exert political influence (time, labour, etc.) are themselves a social cost damaging to economic growth, because these energies could otherwise be spent productively. In extreme cases and in past history, religious and ethnic differences have generated violence and civil war. In less extreme cases, ethnic diversity can simply create social barriers that, by inhibiting communication, waste any investment made in the creation of new knowledge, so reducing the potential accumulation of social capital. The mistrust that this causes, and the likely misappropriation of public goods, clearly hinder social cohesion and economic growth (Mozaffar & Scarrit, 2005).

Collier and Hoeffler (2002), using global data, indicate that civil wars alone cost more than two percentage points of growth on an annual basis, whilst also sowing the seeds of future conflict. The cost to Africa is high, because civil wars have persisted, particularly in the democratisation period of the mid-1980s through the 1990s (Ndulu & O'Connell, 2008). Ncube et al. (2014) describe three categories of costs associated with such conflicts. The first is an opportunity cost. They suggest that fragile states lose an opportunity to double their initial gross domestic product per capita in a twenty-year period. Second, warfare's destruction has enormous costs. In twenty years of fragility, the cumulative economic cost in Liberia, Sierra Leone and Burundi amounted to U.S.$31.8 billion, U.S.$16.0 billion, and U.S. $12.8 billion, respectively. Third, Ncube et al.'s (2014) simulations show that if Central Africa Republic, Liberia, and Sierra Leone had growth rates equivalent to those they modelled in a synthetic country,[1] it would take them 34.5 years, 19.2 years, and 20.8 years, respectively, to recover the level of gross domestic product per capita that would have been achieved had there been no civil war.

The benefits of peace and unity are, therefore, large. The fact that ethnicity has not played a significant role in Tanzania's politics (Barkan, 1994; Erdmann, 2007), has spared the country the economic costs listed in the previous paragraph. Indeed, Miguel (2004), using micro evidence, shows that, in contrast with Kenya, Tanzania's policy of ethnic homogeneity has led to significantly better provision of

---

[1] Ncube et al.'s (2014) synthetic country is a weighted average of a group of countries that display similar characteristics to the fragile state before it became fragile. Fragile countries used in the study include Liberia, Burundi, Sierra Leone, Central Africa Republic, Eritrea, and Guinea Bissau, while their comparable group of countries comprised Bangladesh, Burkina-Faso, Chad, China-PR Mainland, Cameroon, Congo-Republic, Gambia, Guyana, Lesotho, Madagascar, Malawi, Mozambique, Nepal, Nigeria, Sudan, and Uganda.

public goods. Miguel's study compares the two countries' local school funding and facilities and finds that ethnic diversity has lowered public goods funding in Kenya, but not in Tanzania. Similarly, Therkildsen and Tidemand (2007) compared public sector staff management practices in Uganda and Tanzania in 2006. They found that ethnic connections played a much greater role in staff recruitment in Uganda than in Tanzania.

Many have asked the reasons for Tanzania's relative social and political stability. What explains the absence of the violence and instability that can be observed elsewhere in sub-Saharan Africa? We argue that this peculiarity lies in the path dependence of its national unity moulding process. The nature of its ethnic fragmentation is less important than the absence of incentives for divisive political action.

To support this argument, we must consider Tanzania's history. As we shall see, one part of our explanation lies in the unified nature of the Tanzanian nationalist movement in later colonial times, before independence. But that cannot be the whole story, because not all countries with similarly unifying nationalisms experienced the same outcomes. We must, therefore, also consider some of the challenges that Tanzania's early nation-builders faced, and how they overcame these challenges.

3.4 Tanzania's Phased Approach to Nation-Building

Tanzania is a case where elite politicians have been able to turn ethnic diversity into an opportunity for social cohesion and political stability – a process that can be traced in all four phases of government. Efforts in this direction began under Mwalimu Julius K. Nyerere, the founding president of Tanzania (Miguel, 2004). His successful nation-building is the chief explanation for Tanzania's difference from many other comparable African countries (Green, 2009). From its colonial beginnings in 1954, Tanzania's nationalist party, TANU, sought to develop a new national consciousness (Bjerk, 2017, p. 53). This project continued after independence, when the people were rallied along one national goal of fighting the three enemies of poverty, ignorance, and disease (Pratt, 1976, p. 173). In adopting the Arusha Declaration in 1967, the government undertook, as a nation-building project, a series of socialist economic reforms and the consolidation of single party rule (Bjerk, 2017). The combination of these societal, economic, and political policies created a national political culture that set the country on a long-term path of internal peace.

3.4.1 Nation-Building Policies

In the years following independence in December 1961, Nyerere's government adopted a series of policies to build a united Tanzania. These policies included abolishing chiefship in a bid to avoid the divisive forces of tribalism, promoting Swahili as a national language, developing educational policies that promoted national unity, and seeking to ensure equitable resource allocation within the country.

Unity and Fighting Tribalism
The decision to abolish chiefship had its roots in the politics of post-1945 Tanganyika. Chiefs had been a central part of the colonial ruling structure from the interwar period. Donald Cameron, Governor of Tanganyika from 1925 to 1931, came on transfer from Nigeria, where he had seen indirect rule through chiefs in action. On his arrival in Tanganyika, he sought to establish a similar system, which gave considerable power to local chiefs. The structure was implemented in a uniform fashion, both in areas with a long tradition of chiefship and in those where chiefship was a novelty. Even where there was a long history of chiefship, the nature of the office changed in the colonial period, with the powers of chiefs being significantly increased.

This indirect rule structure began to change after 1945, as district councils were introduced across Tanganyika, combining elected African representatives and unelected chiefs and other officials. The nationalist party TANU, formed in 1954 and led by Julius Nyerere, often forged alliances in local areas that opposed chiefs (Nugent, 2012, pp. 130–131). Once in government, TANU soon moved to abolish chiefship, removing chiefs' powers in relation to law and order in 1962 and setting up a new nationwide system of District Councils in 1963 (Nugent, 2012, p. 130). While abolishing chiefship was something Julius Nyerere later regretted (Molony, 2014, p. 41), at the time it seemed to be essential to avoid the division that Nyerere believed tribalism could cause.

The early 1960s saw the development of a distinctive political system that removed the possibility of political coalitions being forged along ethnic, or, for that matter, religious or regional, lines. In 1963, Nyerere's pamphlet "Democracy and the Party System" set out the problems, as he saw them, with a multiparty system of politics. The following year, he established a commission to explore the need for constitutional change. Its report recommended the establishment of a one-party state. Under the system introduced in 1965, elections would see contests only between two members of the same party, TANU; the electoral rules banned any reference to ethnicity (Cliffe, 1967).

If the move to one-party democracy marked a significant expansion of TANU's political role, it was mirrored across social, economic, and cultural life. In 1964, the National Federation of Labour was dissolved and replaced with the National Union of Tanganyika Workers, an organisation more closely supervised by the party and the government. In 1967, the Arusha Declaration strengthened TANU's economic role with the creation of state monopolies. As several authors have argued, while the Arusha declaration did not explicitly set out to decrease the political salience of ethnicity or religion, it nevertheless served to consolidate earlier nation-building policies (Gahnström, 2012; Miguel, 2004; Nyang'oro, 2006).

Language

Together with its steps to take ethnicity out of public political discourse, the government pursued a series of other nation-building measures. By the time of independence, the use of the Swahili language, which had once been limited to the coast and Zanzibar, was increasingly widespread across the country. The expansion of trade routes beyond the coast in the nineteenth century saw Swahili become the language of commerce. In contrast with Kenya and Uganda, colonial-era educational policies allocated a key role to Swahili rather than to vernacular languages. By the 1950s, alongside English, it was the main language of the press and radio. The nationalist party, TANU, used Swahili in its campaigning across the country and after independence continued to promote Swahili, now as a national language (Geiger, 1997, p. 9). The use of ethnic vernaculars was banned in the public media. For the new government, to use Swahili in education, government, and public discourse was a means of political integration and fundamental to the building of a new national culture (Abdulaziz, 1971, p. 160; Barkan, 2012).

Yet vernacular languages remain important in some areas. There are 5.2 million speakers of Kisukuma, the language of the Sukuma of northwestern Tanzania. As Gahnström (2012) found in his study of ethnicity and politics in the Mwanza region, there are frequent reports of politicians using this vernacular in election campaigns, despite this being forbidden in Tanzania's electoral code. Many of his informants told him that knowledge of Kisukuma was essential for politicians seeking election in some areas of the region (Gahnström, 2012, p. 41, p. 78, p. 105).

Education for Nation-Building and National Service

A key area for nation-building after independence was in relation to Tanzania's youth, particularly through education and national service. One legacy of colonial rule was the unequal provision of schools across the country. Some ethnic groups had much better educational provision than others, particularly in their access to secondary schooling (compare Chapter 9). The independent government took steps to remedy this by varying entry requirements for secondary school according to region of origin (Gahnström, 2012, p. 71). School children often moved away from their home regions to attend school; this measure helped to ensure that they spent time with young people from other parts of the country, so contributing to national integration. At the same time, a curriculum was developed that sought to embed a shared national identity.

There was also a major emphasis on adult literacy and civics education through a school curriculum that gave weight to political (*siasa*) education (Green, 2009). The goal of civics education is to mould the masses into good citizens (Kessler, 2006). In the *ujamaa* (socialism) years, for example, good citizens were described as people who loved their country and were willing to work hard and make sacrifices for it (Meienberg, 1966). Since the political liberalisation of the early 1990s, civics education coverage has changed to incorporate the need to create knowledgeable, critical citizens who show their patriotism by critically examining its institutions, by participating in political change, and by demanding that their country does better (Okewa, 1996).

Engaging the youth was particularly important for two reasons. First, some of the most striking changes in a culture happen simply through generational replacement (Almond & Verba, 1963). Engaging the young people therefore helped to commit them to the nation as they grew up. The second reason is that youth are amongst the most volatile segments of any population. According to Kessler (2006), if they support the government, they represent a source of energy, enthusiasm, and physical vigour to help with development. Likewise, if they oppose the government, they represent a major threat to stability. For both these reasons, gaining youth support for the young nation via civics education was a vital step for the Tanzanian government.

Another element in engaging Tanzania's youth was National Service, initially developed in 1963 as a voluntary programme. Those who gained places on the programme received training to undertake two years of nation-building work on various development schemes. It was hugely popular among primary school leavers for whom it provided a basis for secure employment (Ivaska, 2005, p. 90). It was much less popular among the educated youth and, as discussed in Histories of Nation-Building from Below, in late 1965 a plan was developed whereby a period of National Service would be compulsory for all those completing secondary school and higher education programmes (Ivaska, 2005, p. 90). The aims were, among others, for young people to work together to build their sense of nationalism; develop cultural and sociological awareness of other ethnic groups, but in an age-based network of friendship; provide skills, build economic independence, and decrease unemployment; train and develop the youth for national service and to assist the government during natural disasters and calamities; and to build and develop the national economy (Global Security, 2018). Since its inception, the duration of training generally has varied between three months and one year, mainly for individuals leaving secondary school, and two years for volunteers, some of whom, at the end of their training, will join the army or enter employment in the public and private sectors.

Nationalising the Government and the Civil Service
As Julius Nyang'oro explains, in the colonial period opportunities for economic development through growing and selling cash crops were concentrated in particular areas and around particular groups,

notably the Haya, Chagga, and Nyakyusa from the regions of Kagera, Kilimanjaro, and Mbeya (Nyang'oro, 2006, p. 329). As we have seen, educational facilities were also very unequally distributed and were concentrated in the same areas. Many of the first African civil servants to be appointed came from these regions (Nyang'oro, 2006, p. 334).

After independence, official policy was one of nonrecognition of ethnicity, so there was no formal policy of balancing representation in the civil service or in appointments to public office. However, Nyang'oro (2006) suggests that the combination of a government focus on expanding educational opportunities and appointing those with a national outlook to public office ensured equitable representation and distribution of public office (Nyang'oro, 2006, p. 331). Others have suggested that Nyerere's government was more active in its rebalancing of the civil service, by encouraging members of those groups that had had more educational opportunities to "pursue careers within the professional fields, while the less privileged groups in turn were given access to public and political office" (Gahnström, 2012, p. 68).

As for parliamentary elections, Nyang'oro (2006) suggests that, because constituencies were rarely composed of only one ethnic group, ethnicity tended not to be a source of political advantage (Nyang'oro, 2006, p. 332). It is also important to note that Nyerere deliberately appointed officials to serve outside their home areas, a policy that continued after his departure from office. In his study of Tanzanian regional commissioners in post in 2000, Nyang'oro (2006) found that only two regional commissioners were "native to the regions in which they serve" (Nyang'oro, 2006, p. 331).

In January 1964, mainland Tanzania was shaken by an army mutiny. The government responded by completely restructuring the military, replacing the old Tanganyika Rifles with the Tanzanian People's Defence Force. As a recent study by Stefan Lindemann (2010) has emphasised, "[r]ecruitment policies were from the beginning inclusive in nature" and this has continued, so that "the TPDF has always remained a national force that is broadly reflective of the country's ethno-regional diversity" (Lindemann, 2010, p. 4). These various nation-building policies have meant that, rather than mobilising along ethnic lines, individuals have tended to engage in public life through the party and the state.

3.4.2 Histories of Nation-Building from Below

As we have seen, one part of the story of Tanzania's success in terms of social cohesion is a set of nation-building policies. However, none of these policies was inevitably destined to promote cohesion. For example, the policy of promoting the Swahili language involved making choices about which kind of Swahili would be used, and exposed fault lines between the Arabized Swahili of the coast and the Swahili of inland areas. The policy of National Service was also controversial. When it was introduced, Nyerere met with resistance from university students who interpreted it as an attack by the political elite on a younger generation. The controversy culminated in a dramatic confrontation at State House between Nyerere and representatives of the students who opposed the policy, which ended with the students being ordered to leave the university and return to their homes. In the period that followed, TANU's political discourse increasingly came to redefine which 'youth' would play a central role in building the nation, emphasising the role of the TANU Youth League and those who embraced national service at the expense of university students (Ivaska, 2005, p. 100). At the same time, the measures taken to remove ethnicity from public politics and to close down associations formed on ethnic lines provide some explanation of why ethnicity became less politically divisive than in other states, but it does not explain why these moves were accepted without significant dissent.

One way of understanding why this happened in Tanzania but not elsewhere might lie in Charles Tilly's (2005) concept of trust networks. In his 2005 book, *Trust and Rule*, Tilly considers the relationship between trust networks and public politics. Trust networks, he shows, emerge in all places and times; they are not simply a vestige of traditional society (Tilly, 2005, p. 14). But they often "compete with rulers for the same resources", resources such as "labour power, money, information, loyalty, and more" (Tilly, 2005, p. 6, p. 23). This sets up a potentially conflictual relationship. Yet in some cases, trust networks come to be absorbed into public politics, if, for example, the trust network lacks the resources to do what it promised, or rulers are able to offer a better "systems of protection and/or welfare" (Tilly, 2005, p. 23).

Let us now consider how it was that in Tanzania the trust networks, which in other parts of Africa remained localised and defined in ethnic, regional, or religious terms, were to some extent successfully transferred to the national body. To do so, we look again at the question of ethnicity. Although it is true that there was no single dominant ethnic group in Tanzania in the way that there was in Kenya or Uganda, many of the processes whereby ethnic group identity was becoming strengthened, which we see in Kenya and Uganda in the colonial period, were taking place in Tanganyika too (Maddox & Giblin, 2005). As elsewhere in the region, from the 1920s new self-help associations began to be formed, often along ethnic or in some cases religious lines. Those who moved to towns for work and found themselves without the support of family could turn to ethnic associations when times were hard. This was not a reversion to an older form of solidarity; rather, it was a response to the development of new economic forms.

In the 1940s and 1950s, new political associations emerged in some areas, again often along ethnic lines, associations such as the Kilimanjaro Chagga Citizens Union and the Sukuma Union. They engaged in cultural projects to develop a recognisable identity and committed themselves to the development and uplift of members of the community, defined in ethnic terms (Hunter, 2015, p. 118). The precise nature of this uplift, increasingly in the 1940s and 1950s defined in terms of development or *maendeleo*, varied from place to place. Education, and providing educational opportunities for the young, was often a key concern. In areas experiencing increasing land shortage, as in northeastern Tanganyika, new associations could mobilise to ensure that land remained in African hands, so that a younger generation would not find itself without land to farm.

Why, then, did these associations, which defined their remit in ethnic terms, disappear so swiftly after independence? Part of the answer lies in the way in which the government moved to make forming associations on ethnic lines legally impossible. But that does not provide a full explanation. In other settings, such associations might have gone underground or become sites of resistance. Part of the answer must also, therefore, lie in the ways in which the central government took note of the arguments that had been taking place at the local level and the problems that local associations were formed to solve, and sought to solve them at the national level.

In political terms, the historian Steven Feierman (1990) has shown how the arguments taking place in the Usambara mountains in the 1950s over what democracy should mean in practice were picked up by Nyerere and answered at the national level in the 1960s (Feierman, 1990). In terms of education, the government stepped in to take on the responsibility of funding new educational facilities and scholarships, in place of local cooperative societies. In terms of land, complaints about land shortage, which local associations had attempted to resolve at the local level, were transferred to the national level (Hunter, 2017, p. 114). The region of Kilimanjaro in northeastern Tanzania provides a striking example of this process. In the 1950s, local politics was fuelled by the demand of the landless and land poor for land. Local politicians envisaged answers to this problem defined in ethnic terms. The conservative Kilimanjaro Chagga Citizens Union drew up schemes whereby land could be bought and distributed to landless Chagga youth. Nyerere's answer to the problem was different. The mountain was, he said on a visit to the region in 1963, now full and the youth should look elsewhere for land. Local party and government officials now called on the central government to provide loans so that the young could start farming in other parts of the country, or to develop state farms. This process, whereby calls for land were transferred from the ethnic group to the national centre, was further accelerated by the 1967 Arusha Declaration (Hunter, 2017).

More generally, we might view Nyerere's version of African socialism, developed in pamphlets in the early 1960s and then instituted through the Arusha Declaration of 1967, as a response to fears that growing inequality would lead to the sort of political turmoil that other African countries experienced in the 1960s. It was a way of having economic development without a breakdown in social cohesiveness (Hunter, 2017).

As a consequence of these measures, whereas in other settings trust networks persisted clandestinely and in opposition to the state, in Tanzania trust networks were incorporated into national politics. The government intervened to show that the protection offered by smaller scale associations defined along ethnic, religious, or other lines could best be provided by the central state. In this way, cohesive futures were built from divided pasts. But this state of affairs depended on contingent circumstances, and was always fragile.

3.4.3 Subsequent Phases of Government Have Also Preserved the Key Pillars of National Identity and Unity

One of the key features distinguishing Tanzania from other African countries that have attempted to build a unified nation and failed is its path dependence in terms of nationhood and political culture. The process has been guided by the understanding that building a national political culture cannot be a one-time event, but should be slowly built and reinforced over time. The adoption of the Arusha Declaration in 1967 made room for combining societal, economic, and political policies in creating that national political culture. This set the country on a long-term path of internal peace. Mahoney (2001) argues that countries tend to remain on the path they have chosen because values and institutions become self-perpetuating through the inertia of structural persistence. Governments also become committed to the institutions in which they have invested their reputation. Citizens come to see institutions as legitimate and wish for their reproduction out of a belief that it is the right thing to do. After the demise of the socialist and one-party state in Tanzania, the institutions that had created the national values disappeared. However, Mahoney (2001) argues that "path-dependent structures and institutions" may endure in the absence of the processes that first led to their establishment. This implies that, even though the circumstances that created the unique Tanzanian national identity have passed, national identity and values could remain strong and continue to provide a pacifying frame – serving as its national social DNA. As we have suggested, a possible reason for this endurance in Tanzania is that national political culture was not a sudden imposition, but was slowly built and reinforced over several decades, so setting Tanzanian history on a self-perpetuating path, away from violence and division and towards a peaceful political sphere (Kessler, 2006). Since its founding, Tanzania's political leaders have emphasised the importance of just and moral policies. Leaders repeatedly call nation-building a war on poverty, ignorance, and disease. But the degree to which this war has actually been waged set Tanzania apart from many other African states (Kessler, 2006).

Subsequent governments have tended to sustain the national culture initiated by the first phase government. They may have adopted different policies, but always with the stated aim of preserving national identity, unity, and political stability. As an example, the Second Phase Government (1985–1995) moved to reform and liberate the economy as a means to address macroeconomic instabilities for sustainable economic development. Although the liberalisation of the economy was done in a rather unfettered manner, national identity was emphasised. People were to identify themselves as Tanzanians first rather than by their ethnic affiliations (Green, 2009).

Political liberalisation was also carried out in such a way as to reinforce rather than threaten national integration. In many other countries across Africa and beyond, political liberalisation has been characterised by mobilisation along ethnic or religious lines. In Tanzania, the government set up the Nyalali Commission in 1991 to explore how to move from a single party to a multiparty system. A large proportion (77 per cent) of the 40,000 Tanzanians whom the commission interviewed expressed a desire to retain the single-party system, in large part owing to fears of the ethnic conflict that might result if a multiparty system was introduced, as indeed happened in Kenya (Gahnström, 2012, p. 19). The government sought to prevent this outcome by enshrining in the 2002 Political Parties Act the principle that any political party must have support from across Tanzania's regions. Parties were required to have at least "200 registered members in 8 out of the mainland regions and on both Pemba and Zanzibar" (Gahnström, 2012, p. 75). Candidates seeking election to the presidency are required to have support from both mainland Tanzania and Zanzibar. The requirement to use Swahili rather than vernacular languages in campaigning was reinforced in the 2010 Electoral Code of Conduct.

Efforts to reinforce national integration were continued under the Third Phase Government (1995–2005), whose main focus lay in institutionalising the market economy and multiparty democracy. The focus was put on four broad areas: economic reforms, particularly in the financial sector; promotion of private sector participation and improvement in the business environment; setting up of institutions and sharpening rules of engagement for political pluralism and competition, including an efficient electoral commission; and rebuilding social services and universal access to education and health. These policy measures were included in a long-term development plan – the Development Vision 2025. The vision stipulates that peace, stability, and the security of citizens and their property constitute a fundamental and necessary environment for development. The vision also directs every Tanzanian to refrain from acts that may divide them on the basis of religion, tribe, race, gender, or place of origin.

The Fourth Phase Government (2005–2015) encouraged nation-building by creating the infrastructures of sustained high growth. The nation is being connected by communication technology (national fibre optic network and cellular technology) and by consolidating the institutions of market economy and multiparty politics. The main focus has been to reshape the role of the state under public–private partnerships and to repair emerging cracks in the unity of the nation by reintroducing compulsory National Service in 2013 – after its abolition in 1994 – with a view to strengthening youthful patriotism. Moreover, to guarantee universal access to secondary education, schools have been built on a collective basis at the ward level. While a collective school building policy ensures that the government equitably distributes its resources, it also instils local ownership of the obtainable public goods. Meanwhile, the government has reinvigorated and aligned its short-term to long-term development plans to the implementation of the Development Vision 2025. It also initiated a participatory constitutional review process (yet to be concluded) in response to socio-economic and political changes in the country.

For its part, the Fifth Phase Government (since 2015) has resolved to lead the country towards middle-income status. It has, therefore, embarked on an ambitious drive to industrialise. The new backbone infrastructures have this aim in mind, so that industry can exploit the opportunities offered by the country's strategic geographical position and huge natural resources. Equally important are renewed attempts to instil fiscal discipline, obey the rule of law, increase accountability, and pursue development policies that promise inclusive growth. New legislation requires that national resources benefit all the people. The Fifth Phase Government has, therefore, reemphasised moral policies, that unique feature of Tanzania's history, to great popular approval.

The people have been rallied – irrespective of their political, cultural, religious, or ethnic affiliation – towards a commitment to work for national development and unity, while fighting corruption. The government has set up a special high court to speed up the prosecution of criminal corruption. There is a popular consensus that corruption undermines development, deprives people of their due rights, and increases social inequality. To stem graft is thought essential to accelerate inclusive economic development, so advancing the country's social cohesion.

3.5 Self-Reinforcement of the National Identify and Unity

A key question to be asked is whether the nation-building efforts of the five government phases – particularly the pioneering first phase – have indeed created a self-reinforcing political culture of national identity and unity. In 2006, Kessler (2006) conducted a survey among university students to examine the relations between political culture and personal attitudes towards violent conflict among this rising elite. Interestingly, he found that the key building blocks of Tanzania's peaceful political culture, namely, "national identity" and "national pride", remained strong (Kessler, 2006, p. 97). Another basis for sustainable national unity was a "commitment to finding peaceful solutions to political conflicts" (Kessler, 2006, p. 97), a reassuring finding, because violence or inflammatory rhetoric can so rapidly destabilise a state. The fact that key attributes of nationhood have endured even after the active phase of nation-building has passed suggests that the national political culture is indeed sustainable. Even at work, Bannon et al. (2004) note that, in contrast with citizens from other African countries, Tanzanians identify themselves by occupation and class rather than by ethnicity.

Recent surveys also tend to support Kessler's (2006) findings. The Afrobarometer survey of 2012 on attitudes to the constitutional review, the union with Zanzibar, and executive power indicates that about 88 per cent of the respondents did not want the dissolution of the union between Tanganyika and Zanzibar (Afrobarometer, Round 5). In the surveys of 2012 and 2017, when asked to express their feelings on how to be identified, about 68 per cent and 56 per cent, respectively, of the respondents preferred to identify themselves more, or only, as Tanzanians rather than by their ethnic groups (Afrobarometer, Rounds 5 and 6).

In the 2017 Afrobarometer survey (Round 6), 97 per cent of respondents said they had never been discriminated against because of their ethnicity, 98 per cent had never suffered on account of their regional identity, and 93 per cent felt government had never treated their ethnic group unfairly. People also trusted in their institutions.

In the 2017 survey, 51 per cent held a high level of trust in the president, 49 per cent in local government, and 74 per cent in religious leaders. Further, 81 per cent claimed never to have feared violence at a political rally or campaign event in the two years before the 2017 survey, and 92 per cent had never feared violence while taking part in a public protest or march. Tanzanians also feel they can trust members of other ethnic groups (Afrobarometer, Round 6). Kessler (2006) found that 60.5 per cent of his survey respondents agreed that "most people can be trusted" (Kessler, 2006, p. 90); 96 per cent of his respondents either did not care or else liked having people from other ethnic groups as neighbours. In the 2017 Afrobarometer survey, 71 per cent strongly liked people of different regions or and ethnic groups to be their neighbours (Afrobarometer, Round 6).

3.5.1 Challenges to Sustaining National Identify and Unity

Despite Tanzania's achievements in maintaining national identity and unity, the growth of social class differentiation in difficult world economic conditions has the potential to work against social cohesion and political stability. We consider two possible causes of this development. First, with a population growth of 2.9 per cent per year, the country is still experiencing a delayed demographic transition, which is likely to produce a future labour force boom. Second, economic growth has not generated enough jobs to absorb the growing labour force. Agriculture in particular, which still absorbs 75 per cent of the labour force, has been growing by less than 4 per cent on average in the past five years, a rate too low to raise the poor above the poverty line, given the high population growth. Although these conditions have led to high unemployment rates (averaging 12 per cent of the labour force), they also have the potential to create classes of "haves" and "have nots". There is already a huge rural to urban migration of young people. It is estimated that the rate of population increase in Dar es Salaam (the largest city) is about 4 per cent, well above the country's overall population growth rate (Ndulu, 2012). Urban youth unemployment has increased substantially; job creation cannot keep pace. It is also true that a good number of these young migrants have neither the capital to engage in business nor the skills for useful employment. Unsurprisingly, unemployment has fostered political agitation.

Citizens are most committed to peace when they feel that they benefit from economic growth, are being treated fairly, and can participate meaningfully in the political process. It follows that, for a state to get on a self-perpetuating peaceful path, it must pursue policies that incorporate all citizens into the national development and political process. This process involves ensuring equal opportunity in employment, provision of public goods, and participatory political competition. This is a tall order, because the necessary investment in job creating, inclusive, growth is huge and the opportunity for divisive political competition on behalf of the dissatisfied equally so. Although Tanzania has not yet departed from its path of peace, these issues need to be remembered.

One way to address the challenges would be to reinvigorate the nation-building pillars, reassess their viability, and replace those that have been removed with newer, more robust ones. Economic growth, political stability, and national unity are mutually reinforcing. These, together with trustworthy institutions, can help the country to grow faster. Tanzania's strong sense of national unity and identity will have to play a positive role in the years ahead, if the level of poverty and unemployment is to be decreased. Tanzania's growth rate of 7 per cent in the last decade suggests that the economic reforms implemented since the mid-1980s, giving more freedom to markets, have also helped (Ndulu, 2012).

3.6 Conclusion

In this chapter, we have given an account of Tanzania's nation-building efforts as a cornerstone of its social stability and cohesion – an exception to the violence and instability that has been experienced in some other parts of sub-Saharan Africa. The combination of an ethnically very diverse population and sustained, active, nation-building policies has contributed to Tanzania's relatively high political and social stability. Firm and visionary political measures that incorporated alternative trust into the public realm have helped to mould a unified nation and political culture that have endured beyond the pioneering years.

Human conflict is inevitable, but cross-cutting identities such as occupation and, especially, the all-encompassing identity of nationality, can help to decrease the likelihood that conflict will result in division. Diversity may present a challenge to national unity, but it is not destructive provided that the political leadership is committed to deemphasising ethnic group identities in the public sphere and pursues policies designed to improve regional and ethnic equality.

Diversity is not dangerous in itself, even when rich in a multiplicity of languages and cultures; it can be like a many coloured rainbow whose colours coexist without conflict. It becomes a liability only when exploited for political interest or for rent-seeking purposes; it then proves to be a perfect avenue for conflict. The Tanzanian case suggests, however, that it is indeed possible to create a sense of nationhood that can interpret cultural diversity, instead, as the best reason for social tolerance and cultural plurality.

References

Abdulaziz, M. H. 1971 Tanzania's national language policy. In Whiteley, W. (ed.), *Language Use and Social Change*. London: Oxford University Press, pp. 160–178.

Afrobarometer Data, [Tanzania], [Round 5, 6], [2012, 2017]. Retrieved from www.afrobarometer.org.

Alesina, A., Devleeshauwer, A., Easterly, W. Kurlat, S., and Wacziarg, R. 2003. Fractionalization. *Journal of Economic Growth*. 8(2): 155–194.

Almond, G. A., and Verba, S. 1963. *Civic Culture: Political Attitudes and Democracy in Five Nations*. Thousand Oaks, CA: Sage.

Bannon, A., Miguel, E., and Posner, D. N. 2004. *Sources of Ethnic Identification in Africa (Working Paper)*. Cape Town: Afrobarometer.

Barkan, J. D. 1994. Divergence and Convergence in Kenya and Tanzania: Pressures for Reform. In Barkan, J. D. (ed.), *Beyond Capitalism versus Socialism in Kenya and Tanzania*. Boulder, CO: Lynne Reinner Publishers.

2012. Ethnicity Fractionalization and the Propensity for Conflict in Uganda, Kenya and Tanzania. In Herbst, J., McNamee, T., and Mills, G. (eds.), *On the Fault Line: Managing Tensions and Divisions within Societies*. London: Profile Books, pp. 150–169.

Bjerk, P. 2017. *Julius Nyerere*. Athens: Ohio University Press.

Burgess, R., Jedwab, R., Miguel, E., Morjaria, A., and Miquel, G. 2015. The value of democracy: Evidence from road building in Kenya. *American Economic Review*. 105(6): 1817–1851.

Cliffe, L. 1967. *One Party Democracy: The 1965 Tanzania General Elections*. Nairobi: East African Publishing House.

Collier, P., and Hoeffler, A. 1998. *On the Economic Causes of Civil War*. Oxford: Centre for the Study of African Economies.

2002. On the incidence of civil war in Africa. *Journal of Conflict Resolution.* 46(1): 13–28.

Crepaz, M. M., and Damron, R. 2009. How welfare states shapes attitudes about immigrants. *Comparative Political Studies.* 42(3): 437–463.

Easterly, W., and Levine, R. 1997. Africa's growth tragedy: Policies and ethnic divisions. *Quarterly Journal of Economics.* 112(4): 1203–1250.

Erdmann, G. 2007. *The Cleavage Model, Ethnicity and Voter Alignment in Africa: Conceptual and Methodological Problems Revisited (Working Paper).* Hamburg: German Institute of Global and Area Studies (GIGA).

Fearon, J. D. 2003. Ethnic and Cultural Diversity by Country. *Journal of Economic Growth.* 8(2): 195–222.

Feierman, S. 1990. *Peasant Intellectuals: Anthropology and History in Tanzania.* Madison: University of Wisconsin Press.

Gahnström, S. C. 2012. *Ethnicity, region and politics in Tanzania: The 2010 general elections and Mwanza region.* Master's Thesis. University of Helsinki.

Geiger, S. 1997. *TANU Women: Gender and Culture in the Making of Tanganyikan Nationalism.* Oxford: Heinemann.

Global Security. National Service. Retrieved from: www.globalsecurity.org/military/world/tanzania/national-service.htm Accessed 11 May 2018.

Green. E. 2009. The political economy of nation formation in modern Tanzania: Explaining stability in the face of diversity. *Commonwealth and Comparative Politics.* 49(2): 223–244.

Greenfeld, L. 2003. *The Spirit of Capitalism: Nationalism and Economic Growth.* Cambridge, MA: Harvard University Press.

Gurr, T. R. 2000. *Peoples Versus States: Minorities at Risk in the New Century.* Washington, DC: U.S. Institute of Peace.

Horowitz, D. 2001. *The Deadly Ethnic Riot.* Berkeley and Los Angeles: University of California Press.

Hunter, E. 2015. *Political Thought and the Public Sphere in Tanzania: Freedom, Democracy and Citizenship in the era of Decolonization.* Cambridge: Cambridge University Press.

2017. "Economic man in East Africa": Ethnicity, nationalism and the moral economy in Tanzania. In Berman, B. J., Laliberté, A., and Larin, S. J. (eds.), *The Moral Economies of Ethnic and Nationalist Claims.* Toronto: UBC Press, pp. 101–122.

Huntington, S. P. 1996. *The Clash of Civilizations and the Remaking of World Order.* New York: Simon & Schuster.

Ivaska, A. 2005. Of students, "nizers", and a struggle of over youth: Tanzania's 1966 National Service crisis. *Africa Today.* 51(3): 83–107.

Kessler, I. 2006. *What went right in Tanzania: How nation building and political culture have produced forty-four years of peace.* Master's thesis. Georgetown University.

Langer, A. 2013. Comment on "Bonding Ethnic Communities and Building National Cohesion" by Mwabu G. In Hino, H., Lonsdale, J., and John, T. (eds.), *How Can Africa Flourish with Ethnic Diversity?* Kobe: Research Institute for Economic and Business Administration, Kobe University.

Lake, D., and Rothchild, D. 1998. Ethnic Fears and Global Engagement. In Lake, D., and Rothchild, D. (eds.), *The International Spread of Ethnic Conflict: Fear, Diffusion and Escalation*. Princeton, NJ: Princeton University Press, pp. 339–350.

Lindemann, S. 2010. *Civilian control of the military in Tanzania and Zambia: Explaining persistent exceptionalism (Crisis states working papers series No. 2)*. Retrieved from: www.lse.ac.uk/international-development/Assets/Documents/PDFs/csrc-working-papers-phase-two/wp80.2-civilian-control-of-the-military.pdf. Accessed 4 July 2018.

Lonsdale, J. 2012. Ethnic patriotism and markets in African history. In Hino, H., Lonsdale, J., Ranis., G., and Stewart, F. (eds.), *Ethnic Diversity and Economic Instability in Africa. Interdisciplinary Perspectives*. Cambridge: Cambridge University Press, pp. 19–55.

Maddox, G., and Giblin, J. 2005. *In Search of a Nation: Histories of Authority and Dissidence in Tanzania*. Oxford: James Currey.

Mahoney, J. 2001. *The Legacies of Liberalism: Path Dependence and Political Regimes in Central America*. Baltimore, MD: Johns Hopkins University Press.

Meienberg, H. 1966. *Tanzanian Citizen: A Civics Textbook*. Oxford: Oxford University Press.

Miguel, E. 2004. Tribe or nation? Nation building and public goods in Kenya versus Tanzania. *World Politics*. 56(3): 327–362.

Molony. T. 2014. *Nyerere: The Early Years*. Woodbridge, UK: James Currey.

Mozaffar, S., and Scarrit, J. R. 2005. The puzzle of African party systems. *Party Politics*. 11(4): 399–421.

Ncube, M., Jones, B., and Bicaba, Z. 2014. *Estimating the Economic Cost of Fragility in Africa (African Development Bank Group Working Paper No. 197)*. Tunis: African Development Bank.

Ndulu, B. 2012. Keynote Address delivered at the National Conference on "Unleashing Growth Potentials: Lessons and Way Forward in Creating an Inclusive Growth", Economic and Social Foundation (ESRF). Dar es Salaam, 16 May.

Ndulu, B. J., and O'Connel, S. 2008. Policy Plus: African Growth Performance, 1960–2000. In Ndulu, B. J., O'Connel, S., Bates, R. H. Collier, P., and Soludo, C. C. (eds.), *The Political Economy of Economic Growth in Africa 1960–2000*. Cambridge: Cambridge University Press, pp. 249–296.

Nugent, P. 2012. *Africa Since Independence: A Comparative History*. Basingstoke, UK: Palgrave.

Nyang'oro, J. 2006. Ethnic structure, inequality and governance of the public sector in Tanzania. In Bangura, Y. (ed.), *Ethnic Inequalities and Public Sector Governance*. Basingstoke, UK: Palgrave Macmillan, pp. 322–340.

Okewa, M. 1996. *Political Culture of Tanzania*. Lewiston, ME: E. Mellen Press.

Posner, D. N. 2004a. The political salience of cultural difference: Why Chewas and Tumbukas are allies in Zambia and adversaries in Malawi. *American Political Science Review*. 98(4): 529–545.

2004b. Measuring ethnic fractionalization in Africa. *American Journal of Political Science*. 48(4): 849–863.

Pratt, C. 1976. *The Critical Phase in Tanzania 1945–1968: Nyerere and the Emergence of a Socialist Strategy*. Cambridge: Cambridge University Press.

Roeder, P. G. 2001. *Ethnolinguistic Fractionalization (ELF) Indices, 1961 and 1985*. Retrieved from: http://weber.ucsd.edu/~proeder/elf.htm. Accessed 18 September 2018.

Scarritt, J. R., and Mozaffar, S. 1999. The specification of ethnic cleavages and ethnopolitical groups for the analysis of democratic competition in contemporary Africa. *Nationalism and Ethnic Politics*. 5(1): 82–117.

Therkildsen, O. 2009. Competitive Elections, Ethnicity and State Elite Policy Responses, with Examples from Tanzania. Paper presented at *From Asymmetry to Symmetry? The West, Non-west and the Idea of Development as Conceptual Flow*, University of Heidelberg, 13–16 July 2009.

Therkildsen, O., and Tidemand, P. 2007. *Staff Management and Organizational Performance in Tanzania and Uganda: Public Servant Perspectives*. Copenhagen: Danish Institute for International Studies.

Tilly, C. 2005. *Trust and Rule*. Cambridge: Cambridge University Press

4 | Identity, Inequality, and Social Contestation in the Post-Apartheid South Africa

HIROYUKI HINO, MURRAY LEIBBRANDT,
RATJOMOSE MACHEMA, MUNA SHIFA, AND
CRAIN SOUDIEN

4.1 Introduction

Ethnicity in Africa dates back centuries. It evolves in response to the challenges and opportunities provided by geography and demography. It takes its dynamism from the social, economic, and political circumstances that surround the ethnic groups, including inequalities between – and within – those groups (see the Introduction to this book). Directly relevant for this chapter is Lonsdale's description (Chapter 1) of how this process of the making of ethnic identity unfolds. In his useful portrayal of the four ages of ethnicity in Kenya, he explains that the fourth and latest age can be described as the age of "political ethnicity". It is characterised by divisiveness. Lonsdale comes to the conclusion that a more inclusive, fifth age of ethnicity does not seem to be likely, at least in the near future, despite the painful memory of ethnic clashes that claimed more than 1,300 lives only a decade ago and the subsequent adoption of a truly progressive constitution that people hoped could finally usher in a more cohesive society in the country.

In this chapter, we turn to South Africa. It, too, is struggling with the challenge of building a nation where its citizens are bound by a sense of common purpose and belonging. The challenge in South Africa is more complex than it may be in many other countries. It concerns not simply one form of social difference, as may be the case in Kenya, but fractures involving the interplay of multiple differences and identities. The country is constituted around many forms of social difference. These include race, ethnic affiliation and class, in addition to gender, sexuality, religion, language, geography, region and a whole host of other forms of social differentiation.

These differentiations occur, moreover, in contexts of intense social stress. The country, as we explain, is working its way through a long process of transition out of its apartheid past in which the differences of race, ethnicity and class were formative at both individual and social levels. Critical, also, is the challenging economic environment in which South Africa finds itself. Growth has stalled. Unemployment levels grow each year.

These conditions have coalesced to make South Africa one of the most complex countries in the world. While, thus, the country is a place of immense possibility and innovation, it is beset with challenges. These challenges have made the country immensely susceptible to social discontent. It is now one of the most protest-hit countries in the world. Many protests, moreover, have turned violent (Alexander, 2016). The incident at the Marikana platinum mines in the Northwest Province, where more than 60 miners were killed, is one of notable examples of such violent protests. The conditions have also given rise, as communities seek to act in what they think is their best interests, to extreme forms of xenophobia (Hofmeyr & Lefko-Everett, 2014).

The end of apartheid and the coming of democracy in South Africa in 1994 promised for the country a new beginning. It gave birth to hopes of a new inclusive South African identity that would transcend its old apartheid racialised loyalties. The ideal of "a nation united in diversity" or "a rainbow nation" was developed. Moments arose in the last 23 years when it seemed that the dream of the rainbow people was being realised. These moments happened most notably when South Africa won the rugby world cup in 1995 and when it hosted the football world cup in 2010. The big global events came and went, and a hard reality sunk in. It has been difficult to sustain these moments against its history.

Various opinion surveys indicate that South African society might have begun to move towards greater cohesion during the first decade of the democratic dispensation, but thereafter the momentum seems to have given way to the assertion of social divisions as differentiations sharpened and inequality within the country grew, with the widening of inequality both between and within groups. These fractures have taken many forms and can be examined from many perspectives. They manifest themselves in racial, class, gender, regional and a multiplicity of other forms. The fracture of most interest for this chapter is that of race. Contestation between and within racial groups, with class and ethnic overlays, has sharpened over the last decade, manifesting itself in violence, land disputes, workplace conflicts, social frictions and a loss of economic productivity.

Race is prioritised in this discussion because it has historically shaped up as the major form of social identification in the country. This identification, it is important to explain, and the literature on this is voluminous (see, for example, the recent work of Erasmus, 2017), is the direct result of the country's long history of social engineering. This engineering came to a climax in 1950 with the passage of the Population Registration Act, which required that every South African carry an identity document that classified him or her in racial terms. At that point, three racial groups were identified, Whites, Natives (the term was later changed to 'Bantu') and Coloureds (who were subdivided into seven groups that included people classified as Indian and Chinese). Indian people were later separated out as a distinct racial group.

These racial groups were, after 1949, allocated to separate 'group areas', where their whole social and cultural lives were expected to be played out. At the heart of these processes was a system of racial classification that was initially premised on racial biological terms, and later, after this was unable to be sustained on scientific grounds, on cultural grounds. In the process, as definitions shifted towards the cultural, terms such as 'race' and 'ethnicity' became interchangeable.

What the term 'ethnicity' signifies in South Africa is also important to clarify. Although the term is used in this chapter, it is necessary to signal that it has an uncomfortable presence in the social sciences in South Africa. The discomfort felt around it (see, importantly, the clarification of the nuances around this term and others in use in South Africa in Boonzaier and Sharp [1988] and Shepherd and Robins [2008]), is fundamentally about the way the term 'ethnicity', and its correlate 'ethnic groups', has been used as synonym for 'race'. Shepherd and Robins (2008) make clear, for example, how the social sciences have struggled over the idea in the last few decades: "Whereas during the antiapartheid struggle, Left intellectuals and activists believed that outmoded ideas about ethnic and cultural differences would give way to modern, socialist understandings of working-class consciousness and solidarity, political life in post-apartheid South Africa continues to be animated by discourses on 'African tradition' and ethnic difference" (Shepherd & Robins, 2008, p. 7).

This chapter aims to provide a deeper understanding of the social contestation of South African society since the end of apartheid, focusing on the evolution of the character of each of key identity groups – race and ethnicity. We gauge the inclusiveness/exclusiveness of an identity by the extent to which individuals in the identity group engage in or wish to engage in social interactions with those in other identity groups and by their desire to learn customs of others' identities. We then establish how the character of race and ethnicity has changed over the period and investigate if a deepening of inequality helped to trigger those changes. We look closely at how inequalities between and within race groups and those between and within ethnic groups changed over the period, and how they are correlated with the changes of the character of race identities. We measure inequalities in terms of both income and self-assessment of the level of an individual's life satisfaction, the latter being a more comprehensive measure of one's well-being.

We begin with a brief review of identities in South Africa, focusing on how the characters of ethnic and race identities evolved from the precolonial period to the present (Section 2). This discussion is followed by a presentation of vertical, horizontal and intragroup inequalities of race and ethnic groups from 1994 to 2008 and between 2008 and 2015 (Section 3). We then investigate changes in the extent of and the desire to engage in inter-racial social interactions over the two subperiods and how those changes correlate with the trends in various measures of inequality (Section 4). Observations on prospects for forging a more cohesive society conclude the chapter (Section 5).

4.2 Identities of South Africans

According to the 2017 Report of the South African Reconciliation Barometer Survey (Potgieter, 2017), language, i.e., proxy for ethnicity, and race are by far the most prominent identities of South Africans: about one-half of South Africans consider language and race as either their primary or secondary identities. Economic class is listed as the primary or secondary identity by about one-quarter of South Africans. Interestingly, fewer than one in five South Africans consider being South African as his or her primary or secondary identity. The South African Reconciliation Barometer Surveys (SARBS) 2017 also reports that only 4 per cent of the population list language as the first cause of the division in the country, while race is mentioned as the first cause by 24 per cent of the population. In contrast, inequality is listed as the number one cause of division by 31 per cent of the population (Potgieter, 2017, p. 16).

In the official nomenclature in South Africa and in private conversations, as seen, people are routinely classified into four "race" categories – African/Black, White, Coloured and Indian. The Coloured group are offspring of inter-relationships between freed slaves (mainly of Malay origin), the Khoisan, and European colonists. The Indians constitute a small but important ethnic group. The persons of Indian origin first came to the Cape in the community of slaves, and later, the large migration of people of Indian descent occurred during the 1860s when indentured labour was required to work the Natal sugarcane fields. The Indians have remained a relatively homogeneous and internally cohesive group, with strong attachment to their culture and tradition.

South Africans are concurrently classified in "ethnic" categories. There are eleven official languages in South Africa, and they are often used as proxies for ethnicity. Nine of the official languages are those of African origin such as Zulu, Xhosa, Ndebele and Venda, and the other two are European, i.e., English and Afrikaans, a local adaptation of Dutch. Languages broadly correspond with ethnic groups, but not precisely so. Afrikaans is spoken by the Afrikaners, mostly descendants of Dutch settlers, the Coloured and some African ethnicities.[1]

The histories of these groups too have been a source of conflict in the country. Dominant apartheid history sought to hold alive the explanation that African and European people arrived in the country at the same time. The narrative has it that the country was empty and so terra nullius. Anti-apartheid historians have long sought to show the falsity of this claim and have demonstrated that the country was occupied by Bantu-language speakers, never mind the Khoisan who were here many centuries earlier (see Wilson, 2011).

In this section, we briefly review (a) the evolution of ethnicities of African origin over the course of history, (b) the formation of race as a

---

[1] According to StatSA, in 2014, the South African population was composed of African/Black (80.2%), Coloured (8.8%), White (8.4%), and Asian/Indian (2.5%) (StatSA, 2014). In terms of languages spoken at home, IsiZulu (22.7%), IsiXhosa (16.0%), Sepedi (9.1%), Setswana (8.0%), Sesotho (7.6%), Afrikaans (13.5%), and English (9.6%) accounted for 86.5% of total population in 2011 (StatSA, 2013).

statutory imposition and classificatory name, and (c) the emergence and suppression of a unique identity group in the country from intermingling of ethnicities, all with a view to understanding the character of race and ethnic identities at present as well as its interplay with inequality. Class (as in labour vs capitalist) is another key identity impacting social contestation in the country. However, in the context of South Africa, as we will see, class formation is closely interwoven with that of race. It is, therefore, difficult to untangle the impact of class from that of race in our quantitative analysis. For this reason, and because of data limitations, class is not a focus of detailed discussion in this chapter.

4.2.1 Evolution of Ethnicities of African Origin

Ethnicity – as it relates to the kinship groups of African origin – has a bifurcated character. There are linguistic groups that evolved in relatively autonomous ways, much as they would have in other parts of Africa, but there is a distinct colonial hand in the identities that have emerged (see Chanock, 2001; Delius, 2008; Mamdani, 1996). The identities have both self-making and constructed dimension to who they are. With respect to the latter, they take much of their character from the complex structural forces, not least of all British colonialism, which played themselves out around them. These groups sharpened their distinct identities during the apartheid era as a result of the country's homeland policy, which had as its intention the disenfranchising of all South Africans who were classified Bantu and the creation for them of separate homelands. The effects of these developments have been to produce relatively robust ethnic identities.[2]

People of African origins migrated to southern Africa many centuries ago – first, the Sans from further north about 8,000 years ago; then the Khoikhois also from further north about 2,000–3,000 years ago; and finally, the bantu-speaking people probably from east and central Africa between AD 300 and 900 and possibly earlier (Nattrass, 2017). Substantial polities began to develop, and, by the 1760s, a large number of political entities emerged. These jurisdictions have come

---

[2] How these identities, as social collectivities, are referred to has long been controversial in South Africa. The term 'tribe' is avoided by social scientists because of its colonial provenance (see, for example, Wilson & Thompson, 1982).

to be described in the historical literature in different ways. Some texts describe them as chiefdoms, others as kingdoms. Those, of course, were not the terms that people used to describe themselves and the collectivities to which they belonged. But the concepts have an intelligibility that is useful for this work. Chiefdoms typically had a decentralised hierarchy with low intragroup inequality and were not always tightly closed to those outside. People in a chiefdom shared norms of reciprocity and collective protection of kin, and hence a common sense of belonging.

However, the country's geography and ecology made inequality between the distinct groups inherently complex. Moreover, trade with European settlers that had begun in the late seventeenth century, and more generally the dawn of commerce, led to a rise in both intergroup and intragroup inequalities. As population pressures grew and climate change made land less fertile, the search for food and pasture led to large-scale migrations within Southern Africa. This brought groups into direct conflict and, eventually, armed contestations between them. The defeated were absorbed into the victorious, and large polities emerged by the 1830s.

Those polities generally had a three-tiered hierarchy – aristocrat, commoners and war captives – and, consequently, considerable intragroup inequality. People in those polities were structured around leaders who presented themselves as kings and were much less naturally bonded to each other with mutual trust. Group moral ethnicity thus faded, and an identity of exclusive instinct gained strength.

As European settlers increased their presence and advanced into the interior by force in quest for agricultural land and mineral resources, the traditional polities fought long and vicious wars to protect their land and community. They were defeated. The British colonies expanded, and the Boers (mostly Dutch settlers) established two colonial states, Transvaal and the Orange Free State (1852–1854). The traditional institutions were absorbed into the colonial administrations in ways that simultaneously cemented particular identities, weakened others and created new ones. Particularly complex variations of how this process developed can be seen in the creation of new and larger political identities and the dissolution or weakening of older loyalties within the isiXhosa- and isiZulu-speaking communities.

The traditional institutions were revived by the colonial administrations for their own convenience. Those institutions have since been nourished in the post-apartheid governments, and traditional attachment has been used increasingly for political mobilisation (see Claassens and Boyle, 2014). Furthermore, evidently, the memory of injustice – committed by both triumphant kingdoms and the colonial powers – does not fade for centuries. Thus, today, most South Africans of African origin harbour a sense of belonging to their respective lineage, and ethnicities of African origin remain a foundation of South African society with a varying degree of instinct of exclusion and mistrust of others.

4.2.2 Race Formation and Ethnic Identity

South Africans of European origin began to migrate to the country during the 1650s. They are largely those of British and Dutch origin, but also include smaller numbers of French Huguenots, German reformists Protestants and others. These smaller groups of European descendants assimilated quickly into the Dutch. A new culture, a language and an ethnic identity, Afrikaner, emerged through social and economic integration. Between 1835 and the mid-1840s, Afrikaners (Boers) advanced into the interior from the Cape Colony, in search of pasture and land and to escape from the British rule. The Afrikaner identity gathered strength during this "great trek" and was solidified in the Boer Republics, which were established after that. Governance in these republics was meant to erect political, social and economic inequalities in favour of Afrikaners and in detriment to slaves and Africans.

Afrikaners, most of whom had initially arrived as poor settlers and were still relatively poor farmers, went on to engage in ferocious wars against the richer British to secure more land and mineral resources, and, hence, greater equality and self-determination vis-à-vis the British. The Afrikaners eventually lost the second, decisive, Boer war of 1899–1902, and accepted the abrogation of the Boer Republics and the formation of the Union of South Africa in 1910 as a dominion of the British Empire. Nonetheless, the Afrikaners created an internally cohesive identity with "nationalism" for their own advancement and a strong instinct for exclusion of others.

This Afrikaner nationalism exerted a strong influence in successive governments of the Union of South Africa, which began to institutionalise the Whites as an identity group to protect its own for exclusion of others. The union governments were concerned that poor Whites (Afrikaners) became more prevalent in the aftermath of the depression of the 1880s and began to assimilate into communities of Africans and former slaves. The governments feared that such assimilation could endanger the very existence of the Whites as a distinct supreme race. The response of the Union government was to eradicate poverty from the White population altogether, through preferential treatments in favour of the Whites and discrimination against the others (Bundy, 2016).

Thus, a series of aggressive legislations were enacted, all with the aim of removing competition for good jobs for middle class Whites and ensuring a supply of cheap Black labour for rich Whites. Those legislations included (a) the Natives Land Act of 1913, which allocated 87 per cent of land to Europeans and barred African sharecroppers and squatters from farming in White owned farms except as labour tenants, (b) a series of labour laws that created a system of industrial relations under which, for example, skilled jobs were kept only for White workers while unskilled jobs were subject to a minimum wage but only for White workers, (c) large-scale public works programmes, which created jobs for White workers, and (d) extensive public services only for White families, covering education, housing and health (1930s). By the early 1940s, there were no longer poor Whites.

The apartheid period between 1948 and 1994 is particularly significant for the process of race formation and ethnic identity in South Africa. In 1948, the National Party won the Whites-only election in South Africa. It immediately set about institutionalising the policy of 'apartheid'. 'Apartheid' was based on the idea that the people of South Africa were divided into clear racial groups, each of which had a separate social, cultural and economic existence and so should be allowed to develop and live separately. Intrinsic to the idea was the belief that people classified as White were superior to the other groups identified in the policy, i.e., the Africans/Black, the Coloured and the Indians.

The new government introduced a panoply of laws – approximately 300 – to manage the entrenchment of separate development. The most notable of these were the Prohibition of Mixed Marriages Act of 1949; the Population Registration Act, the Group Areas Act, the Suppression of Communism Act, all passed in 1950; the Native Laws Amendment and the Abolition of Pass Laws Acts (which, ironically forced all African people to carry reference books, the hated 'dompas'), and the Bantu Authorities Act, which were passed in 1952; and the Bantu Education Act of 1953. These laws institutionalised discrimination and socialised the Black people of South Africa, those who were not White, into physical and mental states of inferiority. South Africans growing up in this period grew up believing that, unless they were taught otherwise by their parents, teachers or religious and educational institutions, which did happen, their imposed racial classifications were real.

When apartheid was finally forced out and democracy was born in 1994, the ideology of inclusion was formally instituted in the new constitution, which was adopted in 1996. Thus, the new South Africa had an opportunity to be founded on an inclusive sense of what it meant to be African. However, this opportunity faded as government policy to bring about greater equality for the Africans/Blacks ironically cemented race in government institutions and public discourse and inequalities between race groups grew in people's self-assessment of life satisfaction.

More than two decades after the end of apartheid, South Africa still lives in its shadows. The Afrikaner identity remains today, although not as overt as used to be. South Africans of British origin had a privileged position in the society and economy, protected for a long time by the colonial institutions and then apartheid. Growth of land ownership and commercial farming by Africans did occur in rural areas under the British colonial administration, but this development was abruptly reversed by the segregation policy of the colonial administration (Acemoglu & Robinson, 2012; Bundy, 2016). Thus, inequality between the British as an ethnic group and the African ethnic groups steadily increased and remains exceedingly high today. Importantly, colonialism and apartheid ruptured the very foundation of African communities and aroused strong feeling of injustice and social contestation. It continues to do so today.

4.2.3 Emergence and Suppression of the Coloured Community

Enslaved people came largely from the Malay Peninsula in South East Asia, but also from Madagascar and other coastal areas of the Indian ocean. They were first imported in 1658 and increased to as many as 36,000 in the Cape alone by the early 1800s. They were disparate groups with no common identity, disfranchised and dependent on their masters for their meagre living. They were thus unable to organise as an identity group either to protest for their interests or create social conflicts.

After they were emancipated in 1834, a majority of the slaves in the Cape Colony stayed with their masters, but many moved out to work in commercial farms in Western Cape. There, they began to develop their own culture and communities through intermarriages and social interactions. Many other emancipated slaves moved to the District VI area of Cape Town, where they, together with other Muslim immigrants, developed a distinct, ethnically-mixed community with its own culture (see Rasool, Chapter 11 in this volume). Similarly, a vibrant ethnically mixed community emerged in Sophiatown and other urban areas in the country. However, those communities were squashed as the colonial and apartheid administrations forcibly resettled the inhabitants, precisely for fear of the growth of ethnically or racially mixed identity groups and the consequent challenge to White supremacy.

An important component of this group's history has to do with the Khoisan community. Khoisan people were not enslaved, but have a complex history of hostility and rapprochement with the White settler community. The first frontier wars in the relationship between White settlers and the indigenous peoples were fought with the Khoisan in 1658. This inaugurated a long period of conflict which led, as Adhikari (2010) has argued, to what he calls "the genocide" of the San people. After about 1840, when Khoisan people were brought into the economy as indentured people and after slavery was abolished, slave descendants and Khoisan people began to be referred to by the colonial government as "Coloured" people. Out of this history has emerged a relatively identifiable community with cultural practices that include the experiences of slavery, the recovery of Islam at the Cape, conversion to Christianity and the complex effects of racial classification.

To sum up, the race and ethnic landscape in South Africa has historically been complex and continues to be so today. The ethnic groups of African origin contain internal contradictions and contestations, as inequalities between and within the ethnic groups are large; this finding is confirmed in recent surveys. Similar observations could be made about the relationships between Afrikaners and the British, and between these groups and the African ethnic groups. An analysis of social contestation or cohesion in South Africa is incomplete unless narratives of race and ethnic relations are read together with parallel stories of inequalities, to which we now turn.

4.3 Inequalities in the Post-Apartheid Period

While 1994 ushered in a new, nonracial era of equal rights before the law, one cannot legislate at the stroke of the same pen the equalisation across race and ethnicity of access to wealth – including land, human capital and other assets – that was carried into the post-apartheid era as the legacy of the history that was unpacked in the previous section. The incredibly high measured inequalities at the start of the post-apartheid period served as the clearest metrics of this historical legacy and, in the intervening years, have served as key benchmarks of progress in building a flourishing and cohesive new South Africa.

In this section, we analyse holistically the extent and trend of inequalities since the end of apartheid in 1994, namely, in terms of income and life satisfaction; in relation to South African society as a whole and to each race and ethnic group individually; and both within (vertically) and between groups (horizontally). We show that aggregate measures of vertical or horizontal inequality do not necessarily point to an increase in social contestation during the last decade. Rather, undergirding this are the perceptions of inequality based on the lived experience of post-apartheid South Africa and the changing texture of inequalities between certain historically sensitive race or ethnic groups and within certain groups. These inequalities have risen and such "inequality hotspots" require close attention.

The data for income and life-satisfaction inequality analyses are derived from the Project for Statistics on Living Standards and Development (PSLSD) for 1993, and two waves of the National Income Dynamics Study (NIDS) for 2008 and 2015. The PSLSD was conducted just before the first democratic elections in 1994 to give a broad national picture of South Africa at the start of democracy (Southern Africa Labour and Development Research Unit [SALDRU], 1994). The NIDS is the first nationally representative panel survey, which started in 2008 and continues every two years. The latest wave available was conducted in 2015 (SALDRU, 2015).

The inequality analysis in this section extends the literature in two respects. First, the assessment of the extent of inequality in South

Africa has been based largely on income. There is very little research that examines the extent of inequality using multidimensional inequality measures, which more fully reflect the distribution of relative well-being of members of the society (Bhorat & Westhuizen, 2013; Wittenberg & Leibbrandt, 2017). Our analysis makes use of a self-assessment of the degree of life satisfaction, perhaps the broadest measure of one's well-being. Second, the assessment of inequality has focused mostly on vertical inequality, i.e., the distributional pattern of income among individuals in the country. Evidence suggests that such aggregate measures of vertical inequality (e.g., the Gini coefficient) are not strongly correlated with social tension or instability. Rather, it is horizontal inequality and polarisation, i.e., disparities in the level of well-being between competing identity groups, which correlates more closely to social conflicts (Esteban & Ray, 1994; Stewart et al., 2010). Thus, we augment our analysis of vertical inequality with a detailed analysis of horizontal inequality, with respect to both race and ethnic groups.

4.3.1 Inequality at the National Level

We begin our analysis of inequality in South Africa with an examination of vertical inequality in the national distribution between 1993 and 2015. We offer estimates of several indicators of vertical inequality; namely, the Gini coefficient, skewedness at the top and the bottom of distribution and the Palma ratio. We present those estimates for income distribution, and then for the self-assessed level of life satisfaction. Taking the estimates of these inequality indicators together, aggregate income inequality increased notably between 1993 and 2008, and decreased somewhat from 2008 to 2015. In contrast, on the same basis, aggregate life satisfaction inequality decreased strongly from 1993 to 2008 and remained broadly unchanged after that.

National Income Inequality
The first panel of Figure 4.1 displays the distributions of log real income per capita and Lorenz curves for real income per capita for 1993, 2008 and 2015. All incomes are indexed to 2015 prices. The distribution of income shifted slightly to the right from 1993 to 2008,

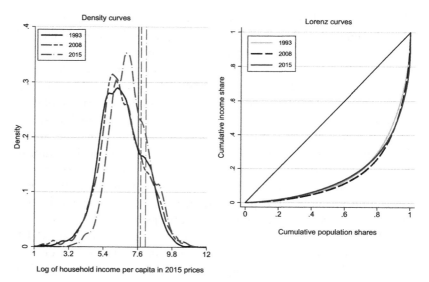

Figure 4.1 Distribution of real income per capita and Lorenz curves (1993–2015)

Source: Own calculations from weighted PSLSD (1993) and NIDS (2008, 2015).

mainly in the middle and in the tails of the distribution and shifted further to the right in 2015 at all levels of the income distribution, except at the very top. These results suggest that, from 1993 to 2015, there has been an increase in real incomes at all levels.

However, it is difficult to discern changes in inequality from this figure. To make progress on this issue, the second panel of Figure 4.1 presents a set of Lorenz curves that provide a clear view on changes in vertical inequality at the national level. Recall that the further a Lorenz curve lies from the 45° line of equality, the more unequal the distribution is and the higher value of the Gini coefficient. In the second panel, the 2008 Lorenz curve is clearly further away from the diagonal line than the 1993 curve. This means that whatever measure one uses, inequality worsened from 1993 to 2008. With regard to the comparison of 2008 and 2015, the Lorenz curves cross, which means we cannot state definitively whether inequality rose or fell between these two observation points. Different measures, with their different value judgements, will reach different conclusions about changes in inequality between 2008 and 2015.

To explore these trends further, we calculated a few different indicators of inequality over time, starting with the Gini coefficient. This coefficient increased from 0.667 in 1993 to 0.698 in 2008 and decreased slightly to 0.678 in 2015. The increase from 1993 to 2008 is expected, given the clear outward shift of the Lorenz curve in Figure 4.1. However, when it comes to assessing the change from 2008 to 2015, the Gini coefficient is more definitive than the Lorenz curve in reflecting a decrease in inequality from 2008 to 2015. Reconciliation comes from the fact that the Gini coefficient is particularly sensitive to changes in the income distribution occurring around mean income. Given South Africa's high inequality, such changes are in the upper middle section of the distribution. Inspection of both panels of Figure 4.1 show that real incomes increased in this upper middle section and larger shares of the income accrued to this section; hence, the declining inequality reflected in the Gini.

Other measures are better than the Gini in giving a sense of changes in the tails of the distribution and in the distance between the rich and the poor. In this regard we also calculated (a) the shares of incomes of the top 10 per cent and the bottom 10 per cent in total income; (b) the distance between the top 10 per cent and the bottom 10 per cent as measured by their ratios to the median income; and (c) the Palma coefficient, which is the ratio of the income share of the top 10 per cent to the income share of the bottom 40 per cent. The Palma coefficient focuses on the top 10 per cent and the lower 40 per cent of distribution, because in most countries, those in the middle deciles tend to capture about 50 per cent of national income (Cobham & Sumner, 2013).

Like the Gini coefficient, each of these five indicators uniformly shows that inequality increased from 1993 to 2008, and then declined from 2008 to 2015. For example, the median income of the richest 10 per cent, which was already exceptionally high in 1993 relative to that of the bottom 10 per cent (69 times), became even more so in 2008 (85 times) before falling back to 65 times in 2015. Likewise, the income share of the top 10 per cent was 52 per cent in 1993, increased to 56.9 per cent in 2008 and declined slightly to 56.5 per cent in 2015. In contrast, the income share of the bottom 10 per cent was only 0.44 per cent in 1993, declined even further to 0.36 per cent in 2008, and then crawled up to 0.6 per cent in 2015. The trends are similar if we look at the Palma coefficient, which increased from 10.1 in 1993 to 12.4 in 2008 and declined to 9.6 in 2015.

The regularity in these inequality trends is striking. In sum then, even if the Lorenz curve reflected some ambiguity, from most vantage points, national income inequality declined from 2008 to 2015. Importantly, this finding does not correspond with perception surveys, which show consistently that the public perceives that inequality continued to rise in recent years. It seems that the unfolding realities of daily life for the majority of South Africans have not evidenced a declining inequality or the move to more integrated socioeconomic circumstances that would lead people to perceive a reality of declining income inequality. We go on to investigate these perceptions in the next subsection.

National Life Satisfaction Inequality
Given that the post-apartheid period was explicitly meant to do away with the race-based discrimination and favouritism, the impact of the birth of the nation on a person's life satisfaction must have been deeply different, depending on his or her race and ethnicity. Divergent patterns in the levels of and disparities in life satisfaction that emerged must have been fundamental in determining social contestation in South Africa.

Figure 4.2 shows the distribution of life satisfaction over time at the national level and for each race group except the Indian/Asian group, which is too small a subsample in NIDS for reliable analysis. As anticipated, there was an upsurge in life satisfaction across the spectrum from 1993 to 2008, followed by a reversal from 2008 to 2015. Large portions, if not most, of those reporting less than satisfied (categories 1 through 4) moved to either neutral or somewhat satisfied (categories 5 and 6). This improvement was more than reversed during 2008 to 2015. In this more recent period, the proportions of the population who ranked their level of satisfaction in the lower half (categories 2, 3 or 4) increased substantially, while those who ranked their level of satisfaction in mid-range (categories 5, 6 and 7) decreased correspondingly.

Most striking is the unmistakable shift of the distribution towards less satisfaction from 2008 to 2015, driven mostly by changes in the assessment of life satisfaction of the African group. From 1993 to 2008, the distribution of life satisfaction of the African group clearly and remarkably shifted upward, i.e., from less satisfied to more satisfied, but then shifted back from 2008 to 2015. The trends of life

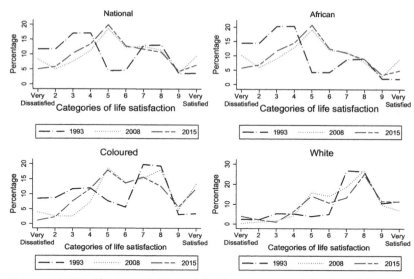

Figure 4.2 Distribution of life satisfaction at national level and by race (1993–2015)
Source: Own calculations from weighted PSLSD (1993) and NIDS (2008, 2015).

satisfaction of the Coloured group broadly mirror those of the African group, although at higher levels of satisfaction. For the White group, the shifts in life satisfaction were subtle. We will return to these trends in Section 5.2, where we discuss horizontal inequality.

Figure 4.3 presents life satisfaction Lorenz curves for 1993, 2008 and 2015. It shows that the Lorenz curve unequivocally shifted inward from 1993 to 2008. This means that vertical inequality of life satisfaction in South African society unambiguously fell from 1993 to 2008. The change from 2008 to 2015 is unclear as the Lorenz curves of 2008 and 2015 are sitting on top of each other. The Gini coefficients confirm this trend (a decline from 0.318 in 1993 to 0.257 in 2008, and a smaller and possibly insignificant decline to 0.242 in 2015). As the Lorenz curve analysis is so clear-cut, we do not augment the Gini coefficient with other measures of inequality.

What are the key takeaways from the discussions of vertical inequalities of income and life satisfaction above? First, it may not be prudent to focus exclusively on the level and trend of income inequality. Income inequality of course is one of the elements that influence life

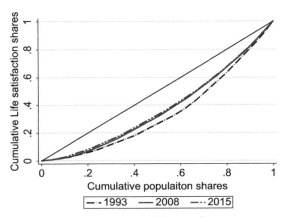

Figure 4.3 Lorenz curves of life satisfaction (1993–2015)
Source: Own calculations from weighted PSLSD (1993) and NIDS (2008, 2015).

satisfaction. But, apparently, there have been other factors that outweighed income in the assessment of life satisfaction by South Africans. Arguably, the latter, i.e., inequality in the degree of life satisfaction, could have a more direct and important role as a link between inequality and social contestation and cohesion. Second, it may be useful to study more carefully both levels and inequalities of life satisfaction – particularly those of race and ethnic groups – to better understand the social cohesion dynamics in the country. The wave of optimism that followed independence seems to have been replaced by a sense of frustration and discontent, and hence stagnation or even a decline in life satisfaction across a broad spectrum of the society over the last decade.

4.3.2 Inequalities between and within Race Groups

As shown in the discussion of identities in Section 2, inequality between groups (horizontal inequality) is most pertinent in understanding contestation of a society. When inequality between two groups rises, members of the group that became worse off tend to come together to protect their interests, leading at times to greater antagonism towards other groups. Additionally, when inequality within a group rises, bonding of its members around their common identity weakens, leading at times to fragmentation of the group.

In this subsection, we examine the horizontal and intragroup inequalities of race groups. We first examine visually the distributions of individual groups in any given year, to see how close they are to each other. We then quantify the closeness by measuring distance between the means of the distribution of pairs of groups and then aggregate all bilateral mean distances into one measure, the group coefficient of variation (GCOV), to produce an aggregate measure of horizontal inequality (Stewart et al., 2010). We further quantify the extent of overlap between two distributions by measuring the ratios of the mean of one distribution to that of the others across all levels of income. This is called the disparity ratio (Stewart et al., 2010). We complement these horizontal inequality measures by Gini coefficients for each group (intragroup inequality). As in the previous subsection, we contrast income and life satisfaction inequalities.

Income Inequality of Race Groups

Figure 4.4 compares income distributions of three race groups (African/Black, Coloured and White). It shows that, in 1993, the three

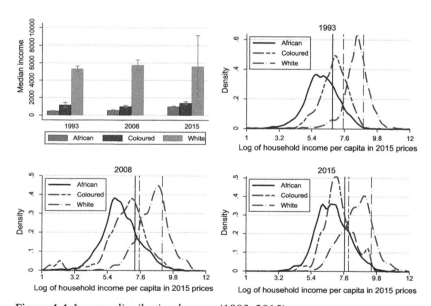

Figure 4.4 Income distribution by race (1993–2015)
Source: Own calculations from weighted PSLSD (1993) and NIDS (2008, 2015). Note: All incomes inflated to 2015 prices.

distributions were quite distant from each other, with a limited overlap between the distribution of the African/Black group and that of the Coloured and almost no overlap between the African/Black group and the White group. This finding is a clear sign of large horizontal inequality. In 2008, the distances became less wide and the overlaps increased, mostly because the distribution of the African/Black group shifted decidedly to the right. Horizontal inequality clearly narrowed. By 2015, the shapes of income distributions of all three groups changed noticeably. The distribution of the African/Black group became more dispersed, with a flattening of the distribution in the middle; the distribution of the Coloured group became more concentrated; and, interestingly, for the White group, the lower ends of the distribution bulged while upper ends shrank. It is not immediately clear if horizontal inequality continued to fall. From the visual inspection, we see no indications that horizontal income inequality was a cause of the apparent rise in racial divisiveness over the last decade.

The distances between the mean incomes of race groups confirm the very large yet declining horizontal inequality we observe. In 1993, the median income of the African/Black group was less than one-tenth of Whites, one-fifth of Indians and about one-half of Coloureds. Likewise, the median income of Coloureds was about one-fifth of Whites and one-half of Indians. From 1993 to 2008, the relative positions of the median incomes between racial groups remained largely unchanged, except that the Coloured group became significantly poorer relative to the White group, and less rich relative to the African/Black group. From 2008 to 2015, however, the relative income positions narrowed significantly across all racial pairs. In particular, the African/Black group continued to improve their relative income position vis-a-vis the Coloured group, while the income gap narrowed between the Coloured group and the White group.

We calculated the GCOV to sum up the trends in horizontal income inequality. This GCOV declined by 15 per cent from 1.034 in 1993 to 0.782 in 2008; and further by 18 per cent to 0.566 in 2015.

Disparity ratios add further texture to this picture. As explained, a disparity ratio estimates the distances between two distributions at every quintile and hence tells how closely two distributions overlap. As shown in Figure 4.5, between the White and the African/Black groups, the distance in mean income at the lower ends of the

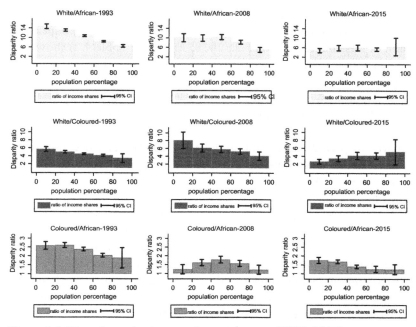

Figure 4.5 Disparity ratios in mean income by race (1993–2015)
Note: All incomes inflated to 2015 prices.
Source: Own calculations from weighted PSLSD (1993) and NIDS (2008, 2015).

distribution declined steadily from 1993 to 2008, and further to 2015. In the middle income ranges, this distance did not fall much from 1993 to 2008 and declined somewhat from 2008 to 2015. Together, these two trends imply that the decline in horizontal inequality between the White and the African/Black group was driven by those in lower income brackets.

Between the Whites and the Coloured groups, the distance in mean income actually increased from 1993 to 2008 in all income quintile ranges, except at the highest end; from 2008 to 2015, the distance declined remarkably at lower ends but increased slightly at the highest end. Between the Coloured and the African/Black groups, mean of the former remained higher than those of the latter at all income levels. However, the distances declined dramatically across all income levels from 1993 to 2008, and the decline continued through 2015, except at the lower ends.

Did income inequality within racial groups fall in tandem with inequality between groups? Data reported in the working paper version of this chapter (Hino et al., 2018, Appendix Table 4.2) show that the answer is a clear no. Measured by Gini coefficients, there have been large increases in intragroup income inequality from 1993 to 2008 for all race groups, although these increases were clawed back partially from 2008 to 2015. A number of studies have documented the changes in between-race versus within-race income inequality over the post-apartheid period (e.g., Leibbrandt et al., 2012). Such decomposition shows that the within-race component rose and the between-race component declined over the post-apartheid period. We redid these calculations for 2015 and this shows a continuation of this trend beyond 2008 to 2015. While there remains a staggeringly high between-group share, it suggests an increasing importance of within-race group inequalities in understanding inequality in South Africa and assessing its implications for social contestation and cohesion.

To sum up, while inter-racial and interethnic horizontal income inequalities clearly fell in aggregate from 1993 to 2015, this does not tell the whole story. Incomes of the Coloured group were squeezed from below from the African/Black group, and, at the same time, pulled apart from above by the White group. The disparity ratio analysis is interesting in showing that gains have only been made between the African bottom and the White bottom. So, in general the African group is aggrieved at the pace of transformation, the Coloured group is very threatened, and the bottom end of the White group is threatened too. Equally important for social contestation are the dynamics arising from the changes in the relative positions within racial and ethnic groups. Similarly, large inequality emerged between ethnic groups of African origin. These dynamics must have had a significant impact on social relations in the country.

Life Satisfaction Inequality of Race Groups

We turn now to horizontal and intragroup inequalities of life satisfaction. Figure 4.6 shows the distribution of life satisfaction for each race group in 1993, 2008 and 2015. In 1993, while the three distributions clearly overlap, they sit apart with some distance between them. The distribution of the White group sits substantially lower than that of the African/Black group in the lower half of the level of satisfaction, and higher in the upper half; the distribution of the Coloured group sits

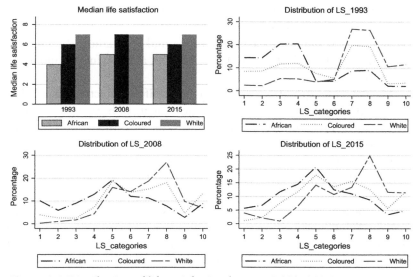

Figure 4.6 Distribution of life satisfaction by race (1993–2015)
Source: Own calculations from weighted PSLSD (1993) and NIDS (2008, 2015).

neatly in between. This again indicates large horizontal inequality. In 2008, the three distributions come much closer together. The distributions of the White and the African/Black groups sit on top of each other from the lower end to the middle of the level of satisfaction, while sizeable gaps remain in the upper half. The distribution of the Coloured group actually crosses over the other two. Horizontal inequality clearly fell.

In 2015, the three distributions moved apart again. The distribution of the White group returns to below that of the African/Black group in the lower half of satisfaction, and even higher than before in the upper half. Interestingly, the distribution of the Coloured group criss-crosses that of the African/Blacks in the lower to middle range of satisfaction and is lower in the upper half of satisfaction. Gaps between the White group and the Coloured group in the upper half of the level of satisfaction are very large indeed. Clearly, horizontal inequality rose from 2008 to 2015.

The differences in median life satisfaction scores between race groups show a similar trend. They were substantial in 1993, but narrowed noticeably in 2008 as life satisfaction of the Africans/Black group and the Coloured group moved closer to that of the White group. The summary measure of horizontal inequality, the GCOV, halved from 0.226 in 1993 to 0.108 in 2008, and fell further modestly to 0.082 in 2015.

Has intrarace group vertical inequality of life satisfaction changed in a way to reinforce the impact of the movements of horizontal inequality on social contestation? In other words, did intrarace group inequality narrow from 1993 to 2008 and further in 2015? Indeed, this is the trend we observe (see Hino et al., 2018, Appendix Table 4.3). The Gini coefficients declined in each race group from 1993 to 2008 – by a large margin in the cases of the African/Black and the Coloured groups. In 2015, inequality of life satisfaction declined for all race groups, except for the White group. However, these aggregate figures do not tell the whole story. As is the case in income inequality, life satisfaction of the Coloured group got worse relative to that of the Whites and the African/Black groups.

4.3.3 Inequalities among and within Ethnic Groups

As regards ethnic groups, trends and notable developments of inter-group and intragroup inequalities are broadly similar to those of race groups with regard to income but were remarkably different in relation life satisfaction. The following four points may be highlighted.

First, as shown in Figure 4.7, income gaps between the ethnic groups of African origin on the one hand and the English and Afrikaans group on the other narrowed substantially from 1993 to 2008, and this trend continued to 2015. Among the ethnic groups of African origin, substantial widening was observed in some bilateral comparisons (e.g., Zulu vs Sotho) from 1993 to 2008 although there were notable declines in others; further, considerable widening occurred in several bilateral relations from 2008 to 2015.

Second, our calculations show that the Gini coefficients were uniformly high within the ethnic groups of African origin in 1993 (except one) and went even higher in 2015 in all ethnic groups, except two relatively small groups; the Gini coefficient ranged between 0.76 and 0.45 in 2015. Apparently, African ethnic groups have become much less uniform in terms of income distribution, both between and within the groups.

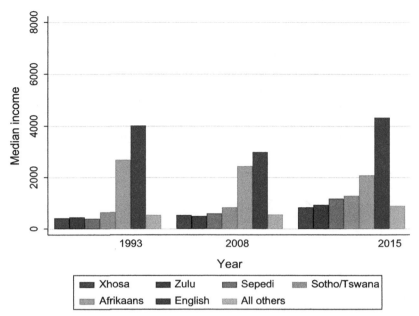

Figure 4.7 Median per capita income of ethnic groups (1993–2015)
Note: All incomes inflated to 2015 prices.
Source: Own calculations from weighted PSLSD (1993) and NIDS (2008, 2015).

Third, regarding life satisfaction, in 1993 the distributions of ethnic groups were quite far apart at both lower and higher levels of satisfaction, except that the distributions of the English and Afrikaans group were close. As can be seen in Figure 4.8, all distributions became remarkably close to each other in 2008 and got even closer in 2015, with all groups bunching in the middle, except again the English and the Afrikaans group. The narrowing of inequality between ethnic groups is seen not only in terms of the entire distribution of life satisfaction, but also in terms of mean satisfaction scores.

Fourth, as shown in Hino et al. (2018, Appendix Table 4.4), intragroup life satisfaction inequality was rather uniform across the ethnic groups of African origin in 1993, but sizable difference emerged since then. In 2015, the Gini coefficient of life satisfaction ranged from a high of 0.674 (Tsivenda) and a low of 0.476 (IsiNdebelele).

To sum up, measured by life satisfaction, vertical and horizontal inequalities in South Africa unambiguously fell from 1993 to 2008,

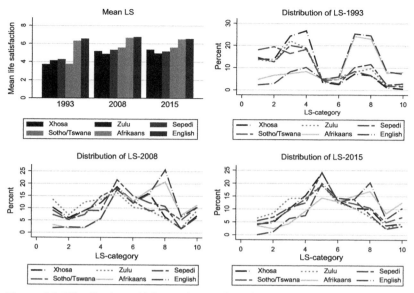

Figure 4.8 Distribution of life satisfaction by ethnicity (1993–2015)
Source: Own calculations from weighted PSLSD (1993) and NIDS (2008, 2015).

although intragroup inequality rose. From 2008 to 2015, however, the level of life satisfaction declined across all race groups. This change must have had a significant negative impact on overall sentiment in the society. Life satisfaction of the African/Black group declined at a pace substantially faster than that of the White group. Life satisfaction of the Coloured group fell at a rate faster than either the White group or the African/Black group, leaving the Coloured group worse off than the White group and less better off than the African/Black group.

Such delicate movements in life satisfaction of underprivileged identity groups – and the consequent rise in inequality between the race groups with a difficult history – would have certainly aggravated social contestation in the country. Similar trends are observed for the relevant ethnic groups. Indeed, this chapter shows that, measured by the extent of and the desire to engage in inter-racial social interactions, race and ethnic groups became significantly more outward looking and inclusive from 1993 to 2008, but this trend stagnated and even reversed from 2008 to 2015. This corresponds closely with the trends of the inequality of life satisfaction. In contrast, we do not find such correspondence between inter-racial social interactions and income inequality.

4.4 Correlation between Inequality and Identity Formation in the Post-Apartheid Period

The previous section has made it clear that, if we are to see how inequality relates to social contestation, it is necessary to go beyond the usual macro measures, such as a Gini coefficient of national income distribution. It is important to identify "inequality hotspots", such as a significant rise in inequality between two identity groups with a difficult past or a large increase in inequality within delicate identity groups.

In this section, we return to the issue of identity formation. We posit that the extent of inter-racial social interaction – both actual and desired – indicates the degree to which a particular race group is inward-looking and exclusive of others and examine the trends of those indicators from 1993 to 2015. We show that inter-racial social interactions, as seen as a composite of actual and desired, rose significantly from 1993 to 2008, but have fallen off since then. We then see which specific aspects of inequality correlate with this trend. We examine how the observed changes relate to various aspects of inequality, such as intragroup (vertical) income inequality or intergroup (horizontal) life satisfaction inequality.[3]

4.4.1 Trends in Inter-Racial Social Interactions

The SARBS ask respondents three questions regarding inter-racial interactions: (1) On a typical day during the week, whether at work or otherwise, how often do you talk to [other race group] people? (2) When socialising in your home or the homes of friends, how often do you talk to [other race group] people? and, (3) If you had a choice, would you want to talk to [other race group] people? Figure 4.9 presents responses to those questions for 2003 to 2013.

---

[3] David et al. (2018) examine how the trends in inter-racial social interactions are correlated to living standard and perceived inequality, based on the data set from SARBS.

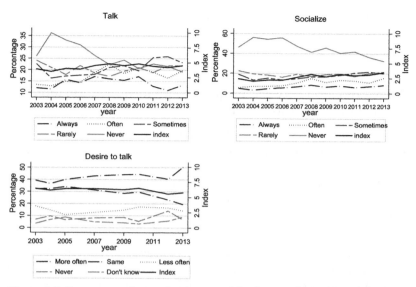

Figure 4.9 Frequency of everyday inter-racial talk, socialisation, and desire to talk (2003–2013)
Note: The index is created as a weighted average of five data points (never / don't know – 0; rarely – 2.5; sometimes – 5.0; often – 7.5; and always – 10.0)
Source: Own calculations from weighted SARBS (2003–2013).

It is striking how limited inter-racial social interactions are in South Africa. This is the baldest statement as to the persistence of the historical legacies of separate development and apartheid planning that were described in Section 2. Even in 2013, only one-third of South Africans often or always talk with someone from a different racial group and only one-quarter of South Africans often or always socialise with someone from a different racial group at his or her home or the home of friends.

Those who often or always socialised with people from a different race group increased considerably from 2003 to 2008, and then fell subsequently. Those who never or rarely socialise with other race groups dropped remarkably from 2003 to 2008 and rose slightly since then. Similar trends are observed for inter-racial talk. To the extent that the paucity of inter-racial socialisation is an indicator of social

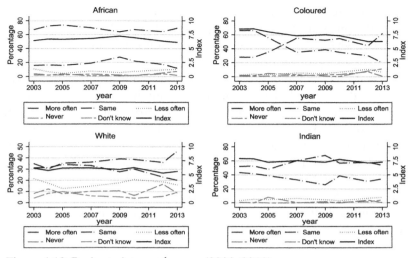

Figure 4.10 Desire to interact by race (2003–2013)
Source: Own calculations from weighted SARBS (2003–2013)

contestation, these trends suggest that social contestation fell from 2003 to 2008, but that progress has halted since then. Similar findings are also suggested in other studies (Mattes, 2014; Tredoux & Dixon, 2009).

The survey results on the desire to talk with other race groups reinforce these findings. From 2008 to 2013, the share of those who desired to talk more with people of other races declined, while those who desired to talk never or less increased. In 2013, about 50 per cent of South Africans wanted to maintain the same level of inter-racial interactions (talk), while 19 per cent of them wanted to interact more often.

As expected, Figure 4.10 shows that there are significant differences in the attitudes towards inter-racial socialisation among race groups. In 2003, only 15 per cent of the White group desired to interact more often; in the case of the other race groups, the share of those who desired to interact more often was at least 30 per cent. Most interesting, however, is that as much as 70 per cent of those in the Coloured group desired to interact more often in 2003, but this share declined steadily and sharply to only 20 per cent by 2013. Note that this is exactly what was predicted from the squeezing of the Coloured observed in the previous section.

The decline in the desire to engage in inter-racial interactions over the last decade could be a response to a rise in frustration and disappointment about (a) poor service delivery, particularly to the poorest, who are still overwhelmingly Africans; (b) massive unemployment, from which younger generations in particular suffer; and (c) the perceived inability of the political leadership to address the exceptionally high racial inequality (see Hofmeyr, 2008, and Lefko-Everett et al., 2011). Indeed, we have witnessed a wave of demonstrations demanding better service delivery across the country during this period.

4.4.2 Correlation between Inter-Racial Socialisation and Inequality

It would be entirely reasonable to conjecture that a rise in inequality is at least in part responsible for the decline in the extent of inter-racial socialisation as posited in the paragraph above. Indeed, as reported earlier, the SARBS 2017 reports that inequality is cited as a principle reason for social division by more South Africans than any other variables, including race and ethnicity.

But which aspects of inequality are most critical in influencing social contestation? Table 4.1 is intended to answer this question. It indicates the direction of change in inequality from 1993 to 2008 and from 2008 to 2015, for vertical inequality, horizontal inequality and intragroup inequality separately, and for income inequality and life satisfaction inequality. Each mark represents a collective assessment of a few relevant measures discussed above. Marks for inequality and those for inter-racial social interactions are colour coordinated, namely, a rise in inequality and a fall in inter-racial social interactions are marked by X in red, while a fall in inequality and an increase in inter-racial social interactions are marked by a star in green.

A few observations are in order. First, in general, income inequality indicators and life satisfaction inequality indicators did not move in the same direction between 1993 and 2015. This means that there were some factors, other than income, that dominated people's assessment

Table 4.1 *Inequality and inter-racial social interactions (1993–2015)*

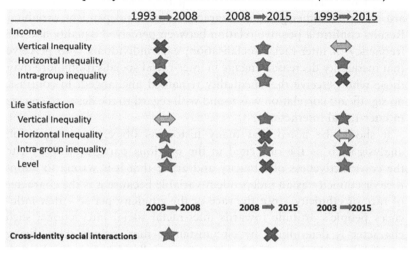

	1993 ➡ 2008	2008 ➡ 2015	1993 ➡ 2015
Income			
Vertical Inequality	✖	★	⬌
Horizontal Inequality	★	★	★
Intra-group inequality	✖	★	✖
Life Satisfaction			
Vertical Inequality	⬌	★	★
Horizontal Inequality	★	✖	⬌
Intra-group inequality	★	✖	★
Level	★	✖	★
	2003 ➡ 2008	2008 ➡ 2015	2003 ➡ 2015
Cross-identity social interactions	★	✖	

Notes: An X indicates an increase in inequality and a decline in inter-racial social interactions. Star denotes a fall in inequality and an increase in inter-racial social interactions.

of life satisfaction. Euphoria about the rebirth of the country in 1994, excitement about hosting the football world cup or disappointment in government performance are some examples of those factors.

Second, for 2008 to 2015, for which comparable data are available, income inequality does not correlate with inter-racial social interaction, except that the direction of change of horizontal inequality is ambiguous. In contrast, life satisfaction inequality indicators correlate with inter-racial social interactions correctly, except intragroup inequality.

Third, it is necessary to go beyond these indicators and identify "inequality hotspots" to better capture impact on inequality on social contestation.

The authors of this chapter, together with two other researchers, have tested correlation between inequality and inter-racial interactions with regression analyses using a different dataset, where the inequality variable was confined to perceived inequality (David et al., 2018). The regression model has the frequency of inter-racial interactions as the dependent variable, and perceived inequality, race, trust, living standard and a few other personal characteristics as independent variables. Results confirm a positive relation between perceived equality and the frequency of inter-racial socialisation; e.g., individuals who perceive that inequality decreased engage in inter-racial socialisation more than those who perceive that inequality remained unchanged. In contrast, no significant correlation was found with regard to the desire to engage in inter-racial interactions.

It should be noted that many historians object to a regression analysis such as the one cited in the previous paragraph. They cite the constructiveness of ethnicity and argue that it is wrong to adopt race or ethnicity as an independent variable because it is the character of race or ethnicity – not the race or the ethnicity per se – that influences people's attitude towards inter-racial social interactions; such character is determined by circumstances that include trust, living conditions and other variables that are typically included as independent variables. This observation does not negate the value of regression analysis, but rather, calls on researchers and readers to be mindful of the interdependence of variables included in a regression model and to interpret regression results with care.

4.5 Conclusion

South Africa remains a divided nation and far from "a nation united in diversity" that was the ideal enshrined in its 1996 constitution. This chapter has offered some evidence that South Africans became less inward-looking and less exclusive of people in other race groups during the early years of post-apartheid period but have reversed this accomplishment over the last 10 years.

A central conclusion of this chapter is that the South African society is still shot through with inequalities no matter what happened to the national trend in income or asset inequality. Inequality needs to be assessed in its entirety; vertical and horizontal; ethnic and racial; class and profession; spatial and time series; and measured by income and by the quality of life. Moreover, it is crucial to look closely into inequalities within individual racial and ethnic groups, at disparities between some of those groups, and at sufficiently small jurisdictions.

Such textured analyses will allow us to identify "inequality hot spots", which need to be addressed if a more cohesive society is to be nurtured in the country.

People see income inequality in their daily lives. For example, the earnings gap has been increasing in factories. (This is one of the manifestations of rising within-group inequalities.) Such material inequality is at the heart of people's daily lives rather than any national Gini coefficient. Thus, even if this national Gini goes down, people will see inequality as increasing and this is not incorrect. It is this inequality that dominates any relationship that we must attempt to pick up in the data between income inequality and other variables, and in the assessment of life satisfaction.

What then are the prospects for South Africa to become less fractious or what could be done for it to become so?

First, address decisively inequalities between and within race and ethnic groups.

'Which one occupies one's mind most and motivates behavior varies over time. An identity may be a productive, inclusive instinct or a destructive exclusive sense of belonging, depending on the circumstances at that time. The history of the African continent shows that ethnic hostility often stems from 'horizontal' inequalities in wealth, power, education or reputation, since ethnic groups generally retain regional homelands. Changes in social differentiation or 'vertical inequality' within an ethnic group can also cause internal conflict and stress, which may foster external aggression'. (Lonsdale, 2012, pp. 21–22)

In the South African context, race is as much a part of the social fabric as ethnicity, given the country's history and the fact that memory of injustice endures decades or even centuries.

It is instructive, as argued by Bundy (2016), that the Union of South Africa government completely eliminated poverty from Afrikaners through large-scale public works programmes, education and other public services and other decisive measures during 1910 to 1942. Consequently, the inequality between the Afrikaners and the British narrowed, although regrettably at the expense of ethnicities of African origin. It may not be realistic to expect similarly ambitious yet socially just programmes, this time, to eliminate poverty from Africans/Blacks. However, decisive measures targeted at "inequality hotspots" are certainly warranted and feasible.

Second, dig beyond a macro picture. Inequality in South Africa is complex. It is deeply rooted in history and society as well as geography. As briefly summarised in this chapter, a complex web of inequalities began to emerge when polities started to develop centuries ago in what was essentially a tribal society. The complexity was magnified, and the inequalities deepened through colonialisation, slave trade, the discoveries of gold and diamonds, industrialisation, government policies of racial and ethnic discrimination, and, more recently, globalisation. Given this complexity, it is not enough to highlight one element of many important aspects of inequality in a society such as the Gini coefficient of the national income distribution or even a multidimensional inequality index in isolation. It is striking that income inequality and life satisfaction inequality indicators often moved in opposite directions during the last 20 years.

Third, foster a common citizenry, a national identity, that will be based on a shared belief that state institutions will ensure equal rights irrespective of the identity of the persons concerned. It will also be based on shared values such as those cherished in the 1996 constitution as well as mutual respect for cultural and other differences. In other words, trust between identity groups and a common sense of belonging will need to be mediated by institutions, rather than personal patronage or kinship.

Fostering such a common citizenry will not be an easy task. More than one-half of South Africans consider that their primary identity is very important, and about three-quarters consider it so because the identity makes him or her feel important and secure (Potgieter, 2017, p. 15). Moreover, South Africans are well known for the "sharply declining radius of trust" (Mattes, 2014). More than 60 per cent of South Africans trust their relatives, but this ratio falls to only 20 per cent when it comes to trusting people of other races or languages (Potgieter, 2017, p. 44). The end of apartheid and birth of democracy may have been an opportunity to cultivate a national identity based on a common citizenry. The hope faded as the government policy cemented race in institutions in the post-apartheid South Africa, ironically to bring about greater equality for the Africans/Blacks. In 2004 and 2005, nearly 80 per cent of South Africans considered it desirable to create a united South Africa, but the proportion of such South Africans declined substantially since (Potgieter, 2017, p. 16).

However, there are encouraging signs in this regard. According to the Afrobarometer survey of 2011, 12 per cent of South Africans consider the neighbourhood where they live as their primary identity while another 8.8 per cent cite 'economic class' as their primary identity (Mattes, 2014). This suggests the emergence of a group of individuals who earn more than enough to merely survive, and value a unified lifestyle of a shared ensemble of choices about people, things and practices, i.e., a "middle class habitus" (Chipkin, 2014).

Indeed, a number of gated communities and other residential developments have emerged where individuals who share such middle-class habitus live in a new post-apartheid "community". Around one million people had moved into those complexes by 2013 that cater for the upper working class and lower middle class. These complexes tend to be very diverse demographically, with young White Afrikaners and young Blacks moving into these diverse, linguistically and racially mixed complexes. These individuals coexist and are all members of the body corporate that governs the community (Chipkin, 2014).

In those middle-class communities, members are not governed by the traditional norms of social interactions. Rather, body corporates produce the social behaviour compliant with regulations and mediate potential conflicts. Members are not bonded with each other by kinship, race or ethnicity. Rather, they are connected through subscription to a common code of conduct stipulated by their body corporate. Members trust others in the community because of the shared background and their belief in the ability of body corporate to regulate and maintain the neighbourhood in which they live. In other words, key constituents of social cohesion – trust, bond and identity – are mediated by institutions. As middle class grows, more people will likely coalesce on this identity, "middle-class habitus".

These communities or local societies are still by far the exception rather than the rule. Most suburbs, schools, health facilities and churches today still bear the legacies of apartheid's racial and ethnic demarcations. This has real consequences in terms of the attitudes and approaches South Africans carry into the workplace and their broader lives. This lived experience is articulated in the surveys as a lack of trust and/or a lack of commitment to forging a new South Africa. Nevertheless, these gated communities signify that democratic institutions can transcend race or ethnicities in building trust, bonding social relations and engendering common citizenry. It is such dynamics in the South African society that leads us to a hopeful conclusion that a common citizenry, a new national identity, may emerge out of new generations of middle-class South Africans.

References

Acemoglu, D., and Robinson, J. A. 2012. *Why Nations Fail: The Origins of Power, Prosperity and Poverty*. New York: Crown Business.

Adhikari, M. 2010. *The Anatomy of a South African Genocide*. Cape Town: UCT Press.

Alexander, P. 2016. Marikana Commission of Enquiry: From Narratives Toward History. *Journal of Southern African History*, 42 (5): 815–839.

Bhorat, H., and van der Westhuizen, C. 2013. Non-monetary dimensions of well-being in South Africa, 1993–2004: A post-apartheid dividend? *Development Southern Africa*. 30 (3): 295–314.

Boonzaier, E., and Sharp, J. S. 1988. *South African Keywords: The Uses and Abuses of Political Concepts*. Cape Town: David Philip.

Bundy, C. 2016. *Poverty in South Africa: Past and Present*. Johannesburg: Jacana Media (Pty) Ltd.

Chanock, M. 2001. *The Making of South African Legal Culture, 1901–1936: Fear, Favour and Prejudice*. Cambridge: Cambridge University Press.

Chipkin, I. 2014. *Breaking through Identity Barriers: Middle Classing in Roodepoort and Polokwane*. Working Paper. University of Johannesburg.

Claassens, A., and Boyle, B. 2014. *Entrenching Inequality in the Name of Custom: Land and Governance in the former Bantustans*. Cape Town: The Rural Women's Action Research Programme (RWAR), The Centre for Law and Society, The University of Cape Town.

Cobham, A., and Sumner, A. 2013. *Is it all about the tails? The Palma measure of income inequality (CGD Working Paper 343)*. Washington, DC: Center for Global Development.

David, A., Guilbert, N., Hino, H., Leibbrandt, M., Potgieter, E., and Shifa, M. 2018. *Social Cohesion and Inequality in South Africa (SALDRU Working Paper No. 219)*. Cape Town: SALDRU, UCT.

Delius, P. 2008. Contested Terrain: Land Rights and Chiefly Power in historical Perspective. In Claassens, A., and Cousins, B. (eds.), *Land, Power and Custom: Controversies Generated by South Africa's Communal Land Rights Act*. Cape Town: UCT Press, pp. 211–237.

Erasmus, Z. 2017. *Race Otherwise: Forging a New Humanism for South Africa*. Johannesburg: Wits University Press.

Esteban, J.-M., and Ray, D. 1994. On the measurement of polarization. *Econometrica: Journal of the Econometric Society*. 62 (4): 819–851.

Hino, H., Leibbrandt, M., Machema, R., Shifa, M., and Soudien, C. 2018. *Identity, Inequality and Social Contestation in the Post-Apartheid South Africa (SALDRU Working Paper No. 233)*. Cape Town: SALDRU, University of Cape Town.

Hofmeyr, J. 2008. *SA Reconciliation Barometer 2008 8th Round Media Briefing*. Cape Town: Institute for Justice and Reconciliation.

Hofmeyr, J., and Lefko-Everett, K. 2014. Xenophobia and reconciliation. In Meyiwa, T., Nkondo, M., Chitiga-Mabugu, M., Sithole, M., and Nyamnjoh, F. (eds.), *State of the Nation, 2014. South Africa 1994–2014: A Twenty-Year Review*. Cape Town: HSRC Press, pp. 223–234.

Lefko-Everett, K., Nyoka, A., and Tiscornia, L. 2011. *SA Reconciliation Barometer Survey: 2011 Report*. Cape Town: Institute for Justice and Reconciliation.

Leibbrandt, M., Finn, A., and Woolard, I. 2012. Describing and decomposing post-apartheid income inequality in South Africa. *Development Southern Africa*, 29 (1): 19–34.

Lonsdale, J. 2012. *What If Anything Is Wrong with Africa and Teaching National History for Divided Nation*. Japan: University of Kobe.

Mamdani, M. 1996. *Citizen and Subject: Contemporary Africa and the Legacy of Late Colonialism*. Princeton, NJ: Princeton University Press.

Mattes, R. 2014. *South Africa: Vertical Integration and Horizontal Separation*. Cape Town: Democracy in Africa Research Unit, Centre for Social Science Research, University of Cape Town.

2015. *South Africa: Vertical Integration and Horizontal Separation*. Building a More Cohesive Society in South Africa. University of Cape Town.

National Income Dynamics Study (NIDS). 2008, 2015. Retrieved from www.nids.uct.ac.za/.

Nattrass, G. 2017. *A Short History of South Africa*. Cape Town: Jonathan Ball Publishers.

Potgieter, E. 2017. *SA Reconciliation Barometer Survey 2017 Report*. Cape Town: Institute for Justice and Reconciliation.

Project for Statistics on Living Standards and Development (PSLSD). 1993. Retrieved from http://opensaldru.uct.ac.za/.

Shepherd, N., and Robins, S. L. 2018. *New South African Keywords*. Athens: Ohio University Press.

Southern Africa Labour and Development Research Unit (SALDRU). 1994. *Project for Statistics on Living Standards and Development*. Cape

Town: SALDRU. Retrieved from www.datafirst.uct.ac.za/dataportal/index.php/catalog/5. Accessed 18 September 2018.

2015. *National Income Dynamics Study*. Cape Town: SALDRU. Retrieved from www.datafirst.uct.ac.za/dataportal/index.php/catalog/570. Accessed 18 September 2018.

South African Reconciliation Barometer Survey (SARBS). 2003–2013. Retrieved from https://reconciliationbarometer.org.

Statistics South Africa (StatSA). 2013. *Census 2011 Mobile Information*. Retrieved from www.statssa.gov.za.

2014. *Mid-Year Population Estimates 2014*. Retrieved from www.statssa.gov.za.

Stewart, F., Brown, G., and Mancini, L. 2010. *Monitoring and Measuring Horizontal Inequalities. Centre for Research on Inequality, Human Security and Ethnicity, (CRISE Working Paper No. 4)*. Oxford: University of Oxford.

Tredoux, C. G., and Dixon, J. A. 2009. Mapping the multiple contexts of racial isolation: The case of Long Street, Cape Town. *Urban Studies*. 46 (4):761–777.

Wilson, F. 2011. *Dinosaurs, Diamonds and Democracy: A Short, Short History of South Africa*. Cape Town: Umuzi.

Wilson, M., and Thompson, L. 1982. Preface to the 1969 Edition. In Wilson, M., and Thompson, L. (eds.), *A History of South Africa to 1870*. London and Canberra: Croom Helm, pp. 31–39.

Wittenberg, M., and Leibbrandt, M. 2017. Measuring inequality by asset indices: A general approach with application to South Africa. *Review of Income and Wealth*. 63 (4): 706–730.

5 | Ethnicity, Development, and Social Cohesion in Africa

Overview

BRUCE J. BERMAN AND MOTOKI
TAKAHASHI

5.1 Introduction

The purposes of this chapter are two-fold: First, we aim to offer an overview of the analysis of ethnicity in Africa in relationship to the political economy of specific countries. Second, we discuss the key issues relating to ethnicity and its relationship to socioeconomic and political development and social cohesion as the basis for the discussion of institutions, policies, social practices and other interventions that could mitigate the destructive impact of rapidly increasing inequalities between and within ethnic communities on politics and, if possible, transform ethnic diversity into a more positive factor for achieving more equitable social and economic development and social cohesion in Africa.

Over the course of the discussions on the theme of this book, the authors and colleagues have come to a common understanding that ethnicity and ethnic diversity per se are neither politically nor economically problematic, but lead to disruptive conflicts and negative socioeconomic effects in the specific political and economic contexts of particular countries. We also understand that ethnicity is a modern, historical construct, deeply influenced by historical circumstances since the imposition of colonial rule in the nineteenth century and continuing today as an open-ended and often highly contested process both within and between ethnic communities. We also realize that ethnicity is a given and often overwhelming dimension of social and political reality for people in most, although not all, countries in Africa. While the factors of political economy have influenced the development of ethnicity over time, the politics and economics of ethnicity have had a reciprocal impact on those factors both by shaping people's everyday life and leading to conflicts with major consequences challenging both economic growth and social cohesion.

During the course of the discussions, we have debated at length the value of quantitative and qualitative evidence in evaluating the development and impact of ethnic diversity. We note that all quantitative measures relating to African societies must be treated with extreme care with regard to both their provenance and methodology regarding not only actual counting, but also the underlying assumptions determining the categories to which the numbers are attached. This has led us to view with skepticism the value of the earlier and highly influential Ethnolinguistic Fractionalisation index (ELF) (see Easterly & Levine, 1997) both for the accuracy of its data (since the number of ethnic groups in many African countries remains in dispute) and the equation of one language with one ethnic group, since there are several instances of a number of modern ethnic communities speaking closely related dialects or of groups changing their language to integrate with other groups through the process of *language shift* (Takahashi, 2010). This index is also based on the false assumption (derived from colonial notions of "tribes") that ethnic groups are ancient, stable communities with fixed customs and boundaries, "atavistic" survivals that cannot effectively interact with modern institutions of states and markets; which leads to the deeply misleading conclusion that ethnic diversity alone accounts for Africa's developmental "failure" (Berman, 2011) and social divisiveness. This reflects a conventional wisdom that ethnic groups or "tribes" are culturally distinct, clearly spatially bounded and ancient communities. Nowadays, it has been already known that ethnic identities, one of the major elements of social cohesion (see the Introduction and Summary) and thus ethnicity itself, can be fluid, multiple, and ambiguous.

The reality is that there have historically been vague boundaries between ethnic communities across which there have been intermarriage, trade, migration and intermingling more often than violent conflict and displacement (Takahashi, 2010). Moreover, large contemporary ethnic communities contain internal cleavages and subgroups, and there can be more conflict internally than with other communities (Tettey et al., 2008). In Kenya the Kalenjin are a recent "super" ethnic group created by the elites of a half dozen distinct communities and the internal politics between those groups is as important as that between the Kalenjin and other ethnic groups. (Lynch, 2011) These facts imply that "radius" of trust, another major element of social cohesion (see Introduction and Summary), is not always determined by rigid ethnic boundaries and could be either strengthened or weakened both inside and outside an ethnic group.

Taking account of the importance of inequality, the third major element of social cohesion (see Introduction and Summary), the authors have, thus, focused on the careful construction of quantitative indices of the horizontal inequalities in the distribution of values between ethnic communities (horizontal inequality indices) that track the changing relationship of ethnic groups with the development of the state and market and provide the essential basis for understanding the sources of ethnic conflict and thus destruction of social cohesion and its anti-developmental consequences in particular contexts (Stewart, 2002, 2008; see also Brown & Langer, 2010). At the same time, we also need to find measurements of the internal inequalities (vertical inequalities) of class that shape the internal politics of ethnic groups.

5.2 An Overview of Ethnicity in Africa: Intragroup and Intergroup Relations

To integrate the quantitative and qualitative evidence regarding ethnicity in Africa we must recognize the contextual influence on such material as much as its impact on the phenomenon itself. Since ethnicity is a historical construct, particularly during the last century, we have to deal with historical evidence, almost all of which, including the numbers, derive from official or state sources, colonial and postcolonial. Like all historical evidence, we need to interrogate such numbers with regard to why and how they were collected and by whom. All such evidence is "impressionistic", based on subjective judgments by officials, often upon unspecified assumptions, especially with regard to the categories under which data is gathered and to which people and communities they are assigned. The degree to which quantitative evidence is an accurate recording of reality and can be employed as objective "data" must be critically assessed, and compared with qualitative sources, both official and unofficial, and both documentary and ethnographic (Berman, 1998, 2011; Kertzer & Arel, 2001).

In other words, the categories and numbers relating to ethnic groups that are official in origin are both products of and active interventions into the historical process and not neutral observations by external observers. The categories and numbers relating to ethnic groups in Africa are political artefacts and cannot be used without careful critical evaluation. As Benedict Anderson notes, official knowledge contained in "census, map and museum" compiled by states are in themselves important factors in the construction of ethnic and national communities (Anderson, 1991). The crucial weakness of the ELF index is that it does not bother to do this and is thus of little or no analytic value. However, although they often do not do so initially, the application of other quantitative indices, including the horizontal inequality indices, can be evaluated in this way and are of greater analytic importance.

Finally, with regard to quantitative data, particularly the calculation of gross domestic product in African countries as the key indicator of economic development, the crucial analysis by economist Morten Jerven (2011, 2013) reveals them to be grossly inaccurate fictions. His careful reanalysis has shown that the gross domestic product of many African countries, including Ghana, Kenya, Tanzania and Zambia ,to be as much as 50% greater than previously thought (Jerven, 2011, 2013, 2014; Jerven & Duncan, 2012). If so, then the assumption of development "failure" is simply false. Instead, as we argue, the issue is how increasingly unequally distributed income and wealth exacerbates horizontal and vertical cleavages between and within ethnic communities, and threatens both political stability and social cohesion.

We believe it is necessary to complement quantitative analyses by extending into the exploration of the complex dynamism and contextual detail related to ethnic diversity through structural and qualitative analyses of historical institutions and practices. We thus focus in this chapter on what we regard as the critical aspects of intraethnic and interethnic relations connecting the internal and external politics of ethnicity in Africa. These interactions deal with both issues of individual identity and belonging and the relations between elites and masses in ethnic communities, as well as the relationship between ethnic communities and links with macro state and market level institutions. Here, we are particularly interested in the processes, internal and external, through which a categorical aggregate of people, sharing broadly similar language, culture and way of life, becomes a self-conscious and politically mobilized ethnic group.

The intragroup relations of a particular community may change over time, and we are particularly interested in how these changes are related to the allocation of values within the group, including changing vertical inequalities, the role of elites in defining the group culturally and politically, and the relationship between identity and belonging, in so far as it governs access to key values that determine production and reproduction within the group. In particular, we focus on the internal processes that were caused by the widening of new inequalities introduced by the modern state and market economy that undermined the traditional moral economy controlling the distribution of key values, which led to new struggles between the elites and masses to redefine the mutual obligations of reciprocity, support and redistribution, as well as the boundaries of the community and those who legitimately belong to it, the issue of ethnic citizenship which we discuss in Section 5.4.2. This is what Bayart (2005) describes as the politics of "authenticity" and Berman (1998) and Lonsdale (1994) call "moral ethnicity", in which the character of ethnic identity and the social and physical boundaries of the community are fought out. The confrontations of moral ethnicity, however, represent the continuity of traditional patron–client authority relations that were institutionalized in the linkages between colonial states and indigenous elites and in postcolonial ethnic patronage networks providing access to resources.

In interethnic relations, it is important that the political elites representing each ethnic group obtain access to and control over state resources and the market. Not only the number of ethnic groups in a nation, but also their relative size and the horizontal inequalities between them resulting from differential access to the state and market are key political factors. The simple number of ethnic groups does not indicate either social fragmentation or cohesion. Some of the most bitter conflicts have occurred in nations like Rwanda and Burundi, with a very small number of ethnic communities, or in ostensibly ethnically homogeneous Somalia, torn apart by clashes of clan and tribe. Kenya and Tanzania are both highly ethnically fragmented, with around 40 in Kenya and some 120 in Tanzania, but the relative sizes of communities and the politicization of interethnic relations are dramatically different. In Kenya, where the five largest ethnic groups account for some two-thirds of the population and there are significant horizontal cleavages between them, ethnicity is the central political fact and the major groups fear domination by one or more of the others, while the smaller groups fear being caught in the conflicts. These are sources for deep and persistent interethnic mistrust among ethnic groups in the country. In Tanzania, where the largest group, the Sukuma, comprises 13–15% of the population and no other group is more than 5%, the political salience of ethnicity is, by comparison, extremely muted and governments have had little difficulty in excluding organized expressions of ethnicity from the political arena, perhaps except for Zanzibar (Central Intelligence Agency, 2003–2013; see also Chapter 3).[1] In other words, in Tanzanian national politics, ethnically based subnational citizenship has seldom mattered.

The state in both the colonial and postcolonial eras generated and regulated a wide range of resources in services and public goods, especially in education, health and infrastructure, as well as access to developing markets, business opportunities and employment that were the central focus of African elites' linkages to the state both for personal accumulation and resources for redistribution in the patronage networks of moral ethnicity. At the same time, the uneven development of the state and market from the colonial era based on regional differentiation of cash crop farming, labor migration, mineral development and urbanization, as well as differential access to modern education and health services, compounded by colonial ethnic bias in the recruitment of police, military or administrative personnel, produced the horizontal cleavages dividing ethnic communities. These cleavages are the basis for the distinctly modern competition and conflict between ethnic communities that Berman and Lonsdale call "political tribalism" (Berman, 1998; Lonsdale, 1994). When members of communities fear exclusion from state resources and the domination of larger and more favored groups, with interethnic mistrust deepened, it provides elites with the basis for political mobilization. Where market deregulation has exacerbated existing vertical and horizontal

---

[1] Historical censuses, even those relatively professionally designed and carried out, show variations in the number of ethnic groups, their populations increasing or decreasing improbably over time and even in their names reflecting and shaping political conflicts. According to Ikeno (2002), Tanzania stopped collecting data on people's ethnic identity after 1967. The survey in that year showed there were 128 African ethnic groups in the country. On the contrary, the Kenyan government had continued to conduct the same survey every 10 years as one of interviews in population censuses, until 2009. During this process, the categorization and thus the number of ethnic group had changed from one census to next (Takahashi, 2010). Influenced by the said changes in Kenya and the lack of recent surveys in Tanzania, on-line sources of information about the number of ethnic groups in either country and the size of their populations vary significantly, suggesting the political character of the numbers. The categorization and counting of ethnic groups and their populations are highly politicized and resulting numbers must always be treated with caution (Kertzer & Arel, 2001).

inequalities, both class and ethnic conflict has often increased and disrupted both development and social cohesion.

The conventional wisdom about Africa for too many years saw modern national identity and supposedly atavistic "tribalism" as mutually exclusive, with the latter undermining and threatening the development of modern nation-states (Argyle, 1969; Berman & Lonsdale, 2013; Hodgkin, 1956). If we understand, however, that both nationalism and ethnicity in Africa are products of the same political and economic forces, then we can understand that national identity and ethnicity are often mutually reinforcing. The reason why horizontal inequality seriously matters for people on the grounds of distributional unfairness is that people with different ethnicity share a common national identity. It should be stressed, however, that horizontal inequality is not simply a source of divisiveness in a nation. In fact, in many countries in Africa, as in many other parts of the world, notions of citizenship have become increasingly "ethnicized", with ethnic groups that regard themselves as true and authentic parts of the nation turning on those whom they regard is strangers and interlopers, leading to the growing conflicts of "autochthony" (Geschiere, 2009; Geschiere & Nyamjoh, 2000). Against the background of historical migration and the intermingling of groups reinforced by colonial sponsored migration, both within and across colonial and now national boundaries, claims of indigeneity or autochthony are almost always ambiguous and contested.

In Kenya, every national election from the restoration of multiparty politics in 1992 up to 2007 brought violence in the western Rift Valley as Kalenjin communities attacked Kikuyu and Luo outsiders or "settlers", not because they were not Kenyan, but because they were not in their legitimate home territory (Lonsdale, 2008; Mueller, 2008). In north western Ghana, the supposed autochthonous groups confronted those they considered recent migrants and outsiders (Lentz, 2006), while in the Côte d'Ivoire, particularly violent conflicts of autochthony brought attacks in the central and southern regions by those who considered themselves the legitimate autochthons against migrants not only from Burkina Faso, but also from the north of the country (Marshall-Fratani, 2006). In Kenya, the attacks were focused on the descendants of landless Kikuyu settled on former European estates in the aftermath of the Mau Mau Emergency of the 1950s, and in the Côte d'Ivoire the attacks focused on migrants encouraged by the colonial regime to increase the production of cocoa. In all of these

instances, elites promoted intraethnic cohesion and focused on excluding the alien "other" and claiming "ethnic citizenship" as the pre-
requisite for residence and access to land.

The harsh interethnic competition over state resources and authority, underpinned by exclusionary ethnic cohesiveness, is a key cause for
the disruption of social cohesion and economic development and the
negative phenomena of the political economy of ethnicity. Combined
with the rampant corruption of political elites, including widespread
private appropriation of public goods, as well as their failure to meet
the obligations of moral ethnicity, the petty corruption and abusiveness
of public officials has severely undermined trust in public institutions.
The sophisticated opinion surveys carried out by Afrobarometer show
widespread and diverse combinations of distrust in public institutions,
especially the police and the judiciary, high levels of belief in the
corruption of public officials and politicians and declining levels of
satisfaction with democracy and the probity of politicians, parties and
elections (Afrobarometer, 2013), undermining the basis for social
cohesion at the national level.

5.3 African Ethnicity in Global Perspective

Understanding ethnicity in Africa and how to deal with its impact on
socioeconomic and political development requires placing Africa in
global context. Just as the social construction and politicization of
modern African ethnicity must be understood in its origin in the political
and economic institutions imposed during an earlier epoch of globalization led mostly by European imperialism, the current circumstances and
future trajectory of African ethnicity and its interaction with effective and
equitable development cannot be understood without reference to the
contemporary context of globalization and the on-going systemic crisis.
By doing so, we can take Africa out of the ghetto of being a continent
apart from the rest, an area of unique developmental "failure" caused by
its idiosyncratic ethnic fragmentation. Instead, we can see that it is an
integral component of six global phenomena that define the context of
confronting the issue of ethnicity, development and social cohesion:

   All societies are increasingly ethnically diverse and migration and multiculturalism are growing issues in almost all nation-states. Unprecedented global migration flows move from south to north, which have

caused exclusionary xenophobic reactions in most of developed countries, with Africa as a major source of migrants to Europe, where growing conflicts of autochthony mirror those in African states.

For 20 years, political scientists have been noting the increasing levels of corruption in politics all over the world and a corresponding decline of trust in political institutions, the basis for social cohesion at the national level.

International networks of organized crime, especially in drugs, arms and human trafficking, have grown relentlessly and both increasingly involved African nations and criminalized governments in Africa and elsewhere.

National governments, especially in the most developed states, have proven increasingly incapable of dealing effectively with the global crisis and international institutions lack the authority and resources for doing so.

The destructive impact of unregulated markets on equity and thus social cohesion in both highly developed and less developed nations is increasingly obvious.

Rapidly growing and destabilizing socioeconomic inequality is a global issue (Stiglitz, 2011; Wilkinson & Picket, 2010).

5.4 Implications of Critical Issues Relating to Ethnicity

All of these factors have implications for the scope and effectiveness of action by African governments and international organizations, and the choices regarding reform of both institutions and practices must be framed with reference to them. This volume examines the implications of the interaction of internal and external factors, national and global, for different dimensions of five key areas of institutional development and public policy in both governance and the market that shape the horizontal and vertical cleavages and the internal and external politics of African ethnic communities and their consequences for social cohesion and equitable development.

1. Democratic institutions and processes
2. Constitutions and devolved forms of governance
3. Ethnicity, citizenship and national cohesion
4. Land holding and group territory
5. Resource development and foreign investment

5.4.1 Building Democratic Institutions

The development of modern political ethnicity in Africa is inseparable from the development of modern state institutions, colonial and post-colonial, and will in the future continue to depend on the character of those institutions. What to change and how to change it, and what the consequences will be for the future development of ethnic politics and, in particular, how to channel it into more positive consequences for socioeconomic development and social cohesion, are the most critical and intractable questions. It is easy to see that developing a civic culture of trust and probity in institutions that provide for the peaceful resolution of conflicts, equitable distribution of public goods, access to essential services and confidence in the rule of law are crucial to containing patronage, nepotism and outright theft and to dealing with the underlying vertical and horizontal cleavages. However, this has not been fully accomplished in North America, Western Europe and East Asia and with corruption worsening even in developed countries, it will be an incredible challenge in most African nations.

While at the level of moral ethnicity, or intraethnically, there is some degree of political discourse around issues of accountability, obligation, redistribution and moral economy within ethnic communities, externally or interethnically, at the level of political tribalism there is little acceptance of a national civic culture of impersonal authority and disinterested administration of policy and allocation of public goods (Berman, 2004a, 2004b). Instead, there is a political free for all among competing, largely ethnically based, patronage networks seeking control over parts of the state apparatus and the resources at its command. In such circumstances, there is little or no public trust in the competence and probity of public institutions. The politics of the belly rules (Bayart, 1993; Berman, 2004a). The one-party states of the early postcolonial decades were widely criticized by external observers and their claims to be democratic summarily dismissed. With hindsight, however, we can now recognize that the one-party states provided under the cover of nationalist rhetoric and unity, although with varying degrees of success, an arena for competing ethnic elites to bargain over the allocation of access to the state and public resources without disruptive open clashes; at the cost, however, of growing authoritarianism and actual increasing horizontal inequalities, reduction of public political participation to empty formality, suppression of internal politics within ethnic communities and of trade unions and other political organizations that raised threatening issues of class division (Widner, 1993)

During the 1980s, under the impact of structural adjustment reforms African states were significantly undermined, with resources being shifted from the "predatory" institutions of the state to the development of "free" markets and the activities of "apolitical" nongovernmental organizations. The effect, however, was not what was widely anticipated. Ethnic conflict increased as competition for the shrinking resources of the state became more intense, while market development and investment still depended heavily on political influence, which elites provided for their own personal advantage through both the appropriation of public goods and accumulation of private assets. The extremely unevenly distributed growth increased the extremity of vertical and horizontal cleavages and produced what Ferguson (2006) called some of the most extreme inequalities in human history and the bitter conflicts of autochthony (Geschiere & Jackson, 2006). By the end of that decade, it was clear that the legitimacy and effectiveness of most states in Africa had been significantly compromised, which led to the external pressures and internal movements for democratization and capacity building expressed in political reform, including new constitutions, the restoration of multiparty politics and elections. Most of these reforms implicitly or explicitly attempted to contain ethnic conflicts and direct them into more positive democratic and developmental channels.

How effective have these reforms been in relationship to the governance of ethnic politics? Leaving aside the constitutional issues for the moment, much of the political infrastructure of democratization has often increased rather than decreased ethnic conflicts and undermined social cohesion. First, the return of multiparty politics has created parties largely organized around a particular ethnic group or a coalition of groups, often from a particular region. The international constraints on African governments to hew closely to the policies of structural adjustment leave little scope for political differentiation around alternative programmes and the economic policies of parties are essentially the same. This pushes political elites to focus on mobilizing their ethnic base of support around issues of horizontal inequalities between communities, deepening interethnic fear and mistrust. While this is not a surprise in Kenya, in Ghana, where ethnic politics has been far less salient, ethnic bloc voting has persisted over the 20 years of democratic elections, intertwined with socioeconomic issues (Gyimah-Boadi, 2009; Jockers et al., 2010). Second, the persistence of first-past-the-post electoral systems at both national and constituency levels means that losing parties and candidates lose all access to the institutions and resources of the state – a stark contrast to the one-party state where elites of all ethnic communities found access to the bargaining process for a piece of the action beneath the carapace of the party. Finally, the very narrow scope of policy and national economic management permitted to elected governments meant that there could be little attention to growing vertical cleavages and issues of class and their impact on social cohesion. These could be addressed only by agreeing (or pretending to agree) with new agenda of poverty reduction of the international aid community, as in Kenya when President Kibaki in early 2003 restored universal free primary education in place of the fee-for-service system following the structural adjustment prescriptions that had excluded the poorest and most vulnerable sectors of the population.

Some form of proportional representation along with larger multi-member constituencies that would give opportunities for representation to both local majority and minority communities might be a more effective way of dealing with ethnic politics at local levels and provide national access, although it is probably inadequate in itself, especially in cases where political struggle has already been strongly mobilized around ethnic issues. And, as has been shown in many Western nations as well as Africa, competitive electoral systems are readily compatible with ethnic patronage networks.

Would a presidential system or a British-style parliamentary system be more effective in promoting social cohesion at the national level and thus national unity? Several countries have experimented with requiring parties in presidential elections to a gain a minimum proportion of votes in all regions of the country, which is supposed to facilitate interethnic alliances in support of different national candidates. This does build, however, on conflicts among different elite factions within communities and does not resolve the problems of losing elite coalitions being excluded from resource allocation, let alone the temptations of electoral fraud. Constitutional engineering is important in defining the terms of conflict resolution and collaboration among competing ethnic elites and can facilitate, although hardly guarantee, the development of civic democratic political culture around national institutions, leading to actual national unity.

Last, the efforts at democratization have been preoccupied with parties and elections, formal institutions and the allocation of power and resources among political elites at the national level, but has tended to neglect the reform of civil service and local government that are the institutions in most direct contact with ordinary citizens and the most important site of patronage distribution and petty corruption. It is here that ethnic bias in the distribution of patronage and public goods is one of the most important sources of the conflicts of both political tribalism and moral ethnicity. Ethnic bias affects public institutions at three levels: recruitment and allocation of posts (Chege, 1994); communal patronage in the form of development projects, schools, health facilities and infrastructure development to particular communities or areas (Barkan, 1984, 1994; Haugerud, 1995); and individual patronage in the form of scholarships, contracts, loans and grants. Control of these resources comes with senior political and bureaucratic positions in the state apparatus. Placing recruitment and selection in the hands of professional civil service commissions using ostensibly neutral and impersonal criteria is not enough, however. Such commissions were present at independence in many states and increasingly ineffective and, moreover, did nothing to address the question of ethnic bias in the civil service that reflects both historic horizontal differences in access to education as well as control of patronage. The question is whether achieving better ethnic balance and professional qualification can be combined in a way that will increase public trust in the even-handed competence of the civil service, a form of affirmative action recognizing and ameliorating past inequities that must be grounded in the mutual agreement of political elites from all ethnic communities. This is linked also to the elimination of horizontal inequalities in access to education up to the university level that is a key issue of social policy in all multiethnic societies in Africa and elsewhere (see Chapter 9).

The most fraught and potentially explosive arena of reform of ethnic bias in the state apparatus is in the security services, especially the police, where ethnic imbalances in recruitment often go back to the preferences of colonial regimes for soldiers and police from particular ethnic communities. A glaring example of the problem came in the postelection violence in Kenya from the end of 2007 to early 2008, when the police were accused of both killing and injuring innocent civilians and selective suppression of or connivance with the ethnic gangs perpetrating the violence (Commission of Inquiry into the Post-Election Violence, 2008).

5.4.2 Constitutions and Devolved Government

In writing new constitutions in ethnically divided societies, the key issue is the devolution of powers and distribution of resources between the central government and regional and local subunits as well as the sharing of power among ethnic elites in the central state. This can take a variety of institutional forms from formal power sharing in centralized states to federations and confederations, forms of regional autonomy, and devolution of powers or decentralization of policy implementation to local units of governance (see also Chapter 7). The relationship between these forms and particular ethnic communities can vary widely. In all instances, however, they represent an accommodation of the interests and allocation of resources to ethnic elites, perpetuating elite domination of ethnic communities. At whatever level of government, the key issue is to "follow the money" and the allocation of goods and services devolved to public institutions and the degree to which they are controlled by ethnic elites.

Africa has two striking examples of ethnic federal systems in Nigeria and Ethiopia. In both, federal state units, six of nine in Ethiopia and all of the thirty-six states in Nigeria, are organized around particular groups that constitute a local majority (see Chapter 12). However, because minority communities are almost always present, the dominance of the majority group and the equitable treatment of minorities is a perennial issue and often leads to demands for separate units of governance. In Nigeria, while there are thirty-six states, there are also demands from various communities for up to fifty more. In Ethiopia, in addition to majority–minority issues in six of the states, in three others that are ethnically diverse and have no majority group, ethnic conflict has grown as the various communities contest for dominance in the state government. In Nigeria, the three largest ethnic communities were each divided into several states to divide and contain their potential domination of the national state and divert politics from the extreme polarization that disrupted Nigerian politics after the civil war in the 1960s (Suberu, 2001). However, tensions between different sectors of the major ethnic groups at the state levels have become an increasing component of ethnic conflict.

In federal systems, another critical issue is the fiscal arrangements between the center and local units. In Nigeria, where more than 90% of the revenue of the federal state comes from oil, the central government allocates such revenue proportionally to each of the states under the "federal principle", and this constitutes more than 90% of each state's revenues, as well (Ejobowah, 2006, 2008; Suberu, 2001). With limited local sources of revenue, the states remain highly dependent on the central government and that undermines some of the formal devolution of powers to them. That the national state remains the overwhelming source of revenue and resources also suggests why demands for regional autonomy, or secession are infrequent in Africa compared with demands for access to state resources and devolution of control to local government units by ethnic elites. More typical constitutionally, therefore, are the district units of government in Ghana and the counties created under the new constitution of Kenya in 2010, with their elected councils and county executives with significant control over local resources, including land, and the delivery of public goods and services.

It should be noted that forms of government devolution do not in themselves constitute significant democratization, although they can provide for significant improvement in political stability and orderly governance (Lentz, 2006; Suberu, 2001). Devolved government is largely about allocating control of public goods and resources to ethnic elites in their claimed territorial homelands. It concerns ameliorating horizontal cleavages and allocating local sources of patronage. Indeed, rather than bringing government closer to the people or increasing the equity of development, it readily reinforces the personal forms of patronage and power of "big men" or *bwana mkubwa*. The significant dependence on resources from the center may intensify political competition among ethnic elites and reinforce their power as political brokers. The guarantee of the minimum proportion of the national revenue to local governments such as stipulated in the 2010 Kenyan constitution could limit space for their power, though it is far from clear enough to eliminate arbitrariness.

And, as well, given the growing ethnic diversity of rural communities, it rouses conflicts of autochthony, minority rights and differential citizenship, all concerned with the identity issue. Even efforts to decentralize the administration of individual development programmes to local communities can, as Peter Geschiere's (2009) research in Cameroon has shown, lead to explosive conflict over sharing the benefits between "original" inhabitants and migrants.

One possible effective means to reduce opportunities of patronage in both the center and localities is to set up a national standard for equitable development of basic public goods providing minimum welfare for every citizen and neighborhood (the national minimum at the nationwide level or the civil minimum[2] at the local government level) as other countries have experienced, though we agree with Lonsdale in seeing past experience of ethnicity and citizenship in the West or elsewhere, overall, as not necessarily helpful for the African present (Lonsdale, 2016). Whatever public goods can be agreed should be universally available to all citizens in a country, like education and health, should be provided at some essential minimum. The provision of them should be related to the fundamental rights of citizenship. There is also the understanding that public services are crucial to the national interest, not just individual rights, by promoting more equitable and effective development and thus social cohesion. In particular, the concept of civil minimum can also be applied to group specific needs in dealing with horizontal inequalities dividing different communities. Yet it should be noted that, on the other hand, this may raise struggles over the issue of "ethnic citizenship" or who are legitimate members of the specific localities.

5.4.3 Ethnicity and Social Cohesion at the National Level: The Media and Education

In the history of the modern state, the development of mass media and universal public education have played key roles in the development of nationalism and ethnic identity and belonging, including the relationship between ethnicity and citizenship and both interethnic and

---

[2] The civil minimum is a concept developed in the period after Japan's high economic growth, which is aimed at ensuring a minimum standard of living in various dimensions for all the residents in a municipality. It can theoretically contribute to not only improving social rather than economic aspects of livelihood of the people, but also reducing individual and group biases in the provision of public resources within a local administrative boundary.

intraethnic relations and, thus, trust. During the first postcolonial decades in Africa government controlled national media, with a monopoly on broadcasting, official print media, and the development of a national educational system as key components of nation-building strategies (Harber, 1994). Both, however, became vehicles of ruling parties and agencies of presidential personality cults, which undermined their credibility and legitimacy.

In the process of democratization, the development of a professional and ethnically neutral press is understood as a key component. The opening of the mass media to competition and the elimination of government monopolies and controls have been among the most positive effects of political liberalization in Africa since the end of the Cold War. It has generated much high-quality investigative journalism, especially in the print media, that has become a significant counterforce in many countries by exposing the corruption of the political elite. Several newspapers in Africa now enjoy favorable reputations, both locally and internationally. The major newspapers and prominent journalists in Kenya, for example, by focusing on the objective and impartial reporting of ethnic conflict and exposing of corruption, have earned high credibility among Kenyan citizens (Wrong, 2009).

Liberalization has also spawned proliferating media in indigenous languages, especially radio stations that target specific ethnic audiences. Unfortunately, in both Rwanda and Kenya, for example, these have been involved in instigating ethnic violence by inflammatory broadcasts including exhortations to attack the ethnic "enemy". The control of print and broadcast media, given constitutionally enshrined freedom of speech and the press, is a complex and difficult issue. Tanzania's prohibition of media in indigenous languages, for example, may not be a feasible and desirable solution throughout Africa (see Chapter 3). Such media can have a positive role in preserving and developing the richness of diverse ethnic cultures as a part of national development, as well as informing a wider public about the diverse communities with which they share citizenship. The Kenyan effort to outlaw hate speech, such as propelled the violence after the 2007 election, might be a useful first step. However, as experience elsewhere shows, expressions of hate speech often simply go underground and surface in code words well understood by perpetrators and victims. Moreover, the anonymous and virtually uncontrollable electronic media are now rapidly spreading access to the internet, social media and the "blogosphere" in Africa, even in rural areas and can serve as the basis for online communities organized around ethnocentrism and racism.

Finally, nothing is more important for the creation of a civic culture of co-existence and inclusiveness and thereby social cohesion than national systems of public education and what is taught in them about ethnic diversity and citizenship (see Harber, 1994). In Kenya, however, where the subject of ethnicity had been so politically charged, there was no national curriculum or guidelines about how to deal with ethnicity in the classroom and it had been apparently left to the discretion of the individual teacher as to whether it had been addressed at all before the postelection violence ending in 2008. In its aftermath, Kenyan educators realized that for the most part children have been left to learn about ethnicity, their own or that of others, from their parents or on the street, where this knowledge consists of a confusion of positive and negative stereotypes, which have provided the basis for the impact of hate speech and the mobilization of youth for violence or political opposition against the ethnic "other". Subsequently, however, progress began with new textbooks of social studies for Kenyan primary schools have started to mention negative effects of "tribalism" on peace and national unity,[3] although education for peace teaching interethnic co-existence is not easy in ethnically homogenous localities (Lauritzen, 2013). More recently, however, Alice Wairimu Nderitu (2016) has produced for the Kenya Institute of Curriculum Development a sophisticated and comprehensive curriculum guide for Kenyan teachers on how to teach about race, ethnicity, diversity and inclusion. What remains is how national education systems in Kenya and other countries can make effective use of radio, television and the internet in increasingly wired societies as an arena for promoting a culture of diversity and social cohesion at the national level. Finally, with regard to ethnicity and national development, education might well be the most important focus for public policy (see Chapter 10 for more details on Kenya's educational system). To be effective, however, it requires a serious commitment on the part of political elites that may be very hard to come by.

---

[3] We have referred to two social studies textbooks (Kamau et al., 2010; Omwoyo, 2011) now used at the Grade 8 in Kenyan primary schools.

5.4.4 Land and Territory

In nations that remain primarily agrarian societies, land remains essential for the survival of the mass of people in Africa and the necessary basis for socioeconomic development. It is increasingly becoming so in the region as rapid population growth and underdevelopment of alternative income sources are making land more and more scarce in the relative term. At the same time, however, land remains one of the most critical sources of conflict within and between ethnic communities. The issue has two dimensions: territory, in the sense of an area claimed as the historic homeland of a particular ethnic community; and land, in the sense of areas of agricultural and grazing land over which individuals and kin groups hold recognized rights of occupation and production (see Chapter 8).

Against the historic background of migration and intermingling of communities on moving frontiers of settlement, the identification of a particular territory with a particular ethnic community was facilitated by colonial administrative boundaries and maps that in a more clearly fixed and delineated manner than before identified specific areas of land as belonging to supposed ancient "tribes", strengthening the sense of homeland and autochthony. While population growth shifted the key scarce resource from people to land, differences have grown between ethnic communities in terms of their perception of land rights, modes of land utilization and variations in commercial value and the acuteness of local land shortages (Berman, 2014).

In precolonial Africa the allocation of land to use by individual families within corporate kin groups, chiefdoms and kingdoms was one of the fundamental powers and obligations of political authorities. Access to land for crops or grazing livestock, along with marriage were the fundamental conditions of survival and recognized belonging in a community, and the fundamental basis of the patron–client relations between the wealthy and powerful and their poorer clients. When land began to acquire a growing cash value in areas of cash-crop production or mineral exploitation, elites began to try to retain control over more and more land for their personal profit and at the expense of their poorer kin and clients. Conflicts of moral ethnicity developed around the violation of traditional norms of land tenure. So-called informal or vernacular markets developed where elites bought and sold tracts of land without sanction or recognition in either customary or modern law (Amanor, 2009; Berry, 2009; Chimhowu & Wood-house, 2006).

In parts of Eastern and Southern Africa, the land issue was further complicated by the alienation of African land for white settlement and commercial development under various forms of long-term tenancy or freehold tenure. In Kenya, settler holdings were a focus of conflict between African communities and the colonial regime. At independence, large settler farms were transferred intact through cheap loans to elites from a number of ethnic communities in so-called low density schemes, while less desirable settler properties became part of high density schemes for large numbers of landless mostly Kikuyu peasants who were given small holdings (Leo, 1984). These transfers, along with the issue of titles to landholders in several African reserves, served to increase the concentration of land holdings in the hands of Kenyan elites. Whether displaced by the wealthy within their own community or by immigrant "outsiders", rural populations have a sense of increasing displacement and marginalization, making both intraethnic and interethnic trust-building very difficult. It is no surprise that the western Rift Valley, where thousands of landless Kikuyu were settled among Kalenjin communities on former settler land that the Kalenjin considered rightfully their own, has been the scene of recurrent violence and attempts at ethnic cleansing during every electoral period between 1992 and 2007.

The processes of informal commodification and privatization of land are strongly elite dominated, with the lead taken by the indigenous authorities of local chiefs and lineage elders, precisely those supposedly trustees of communal tenure, and with urban professionals and businessmen, the new big men of rural Africa, who have kin ties to the area and seek land as an investment in commercial agriculture, a place of retirement and ultimately burial "at home" (Berry, 1993, 2009; Lentz, 2006). Such elites are best equipped to negotiate the legal contradictions and state bureaucratic red tape. Chiefs and elders sell village and lineage land, particularly in peri-urban areas where rural communities are being engulfed by rapid urban expansion and land values rise rapidly, and fail to distribute the proceeds to other members of the community, as well as deny access to the poor on land they want to develop or sell. Vernacular land markets are embedded in the inequalities of wealth and power in African rural society and work consistently to the detriment of the poor, advancing inequality and class formation (Chimhowu & Woodhouse, 2006; Tettey et al., 2008), and becoming the focus of conflicts of moral ethnicity and thus undermining intraethnic trust.

African governments have been very ambivalent with regard to these developments. First, members of the political elite have themselves been deeply involved in informal land acquisition along with powerful local figures that the government relies on for support (Klopp, 2000), and because most of these transfers are never officially recorded, politicians are not necessarily supportive of land reform involving official registration of transfers taken under supposedly communal tenure systems. Second, most African states from independence had wide formal powers, especially in urban areas, for the compulsory purchase of land for public purposes, development and the "national interest" whether it was for market places, public buildings, schools, or for the needs of parastatal corporations, state-run development projects, and foreign-owned mining concessions and other investments, or for the protection of environmentally sensitive areas like the forest reserves and national parks in Kenya. Such "public land" has now become a major source of conflict between dispossessed rural people and governments. In Ghana, legally mandated compensation in cash or equivalent land or direct relocation for those whose land is appropriated has rarely been provided, while the projects for which the land has been taken are often not pursued and the land lies idle while surrounded by increasingly crowded farmland. "Public land" in both Ghana and Kenya has become part of the pervasive patronage networks of politics and among the most notorious forms of political corruption, with choice plots handed out to political cronies (Klopp, 2000; Tettey et al., 2008).

It is no surprise, then, that legal and extra-legal conflicts over land tenure and access are the most important source of conflict and most common cause of social violence in rural areas in both Ghana and Kenya, and in the latter have overwhelmed almost all other local political issues. Peters (2009) notes the connection between distress sales of land by the poor and expressions of social exclusion, class formation and conflict. In Ghana in 2002, the state courts had a backlog of no less than 60,000 land cases pending, while there were thought to be a similar number before the traditional courts of the regional houses of chiefs. Tettey et al. (2008) note that "the nature of some of these conflicts suggest the depth to which they are embedded in local power structures and social groups membership, as they pit host communities against migrants, ethnic groups against one another, one generation against another, and men against women" (p. 2). In Kenya, outbursts of ethnic violence take place repeatedly in the western Rift Valley areas where thousands of landless Kikuyu peasants were given land in official settlement schemes more than 40 years earlier (Kanyinga, 2009).

Land and territory in contemporary Africa is thus a situation of extraordinary confusion and legal ambiguity, with decaying forms of traditional tenure confronting areas of different forms of legal titles complicated by the informal markets and increasing accumulation of land by traditional and modern elites. This chaotic situation is not helped by contradictions in development policy between well-intentioned but misguided attempts to decentralize development projects to local communities and build on "traditional communal tenure" that actually divide increasingly ethnically diverse rural communities; and efforts to develop legal land markets with transferable titles and link Africa into the international food chain that actually result in increasing loss of land by small farmers and their forced movement into the agricultural labor force or migration to the cities (Amanor, 2009), exactly the developments most feared by colonial officials more than 60 years ago (Berman, 1990). And, to add more fuel to the fire, the most recent development in African agriculture has been the long-term lease of tens of thousands of acres by Chinese and other foreign firms from desperate governments with little or no cash payment and only a vague promise of increased employment and future economic benefits, while the population on the land are moved off and promises of employment on the estates rarely materialize. Instead, in the Chinese case, it is said that such projects employ more than 1100 Chinese agricultural experts and more than 1 million Chinese farm laborers, and the food produced is for China, not local markets. The Director of the United Nations' Food and Agriculture Organization, Jacques Diouf, has denounced these projects as "neo-colonialism" (Rubenstein, 2009). It is reported that so-called land grab deals, by not only Chinese but also various land-thirsty foreign stakeholders, in some cases account for over ten percent of the whole arable land in a country, making extensive impacts on rural societies (Friis & Reenberg, 2010).

Peasant impoverishment and dispossession has long been understood as a major cause of revolutions in the twentieth century (Wolf,

1970), and these conditions in which the conflicts of ethnicity and class are intricately intertwined are now being reproduced in twenty-first century Africa. Stable and legally enforceable land tenure systems, whether communally or individually based, are essential to ensure a sustainable livelihood for peasants and a basis for future sustainable development of African agriculture.

5.4.5 Natural Resources and Foreign Investment

Along with land, the problem of the "resource curse" is the most serious threat to more effective and equitable development in Africa and a potent source of conflict between and within ethnic communities. The resource boom, particularly in petroleum, caused by rapid growth in emerging economies like India and China, as well as growing energy demands in developed industrial states, has brought ever-larger amounts of foreign exchange earnings and foreign direct investment into resource-rich countries where the expected boom in national development has not taken place. In Nigeria, the prime African example of the "resource curse", as already mentioned, huge amounts of oil revenue were distributed under the "federal principle" to a growing number of states to contain ethnic and regional conflicts. The actual result was some of the most outrageous corruption of our time, as both military and civilian elites appropriated billions of dollars from oil revenues. Moreover, perceived inequity in the allocation of oil money in oil-producing states of the Niger Delta and deep upset over the environmental contamination caused by oil extraction has led to repeated insurrections in the region (Barnes, 2005; also see Chapter 2).

State monopolies of natural resource extraction and the collection of revenue from the international companies that do the actual production has been the greatest opportunity for elite enrichment in contemporary Africa, as well as strengthening their ability to mobilize their ethnic base of support. The world's leading example of the equitable and democratic management of resource revenue to promote national development is Norway's national trust that manages oil resources and revenues in the public interest and funds the country's outstanding education and health systems. While such a system might be hard to conceive of in most contemporary African states, it can set an example for countries like Kenya and Ghana where oil deposits have only recently been discovered and important decisions can be made about how they will be managed for equitable development. We can also mention Botswana, where its dependence on mineral resources (diamonds) has not led to grand corruption, but in a state with a very small population, comparative ethnic homogeneity and long term political stability.

Finally, with regard to foreign investment in nonresource industries, global free trade has increasingly removed any restraints on the movement and operation of capital and production by international companies. Macroeconomic policy and programmes of national development are increasingly constrained for all nations, with only limited and often ineffectual supranational institutions of global governance. We should look again at the programmes of national development, circa 1950–1980, which attempted diversified and self-sustaining development and in much of Africa actually achieved significant improvement in key factors of human development, especially life expectancy and literacy. And we have to consider the development of effective institutions of global governance to manage the instability and inequity of the global market.

5.5 Achieving Growth with Equity and Cohesion?

To summarize: achieving growth with equity and cohesion is a universal problem, not just an African one, as much an issue in the United States or Britain or Japan as it is in Kenya or South Africa. Under a globalizing market economy, developed countries also have experienced failures in growth, equity and cohesion. Africa cannot, therefore, be confined to a ghetto as a unique example of failures of development and social cohesion. Ethnic conflict is not the source of the crisis, but a response to the impact of globalization on historic vertical and horizontal cleavages and a growing threat to social cohesion. Unregulated markets are not a solution but the essential source of the crisis, as they were in the nineteenth century, the interwar decades of the twentieth century, and, today, since 2008. Africa has been and is both shadow and portent of the contradictions and crises of globalization, while inhumane aspects of free market economy have been causing multifaceted sociopolitical problems everywhere in the world. So-called developed nations are in no position to lecture African governments on "correct" solutions to a crisis that was largely of their own making. The conflicts of political tribalism (ethnicity) and moral ethnicity (class) are now global. The key issues and solutions of the global crisis are political and social and must be part of a much broader understanding of development and social cohesion, and a global approach to achieving greater equity and security for the populations of all nations, including confronting the yawning inequalities of classes and ethnic communities. How to do so in the context of the unresolved crisis of the global economy and increasing chauvinistic tendencies in developed nations, as well as the looming crises of climate change and environmental destruction, the collapse of the global food system, and the threat of global pandemics are daunting challenges, which are common for not only Africans but the whole of humankind.

References

Afrobarometer Data. [All], [Round 5], [2013]. Retrieved from: www.afrobarometer.org.

Amanor, K. 2009. Global food chains, African smallholders and World Bank governance. *Journal of Agrarian Change,* 9(2): 247–262.

Anderson, B. 1991. *Imagined Communities: Reflections on the Origins and Spread of Nationalism.* London: Verso Edition.

Argyle, W. J. 1969. European nationalism and African tribalism. In Gulliver, P. H. (ed.), *Tradition and Transition in East Africa: Studies of the Tribal Element in the Modern Era.* London: Routledge and Kegan Paul, pp. 41–58.

Barkan, J. D. 1984. Comparing politics and public policy in Kenya and Tanzania. In Barkan, J. D. (ed.), *Politics and Public Policy in Kenya and Tanzania.* New York: Praeger, pp. 3–42.

   1994. Resurrecting modernization theory and the emergence of civil society in Kenya and Nigeria. In Apter, D. E., and Rosberg, C. G. (eds.), *Political Development and the New Realism in Sub-Saharan Africa.* Charlottesville: University of Virginia Press, pp. 87–116.

Barnes, S. 2005. Global flows: Terror, oil and strategic philanthropy. *Review of African Political Economy,* 32(1): 235–252.

Bayart, J.-F. 1993. *The State in Africa: The Politics of the Belly.* London: Longman.

   2005. *The Illusion of Cultural Identity.* London: Hurst.

Berman, B. 1990. *Control and Crisis in Colonial Kenya.* London and Athens: James Currey and Ohio University Press.

   1998. Ethnicity, patronage and the African State: The politics of uncivil nationalism. *African Affairs,* 97(388): 305–341.

2004a. A palimpsest of contradictions: The study of politics, ethnicity and the state in Africa. *International Journal of African Historical Studies,* 37(1): 13–31.

2004b. Ethnicity, bureaucracy and democracy: The politics of trust. In Berman, B., Dickson, E., and Kymlicka, W. (eds.), *Ethnicity and Democracy in Africa.* Oxford: James Currey, pp. 38–53.

2011. Of magic, invisible hands and ELFS: How not to study ethnicity in Africa or anywhere else. *ECAS4.* Uppsala, 11–14 June.

2014. Homeland, my land, *not* your land: Ethnic territory, property and citizenship in Africa. In McGarry, J., and Simeon, R. (eds.), *The Limits of Territorial Pluralism.* Vancouver: University of British Columbia Press, pp. 240–264.

Berman, B., and Lonsdale, J. 2013. Nationalism in colonial and post-colonial Africa. In Breuilly, J. (ed.), *Oxford Handbook of the History of Nationalism.* Oxford and New York: Oxford University Press.

Berry, S. 1993. *No Condition Is Permanent: The Social Dynamics of Agrarian Change in Sub-Saharan Africa.* Madison: University of Wisconsin Press.

2009. Building for the future? Investment, land reform and contingencies of ownership in contemporary Ghana. *World Development,* 37(8): 1370–1378.

Brown, G. K., and Langer, A. 2010. *Conceptualizing and Measuring Ethnicity (JICA Institute Working Paper No. 9).* Japan: JICA Research Institute.

Central Intelligence Agency (CIA). 2003–2013. *The world factbook.* Retrieved from: www.cia.gov/library/publications/the-world-factbook/geos/tz.html. Accessed 12–14 February 2013.

Chege, M. 1994. Swapping development strategies: Kenya and Tanzania after their founding presidents. In Apter, D. E., and Rosberg, C. G. (eds.), *Political Development and the New Realism in Sub-Saharan Africa.* Charlottesville: University of Virginia Press, pp. 247–290.

Chimhowu, A., and Woodhouse, P. 2006. Customary vs private property rights? Dynamics and trajectories of vernacular land markets in sub-Saharan Africa. *Journal of Agrarian Change,* 6(3): 346–371.

Commission of Inquiry into the Post-Election Violence (CIPEV). 2008. *Report of the Commission of Inquiry into the Post-Election Violence.* Nairobi: CIPEV.

Easterly, W., and Levine, R. 1997. Africa's growth tragedy: Policies and ethnic divisions. *Quarterly Journal of Economics,* 112(4): 1203–1250.

Ejobowah, J. B. 2006. The new political economy of federal preservation: Insights from Nigerian federal practice. *Commonwealth and Comparative Politics,* 43(2): 178–193.

2008. Integrationist and accommodationist measures in Nigerian constitutional engineering. In Choudhry, S. (ed.), *Constitutional Design for Divided Societies*. New York and Oxford: Oxford University Press, pp. 233–257.

Ferguson, J. 2006. *Global Shadows: Africa in the Neoliberal World Order.* Durham, NC: Duke University Press.

Friis, C., and Reenberg, A. 2010. *Land Grab in Africa: Emerging Land System Drivers in a Teleconnected World (GLP Report No. 1)*. Copenhagen: GLP-IPO.

Geschiere, P. 2009. *The Perils of Belonging: Autochthony, Citizenship and Exclusion in Africa and Europe*. Chicago and London: University of Chicago Press.

Geschiere, P., and Jackson, S. (eds.). 2006. Autochthony and the crisis of citizenship (Special issue) . *African Studies Review*, 49(2): 1–7.

Geschiere, P., and Nyamjoh, F. 2000. Capitalism and autochthony: The seesaw of the mobility and belonging. *Political Culture*, 12(2): 423–452.

Gyimah-Boadi, E. 2009. Another step forward for Ghana. *Journal of Democracy*, 20(2): 138–152.

Harber, C. 1994. Ethnicity and education for democracy in sub-Saharan Africa. *International Journal of Educational Development*, 14(3): 255–264.

Haugerud, A. 1995. *The Culture of Politics in Modern Kenya*. Cambridge: Cambridge University Press.

Hodgkin, T. 1956. *Nationalism in Colonial Africa*. London: Frederick Muller.

Ikeno, J. 2002. *Tanzania' Sekai Minzoku Mondai Jiten (Encyclopedia of Nations and Ethnic Relations)*. Tokyo: Heibon-sha.

Jerven, M. 2011. Revisiting the consensus on Kenyan economic growth, 1964–95. *Journal of Eastern African Studies*, 5(1): 2–23.

2013. *Poor Numbers: How We Are Misled by African Development Statistics and What to Do about It*. Ithaca, NY: Cornell University Press.

2014. *Economic Growth and Measurement Reconsidered in Botswana, Kenya, Tanzania, and Zambia, 1965–1995*. Oxford: Oxford University Press.

Jerven, M., and Duncan, M. E. 2012. Revising GDP estimates in sub-Saharan Africa: Lessons from Ghana. *African Statistical Journal*, 15, pp. 13–24.

Jockers, H., Kohnert, D., and Nugent, P. 2010. The successful Ghana election of 2008: A convenient myth. *Journal of Modern African Studies*, 48(1): 95–115.

Kamau, C. C., Indire, M., Ombongi, G. M., and Rutere, F. 2010. *Our Lives Today: Social Studies 8* (revised edition). Nairobi: Oxford University Press East Africa.

Kanyinga, K. 2009. The legacy of the White Highlands: Land rights, ethnicity and the post-2007 election violence in Kenya. *Journal of Contemporary African Studies*, 27(3): 325–344.

Kertzer, D. I., and Arel, D. 2001. Census, identity formation, and the struggle for political power. In Kertzer, D.I., and Arel, D. (eds.), *Census and Identity: The Politics of Race, Ethnicity, and Language in National Census*. Cambridge: Cambridge University Press.

Klopp, J. 2000. Pilfering the public: The problem of land grabbing in contemporary Kenya. *Africa Today*, 47(1): 7–26.

Lauritzen, S. M. 2013. *Building a culture of peace: Peace education in Kenyan primary schools*. PhD Thesis. University of York.

Lentz, C. 2006. *Ethnicity and the Making of History in Northern Ghana*. Edinburgh: Edinburgh University Press.

Leo, C. 1984. *Land and Class in Kenya*. Toronto: University of Toronto Press.

Lonsdale, J. 1994. Moral ethnicity and political tribalism. In Kaarsholm, P., and Hultin, J. (eds.), *Inventions and Boundaries: Anthropological Approaches to the Study of Ethnicity and Nationalism*. Roskilde, Denmark: Centre for Development Studies, pp. 131–150.

2008. Soil, work, civilization and citizenship in Kenya. *Journal of Eastern African Studies*, 2(2): 305–314.

2016. Unhelpful pasts and a provisional present. In Hunter, E. (ed.), *Citizenship, Belonging & Political Community in Africa: Dialogues between Past & Present*. Athens: Ohio University Press, pp. 17–41.

Lynch, G. 2011. *I Say to You: Ethnic Politics and the Kalenjin in Kenya*. Chicago: University of Chicago Press.

Marshall-Fratani, R. 2006. The war of "who is who": Autochthony, nationalism, and citizenship in the Ivoirian crisis. *African Studies Review*, 49 (2): 9–43.

Mueller, S. 2008. The political economy of Kenya's crisis. *Journal of Eastern African Studies*, 2(2): 185–210.

Nderitu, A. W. 2016. *Beyond Ethnicism: Exploring Ethnic and Racial Diversity for Educators*. Nairobi: Kenya Institute of Curriculum Development.

Omwoyo, F. M. 2011. *Primary Social Studies Standard Eight: Living Together in Kenya and the World*. Nairobi: Kenya Literature Bureau.

Peters, P. 2009. Changes in land tenure and land reform in Africa: Anthropological contributions. *World Development*, 37(8): 1317–1325.

Rubenstein, C. 2009. China's eye on African agriculture. *Asia Times Online*, 2 October.

Stewart, F. 2002. Horizontal inequality: A neglected dimension of development. UNU-WIDER Annual Lecture Series no. 5. Helsinki: UNU-WIDER.

Stewart, F. (ed.). 2008. *Horizontal Inequalities and Conflict: Understanding Group Violence in Multiethnic Societies*. London: Palgrave Macmillan.

Stiglitz, J. 2011. *The Price of Inequality: How Today's Divided Society Endangers Our Future*. New York: Norton.

Suberu, R. T. 2001. *Federalism and Ethnic Conflict in Nigeria*. Washington, DC: U.S. Institute of Peace Press.

Takahashi, M. 2010. Inter-linkage between ethnicity and development: An analytical framework. *Workshop on Ethnic Diversity and Economic Instability in Africa: Policies for Harmonious Development*, New Haven, CT, Yale University, 17 January.

Tettey, W., Gebe, B., and Ansah-Koi, K. 2008. *The Politics of Land and Land-Related Conflicts in Ghana*. Legon, Ghana: Institute of Statistical, Social and Economic Research and USAID.

Widner, J. 1993. *The Rise of the Party State in Kenya: From 'Harambee' to 'Nyayo'*. Berkeley and Los Angeles: University of California Press.

Wilkinson, R., and Picket, K. 2010. *The Spirit Level: Why Equality is Better for Everyone*. London: Penguin Books.

Wolf, E. 1970. *Peasant Wars of the Twentieth Century*. New York: Harper

Wrong, M. 2009. *It's Our Turn to Eat: The Story of a Kenya Whistle-Blower*. New York: Harper.

PART II

Policies and Institutions for Social Cohesion

6 | Redressing Inequalities in Societies
Growth with Equity

FRANCES STEWART[1]

6.1 Introduction

The idea that inequality is necessary to generate growth has quite a long history. Perhaps the best known articulation of this is that of (Okun, 1975), the title of whose book says it all: *Equality and Efficiency: The Big Tradeoff*. The aim of this chapter is to consider whether the "big-tradeoff" indeed exists, by investigating both theoretical arguments and empirical evidence on the question.

But before considering the critical issue of the relationship between inequality and growth, it is necessary to consider definitions. Two important questions are: inequality among whom? And inequality of what?

Among whom: Inequality may be measured among individuals within a particular society, or in a region or in the world as a whole. Inequality among individuals (or households) is most commonly measured within a particular country, but there are some efforts to measure inequality among all citizens of the world. We shall term inequality among individuals (or households) *vertical inequality* (VI).

Alternatively inequality may be measured across groups of people within a society – e.g., ethnic or religious groups, or people grouped by region, age or gender. We shall term this type of inequality *horizontal inequality* (HI). Inequality is also often measured among countries, or groups of countries (like developed and developing countries), which is a type of HI.

Each of these types of inequality is relevant in particular contexts. For example to find out how a particular level of GDP per capita translates into poverty, VI measures are appropriate. HIs (within a nation) are relevant as a source of injustice, which can lead to societal

---

[1] I am grateful to the participants at the Tokyo workshop, July 2012, for helpful comments on a previous draft.

conflict. And inequalities among nations are relevant to issues of global justice and global redistribution policies, such as aid flows.

Inequality in which space: The question of the relevant space or dimension for measuring inequality again depends on the purpose of the enquiry. The well-known debates about the best measure of welfare are equally relevant to the question of inequality. Although traditionally inequality is measured in income space – and this or inequality in consumption is still dominant in measures of VI – income has been widely criticised as a satisfactory indicator of welfare or of development. Sen has been a leading critic (Sen, 1977): he has argued that development is about advancing freedoms or capabilities, defined as what people can do or be, and consequently that inequality should be assessed in the space of capabilities (Sen, 1980, 1999). This suggests a multidimensional concept. Inequality may then be measured independently in relation to each important capability (such as the ability to be well-nourished or healthy), or in the resources needed to achieve each important capability (such as access to food, health services), or through a multidimensional index. Income distribution, nonetheless, remains an important element helping to determine access to various freedoms. However, empirical research shows that the correlation between income distribution and the distribution of various capabilities is not very strong, so one cannot simply substitute the distribution of income for that of other capabilities (Samman et al., 2011).

Some capabilities seem to be of greater importance than others, because they are perceived as intrinsically important or because they are essential for the realisation of other capabilities. For example, life expectancy represents an important capability in itself, and being alive is, of course, essential for all other capabilities, while people who lack education also generally find that their income earning capacity is diminished and they then have less access to many other capabilities. Consequently, it is essential to separate out the important dimensions, sometimes known as *basic capabilities* (Nussbaum, 2000; Sen, 1999), and to measure inequality in the distribution of each one, paying particular attention to the capabilities that affect other capabilities.[2]

---

[2] Wolff and de-Shalit (2007) use the term "fertile functionings" to describe functionings that affect other functionings positively.

In the theoretical discussions, we consider inequality in a range of capabilities; but the empirical evidence on the relationship between growth and inequality has focused primarily on income, for VI, while for HI, where data are much more scarce, we have to make do with whatever is available (frequently non-income, such as years of education, as a major data source for HIs – the Demographic and Health Surveys – do not collect income data).

There has been much consideration of the relationship between VI and growth, both from a theoretical and empirical perspective, but very little work has been done on the relationship between HI and growth. One major complication is that with respect to both types of inequality we can expect a two-way relationship: i.e., the extent of inequality may affect the growth rate; and the growth rate may affect inequality. Another is that the relationships may change as development proceeds, with different ones holding at low levels of income than at high – as would be expected following the Kuznets curve (Kuznets, 1955).[3] Then policies mediate these relationships: countries with policies aimed at reducing inequality may show a different relationship than those that do not adopt such policies.

6.2 VI: The Relationships

6.2.1 From Income Distribution to Growth

In the 1950s and later, it was argued that a more unequal income distribution led to higher growth, via higher savings and incentive effects (e.g., Galenson & Leibenstein, 1955; Okun, 1975). Consequently, it was recommended that countries should grow first and redistribute later. However, this conclusion was challenged, e.g., by (Adelman & Morris, 1973), who argued that a more equal initial income distribution would lead to higher growth on the grounds that investment in humans (better nutrition, health and especially education) would be greater with more equal distribution and this was the most important factor determining growth.

---

[3] At first, societies become more unequal as income per capita rises, but subsequently become more equal with further rises in per capita incomes (inverted U-curve).

A good deal of empirical literature has supported Adelman and Morris (1973) using cross-country data (e.g., see Alesina & Perotti, 1994; Alesina & Rodrik, 1994; Bénabou, 1996; Persson & Tabellini, 1994).[4] However, Fishlow (1995) finds no statistically significant evidence of a relationship between growth and equality, when a dummy variable is introduced for Latin America and Barro (2008) found that inequality was bad for growth in poor countries, but good for growth in rich (i.e., developed) ones. These investigations all use ordinary least squares cross-country estimates. However, using fixed effects, to allow for country-specific influences, Li and Zou (1998) and Forbes (2000) find a very different relationship, with an *increase* in inequality being associated with an *increase* in growth for countries over time, while Banerjee and Duflo (2003), using nonparametric methods, find that a change in inequality in *either direction* is associated with a reduction in growth. Yet, investigations over time in states in the United States showed a positive relationship between greater equality and higher growth, allowing for fixed effects (e.g., Panizza, 1999).

Cornia (2004) has postulated that the relationship between growth and inequality varies according to the extent of inequality. He plotted inequality (as measured by the Gini coefficient of income) against growth of GDP per capita for 1960–1998, showing a concave relationship with growth rising as inequality increases from very low levels, and then declining with a further increase in inequality.

Berg and Ostry (2011) investigating the relationship between inequality and the *persistence* of growth find support for the view that more equality is likely to be good for sustained growth:

> We find that longer growth spells are robustly associated with more equality in the income distribution. For example, closing, say, half the inequality gap between Latin America and emerging Asia would, according to our central estimates, more than double the expected duration of a growth spell. (p. 3)

Taken as a whole, the evidence is ambiguous. While it does not definitively establish that greater equality promotes economic growth, it does not lend support to the opposite conclusion – that inequality should be promoted in order to increase growth, as argued in the early literature.

---

[4] See also Birdsall, Ross and Sabot (1995); Bourguignon (1995); Deininger and Squire (1998).

6.2.2 From Growth to Income Distribution

How about the reverse relationship? Does growth increase (or reduce) VI? The answer must depend on the *nature* of growth and the impact of government. The distributional effects of growth depend on how far earnings are spread via employment; and how far the tax and government expenditure system in place redistributes primary income.

As far as employment is concerned, a rapid increase in labour-intensive activities would be likely to make growth more egalitarian, whereas capital-intensive growth with low employment growth and fast growth in higher-skilled activities relative to less skilled employment would be likely to lead to more inequality. The primary production sector (agriculture and other natural resources) has an important impact here, especially in low-income countries where it dominates. In agriculture, the distributional impact is likely to vary according to land distribution – peasant agriculture tending to be more egalitarian than plantations or large estates. In non-agriculture, oil and mineral production tend to involve concentrated ownership and capital and skill-intensive production and thus lead to more unequal distribution. Both case studies and regression analysis lend support to these broad conclusions. For example:

- Fei et al. (1979) show how the labour-intensive industrialisation of Taiwan contributed to improved income distribution in the 1960s.
- Conversely, Fishlow (1972) and Thorp et al. (2000) show how the pattern of capital intensive import substitution adopted in many Latin American countries in the 1950s and 1960s was associated with low formal sector employment growth and rising inequality.
- Investigations by Bourguignon and Morrisson (1990), among others, on the basis of cross-country regressions conclude that "endowments in mineral resources, land concentration in agricultural exports, trade protection and secondary schooling are shown to be major determinants of differences in income inequality across developing countries" (p. 1113).
- The rise in inequality in the majority of countries in recent decades has been associated with rising skilled/unskilled wage differentials, partly owing to the increasing skill requirements of modern technology (Berman et al., 1997; Wood & Ridao-Cano, 1996).

However, policy matters too. Falling inequality in Latin America in the 2000s, e.g., has been attributed to a rising minimum wage, increasing secondary education across the population, and cash transfers to the poor (Cornia, 2014; Cornia & Martorano, 2011; Lopez-Calva & Lustig, 2012). Distribution is also affected by the incidence of taxation and public expenditure. A number of studies have found that tax incidence in developing countries is broadly neutral with respect to income distribution, while public expenditure is often progressive, particularly social expenditure (Chu et al., 2000; Cornia, 2004; Van de Walle & Nead, 1995). However, a more recent study by Inchauste and Lustig (2017) of low- and middle-income countries found that fiscal systems almost always reduced inequality, but the extent varies greatly. Among developing countries the most egalitarian systems with respect to cash redistribution (taxes and transfers) were found in Uruguay and South Africa. In a quite high proportion of counties, indirect taxes and subsidies were found to be equalising as well as direct taxes and transfers. Expenditures on health and education were invariably (and quite substantially) equalising but more so in the middle income countries than the low-income ones.

In sum, the consequences of growth for VI depend in part on the initial distribution of assets, and the employment and skill intensity of output growth, and in part on the distributional incidence of taxation and public expenditure. It follows that the relationship between growth and changing distribution will vary across countries according to differences in these variables. Indeed, a World Bank study of 14 countries in the 1990s showed that growth was accompanied by rising inequality in many countries (including India, Vietnam and Ghana), but falling inequality in some (Bolivia, Brazil and Burkina Faso; World Bank, 2005).

6.3 HIs: The Relationships

There has been almost no systematic research directly related to the question of the relationship between HIs and economic growth. Moreover, because there is little correlation between HIs in a society and VI, we cannot assume that what has been found for VI also applies to HI (Mancini, 2008; Østby, 2003). Hence, this section is more exploratory than conclusive.

There are many different ways in which people can be classified into groups, and consequently a variety of HIs in any society, depending on the grouping chosen. Group categorisations that frequently have political and personal significance include regional, ethnic, religious, racial and gender divisions. While gender and region are pervasive characteristics, the relevance of religion, ethnicity and race varies across societies. Sharp inequalities across *any* of these categorisations are unjust because people do not choose their group and major inequalities imply inequality of opportunity and past or present discrimination (Stewart, 2013). Moreover, where the inequalities relate to politically salient groups they raise the risk of violent conflict (Cederman et al., 2011; Stewart, 2008).

The variety of categorisations possible complicates the exploration of the relationship between growth and HIs. For example, it is possible that growth is equalising for some groupings (e.g., gender) and disequalising for others (minority ethnic groups), and conversely, the presence of some types of HI may inhibit growth but not others. For example, the exclusion of a small group from economic and social participation involves a large HI for that group, but is unlikely to affect the overall growth rate; yet deprivation of a large group is likely to be deleterious for growth.

To simplify the argument we need to define the categorisation being explored. We start by considering a society with major ethnic inequalities among sizeable groups – e.g., Nigeria's Northern population which accounts for roughly one-half of the population and, on average, is severely disadvantaged in relation to most Southern peoples.

Considering first, the impact of such HIs on economic growth, it is plausible to argue that it is likely to be growth inhibiting for two reasons:

- Underinvestment in health and education for a large group of people is likely to involve a large loss of potential – in this case, in terms of the economic contribution Northerners would make if they had as much access to social and economic resources as Southerners. Though the North may suffer geographic disadvantages that mean that returns to investments there are likely to be lower than in the South, part of the lower returns is due to low levels of investments of all sorts in the North that keep returns down, and not to geography as such – e.g., due to relatively weak physical infrastructure as well as human investments and underdeveloped markets. So with sufficient investment in human and physical resources, returns would rise. Moreover, with greater investment in their capacities, talented Northerners could migrate to the South and make a contribution there.

- Second, some of the relative disadvantage of Northerners is likely to be due to discrimination against them by Southerners who make the majority of the employment and investment decisions, and this implies a loss of efficiency owing to unequal competition.
- Third, the relative disadvantage of the North threatens political stability which has two sorts of costs: one is the perverse (i.e., non-economic) decisions that politicians have to make to appease the discontented. The other, more direct cost, is the loss of output owing to additional investment in security and, especially, to outright conflicts which disrupt markets, reduce investment and cause human and capital flight (Collier & World Bank, 2003; Stewart & Fitzgerald, 2001).

Consequently, on balance, it seems that large HIs between major groups are likely to be bad for growth. It is indeed difficult to think of arguments why high HIs would actually contribute to growth – although in so far as corrective policies are costly, these might worsen growth in the short run.

Similar arguments would apply to alternative groupings, such as by race or religion or gender. In each case, the presence of large HIs mean that the potential productivity of a major group is not being realised, and that the playing field is uneven implying an efficiency loss. However, as noted earlier, where the deprived group is very small, aggregate GDP growth is likely to be unaffected by the extent of HI. There might also be deprived groups who are very difficult to reach (and/or the costs of doing so are very high) – e.g., those in remote areas; and there may be some whose productivity contribution – even with additional resources – are unlikely to reach those of the more privileged because of particular problems, such as among the disabled or the aged. In all such cases, the reduction of inequalities remains a moral imperative, but one would not expect growth to be positively affected – and indeed might be negatively affected if the costs of reducing the HIs were large.

6.3.1 Does Growth Affect HIs?

As with VI, here the nature of growth is all important. Several reasons suggest that growth might worsen HIs at least in the early stages of development:

- Growth often occurs in specific geographic areas, with cumulative causation or growth cycles, owing to the interactive and dynamic returns to infrastructure, educated workers, institutions and markets (Myrdal, 1956). Consequently, regional inequalities may increase with growth. Given the regional location of ethnic groups, these widening regional inequalities may also constitute widening ethnic inequalities.
- Similarly, more educated people are likely to gain relatively more opportunities when growth occurs, and this means people from more privileged groups gain more than the less privileged.
- Insofar as overt discrimination is responsible for HIs, the continuation of this during growth episodes means that HIs will be maintained and possibly widen.

However, there are circumstances when such worsening may not occur, and indeed there could be an improvement.

- Where there is an "ethnic division of labour", growth that changes the structure of production will favour some activities (and groups) over others. This could either increase or reduce HIs depending on the combination of ethnic specialisation and structural change. For example, in West Africa, the Lebanese dominate trading networks, so growth that favours such networks will also favour the Lebanese. In Malaysia, Indians' concentration as plantation workers means that their relative position depends on the fortunes of plantations. In Northern Ireland (NI), a switch away from shipbuilding (dominated by Protestants) to activities where Catholics enjoyed a larger role (such as the public sector) reduced Protestant/Catholic HIs. A similar argument applies to gender inequalities: many activities are gendered, and structural change (such as towards female-dominated textile production in Bangladesh) can change gender HIs.
- New production activities may open up opportunities for previously excluded groups – e.g., new manufacturing activities.
- Special measures to support the productivity of deprived groups (e.g., through training and loan programmes, and/or affirmative

action) may enable them to participate more equally in the growing economy.

- As the economy expands, the supplies of labour from the more privileged groups may become exhausted, opening up opportunities for the previously deprived and reducing inequalities.
- If growth is accompanied by increased competition, inefficient discriminatory practices may be abandoned in favour of more efficient, and less discriminatory, methods.

These arguments suggest that in the early stages of development, unless special measures are taken, growth is likely to contribute to worsening HIs; but as structural change occurs, labour supplies from previously privileged groups may become exhausted and special measures taken to support the excluded, so that HIs may be reduced. Barrios and Strobl (2005) provide evidence for such a Kuznets curve for regional inequalities in the case of European countries.

Four cases studies illustrate the range of possibilities – in Ghana and Peru, in which growth was accompanied by widening economic HIs, although by some reduction in social HIs; and in Malaysia and NI, where growth was accompanied by significant reductions in HIs of all kinds.

6.3.2 Ghana[5]

Ghana's major divide is a regional one (which overlaps with ethnicity). "Five of the seven administrative regions of southern Ghana (Brong Ahafo, Ashanti, Eastern, Central, and Western) are largely populated by Akan, while the other two, Volta and Greater Accra are largely populated by Ewe and Ga-Adangbe, respectively. The three northern administrative regions, (Northern, Upper West and Upper East) are largely populated by the Mole-Dagbani. In general, the South refers to the seven southern regions while the North refers to the three northern regions" (Seini, 2012). There is also a broadly overlapping religious difference, with Christians (about 70% of the population) dominant in the South, and Muslims (16% of the population) largely based in the North. There have been long-term HIs between North and South, in multiple dimensions. In 1999, e.g., per capita income in the South was 2.4 times that in the North. The North is also relatively deprived in

---

[5] This section relies heavily on Seini (2012).

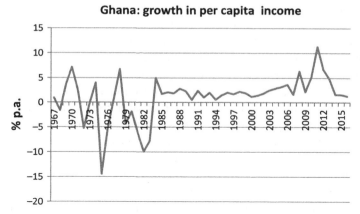

Figure 6.1 Ghana: Growth in per capita income
Source: World Bank, World Development Indicators (Accessed July 2017).

terms of access to schools and electricity, malnutrition and infant mortality.

After prolonged economic decline and stagnation largely owing to political upheavals, which was followed by economic reforms and renewed inflows of aid when political stability was established in the 1980s, the Ghanaian economy resumed economic growth (Figure 6.1). The recovery of production was mainly based on commodities produced in the South – cocoa, gold, diamond, bauxite, manganese and timber and timber products – while Northern cash crops (cotton and rice) suffered a decline, associated with trade liberalisation. The North specialises in food production for subsistence and has fewer non-agricultural activities than the South, which also expanded with growth. Moreover, educated and trained workers are concentrated in the South, and Southerners dominate the civil services. Consequently, in this case, growth was associated with widening economic HIs, basically owing to the geographic location of the production of different products, especially exports, and to the relative advantage of the South in skills, education and non-agricultural activities. From 1992 to 2006, the incidence of poverty fell by about 25 percentage points in Ghana as a whole and more than that in many regions, but it actually rose in the Upper East Region, changed very little in Upper West, and fell by just 11% in the Northern Region (the three regions in the North), while it fell by more than 20% in all other regions apart from

Accra, where it fell by 14% (Cooke et al., 2016). However, between 2006 and 2013, poverty incidence fell by more in Upper East and Upper West Regions than the rest of the country, while Northern Region showed an average decline (Ibid). Yet not all indicators showed a worsening in regional HIs: there was some narrowing in the provision of public assets, such as schools and electricity; while the gap between North and South in female illiteracy and child malnutrition measured by stunting widened, the gap narrowed in infant mortality rates, male illiteracy and malnutrition when measured by wasting (Mancini, 2009). Thus, public policy – with a focus on the provision of public goods in the north strongly supported by aid – was able to counter some of the impact of the rising economic inequalities. But it was insufficient to reverse the economic inequalities. VI also rose over the growth years (Cooke et al., 2016).

6.3.3 Peru[6]

Peru's most salient HIs are between indigenous people and people of mixed or European descent; these are also reflected in geographic inequalities between European dominated Lima and the coast and Ayacucho and the Andes. For example, the illiteracy rate in Ayacucho in 1981 was 45% compared with 21% for Peru as a whole; and within the Ayacucho region, the illiteracy rates of Quecha speakers were nearly three times that of Spanish speakers. Similar differences are to be observed with respect to access to modern sanitation, purified water and electricity.

Peru experienced two decades of good growth from around 1990, interrupted by the 1997–1998 financial crisis. Income per head grew at an annual average rate of 4.2% from 2002 to 2016 bolstered by soaring commodity prices, although incomes fell in 2009 with the global crisis, but growth resumed thereafter (Figure 6.2). The main sources of growth were mining and construction, both located outside the indigenous areas. Commercial agriculture also did well in the Coastal areas. Moreover, the *canon,* a tax on mining, is shared between the centre and the producing regions, so the Andes hardly benefits.[7] The indigenous areas are also those where *coca* is cultivated and there were considerable efforts to reduce the cultivation and sale of

[6] This section draws on Orihuela (2012) and Thorp and Paredes (2010).
[7] For example, Ayacucho received 0.5% of the total, 2004–2008 (Orihuela, 2012).

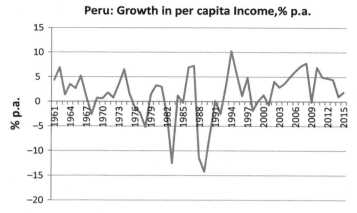

Figure 6.2 Peru: Growth in per capita income
Source: World Bank, World Development Indicators (Accessed July 2017).

this illegal crop with some negative impact on local incomes. Consequently, economic HIs widened with growth. As Orihuela states: "national economic progress does not embrace the Sierra and Selva, widens group inequalities and brings new forms of conflict across the country" (2012, p. 206). However, the booming economy did support the expansion of social and economic infrastructure in indigenous areas. For example, educational inequalities narrowed in terms of access, though quality gaps remained large. In addition, FONCODES (Fondo de Cooperación para Desarollo Social), supported by the World Bank developed thousands of rural development projects directed towards the low-income areas.

Thus, as in Ghana, one finds a mixed picture in the evolution of HIs over time. Between 1996 and 2004, HI in child mortality rose, according to estimates from the Living Standard Measurement Surveys (Thorp & Paredes, 2010), while between 2004 and 2007, poverty incidence rose in the Central-Southern Andes, while falling in Peru as a whole (Orihuela, 2012). But there was some narrowing in the difference in service coverage (electricity, water, education), although the inequalities remained severe. An assessment by Lacavone et al. (2015) found that productivity in manufacturing and mining across regions converged during the growth period of 2001–2014, but that of agriculture and services did not. Poverty incidence did not converge, and some of the highest poverty areas saw least decline in poverty. VI rose in the 1980s and 1990s, but fell from 2000, as in much of Latin America.

6.3.4 NI

Deep HIs in Ireland (and later NI) between Protestants and Catholics ultimately stem from the English invasion of Ireland in the seventeenth century and the subsequent settlement there of Protestants from England, who took the best land and exploited the local population. In 1922, most of Ireland became independent and the Protestant-dominated North joined the United Kingdom. From then until around the early 1980s, such inequalities persisted within NI. For example, in 1981, Catholic men were two and one-half times more likely to be unemployed than Protestant men: Catholics were disadvantaged in every kind of employment (Rowthorn & Wayne, 1988; Todd & Ruane, 2012). With 37% of the economically active population, Catholics had less than 5% of the highest positions in the civil services (Todd & Ruane, 2012). Their housing, education and health levels were also considerably worse than those of Protestants (Stewart, 2002). These inequalities, together with political exclusion, were an important contributor to the violence that occurred in the province from 1970. The violence led to prolonged economic stagnation, but the economy picked up from the late 1980s, and NI then experienced higher growth than the rest of the UK (Figure 6.3).

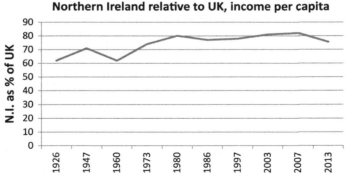

Figure 6.3 Income per capita in Northern Ireland relative to the UK
Source: Brownlow (2012); UK National Office of Statistics.
Note: Data from 1997 are for regional value added per capita.

From the late 1970s, inequalities began to fall as a result of a combination of factors. Discrimination against Catholics in the public sector was recognised as one of the causes of conflict in an official report in 1970. Subsequently, a Standing Advisory Commission on Human Rights was instituted to advise on how to counter discrimination and in 1976 a Fair Employment Act made direct (but not indirect) discrimination illegal in both public and private sectors. But implementation was weak. However, a MacBride principles campaign was initiated, with the support of Irish immigrants in the US, similar to the campaign of the 1970s in relation to apartheid South Africa, which aimed to persuade U.S. companies to support fair employment, and to put pressure on the UK government for stronger action. Action followed with a new Fair Employment Act in 1989. This act not only outlawed indirect as well as direct discrimination, but also had much stronger enforcement clauses, through a Fair Employment Commission and a Fair Employment Tribunal. Subsequently, legislation in 1998 required all public authorities to "work out an equality plan... and to publish impact assessments of their policies in light of the equality plan" (Todd & Ruane, 2012, p. 198).

Other changes also contributed to reduced HIs. One was a massive expansion in the education of Catholics with greater public support, including additional resources, for schools in disadvantaged areas, so by the end of the twentieth century Catholic enrolment rates at all levels were as good as those of Protestants, and by 2015, Protestants were falling behind Catholics. The Equality Commission for NI reported that Catholic children were outperforming Protestant ones in GCSE and A-levels and they were concerned that protestant working class children were falling behind (Equality Commission for Northern Ireland, 2016). In 2015–2016, the proportion of higher education students who were Catholic was 47%, greater than their share of the population in 2011 (40%), while only 30% of higher education students were Protestant, substantially less than their share of the population in 2011 (Northern Ireland Statistics and Research Agency, 2011; McNamee, 2017). Another factor behind the reduction in HIs was the changing structure of the economy. The shipbuilding industry, long dominated by Protestants, suffered major decline (as did manufacturing) while the public sector – which was becoming increasingly less discriminatory – grew. Consequently, economic growth in NI was accompanied by a sharp reduction in HIs. For example, the ratio of high income households to total households among Catholics was just 55% of the Protestant ratio in the later 1970s and had risen to nearly 80% by the late 1990s, while inequalities in unemployment and housing had been greatly reduced. By 2016, the gap in employment had been completely eliminated, with the same ratio of working age Catholics and Protestants in employment (in contrast – the ratio was 70% of Protestants and 54% of Catholics in 1992), and the same proportion in professional jobs (Canning, 2017).

While HIs were falling, VI was probably rising from around 1980 and broadly stable in the 2000s.[8]

While the NI case shows a clear connection between HIs and conflict, there is no apparent relationship between HIs and economic growth. Per capita incomes in NI lagged well behind the UK when NI was first established. Since then the relative position has fluctuated with a catch-up trend, which does not show any obvious connection with the level or change in HIs (Figure 6.3).

From the chart, it appears that neither the violence nor HIs had a major impact on the growth rate. Indeed, the worst violence, as measured by deaths, occurred in the 1970s when there was some catch-up with the rest of the UK. In terms of the effects of growth on HIs, the case supports the conclusion, as suggested, that the consequences of growth for HIs depends in part on ethnic specialisation and the changing structure of the economy, since the decline in shipbuilding and manufacturing and the rise in public sector employment was favourable to Catholics. In addition, on the social side, public policy was critical – with effective policies aimed to reduce disparities in access to publicly provided goods such as education and housing. Moreover, active antidiscrimination policies helped to reduce HIs in both economic and social aspects.

6.3.5 Malaysia

Malaysia provides another example showing that growth can be associated with falling HIs when accompanied by policies towards this end. On independence, Malaya inherited a situation of deep inequalities

---

[8] This assumes that the Gini of Northern Ireland followed that of the UK as a whole in rising sharply in the 1980s (for which there is no separate evidence). Evidence for the 2000s shows inequality in Northern Ireland to be less than the UK, but to move broadly in tandem, with fluctuations and a slight rise over the 2000s (Tinson et al., 2016).

between three communities – the Chinese who formed the commercial class and were substantially the richest group; the *bumiputeras* (an umbrella term for indigenous groups in Malaysia), who were dominantly peasant farmers and were the poorest group; and the Indians – who were divided into two groups – professionals and low-paid plantation workers. The *bumiputera* constituted about two-thirds of the population, and their poverty relative to other groups threatened political stability. Consequently, the New Economic Policy was introduced in 1971, following anti-Chinese riots in 1969, to help secure national unity, aiming to reduce inequalities between the Malays and the Chinese. There was a two-pronged approach: "to reduce and eventually eradicate poverty" and "to accelerate the process of restructuring Malaysian society to correct economic imbalance so as to reduce and eventually eliminate the identification of race with economic function" (Second Malaysian Plan, 1971–1975). In addition to a variety of antipoverty policies (rural development; social services), restructuring policies included expanding the *bumiputera* share of capital ownership to 30%; allocating 95% of new lands to Malays; instituting educational quotas in public institutions in line with population shares; and credit policies favouring Malays, in terms of both credit allocations and more favourable interest rates. At the same time, there was a massive expansion of education (as part of the correction of inequalities in access). Universal primary education was attained, and gross secondary enrolment rose from 34 % in 1970 to more than 77% by 2015 (Faizli, 2012). GDP growth accelerated compared with the pre-independence era; it was nearly 7% in the 1960s almost 8% in the 1970s, and fluctuated between 5% and 7% from 2000 to 2015. This growth was accompanied by structural transformation – with an expansion of manufacturing, whose share of GDP more than doubled from 14.0% in 1970 to 31% in 2000 (but it then fell back to 20% by 2016 with a corresponding rise in the share of services); the share of the public sector (dominated by *bumiputera*) also rose initially, up to the early 1980s, but then fell back again. The combination of structural change and affirmative action policies successfully reduced HIs: the ratio of *bumiputera* average incomes to Chinese moved from 0.44 to 0.70 between 1970 and 2012, the ratio of share ownership from 0.03 to 0.24 (1970–2011), and the *bumiputera* share of registered professionals went from 5% to 51% from 1970 to 2008 (Faaland et al., 2003; Malaysia Government, 2010; Sundaram,

2001; Wahab, N.D.). VI also declined substantially from a Gini of 0.55 in 1975 to 0.4 in 2015 (OECD, 2016)

However, while the policies have been successful in reducing inequalities, they have aroused considerable opposition among the Chinese and Indians. Consequently, the government is considering moving away from direct action, but this, naturally, is meeting powerful opposition from among the *Bumiputera* population (Malaysia Government, 2010).

6.3.6 Conclusions from the Four Cases

Of course, just four cases can only be illustrative and not conclusive. These four cases suggest that the existence of HIs is not an obvious impediment to growth unless they lead to violent conflict which can have serious negative growth consequences. This view is confirmed by some preliminary statistical analysis of the relationship between the level of HIs and growth across African countries.[9] At the same time, growth can be associated with either rising or falling HIs. In the cases of Ghana and Peru, economic HIs seem to have risen while social ones fell owing to active government policy. In NI and Malaysia, in contrast, both economic and social HIs fell during a period of GDP growth – in each case this was due to a combination of structural change favouring the deprived group and deliberate policies to improve their position. Probably both are needed, because structural change is only likely to alter economic inequalities if obstacles to full participation are removed, while action on access to public goods alone without structural change may be insufficient. In South Africa, e.g., there have been efforts to improve the participation of the black population, including antidiscrimination legislation and black empowerment policies, but there has been limited structural change, and slow growth in output and employment, so while black–white differentials have improved on average, this is almost entirely owing to improvements at the top and the position of the black working class remains very poor (Mancini et al., 2008).

The evidence from these four cases shows that changes in VI are unrelated to changes in HIs, as has been shown more systematically

---

[9] By Graham Brown; a lack of data is a problem for carrying out time series, including country fixed effects, which is needed to investigate this issue properly.

elsewhere (Mancini, 2005; Østby, 2003). In these cases, rising economic HIs were accompanied by a falling Gini measure of VI in Peru in the 2000s; while Ghana, with rising economic HIs saw a rising Gini; in the cases where HIs were falling, in Malaysia this was accompanied by falling VI but in NI, we believe it was accompanied by rising VI.

6.4 Policy Conclusions

The evidence does not support the view that greater inequality (VI or HI) is likely to lead to higher growth. Indeed, for VI, Berg and Ostry (2011) have produced evidence to show that lower vertical equality is likely to lead to more sustained economic growth. There is less systematic evidence on HIs and growth, but both a priori arguments and case studies suggest that reducing HIs is likely, if anything, to affect growth positively as societies can draw on the potential of all their populations, while social stability increases.

There are also, of course, strong normative reasons for reducing inequality. Starting with the assumption that all humans are of equal worth, it is difficult to justify substantial inequalities, especially those that lie outside the individual's control. Thus, there is a particularly powerful argument for reducing racial, ethnic and gender inequalities, since these are characteristics which people cannot control (Roemer, 1998). In addition, it is important to reduce the risk of conflict, associated with HIs, both to avoid the human suffering involved and because of the deleterious consequences of violent conflict for the economy.

Yet at a country level, the evidence suggests that VI has been increasing in many countries in past decades, but with evidence of regional variation. Cornia and Sampsa (2001) found that the Gini coefficient rose in two-thirds of seventy-three countries they examined between 1980 and 2000. Ravallion and Chen (2012) using household survey data for 1981–2008 found a large increase in vertical income (or consumption) inequality in East Asia, Eastern Europe and Central Asia, some increase in South Asia, an increase and then a decline in Latin America and the Caribbean, a decline in the Middle East and North Africa and little change in sub-Saharan Africa. Latin America in the 2000s was an important exception with falling VI virtually everywhere (Cornia 2014; Lopez-Calva & Lustig 2012).

The sparse information on the distribution of health and education for 1995–2005 indicates considerable reductions in inequality along both dimensions in six Latin American countries (Cruces et al., 2011; Sahn & Younger, 2006), but little progress on health and some on education in sub-Saharan African countries (Sahn & Younger 2007). However, part of the compression of such inequalities is due to the way performance is measured.

As far as HIs are concerned, the four case studies suggest that economic inequalities tend to rise in developing countries unless there is explicit policy to counter them, but some social inequalities – such as health and education – are more likely to fall as countries move towards the comprehensive provision of services. As noted, an analysis of regional inequalities in Europe (Barrios & Strobl, 2005) indicates a Kuznets-type inverted U curve, with regional inequalities first rising and then falling as development proceeds. Most developing countries would be in the upward portion of the curve. In confirmation of that there is evidence of rising regional economic inequalities in a number of sub-Saharan African countries such as Nigeria, Uganda and Ghana (Langer & Stewart, 2011; Mancini, 2009), while evidence suggests that regional inequalities in China rose earlier and then began to narrow (Fan & Mingjie, 2008).

The widespread acknowledgment that high and rising inequality is undesirable, especially in the context of the high levels of inequality prevalent and the tendencies towards rising inequalities, suggests that systematic policies to reduce inequality are needed. Below we provide a brief outline of policies likely to reduce inequality, first for vertical, then for HI.

6.5 Policies toward VIs

VIs may broadly be divided into policies likely to affect primary (pre-tax and benefits) distribution and those directed toward post-tax and expenditure distribution.

6.5.1 Asset Redistribution

Land reform is the most frequently advocated form of asset redistribution, and historically, it has played an important part in improving primary redistribution, including in South Korea, Taiwan, and a number of Latin American countries (El Ghonemy, 1990; Lipton, 2009). The nationalisation of major industries reduced inequalities in asset ownership in many countries following independence, but privatisation contributed to increasing inequality from the 1980s. Taxation of assets (e.g., on death or in the form of a wealth tax may also reduce asset inequality; Atkinson, 2015; Piketty, 2014). Asset distribution may also be improved by schemes to share wealth from natural assets. An example is the Alaskan Permanent Fund, designed to ensure that the population at large would benefit from the discovery of oil and natural gas. A 1976 amendment to the constitution of the State of Alaska specified that at least 25% of all mineral royalties were to be placed in a permanent fund for the benefit of the whole population.

6.5.2 Income Distribution From Earnings

Increasing access to education can contribute to improving the distribution of earnings from work; minimum wages for unskilled work can also be equalising; and rapid growth of employment, through labour-intensive growth, spreads earning opportunities. Extending education and raising minimum wages are believed to have contributed to the recent improvements in income distribution in some Latin American countries, in addition to cash transfers (Cornia, 2014). In contrast, the improved distribution achieved in some East Asian countries in the 1960s and 1970s has been attributed to a combination of land reform and labour-intensive growth (Fei et al., 1979). Atkinson (2000) argued that incomes at the top are partly determined by convention and norms, and these have been moving in an inegalitarian direction. Hence, a reversal of such norms would assist in reducing inequality at the top. Maximum incomes, in principle, can restrict the earned income of the rich. While this approach has never been adopted systematically, the idea of putting pressure on companies to restrain payments to highest-earning employees is gaining ground.

6.5.3 Policies Towards Secondary Distribution (Post-Tax and Benefits)

Progressive taxation can improve the distribution of both assets (through estate duties and capital taxes as noted above) and income (via income taxes). Yet recently there has been a tendency to move in a regressive direction, with lower marginal income tax rates, reduced rates of corporation tax, an increasing role for indirect taxation, and uniform rates of indirect taxation on all goods (via a value-added tax). Both taxation and expenditures can reduce income inequality. A recent study of selected countries, cited earlier, showed that net direct taxes were invariably equalising, and in a large number of cases, indirect taxes were too. On balance taxes and transfers taken as a whole, were always equalising, the extent varying across countries: "In Ethiopia, Guatemala, Indonesia, Jordan, and Sri Lanka, fiscal income redistribution is quite limited, reducing the Gini by less than 0.03 Gini points, whereas in Brazil, Georgia, and South Africa, fiscal policy reduces the Gini by more than 0.12 Gini points" (Inchauste & Lustig, 2017, p. 9). Public expenditure too on the social sectors was found to be particularly equalising, relative to the impact of fiscal policy, in poor countries such as Bolivia and Indonesia. Consequently, increasing both taxation and expenditure as a proportion of GDP reduces inequality in resource access. Both taxes and expenditures can be designed to be more or less progressive. As far as taxation is concerned, it is a matter of the balance of direct to indirect taxation, and the design of both types. Public expenditure, too, can be made more or less progressive according to its sectorial distribution, with social services generally benefitting poorer people more than others. The nature of sectorial activities can also affect the distribution of benefits across the population, with some sorts of expenditure being more progressive than others (e.g., primary health as compared with hospitals) (Chu et al., 2000; van de Walle & Nead, 1995). A range of benefits in kind or cash can also be targeted to poorer sections of the population. These include conditional and unconditional cash transfers, which can materially affect the secondary distribution (Barrientos & Hulme, 2008). Conditional cash transfers in Brazil, Mexico, and Chile are estimated to have reduced inequality by 15% to 21% at a cost of less than 1% of the GDP (Soares et al., 2007).

Globalisation tends to constrain progressive taxation, because companies and individuals may move to other countries to escape such taxation. This tendency could be overcome by global (and regional) coordination on tax rates, or by changes in the basis of taxation (e.g., by taxing individuals in their country of citizenship irrespective of where they live or where their incomes are earned).

6.6 Policies toward HIs

Here we can differentiate between direct and indirect policies. The former target particular groups (through quotas, etc.), while the latter aim to achieve a similar inequality-reducing effect through general policies, such as taxation or universal services (Stewart, 2008). The first type of policies are often described as affirmative action, and have been adopted quite extensively in multi-ethnic societies (Brown et al., 2012; Simms, 1995). They can be effective in reducing inequalities, but sometimes have some undesirable effects including by entrenching identity distinctions. Specific policies to encourage societal integration are needed to avoid or reduce the enhancement of such divisions.

Indirect policies towards HIs consist in general policies, such as taxation or antidiscrimination law, which have the effect of reducing groups inequalities. Many of the policies towards reducing VI would form part of indirect policies towards HIs, and would tend to reduce HIs as well as VI. In addition, geographic targeting of public expenditure in countries where groups are geographically concentrated is often a relevant indirect policy, and antidiscrimination law can also be a powerful policy if effectively implemented. These policies tend to have weaker impact and to take more time than direct policies, but can be very effective if taken as a complement to direct policies, as in Malaysia and NI.

Like the policies toward vertical distribution, policies towards HIs tend to meet political resistance, but they can also gain strong political support from deprived groups.

6.7 Political Economy of Policy Making

Despite the accepted view that reducing inequality is typically desirable, in general there has only been limited policy change in this direction especially in recent decades. This is generally not owing to lack of knowledge about policies that would be effective, if adopted, but because of political objectives and constraints. Indeed, many policies currently being adopted (often with the support of the international financial institutions) are likely to increase inequality, such as the reduction of marginal rates of income tax, cutbacks in public expenditure, privatisation of public services, and land entitlement schemes, while the (near) unregulated market economy also seems to be unequalising. There is a lack of support for tackling inequalities at the international level too.

Ultimately, the question of reducing inequality comes down to politics. Where there is strong political support for progressive policies—e.g., as a result of social movements, workers' and peasants' associations, or powerful ethnic or religious groups in the case of HI, policies to correct inequalities have been adopted (McGuire, 2010; Polanyi, 1944; Stewart, 2010). But, where poorer groups are badly organised, political parties are weak and non-ideological, and corporate pressure groups are strong, progressive policy change is unlikely. However, in those societies that succeeded in achieving full or near full employment, the relative bargaining and market position of poorer members of society is greatly improved, and policy change to reduce inequality becomes much more feasible. This occurred in Europe after the Second World War, and in several developing countries in recent decades, including Taiwan and South Korea. Currently, China is approaching this situation. Thus, a combination of organisation among poorer groups and rapid employment growth seems to be most propitious for reducing inequality.

6.8 Conclusions

On the basis of a priori arguments, a review of empirical evidence and some country cases, this paper has suggested that there is no trade-off between inequality (either vertical or horizontal) and economic growth. Indeed, there are arguments for concluding that more equality is likely to support economic growth. This is especially so in relation to HI since large group inequalities lead to a failure to use the full potential of those groups who suffer deprivation, and they can also lead to political instability which has severe adverse effects on economic growth. VI can also impede sustained growth because it can lead to economic instability and may lead to less human investments than in more egalitarian societies.

Despite the desirability of more equality – both vertical and horizontal – there has been some tendency for such inequalities to rise in many parts of the world. The chapter explored policy options for reducing inequalities, drawing on the experience of countries that have succeeded in attaining equalising economic growth. There is a large range of feasible equalising policies, which have been adopted successfully in different countries. The major obstacle to such policies is political. They tend to be adopted in situations where there is strong support for more equalising policies usually arising from social and political movements among the poorer members (or groups) in society.

References

Adelman, I., and Morris, C. T. 1973. *Economic Growth and Social Equity in Developing Countries*. Stanford, CA: Stanford University Press.

Alesina, A., and Perotti, R. 1994. The political economy of growth: A critical survey of the recent literature. *World Bank Economic Review*, 8(3), pp. 351–371.

Alesina, A., and Rodrik, D. 1994. Distributive politics and economic growth. *Quarterly Journal of Economics*, 109(2), pp. 465–490.

Atkinson, A. B. 2000. *Is Rising Inequality Unavoidable? A Critique of the Transatlantic Consensus*. Helsinki: UNU-WIDER.

2015. *Inequality: What Can Be Done?* Cambridge, MA: Harvard University Press.

Banerjee, A. V., and Duflo, E. 2003. Inequality and growth: What can the data say? *Journal of Economic Growth*, 8(3), pp. 667–699.

Barrientos, A., and Hulme, D. 2008. *Social Protection for the Poor and Poorest: Concepts, Policies and Politics*. Basingstoke, UK: Palgrave Macmillan.

Barrios, S., and Strobl, E. 2005. *The dynamics of regional inequalities*. Retrieved from www.cepr.org/meets/wkcn/2/2357/papers/barrios.pdf. Accessed 18 March 2013.

Barro, R. J. 2008. *Inequality and Growth Revisited (ADB Working Papers on Regional Integration)*. Manila: Asian Development Bank.

Bénabou, R. 1996. Inequality and growth. In Bernake, B., and Rotemberg, J. (eds.), *NBER Macroeconomic Annual*. Cambridge, MA: MIT Press, pp. 11–74.

Berg, A. G., and Ostry, J. D. 2011. *Inequality and Unsustainable Growth: Two Sides of the Same Coin? (IMF Staff Discussion Note)*. Washington, DC: IMF.

Berman, E., Bound, J., and Machin, S. 1997. *Implications of Skill-Biased Technological Change: International Evidence*. Boston: Boston University.

Birdsall, N., Ross, D., and Sabot, R. 1995. Inequality and growth reconsidered: Lessons from East Asia. *World Bank Economic Review*, 9(3), pp. 477–508.

Bourgignon, F., and Morrisson, C. 1990. Income distribution, development and foreign trade. *European Economic Review*, 34(6), pp. 1113–1132.

Bourguignon, F. 1995. *Comment on 'Inequality, Poverty and Growth: Where do We Stand? (Annual World Bank Conference on Development Economics)*. Washington, DC: World Bank.

Brown, G., Langer, A., and Stewart, F. (eds.). 2012. *Affirmative Action in Plural Societies: International Experiences*. London: Palgrave.

Brownlow, G. 2012. Business and labour since 1945. In Kennedy, L., and Ollerenshaw, P. (eds.), *Ulster Since 1600. Politics, Economy, and Society*. Oxford: Oxford University Press, pp. 291–308.

Canning, M. 2017. Protestant and Catholic Employment Rates Level for the First Time in Northern Ireland. *Belfast Telegraph*, 26 January 2017.

Cederman, L.-E., Weidmann, N. B., and Gleditsch, K.S . 2011. Horizontal inequalities and ethno-nationalist civil war: A global comparison. *American Political Science Review*, 105(3), pp. 478–495.

Chu, K.-Y., Davoodi, H. R., Gupta, S., and World Institute for Development Economics Research 2000. *Income Distribution and Tax, and Government Social Spending Policies in Developing Countries*. Helsinki: UNU-WIDER.

Collier, P., and World Bank. 2003. *Breaking the Conflict Trap Civil War and Development Policy (A World Bank policy research report)*. Washington, DC: Oxford University Press.

Cooke, E., Hague, S., and McKay, A. 2016. *The Ghana Poverty and Inequality report*. Accra, Ghana: UNICEF.

Cornia, G. A. 2004. *Inequality, Growth, and Poverty in an Era of Liberalization and Globalization*. Oxford: Oxford University Press.

2014. *Falling Inequality in Latin America: Policy Changes and Lessons*. Oxford: Oxford University Press.

Cornia, G. A., and Martorano, B. 2011. Democracy, the New Left and income distribution: Latin America over the last decade. In Fitzgerald, V. Heyer, J., and Thorp, R. (eds.), *Overcoming the Persistence of Inequality and Poverty*. London: Palgrave, pp. 172–202.

Cornia, G. A., and Sampsa, K. 2001. *Trends in Income Distribution in the Post-World War II Period Evidence and Interpretation (WIDER Discussion Paper)*. Helsinki: UNU-WIDER.

Cruces, G., Garcia Domench C. G. C., and Gasparini, L. 2011. *Inequality in Education: Evidence for Latin America (WIDER Working Paper)*. Helsinki: UNU-WIDER.

Deininger, K., and Squire, L. 1998. New ways of looking at old issues: Inequality and growth. *Journal of Development Economics*, 57(2), pp. 259–287.

El Ghonemy, M. R. 1990. *The Political Economy of Rural Poverty: The Case for Land Reform*. London: Routledge.

Equality Commission for Northern Ireland. 2016. Key Inequalities in Education. Draft Statement. Retrieved from www.equalityni.org/ECNI/media/ECNI/Publications/Delivering%20Equality/Education-KeyI nequalities_DraftStatement.pdf. Accessed 8 October 2017.

Faaland, J., Parkinson, J. R., and Saniman, R. 2003. *Growth and Ethnic Inequality: Malaysia's New Economic Policy*. Kuala Lumpur: Utusan Publications & Distributors.

Faizli, A. A. 2012. Bumiputera professionals breakdown 1970–2008. Retrieved from http://aafaizli.com/bumiputera-professionals-breakdown-1970–2008/. Accessed 29 September 2017.

Fan, C. C., and Mingjie, S. 2008. Regional inequality in China, 1978–2006. *Eurasian Geography and Economics*, 49(1), pp. 1–20.

Fei, J. C. H., Ranis, G., and Kuo, S. W. Y. 1979. *Growth with Equity: The Taiwan Case*. New York: World Bank (by Oxford University Press).

Fishlow, A. 1972. Brazilian Size Distribution of Income. *American Economic Review* 62(1/2), pp. 391–402.

    1995. *Inequality, Poverty and Growth: Where Do We Stand? (Annual World Bank Conference on Development Economics)*. Washington, DC: World Bank.

Forbes, K. J. 2000. A reassessment of the relationship between inequality and growth. *American Economic Review*, 90(4), pp. 869–887.

Galenson, W., and Leibenstein, H. 1955. Investment criteria, productivity, and economic development. *Quarterly Journal of Economics*, 69(3), pp. 343–370.

Inchauste, G., and Lustig, N. (eds.). 2017. *The Distributional Impact of Taxes and Transfers: Evidence from Eight Low- and Middle-Income Countries*. Washington DC: World Bank.

Kuznets, S. 1955. Economic growth and income inequality. *American Economic Review*, 65(1), pp. 1–28.

Lacavone, L., Sanchez-Bayardo, L. F., and Shrma, S. 2015. *Regional Productivity Convergence in Peru (World Bank Policy Research Working Paper No. 7491)*. Washington, DC: World Bank.

Langer, A., and Stewart, F. 2011. Macroeconomic policies in post-conflict countries. In Langer, A., Stewart, F., and Venugopal, R. (eds.). London: Palgrave, pp. 28–60.

Li, H., and Zou, H.-F. 1998. Income inequality is not harmful for growth: Theory and evidence. *Review of Development Economics*, 2(3), pp. 318–334.

Lipton, M. 2009. *Land Reform in Developing Countries: Property Rights and Property Wrongs*. London, New York: Routledge.

Lopez-Calva, L. F., and Lustig, N. 2012. *Decline in Inequality in Latin America: Technology Change, Educational Upgrading and Democracy.* Washington, DC: Brookings Institution.

Malaysia Government. 2010. *Tenth Malaysia Plan 2011–2015.* Putrajaya: Economic Planning Unit Prime Minister's Department.

Mancini, L. 2005. *Horizontal Inequalities and Communal Violence: Evidence from Indonesian Districts (CRISE Working Paper No. 22).* Oxford: Oxford Department of International Development.

   2008. Horizontal inequality and communal violence: Evidence from Indonesian districts. In Stewart, F. (ed.), *Horizontal Inequalities and Conflict: Understanding Group Violence in Multiethnic Societies.* London: Palgrave, pp. 106–135.

   2009. *Comparative Trends in Ethno-Regional Inequalities in Ghana and Nigeria: Evidence from Demographic and Health Surveys (CRISE Working Papers).* Oxford: Oxford Department of International Development.

Mancini, L., Stewart, F., and Brown, G. K. 2008. Approaches to the measurement of horizontal inequalities. In Stewart, F. (ed.), *Horizontal Inequalities and Conflict; Understanding Group Violence in Multiethnic Societies.* London: Palgrave, pp. 85–105.

McGuire, J. 2010. *Wealth, Health and Democracy in East Asia and Latin America.* Cambridge: Cambridge University Press.

McNamee, M. S. 2017. Revealed: 47% of higher education students are Catholics and 30% Protestants. *Belfast Telegraph,* 28 June 2017.

Myrdal, G. 1956. *Development and Under-Development: A Note on the Mechanism of National and International Economic Inequality.* Cairo: National Bank of Egypt.

Northern Ireland Statistics and Research Agency. 2012. *Census 2011: Population and Household Estimates for Northern Ireland: Laid before the Northern Ireland Assembly Under: Section 4(1) of the Census Act (Northern Ireland)1969.* Belfast, Northern Ireland: Statistics and Research Agency.

Nussbaum, M. 2000. Women's capabilities and social justice. *Journal of Human Development,* 1(2), pp. 219–247.

OECD. 2016. *First OECD Economic Assessment of Malaysia 2016.* Paris: OECD.

Okun, A. M. 1975. *Equality and Efficiency: The Big Tradeoff.* Washington, DC: Brookings Institution.

Orihuela, J. C. 2012. Post-conflict economic policy and group inequalities in Peru. In Langer, A., Stewart, F., and Venugopal, R. (eds.), *Horizontal Inequalities in a Post-Conflict Context.* London: Palgrave, pp. 186–208.

Østby, G. 2003. *Horizontal Inequalities and Civil War*. PhD Thesis. Norwegian University of Science and Technology.

Panizza, U. 1999. *Income Inequality and Economic Growth: Evidence from American Data (IADB Working Paper)*. Washington, DC: Inter-American Development Bank.

Persson, T., and Tabellini, G. 1994. Is inequality harmful for growth? *American Economic Review*, 84(3), pp. 600–621.

Piketty, T. 2014. *Capital in the Twenty-First Century*. Cambridge, MA: Belknap, Harvard.

Polanyi, K. 1944. *The Great Transformation*. Boston: Beacon Press.

Ravallion, M., and Chen, S. 2012. Monitoring Inequality. *Lets Talk Development, A blog hosted by the World Bank's Chief economist*. Retrieved from http://blogs.theworldbank.org/developmenttalk/monitoringinequality. Accessed 18 March 2013.

Roemer, J. E. 1998. *Equality of Opportunity*. Cambridge, MA: Harvard University Press.

Rowthorn, B., and Wayne, N. 1988. *Northern Ireland: The Political Economy of Conflict*. Cambridge: Polity.

Sahn, D. E., and Younger, S. D. 2006. Changes in inequality and poverty in Latin America: Looking beyond income to health and education. *Journal of Applied Economics*, IX(2), pp. 215–234.

2007. *Inequality and Poverty in Africa in an Era of Globalization: Looking beyond Income to Health and Education (UNU-WIDER Research Paper)*. Helsinki: UNU-WIDER.

Samman, E., Ranis, G., and Stewart, F. 2011. *Inequality in Multiple Dimensions of Human Development*. Oxford: Queen Elizabeth House.

Seini, W. 2012. *Trade Policy and Horizontal Inequality in Ghana*. Oxford: Queen Elizabeth House.

Sen, A. K. 1977. Rational fools: A critique of the behavioral foundations of economic theory. *Philosophy and Public Affairs*, 6(4), pp. 317–344.

1980. *Equality of What?* Tanner Lectures on Human Values. Stanford University, 22 May 1979.

1999. *Development as Freedom (DAF)*. Oxford: Oxford University Press.

Simms, M. C. (ed.). 1995. *Economic Perspectives on Affirmative Action*. Washington, DC: University Press of America.

Soares, S., Osorio, R. G., and Soares, F. V. 2007. *Conditional Cash Transfers in Brazil, Chile and Mexico: Impacts upon Inequality*. Rio de Janeiro: International Poverty Centre.

Stewart, F. 2002. *Horizontal Inequality: A Neglected Dimension of Development. UNU-WIDER Annual Lecture Series no. 5*. Helsinki: UNU-WIDER.

Stewart, F. (ed.). 2008. *Horizontal Inequalities and Conflict: Understanding Group Violence in Multiethnic Societies.* London: Palgrave.

2010. Power and progress: The swing of the pendulum. *Journal of Human Development and Capabilities,* 11(3), pp. 371–395.

2013. *Approaches towards Inequality and Inequity.* Firenze: UNICEF.

Stewart, F., and Fitzgerald, V. 2001. *War and Underdevelopment Volume 1: The Economic and Social Consequences of Conflict.* Oxford: Oxford University Press.

Sundaram, J. K. 2001. Malaysia's New Economic Policy and "National Unity". In Banjura, Y., and Stavenhagen, R. (eds.), *Racism and Public Policy.* New York: Palgrave Macmillan, pp. 182–214.

Thorp, R., Cárdenas, E., and Ocampo, J. A. 2000. *An Economic History of Twentieth-century Latin America.* New York: Basingstoke.

Thorp, R., and Paredes, M. (eds.). 2010. *Ethnicity and the Persistence of Inequality the Case of Peru.* New York: Palgrave Macmillan.

Tinson, A., Aldridge, H., and MacInnes, T. 2016. *Economic Inequality in Northern Ireland. (Centre for Economic Empowerment Research Report 14).* Belfast: New Policy Institute.

Todd, J., and Ruane, J. 2012. Beyond inequality? Assessing the impact of fair employment, affirmative action and equality measures on conflict in Northern Ireland. In Brown, Langer, A., and Stewart, F. (eds.), *Affirmative Action in Developing Countries: International Experience.* London: Palgrave, pp. 182–208.

Van de Walle, D., and Nead, K. 1995. *Public Spending and the Poor: Theory and Evidence.* Baltimore, MD: Johns Hopkins University Press (for the World Bank).

Wahab, M. E. A. A. N.D. The myth of high income nation. Achievable. . .but at what cost. Retrieved from www.slideshare.net/effuan/the-myth-of-high-income-nation-72396656. Accessed 29 September 2017.

Wolff, J., and de-Shalit, A. 2007. *Disadvantage.* Oxford: Oxford University Press.

Wood, A., and Ridao-Cano, C. 1996. *Skill, Trade and International Inequality (IDS Working Paper).* Sussex: Institute of Development Studies.

World Bank. 2005. *Pro-Poor Growth in the 1990s.* Washington, DC: World Bank.

7 | Vertical and Horizontal Decentralisation for Equity and Stability

GUSTAV RANIS[1]

7.1 Introduction: Vertical versus Horizontal Decentralisation

Before we explore the interactions between decentralisation and ethnic diversity in sub-Saharan Africa, it is important to first highlight the distinctions between two forms of decentralisation – vertical and horizontal. The vertical form, whether via deconcentration, delegation or devolution, represents some relinquishing of control over public resources and decision making by the central government and extending both towards lower levels of government (Rondinelli et al., 1989). In most cases, it represents some type of delegation, with resources sent down to local governments, usually conditionally, sometimes unconditionally. It infrequently comes close to an actual devolution of power. Privatisation is the last, improbable, step in vertical decentralisation.

Horizontal decentralisation deals with the shift of decision-making power from the finance ministry of the executive branch towards the line ministries concerned with human development-oriented fields, including health and education. It also, significantly, entails a shift of power from the executive branch of government towards the legislative and judicial branches, which is often a sign of democratisation.

The arguments for and against vertical decentralisation are fairly well-known. The main pro argument is that getting close to the people entails better information about local conditions, enhanced efficiency, and lower transactions costs. It gives local governments, often administratively weak at the start, a chance to learn by doing, provides for greater flexibility and scope for innovation, with experimental successes replicable (as in China). The need for some delegation or even devolution becomes more urgent as the economy becomes more complex and more difficult for central authorities to manage efficiently.

---

[1] An earlier version of this chapter has been updated by Frances Stewart, with generous assistance from Rachael Diprose on the Indonesian case.

A second pro argument is that local people may be more willing to raise existing local taxes, or even introduce new ones, when they see the direct benefits of expenditures. The argument is also made that accountability, upward and downward, is enhanced, especially in multi-ethnic contexts. In other words, the local gold fish bowl accountability and transparency context tends to reduce corruption levels. More locally available information reduces all but petty corruption, while at the centre, accountability is diffused and the potential for grand theft corruption increases. On the critical issue of achieving agreement on the quantity and quality of public goods, vertical decentralisation should also be helpful, especially when it is associated with greater ethnic homogeneity. Finally, and critical to the argument, vertical decentralisation increases the chances for horizontal decentralisation and democratisation at both the central and, more important, the local level, i.e., the ability of local people to voice their preferences in relation to local government. It is also important in moving towards a judiciary more independent of the executive branch.

The arguments against vertical decentralisation are equally well-known. The most formidable is that human capacity at local government levels is too weak and too subject to the power of local elites, i.e., corruption may be greater at the local level than it is at the national level, especially when there are many layers of local government and many people expecting extra-legal benefits. It is even claimed that, by diminishing the power of the unifying centre, vertical decentralisation enhances the overall influence of ethnic heterogeneity in the body politic. Moreover there is evidence that the more layers of government, the greater the tendency for resources to be applied to increasing the number of civil service employees and their salaries. This is one reason why the Indonesian fast-track decentralisation of recent years had to be partially reassessed and dialled back. Especially if natural resources are unequally distributed across a country, vertical decentralisation can lead to more dissatisfaction and unrest because it is up to the centre to ensure equity across regions. Overall, vertical decentralisation tends to increase total expenditures on public goods and the share of human development-oriented public goods but increases inequality across regions. Indeed, vertical decentralisation can represent a potential threat to national unity, underlining the need to retain not only macro stability functions at the centre but also to redistribute resources across regions depending on, for example, differential poverty levels.

Country size and the extent of ethnic diversity clearly matter. While small homogeneous units of government favour agreement on public goods, economies of scale may have to be sacrificed. Ethnic homogeneity at the local level may help to foster agreement and enhance the volume and quality of public goods but may reduce national unity. For the advantages of vertical decentralisation to be fully realised, a thoroughgoing devolution of authority would be optimal. A unified government career service – including pay, promotions and transfers – would be an essential accompaniment, but is seldom in evidence.

Most decentralisation efforts instead stop at deconcentration or delegation, with local administrative and revenue raising capacity seen as inadequate by the centre and reduced equity across provinces seen as a threat. Clearly, the centre must retain primary responsibility for horizontal equity as well as macro stabilisation, defence, and major economic infrastructure. But there are always four questions: Who is assigned what tasks and attendant expenditures? Who levies which taxes? How are gaps financed – avoiding borrowing and moral hazards and macro instability? How are horizontal imbalances addressed? The central government determines the extent and nature of progressive, mobile taxes such as the income tax. Local governments levy user charges, property taxes, and other less mobile taxes. Regional projects, national public goods, economies of scale, and equity across provinces indicate where the centre should prevail. Other expenditures under vertical decentralisation redound to local bodies. This means dependence on the centre for fiscal resources. It follows that the centre must continue to exercise control over the most important tax sources. Indeed, in a sample of countries for 2006–2010, developing countries' central government revenues comprise 86% of the total compared with 73% in developed countries (Gadenne & Singhal, 2014). As an economy develops and its complexity increases, the influence of the colonial centre-oriented heritage is diminished. Consequently the predominance of government grants to local bodies – creating perverse incentives – gradually diminishes and local taxes are enhanced. But local taxes still tend to be limited, constrained by the centre and administratively deficient in terms of tax evasion, and a lack of effective controls and sanctions. It also follows that transfers from above, conditional or unconditional, continue to play a critical role, administered, if possible, in a way which does not favour wealthier areas or lead to a disincentive to raise local taxes. Central grants need to be predictable and transparent, not subject to annual bargaining. In some cases local government can borrow domestically or internationally but needs central government approval to obey macroeconomic policy constraints and avoid moral hazard issues. Municipal development funds may provide a good alternative to letting local governments borrow at home or abroad.

Relevant data to be used to measure the level of vertical decentralisation include:

1) Expenditure decentralisation ratios: percentage of government expenditure (not including defence and debt services) spent by local government;
2) Revenue decentralisation ratios: local government revenue as a percentage of total government revenue; and
3) Financial autonomy ratios: locally raised revenue over total local expenditures.

7.2 Decentralisation, Democratisation and Ethnic Diversity

Decentralisation is a political as well as technical issue, part of the transition from authoritarian to democratic rule. Indeed, it is our contention that successful vertical decentralisation requires an accompanying political empowerment or democratisation effort. Of course hybrids are possible, i.e., horizontal decentralisation with some central inputs retained to support technical aspects and enhance overall efficiency. Since local government objectives may differ from the centre's in an authoritarian state, delegation rather than devolution is likely because there exists no counterpower to the centre. But, in a democratic system, popular pressure can move the system towards genuine devolution, even as inevitable conflicts remain. More homogeneous local units produce more public goods. Larger units are likely to be more heterogeneous and produce fewer public goods. Much depends on the extent to which people's preferences are conveyed to decision makers at all levels of government. And the extent of ethnic diversity is critical to this issue. Power sharing at both the centre and lower levels is likely to improve relationships among heterogeneous groups and reduce the likelihood of veto playing and conflict. The quality and quantity of public goods at the local level are bound to be affected by the extent of diversity.

More heterogeneous units are likely to generate less revenue and fewer public goods than more homogeneous units at the local level. It follows that the extent of influence on public sector decision making depends partly on the homogeneity of local units, which in turn depends partly on their size – the larger are more likely to be heterogeneous – and partly on the extent of democratic freedom of action of the local body politic or civil society. Small homogeneous units are more likely to escape capture by minority vested interests but have less impact on collective actions agreed at a higher level. Large heterogeneous units are more likely to succumb to "free riding" and corruption problems. Power sharing at the centre among ethnic groups then becomes critical, especially in small unitary governments. In large countries, federalism becomes a common choice, enhancing vertical decentralisation patterns but encountering more tiers and more corruption. Smaller local units with natural resources can lead to competition and reduce efficiency, while larger subunits can bargain for more central support and weaken macro policy.

Democracy, one of the ingredients of horizontal decentralisation, seems to be more in evidence in countries with higher levels of income, though Przeworski and Limongi (1993) question the relationship between economic growth and democracy at any level of per capita income. Indeed at low levels of income, democracy may be counter-productive. However, Alesina and La Ferrara (2000) find democracy generally helpful for growth in conditions of ethnic diversity. With one-third of sub-Saharan Africa's population living in economies dominated by natural resources, the resulting rents make patronage politics dominant in determining public goods and thus serve to undermine democracy. Local participation is more likely under democratic pluralist national regimes. When the nation state is of the one-party authoritarian variety, vertical decentralisation is likely to be of the deconcentration or delegation variety, leaving little room for civil society participation. At the centre, even in cases of substantial vertical decentralisation, power usually continues to reside in the hands of the dominant ethnic group while horizontal decentralisation can provide a challenge at the local level. Vertical decentralisation needs to be strengthened by political movements, i.e., organised civil society à la Indian Panchayati Raj system. Thus, national unity is preserved but, with vertical decentralisation usually leading to the creation of new districts, local competitive leadership conflicts are encouraged. Vertical decentralization should foster democracy but not if local governments are captured by corrupt elites. Here is where horizontal decentralisation, empowering civil society, comes into play.

One important dimension of the extent of local democracy is whether heads of local legislative bodies are directly elected, indirectly elected, or appointed from above. Moreover, we must ask: What are their functions relative to local government, and who controls the technical cadres, the centre, local government, or local legislative bodies? Small, homogeneous groups create more social capital, and reduce free-riding and competition. Vertical decentralisation may create ethnically heterogeneous units of government likely to enhance local veto playing, free-riding efforts, and corruption. Some of the literature has found, however, that vertical decentralisation, without reference to diversity, tends to increase the total expenditure on public goods as well as its human development-oriented share, if at the aforementioned expense of increased inequality across provinces or regions. With reference to diversity, more homogeneous local units spend more on such public goods. In summary, the quality and quantity of public goods results from the interaction between the public sector at various levels of vertical decentralisation and the legislative branch and civil society at various levels of horizontal decentralisation, and the extent to which this interaction reflects the wishes of ethnic majorities while protecting the interests of ethnic minorities (Laitin & Fearon, 2003). One indicator of the strength of horizontal decentralisation is the percentage of the central budget allocated to the education and health ministries, another the existence of multiparty legislative branches at the centre and locally, and, a third, the prevalence and strength of nongovernmental organisations and other dimensions of civil society. Democracy can be helpful for both upward and downward accountability.

Both forms of decentralisation need to be examined within the context of the considerable ethnic diversity in sub-Saharan Africa. As a comparative reference, we also look at these issues in Indonesia.

7.3 Country Studies: Kenya, Uganda and Indonesia

We now turn to the experiences of Kenya, Uganda and Indonesia, each of which have introduced substantial measures of decentralisation over past decades.

Until 2010, Kenya was highly centralised, with revenue transfers to the local level of around 5% from 1999–2001 to 2007–2008. Menon et al. (2008) describe "the marginalisation of local authorities by the state as it sought to strengthen the powers of the chief executive, starting in the late 1960s" (p. 2). Local government revenue as a share of total current revenue fell from 17% in 1969–1970 to 5% in 1999–2000. There were few checks and balances on presidential power. However, Kenya's constitution of 2010, adopted in reaction the lethal conflicts of 2007–2008, involved substantial decentralisation, both horizontal and vertical. Provisions for greater horizontal decentralisation included the introduction of a second legislative chamber (a senate representing the localities), reforms to the judiciary to increase its independence, and a Bill of Rights. One study estimated that, in terms of separation of powers, this moved Kenya from a situation close to France (with an index of separation of powers compiled by World Bank staff of 5) to one close to the United States (with an index of 9; Ausaid & Worldbank, 2012; see Figure 12.1). It is not possible yet to assess how far these reforms (adopted in 2013) have in practice led to a genuine separation of powers of this magnitude, although the overturning of the results of the August 2017 election requiring a rerun by the judiciary is evidence in support of a diffusion of power.

Vertical decentralisation was also enacted in the new constitution, with the creation of forty-seven county governments, each with an elected governor and assembly. Important functions of government were devolved to the counties, with the centre retaining a monopoly only on security, foreign affairs and water. This involved revenue decentralisation, with a minimum of 15% of total government revenue to be transferred to the counties, in contrast to the 5% previously mandated. From 2013–2014 to 2015–2016, the counties' share of national revenue is estimated at 21%–23% (Cheeseman et al., 2016). Counties also have the right to levy certain taxes, including property taxes, but these are not extensive. Further powers of revenue raising may be granted by national legislation. Local government sources of revenue have risen, but only a few relatively rich counties have raised significant amounts of revenue, to date (Burbidge, 2016). The main revenue raising taxes (income tax and value added tax) remained the responsibility of the central government.

As we can see from Table 7.1, the reforms have greatly increased the proportion of total government expenditure that is the responsibility of

Table 7.1 *Kenya's decentralisation statistics in percentages*

Indicator	1999–2000	2003/2004	2005/2006	2006/2007	2008/2009	201/2014	2014/2015	2015/2016
Expenditure decentralisation ratio (local government expenditures)/(total government expenditures)	—	4	4	5	4	15.51	—	—
Transfers from central government as per cent total central government revenue	5.1	—	—	—	—	21	23	22
Financial autonomy ratio (local government own revenue)/(local government expenditures)	—	94	67	60	59	19[1]	—	—

[1] Estimated by World Bank on the basis of planned changes (World Bank 2012).

Sources: Kenya Human Rights Commission and Social and Public Accountability Network (2010), Mboga (2009), and World Bank World Development Indicators (2012); Dafflon and Madiès (2013); Menon et al. (2008); Cheeseman et al. (2016).

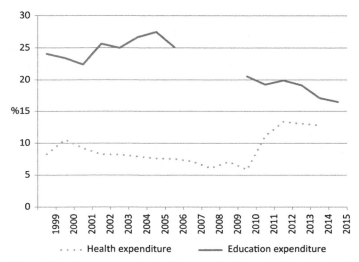

Figure 7.1 Government expenditure on health and education in Kenya as per cent of total government expenditure (1999–2015).
Source: World Bank, World Development Indicators (Accessed July 2017)

local governments, and increased revenue transfers from the central government (though probably not enough to pay for the new responsibilities according to Ausaid and Worldbank [2012]). The financial autonomy ratio of the local governments (the proportion of total funds accounted by their own revenue raising) has decreased substantially, in parallel to the increased central government transfers. But, because most of the transfers are unconditional, the autonomy is much greater than the estimated 19% figure indicates.

Expenditures on health and education, since devolution, have shown contradictory trends. Whereas education expenditure as a per cent of total government expenditure rose in the 2000s, before decentralisation, and fell after 2010 with decentralisation, we observe the opposite trends for health expenditure (Figure 7.1). However, these are aggregate trends and the decentralisation has only recently got under way. Moreover, a good deal of expenditures on both sectors remains the central government responsibility (tertiary education and most hospitals).

Politically, it has been argued, decentralisation has led to the devolution of patronage politics to the local level (D'Arcy & Cornell 2016) and empowered the elected governors who have collectively pushed for greater revenue transfers (Cheeseman et al., 2016). The early assertiveness of governors suggests that they have been empowered by the changes, representing a real diffusion of power, which is likely to make it difficult to reverse them.

It is too early to make an assessment of the Kenyan decentralisation. The reforms would be strengthened by additional revenue-raising powers, but this could be unequalising across counties. It seems likely, in any case, that the poorer counties will struggle with capacity issues. The rather modest equalisation fund is unlikely to be sufficient to compensate for the differences in levels of development. A robust legal and administrative environment for community participation in monitoring local authority is still lacking (UN-Habitat, 2002).

Both the two other cases under scrutiny, Uganda and Indonesia, have a much longer experience of vertical decentralisation, and we can observe some instructive contrasts.

Uganda's (vertical) decentralisation has been described as "one of the most radical devolution initiatives of any country at this time" (Mitchinson, 2003, p. 241). There is also evidence of some limited horizontal decentralisation, as democratic elections were reintroduced in 1995 and multiparty politics permitted from 2005. But the country scores poorly on political rights and freedoms, with a mark of thirty-six out of one hundred for civil and political liberties in 2018. It is classified as "not free" by Freedom House.

Uganda experienced bitter civil wars over the years since independence. There has been relative stability since Museveni acquired power in 1986, although for many years there was continued fighting in the north. Museveni introduced radical measures of decentralisation to the district level, partly to diffuse power and tensions. This process started with the national resistance councils, an outcome of the movement that Museveni led. A succession of reforms followed, notably in 1993 and 1997 (Green, 2008). In 1993, the first thirteen districts were decentralised and local democratically elected councils given the right to retain a proportion of locally generated resources. As a consequence, local tax collections increased substantially. Five District Council levels were created, ranging from higher (LC5) to grassroots (LC1) levels, and the number of districts rapidly expanded, with political pressure from the localities. There were 33 districts in 1986, and by 2016 there were 111. Consequently, Uganda has fewer people per district than any other African country. Most assessments are that the districts are too small for efficiency.

The LC5 or district level retains most of the resources sent down and has most of the decision-making power. In fact, LC1 and LC2 are basically administrative councils and executive committees – both focus on settling civil disputes. LC3, LC4 and LC5, which are more concerned with policy making, are rather remote from citizens' oversight. Youth, women and people with disabilities form one-third of the council, a type of horizontal decentralisation. District chairmen, selected from the elected councillors, hold very powerful positions as the political heads of the district. They nominate the district executive committee secretaries and coordinate and monitor government functions between the district and the government. Councils propose policies which have to be approved at the district level and implemented by civil service staff.

Technical staff were delinked from their parent ministries and placed under the authority of local governments in 1994, while the Central Ministry of local government retains overall supervisory responsibility. The Chief Administrative Officer, an employee of the district council, heads district civil servants and is the accounting officer who is responsible for implementation of council decisions and overseeing the performance of local government officials.

Finance for local government expenditures has been a continual problem. Initially, districts levied a graduated personal tax, accounting for 5% of their total revenues, but this was regressive and unpopular and was abolished in 2005. It was eventually replaced by a tax on hotels and on services, and these new taxes have not yet raised much revenue. Local government taxes as a whole account for less than 5% of their total revenues, although this is believed to be just one-half of the potential revenue from existing taxes (Republic of Uganda, 2016). As the Report of the Auditor General stated, "there is widespread concern that local government financing is not sufficient to meet the level of demand for service delivery" (Republic of Uganda, 2016, p. 2). A sample of thirty-two districts and municipalities showed that almost one-half of the minimum required staff were actually employed, and this was attributed to financial deficiencies (Republic of Uganda 2016).

As Table 7.2 indicates, local revenue provides just a fraction of total local government resources. While transfers from the central government provide the remainder, these have been declining as a

Table 7.2 *Decentralisation ratios in Uganda*

	2003/ 2004	2005/ 2006	2007/ 1008	2009/ 2010	2011/ 2012	2013/ 2014	2015/ 2016
Ratio of central government direct transfers to national budget	25.5	25	23.8	22.3	17.2	15.3	12.9
Ratio of central government transfers to domestic revenue	44.8	38.4	33.6	31.8	26.8	24.6	21
Local revenue as per cent of total				3 (2008/ 2009)		7.6	4.5 (2014/ 2015)
Conditional grants as per cent central government grants						88.5	88.6

Source: Data from Republic of Uganda (2016).

proportion of national revenue. Moreover, the vast bulk of central government transfers are conditional, leaving the local governments very little autonomy. Indeed, it has been suggested that Uganda has experienced some *recentralisation*, including increasing conditionalities of grants, budget restrictions and centralisation of appointments of senior local government officials (Ausaid & Worldbank, 2012). One explanation of this recentralisation is the diffusion of power to opposition groups made possible through decentralisation, which is countered by the central government through the recentralising measures noted (Ojambo, 2012).

There are no notable trends in government expenditure on health and education as a proportion of total government expenditure associated with decentralisation in Uganda (Table 7.3). But standardised public service provisions have been adapted to differing local situations. Teacher and health worker absenteeism remains high: teacher absenteeism, 2004–2011, was estimated at 27% for the country as a whole (wwww.transparency.org), and health worker absenteeism was estimated at 35% in 2011 (IntraHealth, 2017). Considerable variation in standards of provision has been observed, reflecting different capacities, revenues and political connections across districts and municipalities (Lambright, 2009).

An assessment of the impact of decentralisation on rural services – primary health, education, agricultural extension and the management of natural resources – suggests a "mixed scenario" (Bashaasha et al., 2011, p. 21). Great strides were made in increasing primary school enrolment, but quality problems remained; there was little improvement in health services; access to agricultural extension improved, but this was attributed largely to the contribution of nongovernmental organisations, while devolution seems to have improved natural

Table 7.3 *Uganda's government expenditure on health and education as per cent of total government expenditure*

Sector	2000	2002	2004	2006	2008	2010	2012	2014
Education	10.4	—	20.3	—	18.85	10.1	11.5	11
Health	8.8	11.1	12.1	15.1	16	19.5	14.3	11.7
Total	19.2	—	22.4	—	29.43	29.6	25.8	22.7

Source: World Bank, World Development Indicators (Accessed June 2016).

resource management. According to this assessment "most of the literature points to rampant corruption in Uganda's decentralised system" (Bashaasha et al., 2011, p. 6). A study in the early 2000s found that schools received only 13% of the central government grants intended for them (Reinikka & Svensson, 2004).

In multicultural societies subject to violence, like Uganda,[2] decentralisation has been argued to contribute to peace, as a result of the greater diffusion of power. It provides opportunities for power and enrichment at the local level, reaching more communities. This indeed, could be argued to have been achieved in Uganda, where, for the most part, national conflict has been avoided in recent decades. However, in some instances it has led to conflict at the local level (Green, 2008), but in general this is much less damaging than the highly costly national level violence experienced before (Matovu & Stewart, 2001).

In contrast with Uganda, Indonesia opted for a "big bang" rapid vertical decentralisation approach in 1998, but with a lagging horizontal dimension (Diprose, 2009). It should be noted that, with thousands of islands and hundreds of ethnicities, some efforts at vertical decentralisation were inevitable; Indonesia has the sixth highest cultural fractionalisation index in Asia (Fearon, 2003).[3] Data from the Ministry of Home Affairs data indicates Indonesia has thirty-four provinces and special regions, 6,543 districts and subdistricts, and 75,244 villages (Republic of Indonesia, 2018).

By the end of 2001, after the ratification of the decentralisation laws, 2.1 million of civil servants were transferred to the local level government, predominantly to the kabupatan/kota and provincial levels, the latter of which was the main locus of decentralised power. The districts and provinces (with authority mainly for sectoral issues which cross-cut district boundaries), could create policies, local legislation and regulations, and implement these with the support of subdistricts. The desa/kelurahan or villages required kabupatan/kota approval for incorporation in the design of public goods. Provincial and district legislatures (DPRD I and DPRD II) were granted full authority to elect and monitor the heads of government, which gave regional communities sovereignty over their political affairs. DPRDs also had the

[2] Uganda's ethnic fractionalization score is 0.93 and cultural fractionalization score is 0.647.
[3] Indonesia's ethnic fractionalization score is 0.766 and cultural fractionalization score is 0.522.

authority to initiate, legislate and amend regulations, as well as the authority to modify government structures and budgets. Provinces were kept relatively weak, seen as a potential threat to national unity. While civil servants were officially transferred, their wages, standards, and promotions continued to be set by the centre, indicating a de jure rather than de facto decentralisation effort. The fact that until 2004, local government leadership such as district heads and mayors were elected by DPRDs' secret ballot also reduced public accountability and increased vulnerabilities to briberies and other forms of corruption. This changed with the 2004 amendments to the decentralisation laws, allowing for the popular election of governors, district heads and mayors.

Data on fiscal decentralisation show considerable advances for each type of ratio (Table 7.4). Local government expenditure as a share of total public expenditure doubled from 2001 to 2015, reaching more than 40% by 2015. Arrangements were made for sharing revenue for a range of taxes and local governments powers to introduce taxes were increased somewhat. Dependence on transfers from the central government fell, for provinces from 57% in 2001 to 31% in 2013, but municipalities and districts remained heavily dependent on transfers from higher levels of government (Nasution, 2016).

Local governments were not permitted to borrow domestically or internationally, but in practice deficits were financed by the central government. Some advances on the horizontal decentralisation front were instituted (e.g., the heads of the powerful kabupatan were now to be elected), and local preferences were to be articulated with the help of newly created school and health committees.

In 2004, Indonesia took steps to review and curtail some of these big bang decentralisation provisions. As a consequence of the fear of increased levels of corruption at local levels, taking the form of over-staffing and enhanced emoluments for local staff, the provinces' powers were restored, with elections at local levels maintained. Moreover, some of the decentralisation efforts that began in 1998 were dialled back in the sense that central government once again resumed the power to supervise local governments. The new policy empowered local executive units by removing most of local legislatures' authorities to appoint, approve, and monitor the executive. Heads of local government were also to be directly elected instead of through DPRDs.

The virtual doubling of smaller kabupatan units, plus migratory transfers, enhanced levels of local ethnic homogeneity – this

Table 7.4 *Indonesia's decentralisation statistics in percentages*

Indicator	2000/ 2001	2002/ 2003	2004/ 2005	2008	2010	2012	2014	2015
Expenditure decentralisation ratio (local government expenditure)/(total government expenditures)	20	38	43	29	34	34	34	41
Revenue decentralisation ratio (local government revenue/total government revenue)	5	10	10	35	40	42	45	52
Financial autonomy ratio (provinces) (own-local government revenue)/(total local government revenue, province)	39				49		50b	
Financial autonomy ratio (districts and municipalities) (own-local government revenue)/(total local government rev, districts and municipalities	7				7		11b	

Source: Nasution, 2016.

arrangement favoured agreement on the quality and quantity of public goods. Planning proposals could continue to be made at the desa level but with the need for approval at higher kabupatan levels, although this changed somewhat in 2014. At the same time, the fact that, after 2005, the heads of the provinces, districts and municipalities and village heads, were now to be directly elected (rather than appointed) is an indication of enhanced democratisation. Nongovernmental organisations, civil organisations and citizens' forums called the "forum warga" (citizens forum) are quite active in exercising public accountability and serve as channels of democracy in both central and regional politics (Aspinall & Fealy, 2003). While the centre was previously in charge of reconciling the varying public goods preferences of different ethnic groups, this could now be settled at lower levels – and was assisted by the greater ethnic homogeneity at the local level. This combination of vertical and horizontal decentralisation was associated with an increase in education expenditures (from 11.6% of total government expenditures in 2001 to 19.3% in 2009 and 17.7% in 2014) and with more modest increases in health care, as shown in Table 7.5. Health and education together rose from 4.7% of GDP in 2001 to 6.1% in 2014.

On the negative side, the shared revenue formula and the allocation of grants from the centre, which is partly influenced by different natural resource endowments across provinces, tends to increase horizontal inequalities among provinces which is likely to provoke inter-ethnic friction. The continued relatively large size of transfers from the centre may also have affected local tax collections negatively. Furthermore, the competence of local public institutions in delivering public goods such as potable water, electricity, environment, transportation, and health services is still being questioned, as there are few mechanisms for public complaints about public service delivery. Overall, the public service sector is still not transparent enough (Alicias, 2007).

Table 7.5 *Indonesia's public expenditures on education and health (per cent of government expenditure)*

Sector	2001	2003	2005	2007	2009	2011	2013	2014
Education	11.59	16.28	15.15	14.94	19.31	18.01	17.60	17.67
Health	4.54	5.14	4.24	5.53	5.58	5.83	6.03	5.73
Total	16.14	21.41	19.38	20.47	24.89	23.83	23.63	23.40

Source: World Bank World Development Indicators (Accessed June 2016).

However, in 2014, decentralisation was further rolled back. Law No. 23/2014 itemises the responsibilities of the subnational governments (Nasution, 2016), and further strengthens the central government's power – it can freeze the salaries of regional heads and legislators that fail to meet budget approval deadlines and dismiss regional leaders – and that of the provincial governor as the central governments' representative in the regions (mining, forestry fisheries, and maritime affairs are now under the authority of the provincial government). At the same time, the creation of the new Ministry of Villages and the Village Law (Law No.6/2014) has seen budget transfers made direct to villages across the country to finance their own development (equal to 10% of the state budget), only 30% of which can be used to fund village government operations and the rest is to be used for development. The impacts of these changes are yet to be seen.

While vertical decentralisation has regressed with the curtailment of local governments' sovereignties compared to the early years of decentralisation (particularly at the district level), important progress on the horizontal front has been made, including increased emphasis on health, education, and other public goods and enhanced democracy via the incorporation of civil participation in local and central politics. In a large scale study of subnational patterns of violence and its relationship with decentralisation, Pierskalla and Sacks (2017) find that the introduction of the direct elections of district heads and other leaders and district splitting under decentralisation has ameliorated some pressures and reduced the propensity for violence (confirming the findings of Diprose (2009) using a larger dataset), with the exception of elections-related violence. Fiscal transfers seem to have mitigated communal violence in Indonesia, with the exception of violence in Papua (a region under special autonomy laws with special fiscal transfer arrangements), where there is a strong military presence. Yet the proximity of public service delivery to citizens generated by decentralisation, has been found to be positively correlated with the incidence of routine violence, particularly in heterogeneous districts, and particularly in the form of governance and elections-related violence. Under decentralisation, it seems that where public service provision is low overall, there are low rates of violence, but as the provision of public services increases (likely to be accompanied by an increase in expectations), there has been an increase in the frequency of violence as local governments are unable to meet expectations or favour particular groups. However, the propensity for violence to occur then decreases as even higher levels of services are provided, and, presumably, greater degrees of equity are attained (Pierskalla & Sacks, 2017).

In aggregate terms, it seems that decentralisation has been associated with greater expenditure on the social sectors and improved performance. Although teacher absenteeism persisted, a substantial improvement was observed in primary schools where it fell from 19% in 2003 to 10% in 2013, according to a 2013–2014 survey (ACDP Indonesia, 2014). A study of urban health institutions identified an absentee rate of health workers of 23%, again below an earlier (2002) national estimate of 40% (Chaudhury et al., 2006; Ramadhan, 2013).

Like Uganda, assessments suggest that decentralisation has not reduced corruption and patronage politics in Indonesia. In fact it has been argued that "patronage has expanded and become entrenched under decentralisation" (Blunt et al., 2012, p. 70), but it does seem to have been "localised" to a certain extent, involving local officials and local entrepreneurs, potentially entrenching an imperfect form of democratic decentralisation (Blunt et al., 2012).

7.4 Discussion and Conclusion

It seems clear that, especially in the case of large countries, the increased complexity accompanying economic growth calls for vertical decentralisation at least at the deconcentration or delegation level. Such decentralisation generally enhances the quality of public goods as well as the quality of its human development components. This requires increased support of local government by central grants, both conditional and unconditional, hopefully without unduly discouraging local tax efforts. The centre needs to retain control over macro-economic issues, central and regional projects, as well increase its efforts to enhance equity across decentralised units.

It is necessary to examine the extent to which horizontal decentralisation (especially where it has an ethnic dimension) is a complement to the vertical variety. If local governments are accountable to the centre under vertical decentralisation, they are accountable to democratic forces and civil society under horizontal decentralisation. The question is to what extent these democratic forces exert themselves at different levels of the decentralised hierarchy. The extent to which local decision makers are elected or appointed clearly affects the extent to which they pay attention to the preferences for public goods priorities expressed by political parties or civil society.

Finally, ethnicity plays a large role in the definition and effectiveness of vertical decentralisation. The creation of large local units favours ethnic heterogeneity and generally leads to lower levels of public goods as well as to a lower quality of those goods. Smaller local units are likely to be more homogeneous ethnically, leading to the production of more and better quality public goods. The creation of many additional local units in the course of vertical decentralisation enhances the chances of increased homogeneity, but can be costly as evidenced in both Uganda and Indonesia. With respect to corruption, while it is often argued that large-scale corruption at the centre is likely to dwarf petty corruption locally, especially when horizontal decentralisation has been mobilised, the evidence from Indonesia and Uganda suggests that corruption remains but in localised form after decentralisation. Accountability mechanisms are consequently needed at the local level with decentralisation. Clearly, the creation of too many layers of local government, creating higher transaction costs and greater opportunities for petty corruption, needs to be avoided.

In short, successful vertical decentralisation needs to be accompanied by a process of horizontal decentralisation that can provide guidance and accountability to decision makers at all levels. A unitary state with relatively few decentralised levels and an active democratic civil society would seem to yield the best overall outcome.

Over time, the role of local taxes should be enhanced and the role of central grants diminished, as has been the pattern in more developed countries. Gradually, mobile taxes should be made available to local governments. In general, to maintain monetary stability there should be strict limits on the ability of local governments to borrow either domestically or abroad. If they are to borrow from the market it should be as an accompaniment to a reduction of the traditional grants from the centre.

References

ACDP Indonesia. 2014. *Study on Teacher Absenteeism in Indonesia 2014.* Jakarta: Education Sector Analytical and Capacity Development Partnership (ACDP).

Alesina, L. E., and La Ferrara, E. 2000. Participation in heterogeneous communities. *Quarterly Journal of Economics*, 115(3), pp. 847–904.

Alicias, D. 2007. *Decentralization Interrupted: Studies from Cambodia, Indonesia, Philippines, and Thailand*. Quezon City: Institute for Popular Democracy for Learning Initiative on Citizen Participation and Local Governance.

Aspinall, E., and Fealy, G. 2003. *Local Power and Politics in Indonesia: Decentralization & Democratization*. Singapore: Institute of Southeast Asian Studies.

Ausaid and Worldbank. 2012. *Devolution without Disruption. Pathways to a Successful New Kenya*. Washington, DC: World Bank.

Bashaasha, B., Mangheni, M. N., and Nkonya, E. 2011. *Decentralization and Rural Service Delivery in Uganda (IFPRI Discussion Paper 01063)*. Washington, DC: IFPRI.

Blunt, P., Turner, M., and Lindroth, H. 2012. Patronage's progress in post-Soeharto Indonesia. *Public Administration and Development*, 32(1), pp. 64–81.

Burbidge, D. 2016. County financing. In Burbidge, D., and Cheeseman, N. (eds.), *Devolution in Kenya: Research Literature Digest 2015–2016*. Oxford: Department of Politics, pp. 15–22.

Chaudhury, N., Hammer, J. Kremer, M. Muralidharan, K., and Rogers, F. H. 2006. Missing in action: Teacher and health worker absence in developing countries, *Journal of Economic Perspectives*, 20(1), pp. 91–116.

Cheeseman, N., Lynch, G., and Willis, J. 2016. Decentralisation in Kenya: The governance of governors. *Journal of Modern African Studies*, 54(1), pp. 1–35.

D'Arcy, M., and Cornell, A. 2016. Devolution and corruption in Kenya: Everyone's turn to eat? *African Affairs*, 115(459), pp. 246–273.

Dafflon, B., and Madiès, (eds.). 2013. *The Political Economy of Decentralization in Sub-Saharan Africa*. Washington, DC: Agence Française de Developpement and the World Bank.

Diprose, R. 2009. Decentralization, horizontal inequalities, and conflict management in Indonesia. *Ethnopolitics*, 8(1), pp. 107–134.

Fearon, J. 2003. Ethnic and cultural diversity by country. *Journal of Economic Growth*, 8(2), pp. 195–222.

Gadenne, L., and Singhal, M. 2014. *Decentralization in Developing Economies. National Bureau of Economic (NBER) Research (Working Paper No. 19402)*. New York: NBER.

Green, E. D. 2008. Decentralization and conflict in Uganda. *Conflict, Security, and Development*, 8(4), pp. 427–450.

IntraHealth. 2017. *When no one is there: Uganda's absent health workers*. Retrieved from www.intrahealth.org/features/when-no-one-there-uganda%E2%80%99s-absent-health-workers. Accessed 19 September 2017.

Kenya Human Rights Commission (KHRC) and Social and Public Accountability Network (SPAN). 2010. *Harmonization of Decentralized Development In Kenya: Towards Alignment, Citizen Engagement and
Enhanced Accountability.* Nairobi: KHRC and SPAN.

Laitin, D., and Fearon, J. 2003. Ethnicity, insurgency, and civil war. *American Political Science Review,* 97(1), pp. 75–90.

Lambright, G. M. S. 2009. *Decentralization in Uganda: Explaining Successes and Failures in Local Governance.* Boulder, CO: First
ForumPress.

Matovu, J.-M., and Stewart, F. 2001. The social and economic consequences
of conflict: A case study of Uganda. In Stewart, F., and Fitzgerald, V.
(eds.), *War and Underdevelopment Volume 2: Country Experiences.*
Oxford: Oxford University Press, pp. 240–288.

Mboga, H. 2009. *Understanding the Local Government System in Kenya.*
Nairobi: Institute of Economic Affairs.

Menon, B., Mutero, J., and Macharia, S. 2008. *Decentralization and Local
Government in Kenya (International Studies Programme Working
Paper No. 08–32).* Atlanta: Georgia Andrew Young School of Policy
Studies, Georgia State University.

Republic of Indonesia. 2018. Rekapitulasi Jumlah PPID Provinsi,
Kabupaten DAN KOTA. Retrieved from Depdagri.go.id. Accessed
4 April 2018.

Mitchinson, R. 2003. Devolution in Uganda: An experiment in local service
delivery. *Public Administration and Development,* 23(3), pp. 241–248.

Nasution, A. 2016. *Government Decentralization in Indonesia (ADBI
Working Paper Series 601).* Tokyo: Asian Development Bank Institute.

Ojambo, H. 2012. Decentralization in Africa: A critical review of Uganda's
experience. *Potchefstroom Electronic Law Journal,* 15(2), pp. 70–88.

Pierskalla, J. H., and Sacks, A. 2017. Unpacking the effect of decentralized
governance on routine violence: Lessons from Indonesia. *World Development,* 90, pp. 213–228.

Przeworski, A., and Limongi, F. 1993. Political regimes and economic
growth. *Journal of Economic Perspectives,* 7(3), pp. 51–69.

Ramadhan, A. P. 2013. Teacher and health worker absence in Indonesia.
Asian Education and Development Studies 2(2), pp. 149–161.

Reinikka, R., and Svensson, J. 2004. Local capture: Evidence from a central
government transfer programme in Uganda. *Quarterly Journal of Economics,* 119(2), pp. 679–705.

Republic of Uganda. 2016. *Financing of Local Governments in Uganda
through Central Government Grants and Local Government Revenues.*
Kampala: Office of the Auditor General.

Rondinelli, D. A., McCullough, J. S., and Johnson, R. W. 1989. Analyzing decentralization policies in developing countries: A political-economy approach. *Development and Change*, 20(1), pp. 57–87.

World Bank. 2012. *World Development Indicators 201*. Washington, DC: World Bank.

UN-Habitat. 2002. *Local Democracy and Decentralization in East and Southern Africa: Experiences from Uganda, Kenya, Botswana, Tanzania and Ethiopia*. Nairobi: UN-Habitat.

8 | Land Reform

Strengthening Customary Rights under Community Management

KOJO SEBASTIAN AMANOR

8.1 Introduction

Since the 1990s, institutional reform of land administration has gained considerable attention in Africa. The majority of African states have now initiated new land reform policies, processes and laws that accord formal recognition to customary land tenure and attempt to harmonise customary and statutory tenure. The concept of customary land rights is closely associated with ethnicity since customary rights are usually embedded in notions of citizenship rooted in ethnicity and kinship. Therefore, the transformation of customary land relations has considerable implications for ethnicity. Within the framework of customary tenure a tension exists between the two features of ethnicity that Lonsdale (1994, 2012) identifies, moral ethnicity based on a framework of rights, reciprocity and redistribution, and political tribalism based on competition between a narrow circle of elites using the ideology of tribalism to further their control of resources and their integration into the modern world of commodification and social differentiation. Frequently, in policy frameworks, the unseemly side of community relations is brushed aside and the community is represented as a socially undifferentiated site of moral solidarity against a rapacious state (Watts, 2000). This often results in unforeseen circumstances and unintended consequences as market liberal land reforms are implemented.

Colonial indirect rule in Africa integrated land and polity into a complex of customary law, in which traditional rulers exerted considerable political influence through control over land and customary courts. This enabled them to control their subjects and impose taxes, forced labour and other forms of economic and political coercion. As a consequence of this land administration is as much about exercising control over people and gaining political hegemony as it is about conferring rights for economic and livelihood purposes. This often results in conflicts over the interpretation and reinterpretation of customary tenure (Lund, 2008).

In addressing the relationship between land and ethnicity, it is necessary to examine various forms of marginalisation, because ethnic categories are not primordial or static but arise as processes out of competition for resources and perceptions of inequity and injustice (Lentz, 1995). Thus, the mélange of ethnicised conflicts over land includes such phenomena as declining opportunities for poor youth and tensions between young indigenes and migrants; increasing strife between sedentary and mobile populations, including various categories of herders and farmers; gender relations and the wider alliances of women; conceptions of firstcomers and latecomers and of local rights, national citizenship and service to the nation; human rights, the rights of national minorities and indigenous people; and the allocation of blame for environmental degradation to specific groups of people often involved in marginal economic activities. Beyond these tensions lie complex international networks of human rights and the appeals of various groups to national and international bodies, which also influence the ways in which group interests and demands are articulated. Thus, ethnicity needs to be treated as a process of differentiation by ethnicisation rather than as a predefined entity, and as a process that emerges out of the relationship between economic and political factors and a sense of belonging or identity, which is often projected as cultural or spiritual.

This chapter explores the impacts of recent land reforms on ethnicity and ethnic mobilisation. It examines the ways in which contemporary land reforms address issues of inclusive development, and attempt to ameliorate ethnic conflicts or exacerbate ethnic tensions through the intended and unforeseen consequences of policies and policy assumptions. It also examines the impacts of the increasing commodification and scarcity of land on land conflicts. It first examines the framing and rational basis of land administrative reform in the contemporary period, the nature of reforms carried out in specific nations, and the impact of these reforms on rural society. It then identifies the structural relations that generates ethnic conflicts over land and illuminates this by drawing upon a number of case studies in the literature. This discussion is placed within a historical framework, which seeks to contextualise contemporary land policies within the transformation of African societies and the underlying dilemmas that confront land reform.

8.2 Reframing the Land Question and Governance Reforms

In recent years, the majority of African nation states have introduced processes of land administrative reform, through consultative processes to determine the directions for land reform, writing new policies, and enacting new laws. These reforms give recognition to customary forms of land tenure, by either creating new methods for recording customary land rights within government agencies or decentralising land management to traditional authorities or local communities. This emanates from a framework of rolling back the state and decentralising administration that was implemented under Structural Adjustment Programmes. In the 1980s, the World Bank initiated an analysis of the African state, which argued that the postcolonial state had failed in Africa because the project was misconceived. According to this, the attempt to modernise on western lines had produced a state that was alien to the cultures and institutions of Africans. The object of the good governance agenda was to create "close links between governance, cultural relevance and components of civil society" (Landell-Mills, 1992, p. 567) and to "progressively remodel its institutions to be more in tune with traditions, beliefs, and structures of its component societies" (Landell-Mills, 1992, p. 545). However, these "dynamic" traditions of African peoples were recast within a framework that made them accommodating to liberal market values. African traditional values were reframed as aspiring to capitalist accumulation, entrepreneurship and free markets, values that had been constrained and stifled by social democratic states.

In the 1980s and 1990s, the new framework of good governance facilitated an alliance between donors and nongovernmental organisations (NGOs). With the rationalisation and downsizing of public sector employment services, many social and development services originally carried out by the state became contracted out to the private sector, NGOs and community organisations. This gave rise to an emphasis in policy frameworks on civil society linkages and community participation.

By the late 1980s, two distinct policy frameworks had arisen for land management. The first, concerned with opening the economy to foreign investment, sought to improve the transparency and security of land acquisition by streamlining and making processes of land registration more efficient and transparent. Within the agricultural sector, this attempted to make land registration more comprehensive to enable smallholder farmers to use land as collateral to gain access to capital for farm investment. The second approach, which was influenced by the good governance institutional framework, questioned the appropriateness of state-managed centralised land cadastres and examined modalities for decentralising land management to communities. Bruce (1993) rejected the dualist discourse that the source of insecurity in land lay in outmoded traditional systems that needed to be modernised. He argued that land grabbing by "new elites" allied with competition between ethnic groups and arbitrary state appropriations of land were the major sources of insecurity of tenure. Migot-Abdholla et al. (1991) have also argued that the processes of formal land registration have not created clear incentives for agricultural improvement because the necessary input, credit and risk markets are not in place to support investments based on the collateralisation of land. As a result, land registration has often been carried out by rural people for negative defensive reasons of protecting their land from being claimed by others, rather than to gain access to collateral, as in Kenya. Bruce has argued that the main lines of land reform should be away from comprehensive tenure reform, and towards community-based solutions and a "state-facilitated" evolution of indigenous land tenure systems (Bruce, 1993, p. 51).

This position has influenced the subsequent development of land policy research in Africa in which two approaches have crystallised:

1. A communitarian approach based on strengthening community participation within a livelihood framework; and
2. A focus on promoting the gradual evolution of land markets within a new institutional economics framework.

The first recognises that land tenure systems are not static. They have evolved over a long period and are flexible, diverse and dynamic, responding and adapting to economic and social change (Lavigne Delville, 2000; Toulmin & Quan, 2000). The second approach recognises that, while the individualisation of land is the best arrangement to be attained in the long term, group management of property is in the present, under a wide range of situations, the more pragmatic or realistic way of adapting property rights to changing conditions. As the 2003 World Bank report on land policy states:

While the individualisation of land rights is the most efficient arrangement in many circumstances, in a number of cases, for example, for indigenous groups, herders, and marginal agriculturalists, definition of property rights at the level of the group, together with a process for adjusting the property rights system to changed circumstances where needed, can help to significantly reduce the danger of encroachment by outsiders while ensuring sufficient security to individuals. As long as groups can internally decide on individuals' resource access and other issues following basic conditions of representativeness and transparency, securing group rights can contribute to better and more sustainable land management as well as more equitable access to productive resources. (Deininger, 2003, p. 76)

By 2008, the *World Bank Development Report* on agriculture presented a much more "heterogeneous" narrative of rural life, of socially differentiated agrarian producers who are faced with three options: making the transition to commercial smallholders integrated into markets, transforming themselves into labourers, or exiting from agriculture and enabling more efficient farmers to gain access to their land (World Bank, 2008; see also Amanor, 2009a). The 2008 *World Development Report* argues that provisions should be made to facilitate this process of exit by less efficient farmers, either in the form of alternative livelihood options or through social protection.

Recently, land policy has become even more complicated as foreign investors and financial institutions have shown increasing interest in investing in African land. The World Bank has now wavered from its initial position of firm support for smallholder cultivation, on the basis of it being the most efficient form of agriculture, to supporting the viability of both smallholder and large estate cultivation in Africa depending upon the conditions of cultivation, availability of land, and the nature of infrastructure development (World Bank, 2009, 2010). In contrast, other researchers have argued that recent investments in land in Africa constitute a dangerous form of land speculation and land grabbing that threatens to undermine rural livelihoods and food security (Borras & Franco, 2010; Daniel & Mittal, 2009; Zoomers, 2010). Thus, the contemporary land question is marked by debates and conundrums that attempt to balance the role of the state and the market by, on the one hand, ensuring land security for the rural poor and for marginalised groups and, on the other hand, enabling the expansion of commercial agriculture and foreign direct investment in large-scale agriculture with the consequences of displacement, expropriation and land enclosures. However, these processes do not only occur as a result of the movement of external foreign investment into Africa. They are also internal to forms of agrarian accumulation and social differentiation within rural areas (Amanor, 2012; Cotula, 2013). Recent research has noted the emergence of a middle stratum of farmers accumulating land and capital, often originating from civil servants and traders investing in new fields (Jayne et al., 2016).

The land question has rapidly evolved from theoretical framing to applications that seek to resolve problems and enhance the harmonisation of customary and statutory tenure forms. As a consequence, the contemporary land question is characterised by a setting of institutional pluralism and many experimental forms of land management. Section 8.3 examines the major policy innovations in community-based land administration and the attempts to integrate land administration into the processes of "rolling back" the state and into expanding markets. It explores the problems that emerge from attempting to identify community institutions that can manage land, and from the representation of multi-layered and overlapping user rights in land as property rights that can be traded on markets.

8.3 Institutionalising New Approaches to Community-Based Land Management

Several innovative approaches have been devised for creating institutional structures through which customary land tenure can be formally recognised and managed. The first is based on mapping out and recording various customary arrangements and claims on land in national or decentralised district land registers, with provisions for the formal registration of these customary rights. This includes the recording of multiple rights in land involving various categories of land users exploiting different resources; secondary rights in land such as women's access to land through husbands or kin or rights to rented land; and disputed ownership of land in which the nature of the dispute may also be documented. The second approach, in contrast, may be characterised as a minimalist corporate group approach. This decentralises land management to recognised customary or community institutions, records the boundaries of lands under customary claims and leaves it to the community authorities to work out the modalities for allocating plots and managing disputes. This may also involve attempts to make these community groups accountable by making them subject to elections or defining a set of principles against which the performance of the group is evaluated (such as recognition of gender representation and ensuring land rights for women). The third approach devolves land administration to decentralised local government agencies in which the community or traditional authorities are represented.

8.3.1 Mapping Community Lands

The rise of community forestry in the late 1970s and early 1980s in Sahelian francophone Africa has had a major influence on the subsequent development of land reform programmes. During the 1980s, there was a movement in rural development programmes from emphasising technical interventions to community management. There was a realisation that the environmental problems in the Sahel resulted from the interconnection of institutional and economic factors at the national, local and international levels. Agricultural intensification policies had adversely affected the natural resources base, and sector-oriented development projects had been characterised by disappointing performance. The pressures of structural adjustment and state budgetary constraints resulted in pressures to decentralise and divest state services. In this policy environment, *gestion de terroir* developed as an approach to rural development that sought to use community participation as a way of filling the gaps in declining state services and developing a multisectoral approach to rural development, based on clarifying local rights to natural resources and defining a village territory that could be administered by the community (Guèye & Laban, 1992).

The *gestion de terroir* approach sought to create linkages between democratisation, decentralisation and natural resource management. It focused on developing technical interventions to halt environmental degradation and introduce soil and environmental conservation; and institutional reforms that legally recognised the rights of communities to manage their resources. Its aim was to promote environmental management of a village territory by a village group. *Gestion de terroir* used community empowerment and capacity building techniques to enable communities to manage their resources and resolve conflicts emerging from competition over resources. A team of development officers from various government departments were responsible for mobilising villagers to participate in community development. The community councils implemented a management contract for their territory (de Haan, 1998; Guèye & Laban, 1992). This involved the mapping of village lands and the zoning of the land according to land use. Since the World Bank, United Nations Development Programme, and Food and Agriculture Organisation supported it enthusiastically, *gestion de terroir* gained a high profile in international development. Its focus on community-based natural resource management and the rights of local communities to the management of resources has influenced the subsequent evolution of land policies, as they have moved from state managed cadastres to community-based processes. *Gestion de terroir* provided an influential framework for the subsequent development of Rural Land Plans (*le Plan Rural Foncier*, or PRF) in francophone Africa (Gastaldi, 1999).

PRFs were first implemented in Côte d'Ivoire in 1990, and then introduced into Benin, Burkina Faso, Guinea and Madagascar. The PRF approach devises a simple land register in which all existing rights in land are mapped in the territories of rural communities, using aerial photographs, GPS devices and interviews and consultations with rights holders, landowners and community groups. The objective is to record all existing rights in specific plots of land of all landowners and land users within the nation, and the nature of these rights (such as whether the land can be sold or transferred to heirs). Where land is the subject of multiple interlocking rights, which may include claims to ownership and user rights, these are recorded. Where land is the subject of disputed ownership, this is also recorded. This has been used to create a national land title register, in Côte d'Ivoire and to issue land certificates (Gastaldi, 1999; Lavigne Delville 2005; Ouédraogo, 2005). These land certificates could be converted into registered formal private land titles within a 3-year period from the initial registration.

In Madagascar, in contrast, the PRF is institutionalised within a framework of decentralised community land registers (Teyssier et al., 2009). PRFs in Madagascar aim to integrate agriculture with natural resource management and develop contractual relations between decentralised councils and local communities. A community land register is created that maps out all existing land rights over which there is consensus. Since in rural Madagascar there is a common practice of recording rights in land in informal written documents, the land registration process has also taken these documents into consideration and developed a mechanism for regularising and recognising them within the local administrative system. This has facilitated the rapid and comprehensive mapping of land. After the mapping is done land certificates are issued to individuals, which describe the particular rights held in the land. The process seeks to document existing rights and relations in land rather than registering them according to particular preconceived categories (Teyssier et al., 2009). However, PRFs have encountered practical difficulties in representing secondary rights in land (where there may be a series of overlapping rights and different domains in relation to grazing land, rights to the soil for cultivation, and rights in trees) in land certificates (Chauveau et al., 2006).

A similar process to PRFs also occurs in Ethiopia. Since 2003, the government has undertaken a programme of rural land registration in which farmers are presented with land certificates that are issued by subdistrict councils (Adenew & Abdi, 2005; Rahmato, 2009a). These use simple techniques to map out household lands and involve farmers within communities in measuring and mapping out plots, based on indigenous methods of defining plot boundaries, and written descriptions of the plots that describe boundaries in relation to particular landmarks. This has been an effective system that enables rapid mapping out of farmer plots and has served as a basis for redistributing plots according to the growth and decline of household size. Women's rights are also recognised in this system. This provides a degree of security that enables farmers to also lease out and lease in land according to their needs (Adenew & Abdi, 2005). However, youth often find it difficult to gain access to land, because those who were not old enough to gain land when redistribution took place end up landless when they become adults. The main means of dealing with this has been periodic redistributions and reallocations of land.

Although property rights may be secure in Ethiopia, plots are often highly fragmented in high population areas. In some areas plots are fragmented to the extent that one-third of total holdings are less than 0.5 hectares and more than one-half less than 1.0 hectare (Rahmato, 2009b). The process of securing and registering land according to residency requirements based on ethnic origins prevents farmers moving to new areas when they suffer land scarcity. This is exacerbated by policies that zone land into commercial and peasant areas and prevent movements of the peasantry into new areas. While population is high in the peasant farming zones and land scarce, there are large areas of "empty" land in other areas, which are only exclusively available to private investors. Thus, security of land in itself does not guarantee peasant farmers a viable and satisfying livelihood and does not address situations of land hunger or inequitable access to land.

The process of creating land certificates encourages an anticipation of changing land rights, and more powerful groups may attempt to wrestle land from the more vulnerable, as in the case of Côte d'Ivoire where land registration served as a platform for xenophobia, and in which new conditionalities were created to prevent immigrants from Sahelian countries from registering land that they had often purchased.

8.3.2 Delegation of Land Administration to Corporate Customary or Community Groups

In contrast with customary mapping, the delegation of land administration to customary or community groups constitutes a minimalist approach that leaves the actual definition of customary rights and negotiation of customary disputes to a predefined community (Fitzpatrick, 2005). The law merely protects customary rights, which are formally recognised independently of registration or documentation. The major intervention of the state lies in recognising the nature of the local institution responsible for land management and defining the boundaries over which the community group has jurisdiction. This type of jurisdiction can exist where traditional authorities continue to function and play an effective role in resolving disputes over land, or where there are elected village assemblies.

The land reform processes in Mozambique and Uganda are often held up to be ideal examples of this type of solution. In both these countries, customary land rights are recognised as private property rights, which can be registered and transacted, irrespective of whether they are formally registered. The Uganda Land Act of 1998 recognises customary tenure as legal and equal to other forms of tenure. It recognises that user rights to land can be established through long-term occupancy and provides for the registration of customary rights to land through a system of Certificates of Customary Ownership, which can be converted into freehold land title. It creates an institutional framework for decentralised land management at the district level although it does not formally recognise community level institutions. The main institutions for land management include District Land Boards and Area Land Committees (Nsamba-Gayiiya, 1999).

The District Land Boards are responsible for allocating lands that are not claimed by an owner/user and facilitating the registration of land. The Area Land Committees are responsible for verifying boundaries, recording rights over land, and safeguarding the rights of vulnerable people. The Land Act recognises the rights of Community Land Associations, corporate groups that formally register themselves with a constitution defining the group's claims on land, and the rights of members of the group to land. This in theory enables a customary group such as an extended family or a clan to register their claims over the land without defining the individual members of the group and their individual claims to the land. However, in practice, not one single community group in Uganda has as yet been officially recognised as a Community Land Association and received formal documentation of its land (Knight et al., 2012). Although the Land Act recognises customary rights in land, the provisions it makes for the transferral of customary rights into individual title undermine customary rights. Once registered, customary land is easily converted into freehold title and then ceases to be subject to customary claims. Mugambwa (2007) argues that the aim of the Land Law is not to protect customary tenure as such, but to facilitate its conversion into individual tenure and to facilitate the emergence of land markets. Thus, the Ugandan New Land Law occurs in the midst of increasing transactions in land, increasing distress sales, and lack of secure land rights for women, as males transact land in which women previously held economic and productive interests (Adoko & Levine, 2005).

The Land Law in Mozambique reflects a recent political accommodation between the ruling party and chiefs, and a recognition that in the resettlement of the rural areas following the civil war chiefs played a central role in the reallocation of land and in the mediation of disputes over rights to specific parcels of land (Dinerman, 2006; Tanner, 2010). In Mozambique, the 1997 Land Law was a product of a consultative process that sought to resolve the problem of safeguarding user rights while promoting new investments in land. Land continues to be vested in the state, but the legal framework reforms the ways in which the state allocates lands to citizens and investors. The major innovation that has been made in Mozambique is to remove the dualist framework of customary and statutory tenure, recognise the prevalence of customary tenure, and make provisions for formal recognition of customary rights and land transactions within the customary sector. Thus, customary and formal land holdings are integrated into one legal framework in which different types of land rights coexist. Customary land rights are recognised and given full legal equivalence to state registered land (Tanner, 2010). Within the new land reform, the local community is recognised as a legal entity with formal rights in land. The rights of the members of the community are recognised on the basis of the norms within the community, and based on the notion that all community members have equal rights to community property, and equal rights to participate in decision making and dialogue within the community (Knight, 2010; Tanner, 2010). Where users choose to register their rights proof can involve community-based evidence, community participatory mapping, and evidence based on the history of land occupation and the nature of social and production systems (Tanner, 2010).

In Mozambique, community members also have rights to transact their land with investors through a defined process of consultation between the community and investors. This measure ensures that land users are compensated for the loss of their land. However, this process of consultation often works against the interests of the rural poor. Frequently, the rural poor feel pressured into agreeing for their land to be transacted under such consultations by representatives of the state supporting the external investor. They have little experience in negotiating. Consultations are often too short to enable the issues to be discussed fully and frequently community leaders do not involve a broad spectrum of community members in consultations. Community members are usually not aware of the full value of their landed resources and accept low price offers (Tanner, 2010). Tanner (2010) cites cases where community members sold land to investors for beachfront development for U.S. $390 per hectare. The investors subsequently parcelled out these areas as potential holiday homes, selling 10 hectare plots for up to U.S. $200,000. Tanner (2010) also notes a process of concentration of landholdings, in which large areas of land are being formally registered as the land of a relatively small number of applicants. In the Zambezia Province 11% of applicants received 74% of the total area approved as registered transacted land. On the one hand, the New Land Law in Mozambique enables rural people to realise capital from their land resources. It enables joint projects between communities and investors. However, more ominously it is resulting in a gradual expansion of investors into communal lands and the displacement of rural land users.

In Ghana, land administrative reform is implemented through pilot Customary Land Secretariats, which are run by paramount chiefs. The land secretariats register and manage customary land. However, as land becomes more valuable, chiefs are also using their new powers over land to extend their own narrow interests in land and to expropriate migrants and smallholders. They are expropriating customary law by reinventing customary tenure. In the creation of a Customary Land Secretariat in Wassa Amenfi (in the Western Region of Ghana), the chiefs have instigated a land registration process that "renegotiates" tenancies and redesignates migrants who acquired land through outright purchase as "tenants" (Boone & Duku, 2012, pp. 10–11). Boni (2005) reports similar processes within Sefwi, where chiefs are reinventing and renegotiating land transactions and retrospectively converting the land purchases of migrant farmers into tenancy agreements. In many rural areas chiefs often reallocate lands from locals and migrants to new commercial farmers who are willing to pay for land, unlike local farmers. They lease large areas of fallow land to commercial tree planters, which disrupts local farming strategies and prevents youth from getting access to sufficient land (Amanor, 2009b). Ubink (2008) reports that, in peri-urban areas of Kumasi, property developers are willing to pay high prices for land. To reap the benefits of this, chiefs are claiming the land as their own property and evicting indigenous small farmers from the land without compensation. New customary laws are being invented to justify this, such as claims that when the settlement reaches farmland the ownership of the farmland reverts to the chief.

In Tanzania the New Land Act of 1997 grew out of concerns to create tenure reform to facilitate foreign investment in land and natural resources, while appeasing rural concerns about lack of secure access to land and the alienation of customary land to investors (Manji, 2006; Shivji, 2000; Tsikata, 2003). After the enactment of the New Land Act in Tanzania, the corporate community land managing group consists of elected village councils. All members of the village over the age of eighteen are members of the village assembly, and can vote to select the village council. The village council comprises twenty-five members, of which one-quarter must be women. The village council is vested with executive power in all the affairs of the village and also has legislative power, although the district council must approve its bylaws. The village councils register land, allocate land certificates and adjudicate land disputes. All resident members of villages have rights to land, which they can sell (Alden Wiley, 2003; Veit et al., 2008). The Land Act recognises undocumented customary tenure as equal to statutory tenure, provided the claimants can prove that they have been using the land for at least twelve years. It also creates procedures for villagers to register their land and obtain certificates as proof of ownership (Alden Wiley, 2003). A ceiling of 20 hectares has been established on the amount of land villagers can hold as a means of preventing restratification tendencies and land concentration (Alden Wily, 2003, 2008).

This right to transact land enables village councils to claim common grazing land as their property and later sell these to investors. This often works to diminish the land rights of Tanzania's sizeable pastoral population, who find their rangelands are claimed by agricultural villages, and by the wildlife and tourist sector as private game parks (Brockington, 2002; Igoe & Brockington, 1999; Niboye, 2010; Veit et al., 2008). Village land can be sold to external investors provided it passes through a number of laid down procedures, including consultations with the community and agreement on compensation. This paves the way for investors to acquire and convert large areas under customary land (Land Rights Research and Resource Institute, 2010). As in Mozambique, with the collusion of bureaucrats and village council leaders, investors are often able to gain access to village lands at low prices. For instance, a *Daily News* report of 26 December 2009 describes ways in which villagers are "deceived" into releasing land to investors:

[Villagers] claimed to have been short changed by the investors and given as little as 2,000/- or 5,000/- to accept a useless deal. A list of meeting participants in the villagers was shrewdly used to mean that it was a list of village government council which could authorise the offer of land to an investor. A village government member, Mr Saidi Mata said that an investor has invaded his village and 'grabbed' it through a village meeting which was disguised as a village council meeting. We were gathered here in the village about 40 of us and some of the leaders lured us to sign a deal with an investor. The investor paid 6,000/- to each villager who attended the meeting. We are told that we had approved his application just because we appended our signatures. We are now regretting, he said. (Lugungulo, 2009, in Land Rights Research and Resources Institute, 2010)

8.3.3 Land Boards

Land Boards occur where the administration of land is delegated to decentralised government institutions, which are responsible for interpreting customary law and adjudicating land disputes. Traditional authorities and community groups may be represented on these Land Boards, which may also include elected representatives alongside nominated officials from district government ministries. Land Boards dominate the administration of land in Botswana and Lesotho and comprise an element of land administration in Uganda where they are expected to function alongside Area Committees and registered corporate community associations (Fitzpatrick, 2005; Quan, 2000).

In Botswana, authority over land administration was transferred from chiefs to District Land Boards in 1968 when the Tribal Land Act was introduced. The Land Boards hold "the right and title of the chiefs and tribes on trust for the benefit and advantage of the tribesmen of that area and for the purposes of promoting economic and social development of the people of Botswana" (Botswana Tribal Land Act 1968 in Fitzpatrick, 2005, p. 463). The Tribal Lands Act was important in marking the institutional transition from a system of colonial indirect rule to a modern nation state with a system of representative democracy and local government. The Land Boards have ten members, of which one-half are elected by secret ballot by the Village Assemblies and the other one-half are appointed by the Minister of Lands and Housing. The jurisdiction of the Land Boards is based on tribal territorial boundaries. The Tribal Lands Act originally restricted the allocation of land to tribesmen. An exemption by the Minister of Lands and Housing was necessary to enable "nontribal" people to be allocated land. However, this raised much public concern (including from wealthy citizens interested in investing in the ranching sector) that this contravened the constitution of Botswana, which recognises the equality of all citizens. Hence in 1993 the Tribal Lands Act was amended to lift restrictions on tribal affiliation as a criterion for land ownership (Molomo, 2008).

In Botswana, the Land Boards may allocate land for residential, agricultural, grazing and commercial use. The Land Boards demarcate the site of an applicant for land and issue a certificate of Customary Land Grant or a Statutory Lease if the land is required for commercial use. The Land Boards thus manage both customary and statutory tenure within a unitary framework. They enable commercial users to gain access to land without negotiating with traditional rulers or customary land users, but also ensure the customary rights of villagers. Nevertheless, in practice the Land Boards often have a weak institutional capacity to record and survey existing land rights, and to know the history of plots and which particular plots villagers claim. Although the Land Board system recognises customary rights in land, it frequently privileges commercial users. Boards have been known to allocate lands claimed by customary land users to commercial investors. Thus, the administration of land by Land Boards has gone hand in hand with a process of enclosures in which rangelands have been privatised through a policy of fencing since the 1970s. This has resulted in the allocation of considerable land for commercial ranching, which has undermined the land rights of the rural poor, who clearly lack sufficient capital to convert their land into commercial rangeland (Molomo, 2008; Peters, 1994; Quan, 2000; Werbner, 2004).

Land Board administration has also inflamed ethnic tensions, by associating particular areas with the dominant ethnic groups and managing land in accordance with the dominant Tswana customary norms at the expense of national minorities. Increasingly, national minorities are challenging the dominant paradigms of nation building that associate Botswana with Tswana culture and are calling for frameworks that reflect the ethnic diversity within Botswana society (Molomo, 2008; Werbner, 2004). Land rights have sometimes been denied to national minorities, of which the most famous case to attract international attention has been that of the expulsion of the Basarwa hunter gatherers from the Central Kalahari Game Reserve (Hitchcock, 2001; Molomo, 2008; Suzman, 2003).

8.4 Commodification of Customary Land

The dominant contemporary framework for land administration aims to recognise customary rights within national statutory frameworks, by creating institutional structures that merge the management of both customary and individual property. This facilitates the transformation of customary rights into individual property and enables the "owners" or "users" to sell their land. A second objective of contemporary land reform is to create an inclusive framework that recognises secondary and multiple rights in land, including those delegated to other users and the multiple uses of resources in land by different users, such as rights to trees or to pasture land. In practice, it is difficult to reconcile these two objectives since the conversion of customary rights into individual property rights leads to the erosion of secondary and multiple rights.

Women's rights to land are often embedded in secondary rights. Women's rights in land are frequently marginalised within customary settings because women frequently have limited representation within customary institutions and are often admonished to behave within the confines of patriarchal values (Hunt, 2004; Joireman, 2007; Khadiagala, 2001; Manji, 2001; Whitehead & Tsikata, 2003). With the increasing commodification of land, women frequently find that their access to land becomes less secure as the land in which they had user claims increasingly becomes sold, rented or incorporated into more intensives systems of cropping by male farmers. With few channels to represent their interests in land within the community, women's organisations frequently look to other principles than community rights in advancing their interests. Sometimes they appeal to universal women's rights-based declarations, to which most African states are signatories. They pressurise the state to introduce legislation and policy processes that reflect its commitments to women's rights. However, women's livelihoods are also threatened by the appropriation of community land and by the accumulation of land by private investors. They may respond to this by supporting customary land reforms while also calling for reforms of customary codes to reflect women's land rights (Whitehead & Tsikata, 2003).

It is also difficult to represent the rights of highly mobile users, such as cattle herders and some forms of shifting cultivators within maps, site plans and concepts of plots of land under the control of specific users. Frequently mobile land users lose out from the recognition and validation of customary rights as transactable rights.

The mapping of customary land and the creation of customary land certificates often creates expectations and apprehensions, which can lead to attempts to reframe customary land tenure in the process of registration; conflicts between different groups over the precise meanings of rights in lands; and to the increasing marginalisation of the poor, as the wealthy and powerful redefine customary land tenure to meet their narrow interests and their alignments with the processes of capital accumulation at work within the economy. The recognition of customary rights often occurs in frameworks that romanticise the solidarity of the communal and fail to take into account the extent to which communities are marked by social differentiation and integration into regional commodity markets, including regional land markets (Chihowu & Woodhouse, 2006). The community is a site of conflict that defines privilege and access to resources, and which may also divide distinct groups according to ethnicity, gender, hierarchy and cultural values.

The rural rich and traditional authorities are often integrated into dominant national political networks that promote development through capital accumulation. They are empowered by these political networks to represent the locality or community. They adhere to the ideologies of these political networks and contribute various narratives on national and local development. The policies they help to implement frequently undermine the rights of the poor to land and facilitate the accumulation of capital and investment in land resources. The empowerment of the community in land administration frequently facilitates the conversion of customary land into individual and commercial property and has been accompanied by widespread transferral of landed resources to private investors. This practice can clearly be seen in Mozambique, which is widely heralded to have the most progressive framework for customary land management in Africa, but where between 2004 and 2009 the government granted 405 large-scale investment projects more than 2.7 million hectares of land, which constitutes 7% of the nation's arable land (Oakland Institute, 2011).

The positive elements of recent land reforms include more secure recognition of customary rights in land. However, this often secures the claims of the most powerful sections in the community rather than the rural poor – the land hungry with minuscule plots of land have little to secure. The increasing integration of rural lands into land markets promotes intensified competition for land, and opens opportunities for financial gain from securing land with the purposes of transacting it with private sector investors. While this enables "the community" to capitalise its assets in land, it results in a conversion of customary land into individual property, a loss of user rights in land and increasing conflicts over land.

8.5 Land Redistribution and Restitution

Land redistribution is significant as a way of reducing historical inequalities in land ownership resulting from political domination by particular interest groups. Because these inequalities are sometimes based on ethnic categories, land redistribution plays an important part in addressing ethnic and racial strife. While land redistribution seeks to redress inequalities in rights in land, land restitution seeks to address historical injustices that have resulted in the deprivation of the land of particular groups, by reassigning them land based on their historical claims of ownership.

From the 1950s to the 1970s, land redistribution by the state formed an important part of the theory of land reform within international development. Breaking up large *latifundia* and redistributing them to smaller farmers was seen as a way of both addressing equity and efficiency. Under neoliberalism, this dictum has been modified and discourses about land redistribution have shifted from the political to market spheres. Within the neoliberal discourse, it is frequently argued that land concentration emerged from political distortions, and the best way of correcting these distortions is to allow the market to play a role in allocating land from those with surplus to those in need. Redistributive land reform came to the fore in southern Africa during the 1990s with the attainment of political independence in the last white settler colonies in Zimbabwe, South Africa and Namibia. This has resulted in a polarised debate about the merits of market-based redistribution as adhered to by the South African state, and of the forceful seizure of land occupied by white settler farmers in Zimbabwe, which occurred as it abandoned market-based reform and implemented a programme of fast tracking land redistribution (Moyo & Yeros, 2005).

In both countries, the history of white settler colonialism led to a skewed distribution of land. Before independence white settlers held 46% of land in Zimbabwe and 70% in South Africa. The black African population was crowded into tribal reserves, in which there was insufficient land to meet farming needs. While South Africa has instigated a market-based land reform programme, only 3% of agricultural land in South Africa had been transferred to black ownership after 10 years of reform (Hall, 2010). In Zimbabwe, the market-based land reform programme was abandoned in the mid 1990s. This resulted from the government facing increasing problems of legitimacy related to an economic crisis resulting from the inadequacies and unpopularity of the structural adjustment programme (Moyo & Yeros, 2005). Faced with domestic political opposition, pressures for more radical land reform and a social movement of forceful land occupations led by war veterans, the government turned to a process of expropriating white commercial farmers as a way of restructuring the rural economy (Moyo & Yeros, 2005). This has led to tense relations with international donors committed to market liberalisation. However, there is evidence that this reform process has addressed some of the racial legacies of colonialism and created less disparity in holdings. It has extended access to former settler land to more than 150,000 families, with smallholders occupying 72% of the land, and has also reduced the average size of holdings (Moyo & Yeros, 2005). Scoones et al. (2010) have argued, on the basis of recent research conducted in Masvingo Province, that there is evidence of a significant redistribution of land to smallholder farmers and of steady increases in yields in the smallholder sector. This reflects the development of a new agrarian structure, in which a much wider variation of farm sizes now exists, with a more equitable distribution of land and the emergence of new agribusiness sectors and agricultural support services (Scoones et al., 2010).

In South Africa, redistributive land reform has been framed as largely an agricultural issue. The objective of land reform is to create a more efficient agriculture. This framework has enabled the commercial farmer lobby to transform the debate on land redistribution and frame it in the context of promoting efficiency. They argue that the disruption of commercial agricultural production will have large negative impacts on the South African economy. An emerging new class of aspiring black agrarian capitalists also argues that the land question can be resolved through de-racialisation, by encouraging the emergence of black agrarian capitalists. They argue that the breakup of large holdings and their distribution among smallholders constitutes a deliberate attempt to frustrate the emergence of black capital (Hall, 2010). Hall (2010) points out that the framing of land reform as a discourse of agricultural efficiency rather than human rights has frustrated land redistribution to the poor. It has created a situation in which the criterion for land distribution becomes associated with the capabilities of the farmer to engage in commercial production rather than on need and social inclusion. Ntsebeza (2007) argues that the commitment to protecting existing property rights in South Africa represents a fundamental contradiction within land reform policy, which prevents any meaningful land redistribution. Private land rights are most prevalent on commercial white farms and protecting these rights in effect prevents land redistribution. Promoting the market often results in increasing competitiveness and concentration of agricultural production and agricultural property, rather than in creating favourable conditions for smallholder production (Hall, 2007). Thus, tensions between promoting commercial agriculture and capital accumulation as against social inclusion and smallholder linkages within a diversified regional economy underpin debates about land redistribution in southern Africa. These tensions are marked by recent youth and student unrest in South Africa, and deep concerns about the failure of the post-apartheid political regime to address racial and class inequality, reflected in the slogan "Give back the land".

Redistributive land reform has also occurred in Ethiopia in the 1980s under the Mengistu regime and continued under the Ethiopian People's Democratic Front in a decentralised form of land adminis-tration. Land has been redistributed among peasant households according to household size. In contemporary Ethiopia land reform has been implemented within a zoning system, which demarcates land areas under customary management from those that are available for commercial investment. While the areas under customary management are often densely populated, large areas of "unused" lands are reserved for release to foreign investors. Redistribution takes place within a notion of exclusive ethnic boundaries in which peasants gain access to land through their historical links to the settlement and through residency (Rahmato, 2009a).

Within West African Sahelian countries such as Guinea and Senegal, a form of redistributive land tenure was introduced in the 1960s with the transition to independence. This occurred among rural societies that that were historically hierarchically organised with a landlord class and a servile class of peasant producers who worked lands claimed by the landlords and provided them with labour services and a proportion of their crops (Boiro, 1996; Diop, 2007; Lund, 1999; Olivier de Sardin, 1984). In Senghor's version of African socialism, the development of social stratification within Africa was regarded as a corruption of the African communal tradition. He advocated that the state needed to intervene to protect the authentic African communitarian culture (Senghor, 1964). These types of reforms guaranteed land to the cultivator rather than to the overlord. However, no attempts were made to formalise the new rights accorded to the cultivator. As a consequence, they were dependent on recognition by the political regime, which could lead to widespread abuses by the bureaucracy and the contestation of claims with political change, as has occurred in Guinea, where the former landowners in the Futa Jallon are now claiming restitution of the land that was redistributed to former servile cultivators (Boiro, 1996; Diop, 2007).

Land reform programmes in the Sahel were not based on any concept of ceilings or equitable redistribution of land, but on the ability of the cultivator to work the land. This could lead to significant differentiation in holdings as with the expansion of Mourides groundnut cultivation in Senegal. The rationale of this type of land reform was based on a concept of development of the land (*mise en valeur*), in which the objective of recognising land rights was to facilitate the rapid expansion of agricultural production and the opening of new frontier land to agricultural production.

A similar rationale underpinned land rights in the cocoa industry in Côte d'Ivoire, in which user rights of the land were protected by the state and extended to migrants from neighbouring countries. As President Houphouët-Boigny declared in 1962:

There is enough cultivatable land, but a shortage of manpower. The government and the party have decided, in the national interest, to grant all citizens -whether Côte d'Ivoire is their country of origin or adoption – who cultivate a plot of land of whatever size, the right to permanent ownership which can be passed on to their heirs. (quoted by Diaby, 1996, p. 151)

Traditional authorities in the frontier regions of western Côte d'Ivoire were encouraged by the state to release land to migrants under favourable terms (Chauveau, 2000). However, the successful development of the frontier transformed the relationship between land and migrant labour. As land became increasingly scarce and valuable, the framework for granting rights to migrants became challenged by the indigenes of these areas, some of whom were experiencing land hunger.

In contrast with redistribution, land restitution seeks to restore land to specific groups who have been unfairly dispossessed. These groups claim special rights to the land based on a notion of the injustice, of appropriation of the exclusive historical rights of the group (Fay & James, 2009). Land restitution involves the expression of a specific identity that is frequently ethnically based, which defines a historical relationship between an exclusive group of people and a specific territory. Restitution is premised upon moral discourses about righting past injustices and on exclusionary principles that do not redress forms of social differentiation within society. Restitution establishes a distinct form of citizenship in which people are reconstituted as community groups with special relationships to land.

Groups who feel that their rights to land are not properly addressed within the nation-building and modernist development narratives of the state frequently make recourse to restitution claims. In Kenya and Tanzania several pastoral groups have attempted to gain land rights through appeals for the restitution of their ancestral lands and through re-classifying themselves as indigenous peoples. This enables them to claim rights through universal frameworks of human rights enshrined in the International Labour Organisation's Convention on the Rights of Indigenous and Tribal Peoples rather than through concepts of national citizenship (Brockington *et al.*, 2008; Hodgson, 2011; Igoe, 2006). Similarly, in Botswana the case of the Basarwa hunting and gathering people, who have been expelled from the Central Kalahari Game Reserve, has been taken up by international NGOs proclaiming their status as an indigenous people (Hitchcock, 2001; Molomo, 2008; Suzman, 2003).

The notion of what constitute indigeneity is problematic. It is often based on some notion of authenticity, of belonging to a pure ethnic group that has resisted incorporation into the modern world. However, in reality many of the most marginalised and poor pastoralists are made up of a diverse range of displaced people who coalesce together to make the least ethnically distinct group, a coalition of the dispossessed. This notion of authenticity among pastoral peoples, which is often championed by international NGOs, has enabled many of the wealthier pastoral groups to represent themselves as pure pastoral people at the expense of the broader majority and gain access to support from international NGOs and access to land through restitution. Thus, groups such as the Maa-speaking agropastoral Arusha people are now trying to reclaim their Maasai heritage in response to donor and international NGO whims, while those iconic groups that have attained pristine status attempt to further exclude other (competing) groups as lacking authenticity (Brockington et al. 2008; Hodgson, 2011; Homewood, 2002; Igoe, 2006). Because restitution is bound up with historical claims on land and the rights of particular groups to be regarded as holding exceptional rights, it is invariably bound up with ethnicity and perceptions of ethnicity.

8.6 Land and Ethnic Conflicts

Land forms an important element around which ethnic conflicts are organised. Conflicts over land usually emanate from the interaction of several factors including perceptions of exclusion, domination, privilege, and changes in power relations and their impact on access to resources. Four distinct structural conditions can be identified that result in ethnic land conflicts:

1. Political mobilisation based on ethnic affiliations and the use of land as an instrument in building political patronage networks and capital accumulation;
2. Conflicts between migrants and locals over access, use and control of land;
3. Conflicts between different groups in which access to land was historically structured by hierarchy; and
4. Conflicting use of resources between different groups, which threaten and undermine the use of resources by one group. This frequently results in conflicts between sedentary and mobile populations over access to land and its resources of which the prime example in Africa relates to pastoral peoples.

Examples of these various types of conflicts and their structural contexts are presented.

8.6.1 Land, Ethnic Political Mobilisation and Capital Accumulation

Where the emergence of a socially differentiated agrarian population co-exists with landless elements, an agricultural labouring class and high mobility, transcending notions of fixed ethnic boundaries, conditions can exist for ethnic competition over land under state administration of land. Here the state seeks to modernise land tenure by consolidating fragmented holdings and reallocating land. Favourable land allocations are made on the basis of patronage. Rival political parties with similar ideologies organise their networks on the basis of ethnic networks and pacts between ethnic groups. While ethnic solidarity forms the basis for allocation of land, disproportionate allocations are made to the political elite fraction leading to a process of concentration and accumulation of land. With the capture of political power by opposition parties mobilising among other ethnicities, similar patterns of land allocations and reallocations are made to the members of the new ethnic coalitions in power. This leads to ethnic conflicts over land as the poorer groups (the most vulnerable to land expropriations and land hunger), interpret their current land shortage as resulting from appropriations by other groups. Kenya constitutes the quintessential example of this scenario.

Land grabbing and landlessness have a long history in Kenya, originating in the creation of a white settler class. This led to widespread appropriation of African land and displacements of African populations. By the early 1930s European settlers occupied more than one half of the arable land of the country and a sizeable dispossessed class of African "squatters" emerged (Berman, 1990). Outside of the expropriated lands "native reserves" were established based on ethnic affiliation. With the movement of land hungry Kikuyu farmers into the highlands, the scene was set for ethnic conflicts in land. The land reforms and registration processes of the 1950s expropriated the land of Mau Mau fighters and allocated them to loyalists, ushering in patronage politics (Kanyinga, 2000). During the early independence period, the Kenyatta government attempted to accommodate the interests of various factional leaders by facilitating the accumulation of land by dominant political leaders. Through public redistribution programmes a large landed class with political influence has been able to acquire large estates and use the distribution of land to build political factions. State redistribution schemes have targeted both the poor and a class of wealthy farmers, reallocating small plots to the poor and facilitating the consolidation of large estates by the rich (Leo, 1984). Since ethnicity and ethnic alliances have been the main cleavages along which political parties have organised, the redistribution of land through public programmes has acquired ethnic dimensions, particularly as land became increasingly scarce (Kanyinga, 2000; Kanyinga et al., 2008). The redistribution of land has not relieved land hunger, but has led to increasing social differentiation and the significant accumulation of land by the wealthy and the political class. The largest holdings are held by the families of the former presidents, followed by a group of residual white settlers and power brokers, and a few businessmen and farmers owing hundreds of thousands of acres. The Kenyatta family alone is estimated to own more than 500,000 acres situated in the richest arable part of the country (Namwaya, 2004). It is estimated that 20% of Kenyans own more than one-half the arable land, while 67% have holdings of less than 1 acre and 17% are landless (Namwaya, 2004).

Beyond the settlement schemes, land has been accumulated through two main mechanisms. The first involves allocating land to state corporations for public purposes. Parts of these lands would then be excised and allocated to powerful individuals. The second strategy involves evicting squatters from public lands and then allocating the lands to wealthy individuals with political connections. This practice has been particularly prevalent in forest areas in which parts of the reserves have been excised, and then allocated to public corporations in the interests of national development. The public corporations then transfer the land to wealthy individuals and private property developers. Squatters have also been evicted from forests under the pretext of conservation, for the land to be quietly allocated to the private sector at a later date (Klopp, 2000). For instance, in the Maasai Mau forest reserve thousands of squatters were evicted in 2006. About 3,000 hectares of land were excised from the reserve for later allocation to private developers (Mathangani, 2006). Private sector wildlife tourism in Kenya thrives on these expropriations of land for conservation (Brockington et al., 2008).

The forceful eviction of people from land through organised violence has accompanied expropriation by public sector agencies. This is often organised under the façade of ethnicity. In 1991 organised Kalenjin groups, often dressed in pseudo-military uniforms, indiscriminately attacked and killed Luo, Luhyia, Kikuyu and Kisii farmers in the Rift Valley, resulting in the displacement of thousands of people (Kimenyi & Ndung'u, 2005). Similar incidents have occurred periodically in other areas, but systematically arise in election years, leading to the displacement of thousands of people and the occupation of their land by networks from other ethnic political networks. These conflicts serve to enable political control to be established over land and electoral voting (those who flee because of ethnic violence are robbed of their vote), and this enables ethnic patronage networks to impose themselves on the redistribution of land to smallholders (Kayinga, 2000; Kayinga et al., 2008; Kimenyi & Ndung'u, 2005). The redistribution of land to smallholders on the basis of ethnic recruitment becomes a central tension fomenting violence among the land hungry, competing for access to land. This diverts attention away from the huge inequalities in the redistribution of land between the wealthy and the poor across ethnic identities.

Nevertheless, this expropriation and control of land for purposes of capital accumulation by the political elite and its private sector allies has encountered resistance. The poor have organised spontaneous resistance to prevent state agencies encroaching upon their land and claiming it as public land, and organised squatter invasions onto the lands of absentee landowners (Klopp, 2000). Some pastoralist groups have made appeals to international human rights forums based on their position as "indigenous peoples" and instigated legal proceedings to gain back their land (Hodgson, 2011). These struggles have reverberated with middle-class professionals and civil society organisations. They have demanded greater transparency and accountability in land administration. This eventually led to the instigation of a Commission of Inquiry into the Land Law Systems of Kenya (the Njonjo Commission) to bring about legal reforms.

The Kenya case study clearly illustrates the use of state administration of land to support the private accumulation of vast estates by a small politically dominant class, and to organise political support and control of these narrow economic interests by manipulating the divisive politics of ethnicity.

8.6.2 Migrants, Autochthones and Youth

In Côte d'Ivoire, conflicts over land erupted in the south-western forest zone in the late 1990s, when rural youth started expelling Burkinabe migrants from their cocoa plantations and villages, claiming that they were foreigners and had no rights to Ivorian land (Chauveau, 2009; Chauveau & Richards, 2008; Kouamé, 2010; Losch, 2000). The conflict between foreign migrants and locals spiralled out of control and escalated into a civil war between the north and south of the country. Land reform became a platform for xenophobia and a means to blame away the serious economic crisis that confronted Côte d'Ivoire from the late 1990s as world cocoa prices collapsed and multinationals aggressively took over control of the Ivorian cocoa sector from parastatal organisations (Amanor, 2011; Losch, 2002). In the process, the delicate social contract that had governed the Ivorian cocoa sector unravelled. This was based on the state encouraging the rapid expansion of cocoa into new frontier areas, which brought the state considerable revenues through control over the marketing of cocoa. The cocoa frontier occurred in the southwest forest, among communities in which there was little capital accumulation in agriculture. The main investors in the cocoa sector were migrants from the Baule region. The Baule cocoa entrepreneurial class constituted a powerful interest group within the *Parti Démocratique de la Côte d'Ivoire – Rassemblement Démocratique Africain* ruling party. President Houphouët-Boigny's social origins lay in this class of wealthy cocoa farmers. From the 1950s migrant Baule farmers began to make representations within the nationalist movement for rights to land based on national citizenship rather than ethnic affiliation. For instance, Baule migrants in Oume argued:

We regard ourselves as equal in rights with the Gouros with whom we have, in the past, suffered together on European plantations during forced labour, and also at the time of repression. At that time we were brothers and they did not ask us for anything. Now, the land we have been farming for a long time should be ours. We should be able to buy it, be the owners of it, and not the eternal tenants. (Raulin, 1957, p. 57, in Colin & Ayouz, 2006, p. 408)

With attainment of independence, the *Parti Démocratique de la Côte d'Ivoire – Rassemblement Démocratique Africain* regime facilitated the acquisition of land by Ivorian migrants but also by Sahelian migrants from Burkina Faso, Mali and Niger. These were critical in providing the labour for the transformation of high forest into cocoa plantations, and building labour networks from their home regions within the Ivorian forest for the rapid expansion of the Ivorian forest frontier. There was little direct state intervention in the allocation of land, which took place in a neo-customary framework structured by the *tutorat*. The *tutorat* established a relationship between indigenous landlords, family heads or chiefs and migrants that is rooted in a conception of a moral economy and patronage. The migrants are given access to land in return for which they accept social obligations to respect the landowners, provide them with annual gifts of agricultural

produce, contribute towards local development and social expenditures such as funeral costs incurred by their hosts, and perform labour
services. Because this was conceived within a customary framework
rooted in social relations the terms of the transaction were not clearly
defined but evolved over time, in response to developments within the
cocoa sector and the increasing scarcity of land. Over time, the prestations given for access to land grew to reflect the increasing scarcity
value of land, and were understood to consist of payments of land
(Chauveau, 2000, 2006; Chauveau & Colin, 2010; Chauveau &
Léonard, 1996). The communities in the southwest were appeased
through the redistribution of some of the state cocoa revenues, which
created development projects in the area, education, and support for
the movement of rural youth into the urban sector. In the 1970s and
1980s, urban migration from the southwest was viewed as improved
status, and the Burkinabe migrants in the cocoa sector as occupying the
lowest ranks in the rural setting.

This system functioned well within the context of the expansion of
the frontier and an economic boom. However, by the 1990s the
availability of frontier land had declined. The impact of this was
exacerbated by the economic recession and the collapse of cocoa prices
(Losch, 2002). The main avenues for capital accumulation in cocoa
during this period became rehabilitating old plantations rather than
purchasing uncultivated forestland. The cost of rehabilitating old plantations was expensive (Ruf, 2001) at a time when cocoa prices were
low. As a result, Baule investments in extensive cocoa plantations
declined and the main social group now investing in cocoa were small
Burkinabe planters, who had emerged as the most proficient group in
replanting cocoa on small plots of fallow land rather than in mature
forest (Léonard, 1997; Léonard & Oswald, 1997; Ruf, 2001). The rise
of Burkinabe planters was associated with both declining investments
by wealthy Ivorian planters and rising urban unemployment, both of
which resulted in increasing resentment of the presence of the Sahelian
immigrants.

Within political circles there were attempts to blame this crisis on the
influx of Sahelian immigrants. This led to the articulation of *Ivoirité*, a
xenophobic nationalism imbued with slogans such as "Côte d'Ivoire
for the Ivoirians". Under the regime of Bèdié, the concept of *Ivoirité*
sought to differentiate between "Ivoirians with roots going back for
centuries" and "ad hoc Ivoirians" (Babo, 2013). *Ivoirité* became a

major slogan of the Front Populair Ivoirien in its bid to win votes in the southwest, the main areas of rural migrations. Within Côte d'Ivoire these notions of *Ivoirité* and patrimonial rights began to play out in rural development initiatives in the 1990s, particularly since they converged with the emphasis in international development circles on indigenous rights and community participation. These ideas moved out of party political circles into the implementation of rural forestry, rural land administration, and the NGO sector (Chauveau, 2009; Diaby, 1996; Stamm, 2000). Translated into customary land rights, this differentiated between "customary rights conforming with tradition" and "customary rights ceded to third parties", which essentially referred to migrants (Chauveau, 2009). In 1998 a new Land Act was enacted which asserted the pre-eminence of customary law and the exclusive ownership rights of Ivoirians (Babo, 2013). This resulted in the hardening of ethnicity. Without prospects in the urban areas many of the youth from the southwest drifted back to the rural areas, where they found the agrarian economy dominated by Burkinabe migrants. Embracing the slogans of *Ivoirité* and xenophobic nationalism these youths physically attacked Bukinabe migrants, seized their plantations and expelled them from their communities (Babo, 2013; Chauveau, 2006; Kouamé, 2010).

Lesser conflicts with similar elements can be found in cocoa producing areas in Ghana. In the Sefwi area migrants were originally welcomed by chiefs who granted them land freely (Boni, 2005). In this period, migrants were welcome because they were seen as opening the area to development since native Sefwi inhabitants lacked the capital to invest in cocoa (Boni, 2005; Hill & McGlade, 1957). As more migrants moved into the area to cultivate cocoa, the demand for land increased, resulting in the development of a land market. Land was now sold to migrants, who paid substantial sums of money to acquire land. In the 1980s, as the available frontier land for sale declined, Sefwi chiefs began to replace land sales with sharecropping arrangements, which gave them access to lucrative revenues from cocoa plantations without alienating the land. The chiefs also retrospectively converted previous land sales into tenancy agreements and sharecrop arrangements, arguing that the payments by migrants were prestations made in return for the gift of land under customary arrangements rather than a transaction based on alienating the land. This enabled them to extract new sources of revenues from land (Boni, 2005). With little land available in other areas, migrants were forced to accept these arrangements. Custom has been constantly reinvented as land becomes scarcer. Chiefs are able to extract more revenues as demand for land increases and to shape the nature of land markets. When migrants attempted to resist the new extraction of rent the chiefs mobilised disgruntled youth to threaten the migrants with violence (Boni, 2005). Local youths were aggrieved by their lack of land and livelihood opportunities, which they largely attributed to the occupation of their land by migrants.

Similar conflicts between migrants and autochthones and aggrieved youth have also occurred in the eastern Democratic Republic of Congo, in areas under Hunde chiefs. Land tenure was historically based on a system of clientage in which chiefs gained tribute from subjects to whom they allocated land. Thus land conferred on chiefs both political recognition and access to revenues, and on their subjects' membership of an ethnically defined community and rights to land for a livelihood (Vlassenroot & Huggins, 2005). From the sixteenth century, small numbers of Banyarwanda herders from Rwanda moved into the Kivu area, some of them becoming tributary clients of Hunde chiefs. During the early colonial period large numbers of Banyarwanda labourers moved into the Kivu area. During the colonial period as land became increasingly commoditised Banyarwanda migrants began to purchase land from the Hunde (Mararo, 1997). However, population densities were high in the Kivu area and there was limited land that could be given out to migrants. Therefore, chiefs found new ways of expropriating land from indigenous farmers to sell, re-inventing an array of neo-customary conventions regulating land, which enabled them to invoke a "right of return" of land back to the chiefs (Van Acker, 2005). These trends intensified during the 1970s when investments in land became a major source of accumulation for aspiring capitalists (Mararo, 1997).

During the 1970s, the Zairian state enacted new land laws that enabled it to control the process of land alienation and the granting of land to political allies (Mararo, 1997; Vlassenroot & Huggins, 2005). Traditional authorities actively colluded with the state in the alienation of land to aspiring capitalist farmers (Van Acker, 2005; Vlassenroot & Huggins, 2005). Wealthy Banyarwanda benefitted from this process because they had built up a close political relationship with the Mobutu regime. Prunier (2009) writes that by the 1990s land in the Masisi *territoire* of Kivu became extremely concentrated with 512 families, of which 503 were Banyarwanda, claiming more than one-half of the land. The largest holding was 230,000 hectares, while the average holding was less than 1 hectare, including the land occupied by the majority of Banyarwanda people.

This process of land accumulation led to increasing social differentiation and the emergence of a large labouring class among local farmers with very limited access to land. By the early 1990s, these trends resulted in mounting ethnic tensions. Disaffected local farmers began to organise against their chiefs, refusing to recognise them and pay tribute. They also began to form local militias organised against the Banyarwanda, whose numbers were swelled by the increasing arrival of new migrants from Rwanda (Autesserre, 2010; Huggins, 2010; Vlassenroot & Huggins, 2005). In the North Kivu area, in which the Banyarwanda were most concentrated, they came to constitute about 40% of the population by the 1990s (Prunier, 2009, p. 48). In the transition to liberal democracy in the 1990s, a coalition of Nande and Hunde politicians, fearing that they would lose political power to their Banyarwanda rivals, began to organise xenophobic discourses on the illegitimacy of the Banyarwanda as Zairian citizens, in an attempt to exclude them from the political process (Vlassenroot & Huggins, 2005). Local chiefs also attempted to impose new tributary exactions on Banyarwanda landholders, which the Banyarwanda attempted to resist. Faced with increasing difficulty in controlling migrant Banyarwanda and problems of legitimacy with the farming population for alienating large tracts of land, the chiefs then turned on the Banyarwanda as a convenient scapegoat, mobilising "those local youngsters that had shown their preparedness to take up their machetes for the defence of their own community" (Vlassenroot & Huggins, 2005, p. 146). It is estimated that between 6,000 and 10,000 people were killed and 350,000 displaced in the ensuing ethnic violence (Vlassenroot & Huggins, 2005), before it escalated into a civil war.

Ethnic conflicts between autochthones and migrants are often rooted in a complex political economy of social differentiation and accumulation of land by aspiring capitalist farmers with close ties to the political regime. This frequently leads to local immiseration and the rise of a land hungry local class that can only sell its labour or migrate. Alternative livelihoods to those based on land resources are often very limited. Local poor youth are frequently the category that feels most aggrieved by this process, because they are the first to experience difficulty in gaining access to land. This dissatisfaction manifests itself among youth and commoners as a feeling of betrayal by chiefs and elders that have sold out their birthright, and a deep sense of resentment against migrants who are blamed for taking their land. This sense of betrayal does not always manifest itself as ethnic strife. Chauveau and Richards (2008) show the deep affinities between the struggles of youth in southwest Côte d'Ivoire and in Sierra Leone, but in Côte d'Ivoire this resulted in violence against Sahelian immigrants and in Sierra Leone against elders within their own families.

8.6.3 Hierarchy in Communities

A third type of ethnic conflict relates to societies that have been historically structured by hierarchy, in which there is an ethnic division between a noble caste and their captives or slaves. This includes areas such as the Futa Jallon in Guinea, where the Fulani subjugated the Jallonke (Boiro, 1996; Diop, 2007); the Seno area in Burkina Faso in which the Fulani subjugated the Rimaibe (Lund, 1999); and the Songhai-Zarma of Niger and Mali, who conquered and subjugated a number of agricultural people in the nineteenth century (Olivier du Sardin, 1984). In the Futa Jallon, the Jallonke were conquered by Fulani and turned into a class of servile farmers providing labour services and surplus crops to the landowners. The colonial authority maintained a close relationship with the Fulani and allowed them to maintain the Jallonke in servile subjugation (Boiro, 1996; Diop 2007). With deep resentment of colonial rule the Jallonke supported the anti-colonial movement led by the PDG (Schmidt, 2005). Following independence land reforms were introduced granting land to the cultivators, and enabling the Jallonke to gain their own independent land. This continued until the neoliberal reforms of the state in the 1990s, in which a framework was adopted of promoting customary rights of ownership and the restitution of lands expropriated by the state. Following the implementation of a pilot PRF project in the Futa Jallon, former Fulani overlords began demanding the restitution of their land and forcefully ejected Jallonke farmers from land they claimed, resulting in violent conflicts (Boiro, 1996; Diop, 2007). These conflicts show the limitations of approaches based on notions of community participation, when the community is itself structured by hierarchy.

8.6.4 Pastoral Land Conflicts

Pastoralism largely dominates in the arid and semi-arid zones in Africa. In countries within these zones herders contribute considerably to the national gross domestic product (GDP). In the Sudan, it is estimated that pastoralists contribute up to 25% of the GDP, in Mauritania, Mali and Niger about 20% of GDP and in Tanzania, Uganda and Kenya around 10% of GDP (Behnke & Muthami, 2011; Lane, 1998; Mwangi, 2009). In these areas, pastoral land use is a rational adaptation to marginal productive rangeland (Behnke & Scoones, 1993; Brockington, 2002; Homewood & Rogers, 1985; Lane, 1998; Oba, 2013). However, pastoralists are often maligned in national policy frameworks, which present pastoralism as some outmoded way of life that is environmentally destructive and that is better replaced with modern ranching. As a consequence pastoralists are under pressure of displacement from both the expansion of wildlife reserve and tourist parks encroaching into rangelands commons, from large-scale irrigation projects, the intensification and expansion of rain-fed farming, cattle ranching and agro-pastoralism. A process of commercialisation and commodification within pastoralism also results in intense competition for access to and control of resources.

Significant areas of rangeland in east Africa have been converted into wildlife and conservation parks and pastoralists have been evicted from these parks. An alliance between environmental NGOs and international business interests is creating pressures for the conversion of rangeland into other economic activities that benefit investors. Pastoral rangelands have been encroached upon for the creation of game reserves, many of which are run by the tourist industry (Brockington, 2002; Brockington et al., 2008; Galaty, 1999; Homewood & Brockington, 1999; Igoe, 2006).

The introduction of the *gestion de terroir* approach to participatory resource management in the Sahel has tended to erode pastoral land rights by introducing a system of spatially defining land by fixed village boundaries that poorly represents the interests of mobile and migrant communities, and treats the commons as the property of villages (Lund, 1999; Mwangi, 2009). Although the Tanzanian Land Act explicitly recognises the rights of pastoralists, this has not prevented villages registering pastoral grazing land as their own, and the state continues to alienate large pastoral lands for foreign investment

(Mwangi, 2009). This appropriation of pastoral lands sets off a chain reaction of further displacements and intense competition for resources, resulting in pastoral people encroaching upon each other's rangelands and resources. This promotes intensified violent conflicts between different pastoral groups; marked by raids, counter raids, skirmishes and heavy loss of life (Gebre, 2001). These conflicts are not only interethnic, but also intra-ethnic. Competition over resources leads to a distinct process of social differentiation.

From the 1960s to the 1980s, the dominant policy in pastoral areas in eastern and southern Africa was one of supporting the conversion of grazing commons into individual ranches, which was most pervasive in Botswana and Kenya. This has involved costly processes of fencing and titling land, which excludes the majority of poor pastoralists and also the mobile migratory pastoralists with large herds. The development of irrigation projects on arid lands for commercial agriculture has also displaced large numbers of pastoral people and created pressures on their grazing lands (Adams, 1992; Behnke & Kerven, 2013; Mohamed Salih, 1990).

In the Ferlo region of Senegal, Juul (1993) describes how pastoralists have had to compete with groundnut cultivation by members of the Mouride brotherhood, who have colonised large areas of farmland with tractors. While Senegalese laws recognise the rights of herders to grazing commons they also recognise the rights of farmers to use common lands. This prevents herders from excluding farmers from cropping within rangelands, but enables farmers to claim their croplands as their own personal property. Within the Ferlo area, two distinct groups of Fulani herders co-exist. One group follows an agropastoral way of life combining cropping with semisedentary cattle herding. The second group, the Foutanke, have much larger herds than the agropastoralists and use mobile pasture management strategies to exploit a wide range of seasonal pastures. However their access to pasture is diminishing, as the Mourides have been able to claim critical pasture resources as their own farmland and register them as private property. The agropastoralists have also begun to register portions of their land, which enables them to secure critical dry season pasture resources.

There is a trend in East African rangelands for agropastoralists to move towards exclusive use of resources through crop cultivation on dry season grazing lands, which enables them to gain control of these resources and prevents them from being appropriated. However, this also excludes neighbouring mobile pastoralists with large herds from using these rangelands. As a result of the widespread establishment of commercial ranches in the area, mobile pastoralists experience difficulty in gaining access to dry season grazing areas, and in some areas forage resources have become commoditised to the extent that migratory herders are forced to pay grazing fees (Angassa & Oba, 2008; Tache, 2013).

Herders have responded to the loss of land, water, and seasonal grazing resources in several ways. In Tanzania and Kenya pastoral people have organised associations to mount legal claims for the restitution of areas in which they were historically settled (Brockington, 2007; Brockington et al., 2008; Hodgson, 2011; Igoe, 2006). In Kenya, Maasai herders on the Laikipia Plateau have taken to forcefully occupying grazing lands in drought years, backing up their actions with moral discourses about entitlements and the restitution of their land (they argue that Maasai land was originally granted to the British colonisers on a 99-year lease and that the lease has now expired). In the drought of 2000 and 2004, Maasai herders started invading private ranches. The herders were able to eventually negotiate with private ranches to graze their cattle inside the ranches for the duration of the drought (Letai & Lind, 2013). In the drought of 2009 they further negotiated access to grazing in ranches and also negotiated with Kikuyu and Meru smallholder farmers for grazing land and kraals (Letai & Lind, 2013). Some Maasai and Samburu farmers have also turned their fields over to grass production, which they hire out to pastoralists or process into hay for sale. Wealthier pastoralists are also investing in the purchase of land as fodder reserves. Letai and Lind (2013) describe poorer herders moving into a variety of alternative livelihoods, including charcoal burning, fuelwood collection, chicken and egg production, beehive tending and casual labour on horticultural farms and cattle ranches.

The trend towards increasing commercialisation benefits wealthier herders who are able to invest their surplus wealth in gaining control over key resources such as water and grazing. As community resources become privatised, poorer households are excluded from gaining access to water and dry season grazing and struggle to access these resources. This results in a large number of poor pastoral households exiting from pastoral production, or becoming hired herders, or moving out into agriculture, petty trading, other urban occupations, or dependence on handouts. Pastoralism increasingly becomes a livelihood for wealthy herders who can gain control over resources, and expand production to meet new commercial opportunities. With reference to the Dar Hamar of Sudan, Babiker (2001, p. 139) argues that pastoralism has become a "strictly commercial activity" marked by hired labour:

apart from the few transhumant herders, small and large livestock herders are dependent upon hired herds. In the case of small owners, they practise what may be described as group herding whereby herds are pooled together and entrusted, on an annual contract basis, to a hired herder.

Pastoralism is characterised by increasing social differentiation and concentration of production, the expansion of fewer large herds and the impoverishment of many smaller herders (Catley & Aklilu, 2013; Little, 1985).

The displacement of pastoralists from their original grazing land and commercialisation of herding often results in intensified competition for the remaining scarce forage and water resources which have impacted on relations between different groups of herders. Gebre (2001) shows that in the Afar region of Ethiopia the development of agricultural concessions in the north forced the Afar to encroach into the territory of Karrayu pastoralists in the south. The creation of the Awash National Park expropriated a large part of Karrayu territory forcing the group to move to the south into rangelands claimed by the Arsi Oromo. The appropriation of grazing lands of the Arsi Oromo for the creation of the Nura Era Plantations pressurised the Ansi Oromo to encroach into Karrayu wet season grazing areas. This has intensified conflicts between neighbouring pastoral people (Gebre, 2001).

While intensified competition has encouraged the escalation of ethnic conflicts, it has also led to new ethnic identities among those pastoralists that have been forced to move out of mobile pastoralism (Hodgson, 2011; Igoe, 2006). This has resulted in the intermixing of different ethnic groups and the development of new forms of mutual assistance. Within this new flux of identities, wealthy pastoralists have attempted to gain control over the representation of pastoral groupings, using their wealth to build political networks. International NGOs have often supported these wealthier groups. As discussed, notions of indigeneity and of the purity of pastoral people's way of life have often worked to exclude poorer agropastoral groups and have allowed the large commercial transhumant herders to be represented as the true voice of pastoralism (Brockington et al., 2008; Homewood, 2002; Hodgson, 2011; Igoe, 2006), reinforcing the processes of social differentiation and commodification within the wider economy.

8.7 Conclusion

The land question in Africa is underpinned by three structural polarities that impact on ethnic conflicts:

1. The dichotomy between customary tenure and statutory tenure that has existed since the colonial period;
2. Tensions that occur between widespread migrations and displacements of people brought on by the expansion of the market and a customary system that only recognises the rights of indigenes; and
3. Internal contradictions that occur between the articulation of community solidarity and the processes of commodification of resources and labour that lead to increasing social differentiation.

Under indirect rule, the vast majority of Africans held land under customary tenure. However forms of statutory tenure came into existence, which enabled Europeans to gain access to land and register this land as a concession or as private property rights. This dualism was embodied in notions of assimilation that only conferred rights of full citizenship on Africans who were educated and conversant with the intricacies of European culture, as was explicitly articulated in the political ideology of French and Portuguese colonial assimilation. Colonial paternalism sought to preserve the values of African community against the individualism of the market (Cowen & Shenton, 1996). As a consequence the vast majority of rural Africans gained rights through "custom", which effectively tied them as subjects to an ethnically defined traditional or "native" authority (Mamdani, 1996).

Rural citizens gained access to rights in land through the native authority, but in return they had to provide a number of duties, including communal labour, taxation, and regulations and prescriptions on the cultivation of cash crops. This ensured that African producers were tied into export crop production as independent producers working their own land or as migrant labour. Colonial rule was based on an alliance between the colonial administration and chiefs to extract surplus from rural producers and integrate them into export production. This produced the second contradiction: an administrative framework that only recognised the customary rights and obligations of indigenes, yet an agricultural sector characterised by commodity markets, and migrants who purchased land for investment in export crop production or hired themselves out as labourers. The customary domain served to regulate export production in the main cash crop zones and to push out migrant labour to these zones in the labour reserves.

The economic coercion under indirect rule and its lack of recognition of the impact of the market on social transformation resulted in increasing rural social discontent and support for the anti-colonial movement for independence. With the attainment of independence, some of the vestiges of the most oppressive features of indirect rule were removed, but land ownership continued to be structured by the same duality of customary tenure and statutory tenure that underlay the systems of native authorities. The framework defining the two circuits was now based on the dualism of modernisation and tradition rather than racial notions (Mamdani, 1996), with the majority of peasant smallholders gaining access to land through customary claims based on ethnic origins and a small class of aspiring capitalist farmers securing expropriated land through formal registration. To ensure that registration served the interests of securing expropriated land for a select class of aspiring capitalist farmers, cumbersome processes of land registration were introduced to exclude smallholders from land registration.

As long as land was readily available this policy did not prevent those without registered land from participating in the expansion of export crop production and acquiring land in frontier areas. This facilitated the boom in export crop production during the 1960s and early 1970s. It was only when frontier land began to decline, that the framework of unregulated customary rights began to lead to increasing conflicts over land.

The economic crisis of the 1970s forced most African states to approach the IMF for assistance, which imposed structural adjustment measures and the rolling back of the state in the agrarian sector. This led to the reforms in the land sector, which have stressed decentralisation of land administration, community-based natural resource management, harmonisation of statutory and customary land tenure, and promotion of the market as a mechanism for the allocation and transfer of land. There have been some innovations in devising technical solutions to recognising customary land rights, harmonising customary and statutory tenure within a unitary framework, and integrating informal ways documenting and registering customary land rights with formal legal recognition. This enables customary rights to be transacted in land markets.

The framing of the land question has, however, tended to underestimate the extent to which customary land is already integrated into national and regional land markets and processes of capital accumulation and social differentiation. As a consequence, community-based land administration has often intensified conflicts over land and resulted in the community emerging as a site of struggle for the accumulation and control of land. Far from representing the inclusive rights of the community, traditional authorities and village councils are frequently integrated into national and international circuits of capital accumulation and use their power within communities to further the reach of these commercial networks into the rural landscape. They are involved in the redefinition of community and community values to facilitate processes of capital accumulation and dispossession.

The land question cannot be reduced to technical prescriptions that solve what are deep and complex social problems. There are no "magic bullets", no "best practice" scenarios that can be implemented to solve the problems. Underlying the land question are intractable conundrum of how to ensure that land policy meets the social needs of the poor and provides them with access to viable livelihoods when few other options exist, while enabling land to support economic growth and capitalist accumulation.

Part of the solution will lie in developing dynamic new sectors that are not based on natural resources and which link the rural with urban sectors. However, the land question needs to be reframed to take into account wider patterns of national and regional development, including the extent of rural mobility and movement of labour. Since the early colonial period agricultural export production has been premised on migration and the development of migrant communities throughout national territories. These migrants are vital to a modern economy and must be granted full citizen rights in the areas in which they have been economically and socially integrated, in which they have raised their families and the new generation. However, this process should not result in the dispossession of the local peasantry of their land and natural resources in the name of a national development that fuels capitalist accumulation and the consolidation of wealth by the few.

Part of the solution will also lie in providing agricultural support services to the poor, which will enable them to develop their land resources on their own terms, rather than increase their vulnerability to market shocks and distress sales. Despite the rhetoric about the superiority of modern technology and the need to open up agriculture to external investment, smallholders and pastoralists already make important and dynamic contributions to African economies. Modernisation should not be an excuse for expropriation.

Land rights need to be framed outside narratives of ethnic belonging and ethno-patriarchal privileges. It is this framing that provides the context for ethnic strife, in which the rural poor perceive the process of social differentiation and commodification that undermines their livelihoods as a denial of their ethnic birthrights by an influx of migrants. These perceptions enable local political elites to collaborate in the process of land accumulation while pointing the finger at relatively weak groups of migrants as the causal agents. The movement of migrant labour is a reflection of the development of markets: markets cannot flourish without the free movement of people. Therefore, ethnic land disputes cannot be solved by delegating the power of administration to community institutions, by representing community elders and traditional authority as the voice of the community. This only serves to close down the voices of the dispossessed (Boone & Duku, 2012; Chauveau & Richards, 2008), and fails to recognise the social diversity of rural communities.

Notions of citizenship rooted in abstract human rights to property and property ownership or notions of liberal democratic rights are not without problems. The literature on new institutional economics presents a framework in which the West was able to develop because it evolved institutions that upheld property rights, judicial systems and democratic freedoms (North, 2005). But these property rights did not exist for all. Historically, with the advent of capitalism in Britain, the property rights of the emerging capitalist class were protected to the exclusion of the rural poor, who were expropriated though the enclosure of their user rights and common land (Meiksins Wood, 2012; Thompson, 1993). In Locke's framework, which came to define modern conceptions of property, the main objective of civil society was the preservation of property. Property rights came to define an exclusive citizenry in which political participation and voters rights were defined by ownership of property. Those without rights as full citizens experienced the expropriation of their customary rights in land in the name of "improvement" and progress. Universal male suffrage only became to be established in Europe in the mid nineteenth century and in Britain as late as 1918, by which time the consolidation of capitalist property prevented any meaningful debate about reforming property rights (Meiksins Wood, 2012). The conditions of the western working class has been characterised by the lack of property rights, a factor which continues to be reified in the gentrification of the inner city areas, in the mortgage crisis, in soaring rents in the main cities, and the consolidation of wealth and property by the richest stratum of the population (Fuentes-Nieva & Galosso, 2014; Piketty, 2014).

Debates about what constitutes citizenship in contemporary Africa are closely associated with the creation of exclusive rights in land. In many cases, citizenship is used to create an alliance between those who are able to control land within specific localities and private investors. While property rights are construed as a central tenet of liberal democracy, the ways in which they are fashioned often lead to a process of exclusion and alienation and to perceptions of inequality. While this process is justified as bringing about development, and allowing those with the ability to invest to acquire land, the inequalities and grievances that emerge often lead to demands for the rights of the autochthones, as has been apparent in both Côte d'Ivoire and Kivu in the Democratic Republic of Congo. Migrants are blamed as the weakest link in the underlying patterns of accumulation, market expansion and commodification of land. This playing out of ethnic and nationalistic conflicts in the context of increasing economic woes, is a terrain not unfamiliar to the recent anti-immigrant outpourings in Europe.

The harmonisation of customary and statutory rights within a framework of property rights tends to subvert customary rights. Recognition of customary user rights as individual property tends to transforms them into commodities that can be transacted on markets, opening up their acquisition by investors. The recognition of customary land rights as potential individual property rights and fields for capitalist investment leads to an alliance between forms of accumulation from below within rural areas and accumulation by international and national capital. This alienates increasing numbers of people who lose their access to resources and are forced to migrate to gain a living, which results in increasing land pressures in other areas. Those with customary user rights in land find these rights increasingly subverted by the market, which also subtly transforms their identities, as in the case of poor pastoralists whose lack of access to pasture results in a refashioning of ethnic identities. Those pursuing forms of mobile economy that do not comply with notions of modern property and commercial activities find their property rights undermined, as other land users integrated into commercial production make fresh claims upon their land, leading to a process of the emergence of new forms of land enclosure by commercial land users. This process of revalidating and redefining customary rights and social identities leads to both conflicts and the rapid economic transformation of rural areas.

The shortcomings and unforeseen consequences of a narrow approach to community-based land administration have resulted in a growing awareness of the importance of political economy in understanding the land question (Chauveau & Richards, 2008; Peters, 2004). African rural agrarian economies are characterised by complex linkages of agrarian production to international, national and regional markets. They are marked by social differentiation, processes of concentration of capital and land, and a diversity of coping mechanisms and strategies for accumulation capital. Although it is difficult and unwise to make simple policy prescriptions to resolve the land question at this juncture in time, it is this growing awareness of the complex linkages of communities to wider economies and markets that is likely to provide a new framework for addressing the land question in Africa and conflicts in land.

References

Adams, W. M. 1992. *Wasting the Rain: Rivers, People and Planning in Africa*. London: Earthscan.

Adenew, B., and Abdi, F. 2005. *Land Registration in Amhara Region, Ethiopia*. London: IIED.

Adoko, J., and Levine, S. 2005. *Land Rights: Where Are We and Where Do We Need to Go?* Kampala: Land Equity Movement in Uganda (Lemu).

Alden Wily, L. 2003. *Community-Based Land Management: Questions and Answers about Tanzania's New Village Act, 1999 (Drylands Programme Issue Paper no 120)*. London: IIED.

Alden Wiley, L. 2008. Custom and commonage in Africa: Rethinking the orthodoxies. *Land Use Policy*, 25(1): 43–52.

Amanor, K. S. 2009a. Global food chains, African smallholders and World Bank governance. *Journal of Agrarian Change*, 9(2): 247–262.

2009b. Tree plantations, agricultural commodification, and land tenure security in Ghana. In Ubink, J. M., Hoekema, A. J., and Assies, W. J. (eds.), *Legalising Land Rights: Local Practice, State Responses and Tenure Security in Africa, Asia and Latin America*. Leiden: Leiden University Press, pp. 133–162.

Amanor K. S. 2011. Youth, migrants and agribusiness in cocoa frontiers. Land, labour, child trafficking and the crises of governance in West Africa. In Jul-Larsen, E., Laurent, P.-J., Le Meur, P.-Y., and Léonard, E. (eds.),*Une anthropologie entre pouvoirs et histoire: Conversations autour de l'oeuvre de Jean-Pierre Chauveau*. Paris: Karthala, pp. 93–124.

2012. Global resource grabs, agribusiness concentration and the smallholder: Two West African case studies. *Journal of Peasant Studies*, 39 (3–4): 731–749.

Angassa, A., and Oba, G. 2008. Herder perceptions on impact of range enclosures, crop farming, fire ban and bush encroachment on the rangeland of Borano, Southern Ethiopia. *Human Ecology*, 36(2): 201–215.

Autesserre, S. 2010) *The Trouble with the Congo: Local Violence and the Failure of International Peacebuilding*. Cambridge: Cambridge University Press.

Babiker, M. 2001. Resource competition and conflict: Herder/farmer or pastoralism/agriculture. in Mohamed Salih, A., Dietz, T., Ahmed, A. G. M. (eds.), *African Pastoralism: Conflict, Institutions and Governance*. London: Pluto Press, pp. 134–144.

Babo, A. 2013. The crisis of public policies in Côte d'Ivoire: Land law and the nationality trap in Tabou's rural communities. *Africa*, 83(1): 100–119.

Behnke, R., and Kerven, C. 2013. Replacing pastoralism with irrigated agriculture. In Catley, A., Lind, J., Scoones, I. (eds.), *Pastoralism and Development in Africa: Dynamic Change at the Margins*. London: Earthscan, pp. 57–70.

Behnke, R., and Muthami, D. 2011. *The Contribution of Livestock to the Kenyan Economy (IDAD LPI Working Paper No. 03–11)*. Djibouti: IGAD Livestock Policy Initiative. Intergovernmental Authority for Development.

Behnke, R. H., and Scoones, I. 1993. Rethinking range ecology: Implications for rangeland management in Africa. In Behnke, R. H., Scoones, I., Kerven, C. (eds.), *Range Ecology at Disequilibrium: New Models of*

Natural Variability and Pastoral Adaptation in African Savannahs.
London: Overseas Development Institute, pp. 1–30.

Berman, B. 1990. *Control and Crisis in Colonial Kenya: The Dialectic of Domination.* London: James Currey.

Boiro, I. 1996. The Guinean land tenure system: A methodological approach to sustainable resource management. Case study Kollangui-Pita (Fouta Djallon). In *Managing Land Tenure and Resource Access in West Africa: Proceedings of a Regional Workshop Gorée,* Senegal, November 18–22, 1996, Convened by L'Université de Saint-Louis, GRET, IIED, Ministére Français de la Coopération and British Overseas Development Administration. London: IIED, pp. 71–83.

Boni, S. 2005. *Clearing the Ghanaian Forest: Theories and Practice of Acquisition, Transfer and Utilization of Farming Titles in the Sefwi-Akan Area.* Legon: Institute of Africa Studies, University of Ghana.

Boone, C., and Duku, D. K. 2012. Ethnic land rights in western Ghana: Landlord-stranger relations in the democratic era. *Development and Change,* 43(3): 671–693.

Borras, S. M. Jr., and Franco, J. C. 2010. Contemporary discourses and contestations around pro-poor land policies and land governance. *Journal of Agrarian Change,* 10(1): 1–32.

Brockington, D. 2002. *Fortress Conservation: The Preservation of Mkomazi Game Reserve, Tanzania.* London: James Currey.

    2007. Forests, community conservation, and local government performance: The village forest reserves of Tanzania. *Society and Natural Resources,* 20(9): 835–848.

Brockington, D., Duffy, R., Igoe, J. 2008. *Nature Unbound: Conservation, Capitalism and the Future of Protected Areas.* London: Earthscan.

Bruce, J. W. 1993. Do indigenous tenure systems constrain agricultural development? . In Basset, T. J., and Crummey, D. E. (eds.), *Land in African Agrarian Systems.* Madison: University of Wisconsin Press, pp. 35–56.

Catley, A., and Aklilu, Y. (2013. Moving up or moving out? Commercialization, growth and destitution in pastoral areas. In Catley, A., Lind, J., Scoones, I. (eds.), *Pastoralism and Development in Africa: Dynamic Change at the Margins.* London: Earthscan, pp. 85–97.

Chauveau J.-P. 2000. Question foncière et construction nationale en Côte d'Ivoire. Les enjeux silencieux d'un coup d'État. *Politique Africaine,* 78(2): 94–125. Also in English as The *Land Question in Côte d'Ivoire: A Lesson in History (IIED Drylands Programme Issues Paper No. 95).* London: IIED.

Chauveau, J.-P. 2006. How does an institution evolve? Land, politics, intergenerational relations and the institution of the *tutorat* amongst autochthones and immigrants (Gban region, Côte d'Ivoire). In Kuba, R., and Lenz, C. (eds.), *Land and the Politics of Belonging in West Africa*. Leiden and Boston: Brill, pp. 213–240.

2009. La loi de 1998 sur le domaine rural dans l'histoire des politiques foncières en Côte d'Ivoire: La politique des transferts de droits entre 'autochtones'et 'étrangers' en zone forestière. In Colin, J. P. Le Meur, P.-Y., and Léonard, É. (eds.), *Les politiques d'enregistrement des droits fonciers: Du cadre legal aux pratiques locales*. Paris: Karthala, pp. 105–140.

Chauveau, J.-P., and Colin, J.-P. 2010. Customary transfers and land sales in Côte d'Ivoire: Revisiting the embeddedness issue. *Africa*, 80(1): 81–103.

Chauveau, J.-P., Colin, J.-P., Jacob, J.-P., Lavigne Delville, P., and Le Meur, P.-Y. 2006. *Changes in Land Access and Governance in West Africa: Markets, Social Mediations and Public Policies*. London: IIED.

Chauveau, J.-P., and Léonard, E. 1996. Côte d'Ivoire's pioneer fronts: Historical and political determinants of the spread of cocoa cultivation. In Clarence-Smith, W. G. (Ed.) *Cocoa Pioneer Fronts since 1800: The Role of Smallholders, Planters and Merchants*. Basingstoke: Macmillan, pp. 176–194.

Chauveau, J.-P., and Richards, P. 2008. West African Insurgencies in Agrarian Perspective: Côte d'Ivoire and Sierra Leone Compared. *Journal of Agrarian Change*, 8(4): 515–552.

Chihowu, A., and Woodhouse, P. 2006. Customary vs private property rights? Dynamics and trajectories of vernacular land markets in sub-Saharan Africa. *Journal of Agrarian Change*, 6(1): 346–371.

Colin, J.-P., and Ayouz, M. 2006. The development of land markets? Insights from Côte D'Ivoire. *Land Economics*, 82(3): 404–423.

Cotula, L. 2013. *The Great African Land Grab? Agricultural Investment and the Global Food System. London: Zed Books*

Cowen, M. P., and Shenton, R. W. 1996. *Doctrines of Development*. London: Routledge.

Daniel, S., and Mittal, A. 2009. *The Great Land Grab: Rush for World's Farmland Threatens Food Security for the Poor*. Oakland, CA: The Oakland Institute.

de Haan, L. 1998. Gestion de Terroir at the frontier: Village land management including both peasants and pastoralists in Benin. In Bruins, H. J., and Lithwick, H. (eds.), *The Arid Frontier. Interactive Management of Environment and Development*. Boston: Kluwer Academic Publishers, pp. 209–277.

Deininger, K. 2003. *Land Policies for Growth and Poverty Reduction*. Washington: World Bank and Oxford: Oxford University Press.

Diaby, N. 1996. Land disputes in the South-West Region of Côte d'Ivoire. In *Managing Land Tenure and Resource Access in West Africa: Proceedings of a Regional Workshop*, Gorée, Senegal, November 18–22. Convened by L'Université de Saint-Louis, GRET, IIED, Ministére Français de la Coopération and British Overseas Development Administration. London: IIED, pp. 158–166.

Dinerman, A. 2006. *Revolution, Counter-Revolution and Revisionism in Postcolonial Africa: The Case of Mozambique 1975–1994*. Abingdon, Oxford and New York: Routledge.

Diop, M. 2007. *Réformes foncières et gestion des resources naturelles en Guinée: Enjeux de patrimonialité et de propriété dans le Timbi au Fouta Djalon*. Paris: Karthala.

Fay, D., and James, D. 2009. "Restoring what was ours": An introduction. In Fay, D., and James, D. (eds.), *The Rights and Wrongs of Land Restitution: Restoring What Was Ours*. Abingdon, Oxon: Routledge-Cavendish, pp. 1–24.

Fitzpatrick, D. 2005. "Best practice" options for the legal recognition of customary tenure. *Development and Change*, 36(3): 449–475.

Fuentes-Nieva and Galosso, N. 2014. *Working for the Few: Political Capture and Economic Inequality. Oxfam International*. Available at: www .oxfam.org/sites/www.oxfam.org/files/bp-working-for-few-political-capture-economic-inequality-200114-summ-e. Accessed 16 May 2016.

Galaty, J. 1999. Grounding pastoralists: Law, politics and dispossession in East Africa. *Nomadic Peoples*, 3(2): 56–73.

Gastaldi, J. 1999. Le Plan Foncièr Rural en Afrique de l'Ouest. *Etudes Foncières*, 83, pp. 37–41.

Gebre. A. 2001. Conflict management, resolution and institutions among the Karrayu and their neighbours. In Mohamed Salih, A., Dietz, T., Ahmed, A. G. M. (eds.), *African Pastoralism: Conflict, Institutions and Governance*. London: Pluto Press, pp. 81–99.

Guèye, I., and Laban, P. 1992. *From Woodlots to Village Land Management in the Sahel (Dryland Issue Paper No. 35)*. London: IIED.

Hall, R. 2007. Transforming rural South Africa? Taking stock of land reform. In Ntsebeza, L., and Hall, R. (eds.), *The Land Question in South Africa: The Challenge of Transformation and Redistribution*. Cape Town: HSRC Press, pp. 87–106.

2010. Two cycles of land policy in South Africa: Tracing the contours. In Anseeuw, W., and Alden, C. (eds.), *The Struggle over Land in Africa: Conflicts, Politics and Change*. Cape Town: Human Sciences Research Council, pp. 175–192.

Hill, P., and McGlade C. 1957. *An Economic Survey of Cocoa Farmers in Sefwi-Wiawso*. Legon: Cocoa Research Series no 2, Economic Research Division, University College of Ghana.

Hitchcock, R. K. 2001. Hunting is our heritage: The struggle for hunting and gathering rights among the San of Southern Africa. In Anderson, D. G., and Ikeya, K. (eds.), *Parks, Property and Power: Managing Hunting Practice and Identity within State Policy Regimes*. Osaka: National Museum of Ethnology, pp. 136–156

Hodgson, D. L. 2011. *Being Maasai, Becoming Indigenous: Postcolonial Politics in a Neoliberal World*. Bloomington: Indiana University Press.

Homewood, K. 2002. Elites, entrepreneurs and exclusion in Maasailand. *Human Ecology*, 30, pp. 107–138

Homewood, K., and Brockington, D. 1999. Biodiversity conservation and development in Mkomazi Game Reserve in Tanzania. *Global Ecology and Biogeography*, 8(3–4): 301–313.

Homewood, K., and Rodgers, W. A. 1985. Pastoralism, conservation and the overgrazing controversy. In Anderson, D., and Grove, R. (eds.), *Conservation in Africa: Peoples, Policies and Practice*. Cambridge: Cambridge University Press, pp. 111–128.

Huggins, C. 2010. *Land, Power and Identity: Roots of Violent Conflict in Eastern DRC*. London: International Alert.

Hunt, D. 2004. Unintended consequences of land rights reform: The case of the 1998 Uganda Land Act. *Development Policy Review*, 22(2): 173–191.

Igoe, J. 2006. Becoming Indigenous peoples: Difference, inequality and the globalisation of East African identity politics. *African Affairs*, 105 (420): 399–420.

Igoe, J., and Brockington, D. 1999. *Pastoralist Land Tenure and Community Conservation: A Case Study from Northeast Tanzania*. London: IIED.

Jayne, T. S., Chamberlin, J., Traub, L. Sitko, N., Muyanga, M., Yeboah, F. K., Anseeuw, W., Chapoto, A., Wineman, A., Nkonde, C., and Kachule, R. 2016. Africa's changing farm size distribution patterns: The rise of medium-scale farmers. *Agricultural Economics*, 47(Suppl. 1): 197–214.

Joireman, S. F. 2007. Enforcing new property rights in sub-Saharan Africa: The Ugandan Constitution and the 1998 Land Act. *Comparative Politics*, 39(4): 463–480.

Juul, K. 1993. Pastoral tenure problems and local resource management: The case of northern Senegal. *Nomadic Peoples*, 32, pp. 81–90.

Kanyinga, K. 2000. *Redistribution from Above: The Politics of Land Rights and Squatting in Coastal Kenya*. Uppsala: Nordiska Afrikainstitutet

Kanyinga, K., Lumumba, O., and Amanor, K. S. 2008. The struggle for sustainable land management and democratic development in

Kenya: A history of greed and grievance. In Amanor, K. S., and Moyo, S. (eds.), *Land and Sustainable Development in Africa*. London: Zed Books, pp. 100–126.

Khadiagala L. S. 2001. The failure of popular justice in Uganda: Local councils and women's property rights. *Development and Change*, 32 (1): 55–76.

Kimenyi, M. S., and Ndung'u, N. S. 2005. Sporadic ethnic violence: Why has Kenya not experienced a full blown civil war? In Collier, P., and Sambanis, N. (eds.), *Understanding Civil War: Evidence and Analysis. Vol. 1 Africa*. Washington: World Bank, pp. 123–156.

Klopp, J. M. 2000. Pilfering the public: The problem of land grabbing in contemporary Kenya. *Africa Today*, 47(1): 7–26.

Knight, R. S. 2010. *Statutory Recognition of Customary Land Rights in Africa: An Investigation into Best Practices for Lawmaking and Implementation (FAO Legislative Study 105)*. Rome: FAO.

Knight, R. S., Adoko, J., Auma, T., Kaba, A., Salomao, A., Siakor, S., and Tankar, I. 2012. *Protecting Community Land and Resources: Evidence from Liberia, Mozambique and Uganda*. Rome: International Development Law Organization.

Kouamé, G. 2010. Intra-family and socio-political dimension of land markets and land conflicts: The case of Abure, Côte d'Ivoire. *Africa*, 80(1): 126–146.

Land Rights Research and Resources Institute. 2010. *Accumulation by Land Dispossession and Labour Devaluation in Tanzania: The Case of Bio-fuel and Forestry Investments in Kilwa and Kilolo*. Dar-es-Salam: Land Rights Research and Resources Institute. Available at: http://landportal .info/sites/default/files/land_grab_case_studies_in_tanzania.pdf. Accessed 10 January 2013.

Landell-Mills, P. 1992. Governance, cultural change and empowerment. *Journal of Modern Africa Studies*, 30(4):543–567.

Lane, C. 1998. Introduction: Overview of the pastoral problematic. In Lane, C. R. (Ed.) *Custodians of the Commons: Pastoral Land Tenure in East and West Africa*. London: Earthscan, pp. 1–25.

Lavigne Delville, P. 2000. harmonising formal law and customary land rights in French-speaking West Africa. In Toulmin, C., and Quan, J. (eds.), *Evolving Land Rights, Policy and Tenure in Africa*. London: IIED, pp. 97–122.

2005. Registering and administering customary land rights: Current innovations and questions in French-Speaking West Africa. In van der Molen, P., and Lemmen, C. (eds.), *Proceedings. Secure Land Tenure "New Legal Frameworks and Tools"*. Denmark: FIG Commission 7.

Lentz, C. 1995. Tribalism and ethnicity in Africa: A review of four decades of anglophone research. *Cahiers des Sciences Humaines*, 31(2): 322–324.

Leo, C. 1984. *Land and Class in Kenya*. Toronto and London: University of Toronto Press.

Léonard, E. 1997. Crise écologique, crise économique, crise d'un modèle d'exploitation agricole: Ajustements et recomposition sociale sur les anciens fronts pionniers ivoiriens. In Contamin, B., and Memel-Foté, H. (eds.), *Le modèle ivoirien en question: Crises, ajustements, recompositions*. Paris: KATHALA and L'ORSTOM, pp. 393–413.

Léonard, E., and Oswald, M. 1997. Cocoa smallholders facing a double structural adjustment in Côte D'Ivoire: Responses to a predicted crisis. In Ruf, F., and Siswoputranto, P. S. (eds.), *Cocoa Cycles: The Economies of Cocoa Supply*. Cambridge: Woodhead Publishing Limited, pp. 125–150.

Letai, J., and Lind, J. 2013. Squeezed from all sides: Changing resource tenure and pastoralist innovation on the Laikipia Plateau, Kenya. In Catley, A., Lind, J., and Scoones, I. (eds.), *Pastoralism and Development in Africa: Dynamic Change at the Margins*. London: Earthscan, pp. 164–176.

Little, P. 1985. Social differentiation and pastoral sedentarization in Northern Kenya. *Africa*, 55(3): 243–261.

Lonsdale J. 1994. Moral ethnicity and political tribalism. In Kaarsholm, P., and Hultin, J. (eds.), *Inventions and Boundaries: Historical and Anthropological Approaches to the Study of Ethnicity and Nationalism*. Roskilde, Denmark: Institute for Development Studies, pp. 131–150.

Lonsdale, J. 2012. Ethnic patriotism and markets in Africa. In Hino, H., Lonsdale, J., Ranis, G., and Stewart, F. (eds.), *Ethnic Diversity and Instability in Africa: Interdisciplinary Perspectives*. Cambridge: Cambridge University Press, pp. 19–55.

Losch, B. 2000. Introduction au thème: La Côte d'Ivoire en quête d'un nouveau projet national. In 'Côte d'Ivoire: La tentation ethnonationaliste. *Politique Africaine*, 78, pp. 5–25.

2002. Global restructuring and liberalization: Côte d'Ivoire and the end of the cocoa market?' *Journal of Agrarian Change*, 2(2): 206–227.

Lund, C. 1999. A question of honour – Property disputes and brokerage in Burkina Faso. *Africa*, 69(4): 575–594.

2008. *Local Politics and the Dynamics of Property in Africa*. Cambridge: Cambridge University Press.

Mamdani, M. 1996. *Citizen and Subject: Contemporary Africa and the Legacy of Colonialism*. Princetown, NJ: Princetown University Press.

Manji, A. 2001. Land reform in the shadow of the state: The implementation of new land laws in sub-Saharan Africa. *Third World Quarterly*, 22(3): 327–342.

2006. *The Politics of Land Reform in Africa: From Communal Tenure to Free Markets*. London: Zed Books.

Mararo, B. 1997. Land, power, and ethnic conflict in Masisi (Congo-Kinshasa), 1940s– 1994. *International Journal of African Historical Studies*, 30(3): 503– 538.

Mathangani, P. 2006. Fresh Protests as Government Hives Off Mau Forest. *East African Standard*, August 16.

Meiksins Wood, E. 2012. *Liberty and Property: A Social History of Western Political Thought from Renaissance to Enlightenment*. London and New York: Verso.

Migot-Adholla, S., Hazell, P., Blarel, B., and Place, F. 1991. Indigenous land rights systems in sub-Saharan Africa: A constraint on productivity?' *World Bank Economic Review*, 5(1): 155–175.

Mohamed Salih, M. A. 1990. Government policy and options in pastoral development in the Sudan. *Nomadic People*, 25(7): 65–78.

Molomo, M. G. 2008. Sustainable development, ecotourism, national minorities and land in Botswana. In Amanor, K. S., and Moyo, S. (eds.), *Land and Sustainable Development in Africa*. London: Zed, pp. 159–183.

Moyo, S., and Yeros, P. 2005. Land occupation and land reform in Zimbabwe: Towards the national democratic revolution. In Moyo, S., and Yeros, P. (eds.), *Reclaiming the Land: The Resurgence of Rural Movements in Africa, Asia and Latin America*. London: Zed and Cape Town: David Philip, pp. 165–208.

Mugambwa, J. 2007. A comparative analysis of land tenure law reform in Uganda and Papua New Guinea. *Journal of Pacific Law*, 11(1): 39–55.

Mwangi, E. 2009. Property rights and governance of Africa's rangelands: A policy overview. *Natural Resources Forum*, 33(2): 160–170.

Namwaya, O. 2004. Who Owns Kenya?' *The Standard Online Edition, 1st October*. Available at www.marsgroupkenya.org/pdfs/crisis/2008/02/large_landowners_in_Kenya.pdf. Accessed 26 March 2013.

Niboye, E. P. 2010. *The Impact of Changing Pastoral Strategies on Environmental Resources and Livelihoods in Tanzania's Lake Victoria Basin*. Addis Ababa: Organisation for Social Research in Eastern and Southern Africa.

North, D. C. 2005. *Understanding the Process of Economic Change*. Princeton and Oxford: Princeton University Press.

Nsamba-Gayiiya, E. 1999. Implementing Land Tenure Reform in Uganda: A complex task ahead. *DFID Workshop on Land Rights and*

Sustainable Development in sub-Saharan Africa, 16–19 February, Berkshire, UK.

Ntsebeza, L. 2007. Land redistribution in South Africa: The property clause revisited. In Ntsebeza, L., and Hall, R. (eds.), *The Land Question in South Africa: The Challenge of Transformation and Redistribution*. Cape Town: HSRC Press, pp. 107–131.

Oakland Institute. 2011. *Understanding Land Investment Deals in Africa. Country Report: Mozambique*. Oakland, CA: Oakland Institute.

Oba, G. 2013. The Sustainability of Pastoral Production in Africa. In Catley, A., Lind, J., Scoones, I. (eds.), *Pastoralism and Development in Africa: Dynamic Change at the Margins*. London: Earthscan, pp. 29–36.

Olivier de Sardin, J.-P. 1984. *Les societes Songhay-Zarma (Niger, Mali): Chefs, guerriers, esclaves, paysans*. Paris: Karthala.

Ouédraogo, H. M. G 2005. Etude comparative de la mise en oeuvre des Plans fonciers ruraux en Afrique de l'Ouest: Bénin, Burkina Faso, Côte d'Ivoire. *Etudes Juridique en Ligne*, 42, FAO: Rome.

Peters, P. 1994. *Dividing the Commons: Politics, Policy and Culture in Botswana*. Charlotsville: University of Virginia Press.

2004. Inequality and Social Conflict over Land in Africa. *Journal of Agrarian Change*, 4(3): 269–314.

Piketty, T. 2014. *Capital in the Twenty-First Century*. Cambridge, MA: Belknap Press of Harvard University Press.

Prunier, G. 2009. *From Genocide to Continental War: The "Congolese" Conflict and the Crisis of Contemporary Africa*. London: C. Hurst & Co.

Quan, J. 2000. Land boards as a mechanism or the management of land rights in Southern Africa. In Toulmin, C., and Quan, J. (eds.), *Evolving Land Rights, Policy and Tenure in Africa*. London: IIED, pp. 197–206.

Rahmato, D. 2009a. Peasants and agrarian reform: The unfinished quest for secure land rights in Ethiopia. In Ubink, J. M., Hoekema, A. J., and Assies, W. J. (eds.), *Legalising Land Rights: Local Practice, State Responses and Tenure Security in Africa, Asia and Latin America*. Leiden: Leiden University Press, pp. 33–58.

2009b. Land rights and tenure security: Rural land registration in Ethiopia. In Ubink, J. M., Hoekema, A. J., and Assies, W. J. (eds.), *Legalising Land Rights: Local Practice, State Responses and Tenure Security in Africa, Asia and Latin America*. Leiden: Leiden University Press, pp. 59–96.

Raulin, H. 1957. *Mission d'Étude des Groupements Immigrés en Côte d'Ivoire*. Paris: ORSTOM.

Ruf, F. 2001. Tree Crops as Deforestation and Reforestation Agents: The case of cocoa in Côte d'Ivoire and Sulawesi. In Angelsen, A., and

Kaimowitz, D. (eds.), *Agricultural Technologies and Tropical Deforestation*. Wallingford: CAB International, pp. 291–316.

Schmidt, E. 2005. *Mobilizing the Masses: Gender, Ethnicity and Class in the Nationalist Movement in Guinea, 1939–1958*. Portsmouth, NH: Heinemann.

Scoones, I., Marongwe, N., Mavedzenge, B., Mahenehene, J., Murimbarimba, F., and Sukume, C. 2010. *Zimbabwe's Land Reform: Myths and Realities*. Woodbridge: James Currey.

Senghor, L. S. 1964. *On African Socialism*. New York: Praeger.

Shivji, I. 2000. Contradictory Perspectives on Rights and Justice in the Context of Land Reform in Tanzania. In Mamdani, M. (Ed.) *Beyond Rights Talk and Culture Talk: Comparative Essays on the Politics of Rights and Culture*. New York: St Martin's Press, pp. 37–60.

Stamm, V. 2000. *The Rural Land Plan: An Innovative Approach from Côte d'Ivoire (IIED Drylands Programme Issues Paper no 91)*. London: IIED.

Suzman, J. 2003. Kalahari Conundrums: Relocation, resistance, and international support in the central Kalahari, Botswana. *Before Farming*, 3–4(12): 1–10.

Tache, B. 2013. Rangeland Enclosures in Southern Oromia, Ethiopia; An innovative response to the erosion of common property resources. In Catley, A., Lind, J., and Scoones, I. (eds.), *Pastoralism and Development in Africa: Dynamic Change at the Margins*. London: Earthscan, pp. 37–46.

Tanner, C. 2010. Land Rights and Enclosures: Implementing the Mozambican Land Law in practice. In Anseeuw, W., and Alden, C. (eds.), *The Struggle over Land in Africa: Conflicts, Politics and Change*. Cape Town: HSRC Press, pp. 105–131.

Teyssier, A., Andrianirina Ratsialonana, R., Razafindralambo, R., and Razafindrakoto, T. 2009. Décentralisation de la gestion des terres à Madagascar: Processus, enjeux et perspectives d'une nouvelle politique foncière. In Colin, J.-P., Le Meur, J.-Y., and Léonard, É. (eds.), *Les politiques d'enregistrement des droits fonciers: Du cadre legal aux pratiques locales*. Paris: Karthala, pp. 273–298.

Thompson, E. P. 1993. *Customs in Common*. London: Penguin.

Toulmin, C., and Quan, J. 2000. Evolving land rights, tenure and Policy in Sub-Saharan Africa. In Toulmin, C., and Quan, J. (eds.), *Evolving Land Rights, Policy and Tenure in Africa*. London: IIED, pp. 1–30.

Tsikata, D. 2003. Securing Women's Interests within Land Tenure Reform: Recent debates in Tanzania. *Journal of Agrarian Change*, 3(1–2): 149–183.

Ubink, J. M. 2008. Negotiated or negated? The rhetoric and reality of customary tenure in an Ashanti village in Ghana. *Africa*, 78(2): 264–287.

Van Acker, F. 2005. Where did all the land go? Enclosure and Social Struggle in Kivu (DR Congo) . *Review of African Political Economy*, 32(103): 79–98.

Veit, P., Nshala, R., Odhiambo, M. O., and Manyindo, J. 2008. *Protected Areas and Property Rights: Democratizing Eminent Domain in East Africa.* Washington: World Resource Institute.

Vlassenroot, K., and Huggins, C. 2005. Land, Migration and Conflict in Eastern DRC. In Huggins, C., and Clover, J. (eds.), *From the Ground Up: Land Rights, Conflict and Peace in Sub-Saharan Africa.* Nairobi: African Centre for Technology Studies and Pretoria: Institute for Security Studies, pp. 115–194.

Watts, M. J. 2000. Contested Communities, Malignant Markets, and Gilded Governance: Justice, resource extraction, and conservation in the tropics. In Zernor, C. (Ed.) *People, Plants and Justice: The Politics of Nature Conservation.* New York: Columbia University Press, pp. 21–51.

Werbner, R. P. 2004. *Reasonable Radicals and Citizenship in Botswana: The Public Anthropology of Kalanga Elites.* Bloomington, IN: Indiana University Press.

Whitehead, A., and Tsikata, D. 2003. Policy discourses on women's land rights in Sub-Saharan Africa: The implications of the return to the Customary. *Journal of Agrarian Change*, 3(1–2): 67–112.

World Bank. 2008. *World Development Report 2008.* Washington: World Bank.

2009. *Awakening Africa's Sleeping Giant: Prospects for Commercial Agriculture in the Guinea Savannah Zone and Beyond.* Washington, DC: World Bank.

2010. *Rising Global Interest in Farmland: Can It Yield Sustainable and Equitable Benefits?* Washington, DC: World Bank.

Zoomers, A. 2010. Globalisation and the foreignisation of Space: Seven processes driving the current global land grab. *Journal of Peasant Studies*, 37(2): 429–447.

9 | Protecting Education from Ethnic Politics

ERIC KRAMON AND DANIEL N. POSNER

9.1 Introduction

An educated population is both a development goal and an instrument for development. Education improves a country's stock of human capital and its rate of economic growth (Barro & Lee, 2010; Hanushek & Woessman, 2007). It unlocks economic opportunities for individuals and increases household incomes (Krueger & Lindahl, 2000), while also improving a range of non-market outcomes, notably the health of educated adults and their infants and children (Gakidou et al., 2010; Grossman, 2006). By equipping individuals with the skills they need to make effective choices and live productive, meaningful lives, education is an essential part of what it means to be free (Sen, 1999; World Bank, 2018).

By fostering an informed citizenry, education is essential for active political participation and improving the quality of governance (Bleck, 2015; Brady et al., 1995; Dahl, 1971; Lipset, 1959). Educated individuals are, moreover, more likely to support democracy and express democratic values (Diamond, 1999). Closer to the concerns of this volume, modernization theory suggests that increasing education may be associated with a reduction in individual attachments to localised ethnic identities and a concomitant increase in social cohesion. Indeed, survey evidence from a number of African countries shows that more educated individuals feel a stronger connection to their national identity relative to their ethnicity (Robinson, 2014). To the extent that building a common sense of identification with the nation is an important element of development (Gellner, 1983), education is likely to play a key role. (See Chapter 3 for a case study of Tanzania.) Insofar as education provides opportunities for upward advancement for economically disadvantaged individuals and groups, it may also play a role in reducing both vertical and horizontal inequality. (Chapter 10 discusses language in education as a means of fostering social cohesion.)

Education is thus central to economic and political development. Yet precisely because of its importance to people's current and future well-being (and also because of the size of the budgets and the number of jobs located in the education sector, as well as the number of interest groups with stakes in educational policy decisions)[1] education policy tends to be highly politicised. This leads to inefficiencies, distortions, inequalities in education outcomes, and a general lack of prioritization of student learning. Hence the importance – but also the challenge – of protecting education from politics.[2]

Politics can undermine educational outcomes through multiple channels (World Bank, 2018). One is through corruption and the leakage of funds allocated to build schools, provide educational materials or pay teachers (Reinikka & Svensson, 2004). Where governments are unable to reduce the leakage of funds or where they permit (or even promote) such leakage for political purposes, the quality and quantity of educational services – and with it the quality of learning and the degree of human capital formation that schooling generates – are diminished. Politics can also pervert educational outcomes through partisan and interest group favouritism. The demands of electoral politics may create incentives for governments to disproportionately target educational resources to important voting blocs, thus leading to inefficiencies. Teachers' unions and other organised interest groups may resist educational reforms that might improve children's learning (Bruns & Luque, 2015; Kingdon & Teal, 2010; Taylor et al., 2003).

In this chapter, we focus on a particular – and, in the context we study, particularly important – type of political favouritism: that directed along ethnic lines. Specifically, we investigate whether presidents in Kenya have disproportionately favoured members of their own ethnic groups in the allocation of resources that affect educational outcomes. We focus on ethnic favouritism by the president because the literature on African politics has long assumed that African presidents

---

[1] Education has comprised between 15% and 20% of Kenya's total budget since the 1970s. The government employs roughly 240,000 teachers, making the Kenya Teachers Service Commission the largest public sector employer in East and Central Africa (Hornsby, 2013, p. 650).

[2] In some settings, the politics surrounding education extend to the contents of the educational curriculum – for example to questions about how the country's history is to be taught or about the language(s) of instruction used in schools. We limit our focus in this chapter to noncurricular issues.

enjoy substantial discretion over the distribution of government resources (van de Walle, 2007).[3] Although ethnic favouritism (by the Kenyan president and other power holders) has long been assumed by both Kenyan citizens and scholars, it turns out to be tricky to document empirically, because doing so requires comparing the patterns of resource distribution that we observe with the counterfactual pattern that we would have observed had a leader from another ethnic community been in office. This is, of course, impossible because history only provides us with one leader at a time. Our empirical strategy, which involves comparing the fortunes of citizens when a member of their own ethnic group is in power with their fortunes when a member of a different ethnic group is in power, provides a very close approximation to the ideal, but impossible, comparison.

Using data on the educational attainment of about 50,000 Kenyans since independence in 1963, we show that children who share an ethnicity with the president are substantially more likely to attend primary school, to complete primary school and to be literate as adults. Although these measures do not capture the full set of ways in which the president's co-ethnics may have benefited educationally from their political connection to the leader – and certainly not the full set of ways they may have benefited in other spheres (Kramon & Posner, 2013) – they capture central aspects of educational attainment. They have the virtue of permitting an analysis of change over time (which, as we explain below, is crucial for estimating the causal effect of having a coethnic president).

We then discuss the broader implications of such ethnic bias. We emphasise that the most important impact may stem not from the direct effect of educational favouritism itself but from the effect it has in reinforcing perceptions of a more general ethnic bias in government allocation decisions. Especially in a context of weak social cohesion, such perceptions can foster resentments between ethnic groups, undermine trust in government and, by making prospective electoral losers fear exclusion from government benefits, raise the stakes of elections. This, in turn, may promote tensions between ethnic groups at election-time, incentivise political actors to engage in corruption to amass campaign war chests, and increase the likelihood of political violence.

---

[3] In other work, we also explore favoritism by the minister of education and other political actors. See Kramon and Posner (2016).

Indeed, post mortems of the post-election violence that swept across Kenya in early 2008 and, to a somewhat lesser degree, in 2017, implicate precisely these factors as having contributed to the conflict (Chege, 2008; Mueller, 2011).

We conclude with a discussion of how education might be protected from ethnic politics in countries such as Kenya. We emphasize three potential channels: institutional changes, such as devolution, that limit executive power and discretion over the distribution of resources; the creation of public awareness and social mobilisation in favour of more equity in the education sector; and the promotion of private schools as an alternative to the state-sponsored educational sector. (See Chapters 7 and 13 for related discussions.)

9.2 Inequalities in Education Outcomes in Kenya

The pledge to provide universal primary education has been a promise of every Kenyan president since independence (Nungu, 2010; Sifuna, 2005). It featured prominently in the Kenya Africa National Union's post-independence manifestos of 1963 and 1969 and in the country's first 5-year development plan (1964–1969) (Oketch & Rollenton, 2007). It was the rationale behind President Jomo Kenyatta's abolition of school fees for the first 4 years of primary education in 1973. It motivated Kenyatta's successor, Daniel arap Moi, to scrap building levies and introduce a free school milk programme in 1979 (Amutabi, 2003; Oketch & Rolleston, 2007). It inspired the curricular reforms that Moi initiated in 1984, which were designed to reduce dropout rates by making primary schooling more practically oriented (Nungu, 2010). Universal free primary education was a major campaign promise of President Mwai Kibaki, whose Rainbow Coalition defeated the Kenya Africa National Union in the 2002 elections. More recently, President Uhuru Kenyatta has announced the extension of free education to secondary schools by 2019 (*The Star*, 2016).

Yet, despite these policy promises and initiatives, access to education in Kenya is far from universal. Substantial inequalities in educational attainment persist across Kenya's citizens, with inequalities across ethnic groups being especially pronounced. In the 1990s, members of Kenya's largest and best-educated ethnic group, the Kikuyu, had on average 20% more years of schooling than members of minority ethnic groups and 11% more years of schooling than the national average.[4] Adult literacy rates are similarly imbalanced, with a gap of 16 percentage points between the Kikuyu and members of minority groups.[5]

Cross-group differences in primary school attainment are, of course, driven by multiple factors, with ethnic favouritism being only a part of the explanation. Differential rates of access to education during the pre-independence era gave some groups a leg up in terms of educational attainment, and this early access to schooling has had long-term consequences (Gallego & Woodberry, 2010; Nunn, 2014; Oyugi, 2000; Rothchild, 1969). For example, the Kikuyu have a long history of building their own schools through the colonial era's Kikuyu Independent School Association, and many of these schools continue to operate today. The economic advantages afforded by the growth of agriculture also provided the Kikuyu (along with the Luo and Luhya) with a distinct advantage in the educational realm, in part by providing the resources to support harambee schools, which were a major source of school construction during the first decade after independence.[6] Thus, observing that Kikuyus are still advantaged educationally today could simply mean that these early advantages were perpetuated over time, not that public policy or a biased allocation of educational resources favoured the Kikuyu during the post-independence era.

Educational attainment is also shaped by a range of private and social factors unrelated to politics and policy such as a family's socioeconomic status, religious affiliation, local norms about girls' education, and the expected returns to investing in schooling (Clemens, 2004). The challenge in estimating the impact of ethnic favouritism on educational inequalities thus lies in controlling for these other potential explanations. The strategy we outline below accounts for

---

[4] Minority ethnic groups are defined here as groups other than the five largest (Kikuyu, Luo, Kamba, Luhya and Kalenjin). In the 1990s, Kikuyu children completed an average of 6.7 years of primary school compared to 5.35 years for members of minority groups and 5.96 years for all Kenyans. Calculations are based on DHS data, as described.

[5] Literacy rates among the Kikuyu in the 1990s were 89, compared to 73 among members of minority ethnic groups (as defined). Calculations are, again, based on DHS data, described elsewhere herein.

[6] So close was the link between the growth of agriculture and advances in education that Lonsdale terms it the "agrarian-educational revolution" (see Chapter 1).

these historical factors and provides an estimate of the *additional* contribution made by ethnic favouritism to the patterns of cross-group inequality we observe today.

9.3 Testing for Ethnic Favouritism in Education

To empirically test for ethnic favouritism in primary education in Kenya, we use data from multiple rounds of the Demographic and Health Survey (DHS). DHS are periodic, nationally representative surveys that collect information on population, health, and nutrition at the household level in more than 85 developing countries. We pool the individual-level data from the DHS surveys from the Kenyan survey years of 1989, 1993, 1998, 2003 and 2008. The DHS interviews every woman in the households it samples, along with male household members in a subsample of households. We combine the male and female data sets, generating a master data set with more than 50,000 observations that includes age cohorts, based on the year in which an individual began primary school, that stretch from the mid 1950s to the late 1990s.

In this chapter, we focus our analyses on three outcomes that capture different aspects of primary school attainment: primary school attendance, primary school completion and adult literacy. To measure primary school attendance, we create a dichotomous variable that takes a value of 1 if the respondent attended any primary school and a value of 0 if the respondent did not. To measure primary school completion, we create another dichotomous measure indicating whether or not the respondent finished primary school, conditional on having started. To the extent that finishing primary school constitutes a real achievement – providing the opportunity to attend secondary school and increasing employment options – this measure has the advantage of capturing something tangible and potentially important for real-world outcomes. Finally, we generate a measure of each respondent's literacy, using responses to a DHS question that asks each respondent to read a simple sentence in the language of his or her choice. We code a person as literate if he or she is able to read the sentence completely. The literacy measure is important, because the ability to read and write is what links access to education to improvements in income and well-being more generally, and schooling attendance is no guarantee of actual learning (Uwezo, 2014).

Our main explanatory variable, which we use to test whether ethnic favouritism might help to explain variation in these outcomes, is an indicator variable that takes a value of 1 if the individual was a member of the same ethnic group as the president who was in office at the time that the individual attended primary school, and a value of 0 otherwise. Following Franck and Rainer (2012), we determine an ethnic match with the president by connecting the ethnicity of the individual to the ethnicity of the president when the individual was between 6 and 13 years old.[7] Integrating a 2-year time lag into our coding rule to account for the fact that policies put in place by a president are not likely to have an immediate impact (and that policies put in place by a president's predecessor are likely still to shape educational outcomes for a period of time after he has left office), we code a presidential ethnic match based on the ethnicity of the president when the respondent was aged 4 to 11 years.[8] If a change in the president occurred during a child's primary school years, the match is coded based on the ethnicity of the president who was in power for the majority of the time that the child was in primary school (i.e., for 4 or more years, subject to the 2-year lag).

A drawback of using the DHS data for our purposes is that the DHS surveys are administered to adults, whereas the main outcome we are interested in – primary educational attainment – took place when the survey respondents were children. Because a survey respondent's circumstances may have changed between childhood and the time that he or she was interviewed, we (unfortunately) cannot use most of the rich individual- and household-level information that the DHS collects to control for the circumstances facing an individual's family at the time he or she was of primary school age.[9] Our models are therefore by

---

[7] The Kenyan education system is designed for students to begin at age six (or sometimes seven) and to last for 7 (until 1985) or 8 (after 1985) years. Primary school age is thus roughly ages 6 to 13. To the extent that students delay entry into primary school, withdraw for a period and return when they are older or acquire literacy after their primary school years this will bias our analyses against finding an effect of ethnic favoritism

[8] Our results are robust to changing the lag to one year, as well as to omitting the lag altogether. Extending the lag to 3 or 4 years weakens the results. For robustness tests, see Kramon and Posner (2016).

[9] An analogous issue complicates our interpretation of the literacy results. Literacy may have been acquired after a person left school, in which case the ethnic match between the person and the president during the person's school-aged years may have little to do with the literacy they acquired later on. For this reason, we attach

necessity sparse, although we can and do control for whether the individual spent his or her childhood (and thus attended primary school) in a rural area and for the individual's religion (Catholic, Muslim or Protestant).

As noted, the major challenge in estimating the impact of ethnic favouritism on educational attainment is to isolate the effects of such favouritism from individual- and group-specific (including historical) factors that might also affect schooling outcomes. For example, if we found that, on average, members of the president's ethnic group completed more years of primary schooling than members of other ethnic groups, it would be difficult to know whether this association was a product of ethnic favouritism by the president or of deeper causes such as the group's earlier exposure to colonial education, its proximity to the national capital, its higher than average wealth or greater job opportunities (both of which might affect the cost–benefit decisions families make about whether to send their children to school), or some other group-specific natural advantage.

Our strategy for solving this inferential problem is to leverage changes in the ethnicity of the president (which happened in 1978, when Kenyatta, a Kikuyu, was succeeded by Moi, a Kalenjin, and in 2002, when Moi was succeeded by Kibaki, a Kikuyu) and to run our models with ethnic group fixed effects, which control for unchanging group-specific factors that may predispose members of one group to over- or under-perform others. This set up allows us to study the changing fortunes of each group over time, comparing the group's primary school attainment rates (and other outcomes) during periods when it has a president in the state house and when it does not, thereby holding group-specific characteristics constant. Kikuyus whose primary schooling years took place under Kenyatta and Kibaki receive an equal advantage from their history of Kikuyu Independent School Association and harambee schools, their generally greater wealth and their closer proximity to Nairobi compared with Kikuyus whose primary schooling years took place when Moi was president. By comparing their fortunes, on average, during these different regimes, it becomes possible to separate the relative contributions of having a coethnic in power from the

less weight to our literacy findings than to our findings with respect to primary school attendance and completion.

presumably unchanging group-specific factors that are positively (or, in the case of some other groups, negatively) associated with educational achievement.

In addition to ethnic-group fixed effects, each of our regression models also include age cohort-specific fixed effects, whose inclusion helps to control for time-specific shocks that might impact primary education attainment differently across different age cohorts. This might be an issue for the associations we are trying to estimate if, e.g., a president's tenure in office coincided with a severe economic downturn that caused parents to keep their children home from school (because they could not afford school fees or uniforms, or so that the children could help to generate income for the household). In such a scenario, it would be hard to separate out the impact of the president's efforts to help his group from the impact of the negative shock that happened to coincide with his presidency. The inclusion of age cohort fixed effects helps control for this possibility.[10]

9.4 Evidence of Ethnic Favouritism in Primary Education

To test for the effect of having a coethnic president during childhood on our three primary school outcomes, we ran a series of logistic regressions in which the outcomes are primary school attendance, primary school completion and adult literacy. Figure 9.1 presents the main results.[11] We calculate and plot the average marginal effect of co-ethnicity with the president on each outcome (the solid dot). We also plot the per cent change over the mean of each outcome implied by these average marginal effects (the triangles).

On each dimension, we find evidence that co-ethnics of the president achieve better educational outcomes.[12] With respect to primary school

---

[10] We also include robust standard errors, clustered at the ethnic group-president level (because this is the level at which the treatment – presidential favoritism – is applied). Our results are robust to alternate specifications in which we cluster at the ethnic group age cohort and ethnic group levels and when we compute standard errors using block bootstrap, as suggested by Bertrand, Duflo and Mullainathan (2004). In addition, our findings are robust to the inclusion of ethnic group-specific linear and quadratic time trends. See Kramon and Posner (2016) for details.

[11] For complete regression results, see Kramon and Posner (2016).

[12] In Kramon and Posner (2016), we show that ethnic favoritism extends beyond the president's own ethnic group to his broader ethnic-political coalition (e.g., to the Embu and Meru under Kenyatta/Kibaki and to the Maasai, Turkana and

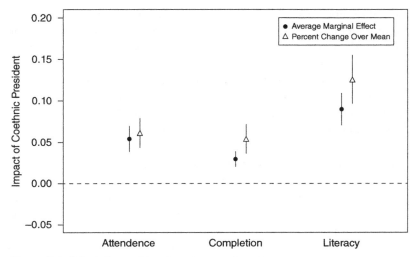

Figure 9.1 Ethnic favouritism in primary education outcomes

Note: The figure presents the effect of an ethnic match with the president during one's primary school-age years on the probability of attending primary school, completing primary school, and being literate as an adult. Estimates are derived from ordinary least squares regression models that include controls for childhood in a rural area and religion, ethnic group fixed effects, and age cohort fixed effects. The solid dot represents the average marginal effect of having a coethnic president. The triangles represent the per cent change over the mean implied by each average marginal effect.

attendance, co-ethnics are on average around 6 percentage points more likely to have ever attended primary school, which represents a 6% increase over the mean (in the full sample, the attendance rate is already quite high at 88%). With respect to primary school completion, co-ethnics of the president are on average about 3 percentage points more likely to complete primary school. This effect represents an almost 6% increase over the full sample completion rate of 56%. Finally, with respect to literacy, adults who had a coethnic as president when they were children are about 9 percentage points more likely to be literate, an improvement of 12% over the full sample literacy rate of 72%. This last finding is particularly striking, because adult literacy is likely a product of language acquisition that continues long after one's

Samburu under Moi). This finding underscores that there is nothing special about ethnic categories as commonly defined in census classifications: what matters is the affinity group writ large, and this group can be defined in multiple ways.

primary school years. Hence, a coethnic president's contribution to an adult's literacy – at any rate the contribution that runs through the president's impact on primary schooling – is less direct than for the other outcomes we discuss.

These effects are roughly comparable to the effects of a number of other policy interventions designed to improve educational outcomes in developing countries. In Kenya, for example, Miguel and Kremer (2004) find that improvements in student health achieved by the allocation of de-worming drugs decrease absenteeism by 7 percentage points. Evans et al. (2008) find that distributing free school uniforms increases attendance by about 6 percentage points. Vermeersch and Kremer (2004) analyse the impact of a school breakfast programme in preschools in Kenya, and find that enrolment in schools where the breakfast was served was about 30 percentage points higher – an effect substantially larger than our own. In Mexico, Schultz (2004) leverages the randomised nature of the Progresa conditional cash transfer programme and finds that the cash payments to parents increased enrolments by about 3 percentage points. And in Colombia, Angrist et al. (2002) find that a lottery that randomly subsidised private schooling for some students increases completion of the eighth grade by 10 percentage points. That the effect of having a coethnic president is of similar magnitude to policy initiatives deliberately designed to improve educational outcomes attests to the importance of ethnic ties in the Kenyan context.

Another way of thinking about the importance of our results is to recharacterise them in terms of the total human capital accumulated by the president's ethnic group as a consequence of his having occupied the presidency. To do this, we use data from the Kenyan census to estimate the number of the president's co-ethnics whose primary school years coincided with his tenure (subject to the 2-year lag). We then multiply this by the average number of years of additional schooling that we estimate are associated with having a coethnic president. These calculations suggest that the Kikuyu ethnic group acquired an extra 236,000 person-years of schooling as a consequence of having had a kinsman in the state house for 16 years and that the Kalenjin community acquired an extra 357,000 person-years of schooling owing to its control of the presidency from 1978 to 2002. Viewed in this way (which allows for the possibility – no doubt borne out in fact – that the benefits of having a coethnic occupying the presidency manifest themselves not as an additional fraction of a year of schooling for every one of the president's coethnics but as many additional years of schooling for an elite subsection of the president's community), the benefits that accrue to an ethnic community from having a coethnic in a position of high power are unambiguously large.

9.5 The Broader Impact of Ethnic Favouritism in Primary Education

What is the broader impact of the ethnic favouritism we have documented in the educational sector? With the data at hand, it is difficult to speak to direct effects. Access to education, especially primary education, has gradually expanded for all groups in Kenya since independence, despite the ethnic favouritism we identify. Average years of primary schooling rose from 4.19 years in the colonial era to 6.13 years by the 1980s, though it dropped to 5.96 years in the 1990s. Adult literacy rose from 20% at independence to 91% by 2005 (Hornsby, 2013, pp. 446; World Bank Development Indicators). Whether this net amount of human capital formation in Kenya would have been greater without ethnic favouritism is hard to establish. But it is almost surely the case that the increase in the average number of years of schooling provided to Kenyan children matters at least as much for the country's development fortunes as whether children from some subgroups received more schooling than others.

Moreover, it is not clear that an equitable distribution of educational resources would even be optimal from an economic development point of view. Lavishing more educational resources on children who already have higher than average levels of schooling (or whose parents have had more education) may be more economically efficient than investing resources in children with lower schooling levels (or in children of poorly educated parents). On the other hand, it is equally plausible that channelling resources to children with lower levels of educational attainment will generate more poverty reduction and better long-term development outcomes. The point is simply that, from a contribution-to-economic-development standpoint, the large increases in levels of schooling *on average* are almost certainly a much more important feature of Kenya's postindependence history than the (more modest) inequality in schooling attainment across ethnic groups.

In addition to bolstering economic development directly, the general increase in schooling may also have an indirect (and positive) impact on development outcomes through its effect on social cohesion. In Western Europe, the growth of education went hand-in-hand with the breakdown of parochial group loyalties and the fostering of national identities. To the extent that increasing citizens' access to education has this effect, and to the extent that the weakening of subnational identities increases social cohesion and reduces the likelihood of intergroup conflict, the increase in schooling since independence could be development promoting – even if the increase is distributed in a biased way.

On the other hand, recent research suggests that, rather than increase social cohesion, education may actually reinforce or exacerbate ethnic divisions in society. In a study in Kenya, Friedman et al. (2016) find that increasing educational attainment was associated with an increase in the importance that people attached to their ethnic identities, although this result is not statistically significant. Miguel (2004) argues similarly that the curriculum and language policies in Kenyan primary schools may contribute to ethnic tensions (although it is not clear from his paper whether this is in absolute terms or simply relative to Tanzania, his comparison case). Because most of the beneficiaries of ethnic favouritism in education – and of the expansion of educational opportunities more generally – do not advance beyond primary school, it is possible that the increase in access to primary education that has occurred in Kenya over the past 50 years has had the effect of exposing more students to an experience that *reinforces* ethnic division and *undermines* social cohesion.[13]

There are also concerns about the quality of the education that students receive – an important issue that our data on educational attainment cannot address.[14] If expansions in educational opportunity do not correspond with increases in the quality of education (as research by Harding & Stasavage [2014], among others, suggests is often the case – or worse, are associated with decreases in the quality of

---

[13] As is emphasized in the Introduction to this volume, Europe's experience points to how the fostering of national identities can generate costly interstate conflicts – even if such identities may generate national social cohesion in the longer term. So, to the extent that education fosters identifications with the nation, it can be conflict generating.

[14] Groups like Uwezo have documented broad shortcomings in children's learning in Kenya, notwithstanding significant increases in the number of children in school and the number of years they attend. See, for example, Uwezo (2014).

education), then we should not expect education to have much of an impact on broader patterns of ethnic politics (or development more generally). The impact of education on ethnic politics is thus debatable. It will be important for future research to examine this potentially complex relationship in greater detail.

An impact that is much less ambiguous, however, is the effect of the kind of ethnic bias we have documented on perceptions of the government's (lack of) even-handedness in distributing public resources – perceptions which have a direct impact on social cohesion and ethnic relations. Survey data in Kenya reveal strong perceptions of ethnic favouritism, with perceptions of fair treatment by the government strongly associated with whether or not the respondent is a member of the president's ethnic group. For example, in a 2008–2009 survey, whereas fully 90% of Luos and 82% of Luhyas reported that members of their group were at least sometimes treated unfairly by the government, just 60% of President Kibaki's Kikuyu co-ethnics reported feeling this way (Afrobarometer, 2008–2009). Although these perceptions are no doubt driven by factors that go beyond the ethnic imbalance in educational attainment, inequality in the education sphere does nothing to weaken these perceptions, and quite likely reinforces them.

Perceptions of ethnic favouritism in the distribution of government resources have a number of important consequences for development and social cohesion. First, they can undermine trust between ethnic groups and between out-of-power ethnic groups and the state. As Lonsdale argues in chapter 1, "only a widespread trust in the state's protection of a common citizenship could usher in a fifth stage of ethnic relations, in which cultural difference is of no consequence". Survey evidence suggests that levels of interethnic trust in Kenya are low: 22% of Afrobarometer respondents report that they trust members of other ethnic groups "not at all" and a further 44% report that they trust members of other groups "just a little". Strikingly, only 7% of Kenyan Afrobarometer respondents trust members of other groups "a lot" (Afrobarometer, 2005–2006).[15] In the Kenya Institute of Public Policy Research and Analysis (KIPPRA, 2014) study

---

[15] The 2005–2006 Afrobarometer surveys were the last versions to include questions about trust in members of other ethnic groups.

described in Chapter 7, the results are somewhat more optimistic, but still suggest that interethnic trust is weak.[16]

This lack of trust extends to the political arena. Whereas 78% of Kikuyus polled in 2012 said they trusted President Kibaki, a fellow Kikuyu, "a lot" or "somewhat", only 29% of Luo and 40% of Luhya reported such levels of trust in the president (Afrobarometer, 2012). Meanwhile, whereas only 37% of Kikuyu reported trusting Prime Minister Raila Odinga "a lot" or "somewhat", 76% of Odinga's coethnic Luos reported such levels of trust in the prime minister (Ibid).

Such sentiments have implications for economic and political development. A large literature suggests that low levels of interpersonal trust are associated with lower rates of economic growth (Beugelsdijk et al., 2004; Knack & Keefer, 1997). Low levels of trust also diminish the ability of politicians to make credible programmatic and policy promises to voters from other ethnic groups. This may undermine democratic accountability by reinforcing patterns of ethnic voting and incentivising clientelist mobilization and vote-getting strategies (Keefer & Vlaicu, 2008).

Real and perceived ethnic favouritism by presidents also substantially raises the stakes of presidential elections, as people fear exclusion from future benefits should the candidate associated with their group lose the election. This has led to the emergence of a "do or die" mentality surrounding elections in Kenya (Mueller, 2011). This mentality has a number of problematic side effects. In the first place, it generates incentives for vote buying, electoral fraud, and other forms of election-related corruption. The need to amass resources to win a campaign can provide a justification for other sorts of corruption as well (Wrong, 2009). Such election-inspired corruption may be particularly hard to stamp out, because voters – or at any rate voters who are co-ethnics of the corrupt politician – may be less likely to object to illegal activities carried out in the name of protecting the livelihood of their ethnic community. The political elite can thus exploit voter fears of exclusion by out-group leaders in order to engage in corruption and extract rents without losing support from their ethnic electoral base (Padro i Miquel, 2007).

---

[16] In the Kenya Institute of Public Policy Research and Analysis study, 13.7% of respondents say they trust people from other ethnic groups "not at all" and only 38.3% say they trust people from other ethnic groups "completely".

High-stakes elections can also fuel election violence, which has been common to each of Kenya's multiparty elections held since 1992 (Mueller, 2011). More recently, this was manifest in the violence that killed more than 1,000 people and displaced roughly 700,000 after the disputed elections of 2007. Though the proximate cause of the violence was a dispute over the true winner of the election and allegations of fraud, the underlying grievances that facilitated the violence were in large part related to perceptions of biased and inequitable distribution of resources across Kenya's ethnic groups. Thus, to the extent that ethnic favouritism in the education sector contributes to the perceptions that power holders will discriminate on behalf of their kin, it may undermine development by generating mistrust, corruption and instability.

9.6 Protecting Education from Ethnic Politics

Given the significant development implications of ethnic favouritism in the education sector, it is natural to inquire how education might be protected from ethnic politics. Three broad responses appear promising. The first involves the introduction of institutional reforms that limit executive discretion. In Kenya, a series of institutional changes in the postindependence period centralised power in the office of the president and led to the emergence of what many Kenyans refer to as the "imperial presidency" – a system in which the president enjoys almost limitless power (Widner, 1992; Hornsby, 2013). The combination of this unconstrained power and the desire to favour one's ethnic kin – born from a combination of in-group affection, social pressure and strategic political considerations – has led to the patterns of favouritism and horizontal inequality we have documented in this chapter.

Kenya's new constitution, adopted through popular referendum in 2010, contains a number of provisions that, if fully implemented, hold promise of constraining executive power and promoting a more equitable distribution of resources (Kramon & Posner, 2011).[17] For example, the constitution devolves significant powers to forty-seven county governments, which are responsible for primary health care,

---

[17] Whether these provisions will be fully implemented is an open question, however. As Ranis makes clear in Chapter 10, the implementation of Kenya's devolution has been weak and uneven. Further, devolution can also create new more localized forms of ethnic conflict over resources (Cheeseman et al., 2016).

agricultural policy, and the provision of a number of other public goods. Also, whereas budgetary power was previously centralised in the executive, and hence subject to presidential manipulation, under the new system a set percentage of the national budget is disbursed to the countries, with the allocation formula determined by an elected Senate. Although primary education remains under the purview of the central government, the constitutional reforms create less favourable environment for ethnic favouritism – at least centralised ethnic favouritism controlled by the president.[18] (See Chapter 7 for a further discussion of devolution.)

In addition to formal institutional constraints on presidential power, ethnic bias in the education sector may be reduced by increased transparency regarding both how education-related resources are distributed and the unequal outcomes that result. Greater citizen awareness about the extent of the bias, generated through enhanced media coverage and civic education campaigns, can lead to social mobilization on behalf of a more equitable distribution of resources and, perhaps, a growing wiliness of voters to sanction politicians that have engaged in ethnic favouritism and to reward those who have not.

An additional solution is to provide opportunities for students to exit the government education system altogether through the promotion of private schools.[19] The development of a viable exit option can both create pressure on government to improve the quality of traditionally disfavoured schools and offer opportunities for children from disfavoured ethnic groups to receive educational training closer to that of their favoured peers.[20]

9.7 Conclusion

In this chapter, we provide empirical evidence of ethnic favouritism in the education sector in Kenya. Drawing on data on the educational

---

[18] For a further discussion of the effects of decentralization in ethnically diverse settings, see Ranis, Chapter 7.

[19] In some poor neighborhoods in Nairobi, more than 40% of the poorest families send their children to private schools, in part because they believe that private schools provide better education at comparable costs, once one has accounted for the informal fees charged in public schools (World Bank, 2018).

[20] To the extent that such schools have a religious orientation or provide instruction in a language other than the national language, however, they may undermine state legitimacy and social cohesion (Bleck, 2015).

attainment of roughly 50,000 Kenyans since independence, we document that Kenyans are substantially more likely to have attended and completed primary school and to be literate as adults if their primary school-age years coincided with the tenure in office of a president from their ethnic group.

Given the strong empirical connections between education and a range of desirable development outcomes (including increased income, better health and greater democratic political participation), such favouritism may exacerbate existing horizontal inequalities between ethnic groups. Additionally, and in part through its impact on these other outcomes, favouritism in the education sector can reinforce perceptions of ethnic bias by the government, thereby reducing trust between ethnic groups, undermining faith in government, destroying social cohesion, and creating a "do or die" mentality surrounding presidential elections. The impact of ethnic favouritism in education thus extends well beyond the education sector and constitutes a major challenge for development. Protecting education from ethnic politics will require both institutional change and vigilance on the part of citizens to ensure that institutional reforms translate into greater equality in education's provision. Attending to these tasks will be an important ingredient in moving Kenya from an ethnically divisive past to a more cohesive future.

References

Afrobarometer Data, [Kenya], [Round 3, 4, 5], [2005, 2006, 2008, 2008, 2012]. Retrieved from www.afrobarometer.org.

Amutabi, M. N. 2003. Political interference in the running of education in post-independence Kenya: A critical retrospection. *International Journal of Educational Development.* 23(2): 127–144.

Angrist, J., Bettinger, E., Bloom, E., King, E., and Kremer, M. 2002. Vouchers for private schooling in Colombia: Evidence from a randomized natural experiment. *American Economic Review.* 92(5): 1535–1558.

Barro, R. J., and Lee, J. W. 2010. *A New Data Set of Educational Attainment in the World, 1950–2010 (NBER Working Paper No. 15902).* Cambridge, MA: National Bureau of Economic Research.

Bertrand, M., Duflo, E., and Mullainathan, S. 2004. How much should we trust differences-in-differences estimates. *Quarterly Journal of Economics.* 199(1): 249–275.

Beugelsdijk, S., de Groot, H., and van Schaik, A. 2004. Trust and economic growth: A robustness analysis. *Oxford Economic Papers*. 56(1): 118–134.

Bleck, J. 2015. *Education and Empowered Citizenship in Mali*. Baltimore, MD: Johns Hopkins University Press.

Brady, H.E., Verba, S., and Lehman Schlozman, K. 1995. A Resource Model of Political Participation. *American Political Science Review*. 89(2): 271–294.

Bruns, B., and Luque, J. 2015. *Great Teachers: How to Raise Student Learning in Latin America and the Caribbean*. Washington, DC: World Bank.

Cheeseman, N., Lynch, G., and Willis, J. 2016. Decentralization in Kenya: The governance of governors. *Journal of Modern African Studies*. 54(1): 1–35.

Chege, M. 2008. Kenya: Back from the brink?' *Journal of Democracy*. 19(4): 125–39.

Clemens, M. A. 2004. *The Long Walk to School: International Education Goals in Historical Perspective (Center for Global Development Working Paper 37)*. Retrieved from https://ssrn.com/abstract=1112670 or http://dx.doi.org/10.2139/ssrn.1112670. Accessed18 September 2018.

Dahl, R. 1971. *Polyarchy: Participation and Opposition*. New Haven, CT: Yale University Press.

Diamond, L. 1999. *Developing Democracy: Toward Consolidation*. Baltimore, MD: Johns Hopkins University Press.

Evans, D., Kremer, M., and Ngati, M. 2008. *The Impact of Distributing School Uniforms on Children's Education in Kenya*. Washington, DC: World Bank.

Friedman, W., Kremer, M., Miguel, E., and Thornton, R. 2016. Education as liberation? *Economica*. 83(329): 1–30.

Franck, R., and Rainer, I. 2012. Does the leader's ethnicity matter? Ethnic favoritism, education and health in sub-Saharan Africa. *American Political Science Review*. 106(2): 294–325.

Gakidou, E., Cowling, K., Lozano, R., and Murray, C. 2010. Increased educational attainment and its effect on child mortality in 175 countries between 1970 and 2009: A systematic analysis. *Lancet*. 376(9745): 959–974.

Gallego, F., and Woodberry, R. 2010. Christian missionaries and education in former African colonies: How competition mattered. *Journal of African Economies*. 19 (3):294–329.

Gellner, E. 1983. *Nations and Nationalism*. Ithaca, NY: Cornell University Press.

Grossman, M. 2006. Education and nonmarket outcomes. In Hanushek, E., and Wlech, F. (eds.), *Handbook of the Economics of Education, vol. 1.* New York: Elsevier, 577–633.

Hanushek, E., and Woessmann, L. 2007. *Education Quality and Economic Growth.* Washington, DC: World Bank.

Harding, R., and Stasavage, D. 2014. What democracy does (and doesn't do) for basic services: School fees, school inputs, and African elections. *Journal of Politics.* 76(1): 229–245.

Hornsby, C. 2013. *Kenya: A History Since Independence.* London: I.B. Tauris.

Keefer, P., and Vlaicu, R. 2008. Democracy, credibility, and clientelism. *Journal of Law, Economics, and Organization.* 24(2): 371–406.

Kingdon, G., and Teal, F. 2010. Teacher unions, teacher pay, and student performance in India: A pupil fixed effects approach. *Journal of Development Economics.* 91(2): 278–288.

Knack, S., and Keefer, P. 1997. Does social capital have an economic payoff? A cross-country investigation. *Quarterly Journal of Economics.* 112(4): 1251–1288.

Kramon, E., and Posner, D. N. 2011. Kenya's new constitution. *Journal of Democracy.* 22(2): 89–103.

2013. Who benefits from distributive politics: How the outcome one studies affect the answer one gets. *Perspectives on Politics.* 11(2): 461–474.

2016. Ethnic favoritism in education in Kenya. *Quarterly Journal of Political Science.* 11(1): 1–58.

Krueger, A. B., and Lindahl, M. 2000. *Education for growth: Why and for whom? (NBER Working Paper No. 7591).* Cambridge, MA: National Bureau of Economic Research.

Lipset, S. M. 1959. Some social requisites of democracy: Economic development and political legitimacy. *American Political Science Review.* 53(1): 69–105.

Miguel, E. 2004. Tribe or nation? Nation building and public goods in Kenya versus Tanzania. *World Politics.* 56 (3): 328–362.

Miguel, E., and Kremer, M. 2004. Worms: Identifying impacts on education and health in the presence of treatment externalities. *Econometrica.* 72 (1): 159–217.

Mueller, S. 2011. Dying to win: Elections, political violence, and institutional decay in Kenya. *Journal of Contemporary African Studies.* 29(1): 99–117.

Nungu, M. 2010. Universalizing access to primary education in Kenya: Myth and realities. *Canadian Journal for New Scholars in Education.* 3(2): 1–10.

Nunn, N. 2014. Gender and missionary influence in colonial Africa. In Akyeampong, E., Bates, R., Nunn, N., and Robinson, J. (eds.), *Africa's Development in Historical Perspective*. Cambridge: Cambridge University Press, pp. 489–512.

Oketch, M., and Rolleston, C. 2007. Policies on free primary and secondary education in East Africa: Retrospect and prospect. *Review of Research in Education*. 31, 131–158.

Oyugi, E. 2000. *The Legacy of Colonialism*. Nairobi: Kenya Coalition for Social Watch.

Padro i Miquel, G. 2007. The control of politicians in divided societies: The politics of fear. *Review of Economic Studies*. 74(4): 1259–1274.

Reinikka, R., and Svensson, J. 2004. Local capture: Evidence from a central government transfer programme in Uganda. *Quarterly Journal of Economics*. 119(2): 679–705.

Robinson, A. 2014. National versus ethnic identification in Africa: modernization, colonial legacy, and the origins of territorial nationalism. *World Politics*. 66 (4): 709–746.

Rothchild, D. 1969. Ethnic Inequalities in Kenya. *Journal of Modern African Studies*. 7 (4):689–711.

Sen, A. K. 1999. *Development as Freedom*. New York: Anchor Books.

Schultz, P. T. 2004. School subsidies for the poor: Evaluating the Mexican PROGRESA Poverty Programme. *Journal of Development Economics*. 74(1): 199– 250.

Sifuna, D. N. 2005. The illusion of universal free primary education in Kenya. *Wajibu*. 19(2): 5–8.

Taylor, N., Muller, J., and Vinjevold, P. 2003. *Getting Schools Working: Research and Systemic School Reform in South Africa*. Cape Town: Pearson Education South Africa.

The Star. 2016. Secondary education to be free in 2019, Says Uhuru. 22 June 2016.

Uwezo. 2014. *Are Our Children Learning? Literacy and Numeracy across East Africa 2013*. Nairobi: Twaweza.

van de Walle, N. 2007. Meet the new boss, same as the old boss? The evolution of political clientelism in Africa. In Kitschelt, H., and Wilkinson, S.I. (eds.), *Patrons, Clients, and Policies: Patterns of Democratic Accountability and Political Competition*. Cambridge: Cambridge University Press, pp. 50–67.

Vermeersch, C., and Kremer, M. 2004. *School Meals, Educational Attainment, and School Competition: Evidence from a Randomized Evaluation (World Bank Policy Research Working Paper No. WPS3523)*. Washington, DC: World Bank.

Widner, J. 1992. *The Rise of a Party-State in Kenya: From "Harambee!" to "Nyayo!"* Berkeley: University of California.

World Bank (2018). *World Development Report 2018: Learning to Realize Education's Promise.* Washington, DC: World Bank.

Wrong, M. 2009. *It's Our Turn to Eat: The Story of a Kenyan Whistle-Blower.* New York: Harper Collins.

10 | Building Social Cohesion through Education in Africa? Lessons from Côte d'Ivoire and Kenya

LINE KUPPENS AND ARNIM LANGER

Increasingly, studies have focused on the potential of the education system to enhance social cohesion, in particular in multi-ethnic societies. It is suggested that the education system can strengthen social cohesion by providing learners from diverse groups equal learning opportunities. Moreover, schooling can impart the "rules of the game" in a democracy and contribute to developing a common sense of belonging. In this chapter, we reflect on three strands of education that are generally not explicitly linked to social cohesion, but that could play a particularly promising role in this regard: multicultural education and citizenship and peace education. While the African continent is often overlooked in the current literature, we analyse education in two African countries: post-conflict Côte d'Ivoire and in the ethnically divided society of Kenya. Notwithstanding promising contributions in each country, we identify a number of hurdles to advancing social cohesion through education, including, most important, remaining biases and negative intergroup attitudes among teachers.

10.1 Introduction

In recent years, an increasing amount of research has focused on the role and impact of education in building social cohesion in multi-ethnic societies around the world (see, e.g., Colenso, 2005; Green & Preston, 2001; Heyneman, 2003; Loader & Hughes, 2017; Sayed et al., 2016; Tawil & Harley, 2004). Here we define social cohesion as a situation in which "relationships among members and groups in society are sufficiently good that all feel a sense of belonging, that they perceive the whole society as greater than the parts, and when differences develop, they can be dealt with peacefully" (Langer et al., 2017, p. 322).

While education may contribute towards improving social cohesion, this is not always the case. Indeed, it is widely accepted that education has "two faces" (Bush & Saltarelli, 2000). On the one hand, education may contribute to the polarisation and possibly the violent disintegration of societies by reflecting and reinforcing existing unequal distributions of power and group status as well as by propagating narratives of bigotry, exclusion and intolerance (Kuppens & Langer, 2019; see also Brown, 2011; King, 2015; Novelli et al., 2017). On the other hand, education may contribute to social cohesion in ethnically divided societies threatened by severe political and ethnic tensions, by providing equal educational opportunities to all students; creating inclusive school and classroom climates; teaching civic and democratic principles and values; and/or by developing a common sense of identity among pupils from diverse backgrounds and groups among other factors (Heyneman, 2000, 2003; see also Colenso, 2005). Although rarely explicitly linked to social cohesion, education in citizenship, multicultural education and peace education are particularly relevant in this regard. Whereas citizenship education is considered crucial for building a strong democracy (e.g., Almond & Verba, 1963; Torney-Purta, 2002); multicultural education aims to ensure all groups equal learning opportunities and to create inclusive classrooms (Banks & Banks, 2001; Stephan & Stephan, 2001); and peace education aims to impart peaceful and nonviolent behaviour (e.g., Davies, 2004; Harris & Morrison, 2003; Salomon, 2002). While it could be argued that each of these educational approaches is distinct in theory, scope and practice, we argue that together the three approaches could make a significant contribution to promoting and strengthening intergroup relations and social cohesion more generally.

In this chapter, we aim to analyse the role of education in advancing social cohesion in African countries. More specifically, we analyse how far the education system was used to advance social cohesion in Côte d'Ivoire and Kenya and reflect upon possible lessons learnt from both countries' experiences. In this respect it is important to note that both Côte d'Ivoire and Kenya have highly diverse ethnic populations (like many other African countries) and have both been confronted with serious political violence in their recent histories. In particular, while Côte d'Ivoire experienced serious political violence in the periods 2002–2003 and 2010–2011 (for a chronology of events see, e.g., Bouquet, 2011; McGovern, 2011), in Kenya, ethnic tensions boiled over after the presidential elections of December 2007 and resulted in the death of an estimated 1,113 people in the period January 2008 to

March 2008 (see, e.g., Berman et al., 2009; Human Rights' Watch, 2008). The political violence and turmoil in both countries had a clear ethnic dimension and since the end of hostilities violence and serious ethnic tensions have at times recurred (see, e.g., Akindès [2017] and Piccolino [2017] on Côte d'Ivoire; Amnesty International & Human Rights' Watch [2017] on Kenya). What is more, following the emergence of severe political tensions and violent conflicts, both countries have integrated elements of peace, multicultural and citizenship education in their formal school curricula.

Notwithstanding promising steps forward, the current chapter shows that the contribution of these educational approaches towards promoting and strengthening social cohesion seems to be quite limited in Côte d'Ivoire and Kenya. First, the curricula in both countries deal rather superficially with democratic principles and notions of tolerance and respect for diversity, imparting only a shallow understanding of these critical notions. What is more, rather than democratic and free of violence, the overall school climate in Côte d'Ivoire and Kenya is characterised by occasional violence and authoritarian teacher-pupil relations, clearly contradicting what is taught on paper. Second, neither country systematically addresses and/or explains their country's violent and divisive past in the classroom. By consequence, pupils gain very little understanding of the root causes of conflict, and how they can be averted from turning violent in the future. More fundamentally, we also show that teachers are no tabula rasa. Indeed, teachers seem to be as prejudiced, divided and traumatised as the rest of the society. Hence, at times, they can become clear obstacles to social cohesion building. Last, instead of promoting unity in diversity, the education system in both countries emphasises unity at the expense of diversity.

The chapter proceeds as follows. In Section 10.2, we offer some theoretical reflections on how education may contribute towards advancing social cohesion in multi-ethnic societies, subsequently discussing multicultural, peace and citizenship education in particular. In Sections 10.3 and 10.4, we analyse how Côte d'Ivoire and Kenya have each attempted to deal with their country's divisive pasts in their education systems and to what extent schooling has contributed towards building social cohesion in both countries. Section 10.5 concludes. Here we draw a number of lessons from the Ivorian and Kenyan cases that seem to have wider relevance in Africa.

10.2 Education for Social Cohesion: Some Conceptual Reflections

Langer et al. (2017) distinguish three dimensions of social cohesion: (1) the extent of perceived horizontal and vertical inequalities, (2) the level of trust among people more generally and towards other groups and the state in particular and (3) people's sense of national belonging. Education can play a key role with respect to all of these dimensions. While disproportional allocations of educational resources between groups and/or regions have been found to amplify conflict (see Chapter 9; in addition see, e.g., Brown, 2011; King, 2015) and more equitable resource allocation can conversely be adopted to promote peace (see Dupuy, 2008); here, we focus on multicultural education, peace education and citizenship education, and their relation to social cohesion building. Before discussing differences and commonalities between these different types of education, we briefly explore how these concepts have been defined in the relevant literature and how they may contribute towards advancing social cohesion in multi-ethnic societies.

10.2.1 Multicultural Education

Banks and Banks (2001) define multicultural education as follows: "An idea or concept, an educational reform movement, and a process" (Ibid, p. 3) that aim "to change the structure of educational institutions so that students from all social class, gender, racial, language, and cultural groups will have an equal opportunity to learn" (Ibid, p. 4). They further argue that it may involve "a wide variety of programmes and practices related to educational equity, women, ethnic groups, language minorities, low-income groups, and people with disabilities" (Banks & Banks, 2001, p. 6). To enhance the achievements of minority groups and to promote equity, multicultural curricula and pedagogies build on the cultural knowledge, frames of reference and prior experiences of pupils (Gay, 2013; Ladson-Billings, 1995; Stephan & Stephan, 2001). More than simply integrating multicultural content into school curricula, multicultural education is about challenging cultural assumptions, prejudices and dominant paradigms and empowering students from diverse racial, ethnic and social class groups as well (see, e.g., Banks, 1993; Banks & Banks, 2001). Multicultural education is closely related to "a culturally responsive pedagogy" (Gay, 2013; Sleeter, 2011), "intercultural education" (Bennett, 2009) and "an antiracist education" (Nieto, 1996). Importantly, multicultural education is not only relevant in highly diverse classrooms, but also in homogeneous classrooms and schools, providing learners a unique opportunity to get to know "the Other".

In its attempt to provide equal educational opportunities to all learners, multicultural education clearly contributes to advancing social cohesion by attenuating (perceived) horizontal inequalities in educational opportunities and outcomes between groups. Although at times criticised for heightening and deepening group identities at the expense of nationality, it is important in a socially cohesive society to value both group and national identity (Gay, 2013; Kymlicka, 2004). Also, recognising that identities are multiple, nested and overlapping (Kymlicka, 2004) can contribute to a shared sense of belonging, bridging group differences and avoiding alienating minority group members (Stephan & Stephan, 2001). Only when group identities take strong precedence over national identity is national cohesion possibly threatened (Langer et al., 2017).

10.2.2 Peace Education

Peace education is an amorphous concept, which lacks a commonly accepted definition. Illustratively, while Bajaj (2008) emphasises that peace education aims to transform the "educational content, structure, and pedagogy to address direct and structural forms of violence at all levels" (Bajaj, 2008, p. 135), Salomon (2002) puts forth four objectives: "accepting as legitimate the other's narrative and its specific implications; being willing to critically examine one's own group's actions toward the other group; being ready to experience and show empathy and trust toward the other; and being disposed to engage in nonviolent activities" (Salomon, 2002, p. 9). The common denominator of the different approaches to peace education is the preoccupation with what Reardon (1988) called "the core" of peace education, namely the eradication of violence (Reardon, 1988, p. 31; see also Bajaj & Hantzopoulos, 2016; Harris & Morrison, 2003). In many ways, peace education is an umbrella concept which incorporates a wide variety of subconcepts, including, e.g., "Learning to Live Together" education (Sinclair et al., 2008), peacebuilding education

(Bush & Saltarelli, 2000; UNICEF, 2011), human rights education (Tibbitts, 2002, 2008), and education for social cohesion and social and civic reconstruction (Tawil & Harley, 2004). Peace education is also sometimes referred to as education for a culture of peace and nonviolence (United Nations, 1999).

Peace education is particularly relevant to the promotion and strengthening of social cohesion in multi-ethnic, and especially (post-) conflict, societies in two regards. First, peace education prepares learners to react peacefully when differences develop – hence preventing the disintegration of social cohesion. And, second, many peace education programmes set up encounters between opposing groups to improve intergroup relations and build trust (see, e.g., Bekerman, 2016; Loader & Hughes, 2017).

10.2.3 Citizenship Education

Citizenship education – also referred to as civic education – aims to impart "the knowledge, skills, attitudes and experiences to prepare someone to be an active, informed participant in democratic life" (Campbell, 2012, p. 1; see also Russell & Quaynor, 2017). In recent decades, various countries have introduced citizenship education in response to decreases in political participation, the surge in migration flows and globalisation more generally, and the growth of antidemocratic movements among other elements (Campbell, 2012; Osler & Starkey, 2006). Increasingly, (post-) conflict societies have introduced citizenship curricula as well (Quaynor, 2012). Osler and Starkey (2005) put forward three dimensions of citizenship education: status, feeling and practice. Whereas status is about teaching about the rights and responsibilities of citizens in a democratic state, the second dimension is concerned with developing a sense of belonging to the state, while the third dimension is about encouraging active citizenship and upholding democracy and human rights (see also Russell & Quaynor, 2017). More than teaching civic content and skills, it is crucial in this respect that schools ensure an open classroom climate, emphasise the importance of political participation, and lead by example by giving pupils voice at school (Torney-Purta, 2002).

More than contributing to people's sense of national belonging (dimension three of social cohesion), citizenship education contributes to and strengthens social cohesion by inculcating "the rules of the game", which include citizens' rights and responsibilities, the duties of political leaders and parties, and the consequences of not adhering to legal and social principles (Heyneman, 2003, p. 29). It is crucial in this respect that citizenship education imparts a notion of civics and citizenship that acknowledges heterogeneity and is based on equal rights and democratic principles instead of instilling nationalism, patriotism and notions of exclusion (Davies, 2004).

10.2.4 Towards a Common Denominator

It is clear from our discussion that multicultural, peace and citizenship education each have a somewhat different immediate objective. Whereas citizenship education is considered crucial for building a strong democracy (e.g., Almond & Verba, 1963; Torney-Purta, 2002); multicultural education aims to ensure all groups equal learning opportunities and to create inclusive classrooms and respect for each other (Banks & Banks, 2001; Stephan & Stephan, 2001); while peace education aims to impart peaceful and nonviolent behaviour (e.g., Davies, 2004; Harris & Morrison, 2003; Salomon, 2002). Having said this, there are also important parallels and commonalities between these three educational approaches.

First, each of these educational approaches is explicitly normative in the sense that they do not just aim to educate about, but also explicitly educate *for* inclusion and international understanding, peace, and democracy (e.g., Bajaj, 2008; Bajaj & Hantzopoulos, 2016). Second, more than conveying knowledge alone, all three types of education aim to impart values, skills and competencies. Some values or skills are common to peace, multicultural and citizenship education, whereas others are specific to one field alone. Critical thinking, for instance, is a major component of all three areas. Third, to impart their respective values and skills, the three fields of study also build on a similar set of pedagogies, whether participative, cooperative or critical. Like peace education, citizenship education and multicultural education in particular build strongly on the insights of critical pedagogues Freire (1970) and Giroux (1983).

While peace, citizenship and multicultural education may be conceived of as three separate fields of study, in practice these three types of education are hard to distinguish from each other. Salomon and Cairns (2010) pointedly note in this regard: "Education for democracy could easily be regarded as a variant of the prototype of peace education and at the same time the prototype of the category of civil education" (Salomon & Cairns, 2010, p. 6). In practice, textbooks and curricula are likely to contain elements of all three educational approaches, as is the case in Côte d'Ivoire and Kenya (as discussed in Section 10.3).

10.3 Côte d'Ivoire: Divided We Teach[1]

The political turmoil in Côte d'Ivoire, which escalated into large-scale violence in 2002–2003 and again in 2010–2011, can be traced back to the power struggle that was unleashed in 1993, after the death of President Felix Houphouët-Boigny, who had ruled the country from independence in 1960 (Langer, 2005, 2010). After his death, political leaders started to use a discourse of ethnonationalism and xenophobia under the slogan of Ivoirité ("Ivorian-ness"). This concept limited citizenship to those born from an Ivoirian mother and father. Although allegedly introduced to promote a sense of cultural unity in Côte d'Ivoire, the concept increasingly excluded the northern population of the country politically and economically as they were considered foreigners because of their seemingly foreign patronym. In 2002, the persistent and deepening discrimination against the North, epitomised by the repeated exclusion of the popular northern politician Alassane Ouattara from participating in the country's presidential elections, led to the emergence of a northern-dominated rebel group, who became known as the Forces Nouvelles ("New Forces"; Akindès et al., 2010). The rebellion de facto split the country in two, with the North being controlled by the rebels and the South remaining under the control of the then President Laurent Gbagbo. This situation lasted for 7 years. It was not until 2010 that the conflict parties agreed to hold new presidential elections in which Ouattara was allowed to stand. While it was hoped that the December 2010 presidential elections would pave the way towards the peaceful reintegration of the country, in the wake of the second-round run-off between Gbagbo and Ouattara, large-scale violence erupted in Abidjan and other areas of the country between

---

[1] This section draws heavily on the following paper: Kuppens L., and Langer A. 2016. Divided we teach? Teachers' perceptions of conflict and peace in Côte d'Ivoire. *Peace and Conflict: Journal of Peace Psychology*, 22(4): 329–333.

pro-Gbagbo and pro-Ouattara forces. While Ouattara had clearly won the presidential elections (International Crisis Group, 2011), Gbagbo refused to acknowledge defeat and tried to stay in power through force. The violence resulted in more than 3,000 casualties (Amnesty International, 2013, p. 8) and lasted until pro-Ouattara forces captured Gbagbo in April 2011. One month later, Ouattara was inaugurated as president of Côte d'Ivoire and was re-elected in October 2015. Under his presidency, the country has improved significantly at the macroeconomic level. At the household level, progress has been much slower, however, causing resentment among the general population (Akindès, 2017). Besides, divisions remain between supposedly pro-Ouattara "Northerners" (Malinké, Sénoufo, immigrants from Burkina Faso, etc.) and so-called Natives of the West (i.e., ethnic Krou, as well as certain Southern Mande groups, such as the Gouro), allegedly pro-Gbagbo (Piccolino, 2017). Indeed, Ouattara's depoliticised policies have insufficiently promoted reconciliation and rapprochement, and have left unaddressed lingering legacies of conflict, including most notably the issue of land titles and tensions within the army (e.g., Akindès, 2017; Piccolino, 2017).

In Côte d'Ivoire, schooling starts at the age of six, with 6 years of primary schooling. This is followed by seven years of secondary education. Secondary education is split into two cycles: lower secondary education (12–15 years old) and higher secondary education (16–19 years old). Further, primary and secondary schools can either be public or private. While public schools are always secular, private schools may be secular or religious. Côte d'Ivoire has a relatively large primary and secondary teacher corps, with about 129,000 schoolteachers in 2013–2014 (Direction de la Planification, de l'Evaluation et des Statistiques du Ministère de l'Education Nationale et l'Enseignement Technique, 2014). Teachers are trained in six different teacher-training colleges. While the main teacher training college for primary school teachers (i.e., Centre d'Animation et de Formation Pédagogique) has schools throughout the country, teacher-training colleges for secondary school teachers are located in Abidjan, the de facto capital of the country. Depending on prospective teachers' educational background (in particular, whether or not they already have a bachelor or master degree in a specific area), teacher-training programmes can last between 2 and 6 years.

The political turmoil and violence in the last two decades have severely damaged Côte d'Ivoire's educational infrastructure and unsurprisingly educational attainment levels have also dropped significantly (Dabalen & Paul, 2014; Lanoue, 2007; Sany, 2010). While the country's educational structures and curricula largely remained the same throughout the political turmoil, the Ivorian educational system underwent an important change following the formal end of the hostilities in 2011 with the introduction of a new course on human rights and citizenship (i.e., *"Education aux Droits de l'Homme et à la Citoyenneté"*; Kuppens & Langer, 2018a). An important objective of this course was to contribute towards reconciling past divisions and facilitating a transition towards a culture of peace. The *Education aux Droits de l'Homme et à la Citoyenneté* (EDHC) curriculum is built around five core competencies: (C1) children's rights, human rights and international humanitarian law, (C2) citizenship and democratic principles, (C3) road safety education, entrepreneurship and community life, (C4) health preservation and sex education, and (C5) environmental sanitation and environmental protection (Ministère de l'Education Nationale, 2012a, 2012b). These competences are taught on the basis of age-specific themes. Our results from a large-scale survey (N = 984) and insights from six focus group discussions show that teachers on average welcome the course and believe that it can contribute to a more peaceful and socially cohesive Côte d'Ivoire. But, even though the EDHC course incorporates issues of human rights and citizenship education, teachers also indicate that the themes are only addressed superficially and that controversial topics are avoided. In particular, the course does not attempt to explain the differences, tensions and opposing narratives, which exist in Côte d'Ivoire regarding the origins of the recent violence and conflicts. Nor does any other course explicitly engage with Côte d'Ivoire's past conflict for that matter. What is more, contrary to the spirit of the course, classroom observations have shown that the overall school climate in Côte d'Ivoire remains undemocratic and that corporal punishment remains common (see Kuppens & Langer, 2018a).

Making matters worse when it comes to dealing constructively with Côte d'Ivoire's divisive past is the observation that Ivorian teachers remain extremely divided with respect to the causes of their country's past conflict as well as the nature and modalities of the current peace and reconciliation process. In particular, based on a large-scale survey among 984 secondary school teachers in Abidjan, Kuppens and Langer (2016) found that teachers' perceptions of peace and conflict were to a large extent driven by their ethnoreligious background. Thus, while Muslim teachers from a northern ethnic background saw the exclusion and discrimination against the North, in both economic and political terms, as the main reason for the emergence of the violent conflict in Côte d'Ivoire, in contrast, teachers belonging to the ethnic group of the Krou (a demographically important ethnic group in the Southwest of the country), were much more likely to perceive the country's past conflict to have been caused by French and foreign interests as well as the lust for political power by Alassane Ouattara, the political leader of the main northern political party, the *Rassemblement des Républicains*. Importantly, as the principal mediators of curricula, teachers build on what they have been taught, or, in the absence of any training, on what they have experienced. Since their experiences and views can challenge the peace-building narrative, it is crucial to train and "reform" teachers' attitudes, perceptions and skills to teach peace and tolerance in a constructive manner. Hence, teacher training can be considered to be of overriding importance and should precede implementation of curricular reform.

10.4 Kenya: Let's Not Talk about the Elephant in the Room[2]

Since the return to multiparty democracy in 1991, the political climate in Kenya has been consistently tense around elections times, causing sporadic outbursts of intergroup violence (Ajulu, 2002). At the time of the 1992 and 1997 presidential elections, more than 1,500 people died particularly in the Rift Valley and to a lesser extent in and around Mombasa (Harneit-Sievers & Peters, 2008, p. 134). After peaceful elections in 2002, violence once more took to the streets in the aftermath of the disputed 2007 elections, between supporters of the incumbent Kikuyu president, Mwai Kibaki, and the main opposition candidate and Luo strongman, Raila Odinga. The clashes had a strong ethnic dimension, and cost the lives of an estimated 1,113 people, wounded another 3,561 and caused more than 350,000 Kenyans to flee their homes (e.g., Dercon & Guitérrez-Romero, 2012, p. 735; Harneit-Sievers & Peters, 2008, p. 137; Human Rights' Watch,

---

[2] This section draws heavily on the following paper: Kuppens L., Ibrahim, S., and Langer A. 2019. Unity over diversity? Teachers' perceptions and practices of multicultural education in Kenya. Compare: A Journal of Comparative and International Education, DOI: 10.1080/03057925.2018.1557037.

2008, p. 22). Despite renewed mistrust and tensions no large-scale violence erupted in the run-up and aftermath of the August 2017 elections. The elections led to a political impasse, however, after the electoral results were annulled in a historical court decision because of irregularities and were followed by opposition leader Raila Odinga's boycott of the subsequent October 2017 elections (International Crisis Group, 2018). Moreover, at least forty-five Kenyans were killed after the first elections alone, largely as a result of unlawful and excessive police violence (Amnesty International & Human Rights' Watch, 2017). Ethnic tensions are not so much about ethnicity, as such, as they are the articulation of underlying historical grievances that date back to colonial times and continue to persist under the postcolonial state, including most notably issues of land ownership (Hornsby, 2013). As a legacy of the British colonial administration, post-independence parliamentary constituencies remained aligned with ethnic boundaries, instigating ethnic politics and favouritism (e.g., Burgess et al., 2015, p. 1825; Li, 2018, p. 194; for a more extensive review, see Berman et al., 2009).

The Kenyan education system is based on the promotion of eight national goals, which include fostering national unity and promoting social equality and respect for the country's rich and varied cultures (see Mwaka et al., 2013). At the age of six, Kenyan pupils start attending primary school normally until the age of fourteen. Then, they enrol in secondary education, which lasts 4 years. To obtain a university degree, students attend four more years of schooling, although this so-called 8–4–4 system is under review (Daily Nation, 2018). Pupils can choose to be taught the first 3 years of primary school in their mother tongue. Subsequent years are taught in English. Primary and secondary education is compulsory in Kenya and theoretically free of costs (Smith et al., 2016). Education in Kenya is highly exam oriented. Admittance to secondary schooling is conditional on pupils' performance on the national examinations organised at the end of primary education. Depending on their score, pupils attend one out of four types of public secondary schools, i.e., national, extra-county, county and subcounty schools. The best-performing pupils are admitted to national schools and the lesser performing ones attend sub-county schools, which are the most common type of school (70% of public schools). In addition, public schools admit pupils based on regional quota (Table 10.1): national schools are the most diverse,

Table 10.1 *Regional quota of public schools in Kenya*

Type of School	Number	Regional Quota
National	103	100% national
Extra-county	328	40% nationally; 40% host county; 20% host subcounty (former district)
County (former provincial)	993	80% host county; 20% host subcounty
Subcounty (former district)	6,982	100% host subcounty

Source: Committee on Review of Form One Selection Guidelines (2015)

accepting students countrywide, whereas subcounty schools only admit students from within the subcounty. County and extra-county schools form the middle tier (Lewin et al., 2011; Nyatuka & Bota, 2014).

Schools are either public or private. In the past, so-called Harambee (KiSwahili for "pulling together") schools existed as well. These community schools were largely established in response to the shortage of government and private low-cost schools, but have been taken over by the government since 1988 (Amutabi, 2003, p. 130). Private schools generally offer better quality of education and have better facilities (Nyatuka & Bota, 2014). Primary school teachers go through a training of two years, dispensed by one of the many teacher training institutes in the country – twenty public and seventy private (Ole Katitia, 2015). To teach at the secondary level, a Bachelor diploma of Education is required or a diploma from one of the three teacher colleges for secondary education. To advance social cohesion, teachers are encouraged to take a teaching position outside of their region of origin. In practice, teachers seem reluctant to be posted elsewhere, however (Smith et al., 2016).

The postelection violence temporarily halted the education of many students in conflict-affected areas in Kenya, while sixty-five schools were looted. Education itself is, however, to some extent complicit in fuelling ethnic resentment and deepening ethnic divides. Historically, the political elites have allocated educational resources disproportionally to those areas where their ethnic group(s) were predominant, resulting in disparities in access to education and in educational outcomes – however, at the primary level, gaps have largely been closed nowadays (see Chapter 9; in addition see, e.g., Alwy & Schech, 2004, p. 267; Li, 2018). Importantly, the Final Report of the Truth, Justice, and Reconciliation Commission of Kenya (2013) recognised these disparities and hence recommends addressing them. In response to the postelection violence, the Kenyan Ministry of Education, Science, and Technology has moreover integrated and mainstreamed peace education. In 2008, a Peace Education Programme was implemented at the primary school level. The Peace Education Programme was originally developed and implemented by the United Nations High Commissioner for Refugees in the refugee camps of Kakuma and Dadaab (e.g., Mendenhall & Chopra, 2016; Obura, 2002). At the secondary level, peace education was introduced in courses such as life skills, religion, social studies and history and government. In addition, an accompanying Education Sector Policy on Peace Education has been in place since 2012 "to promote and nurture a culture of peace and appreciation for diversity in the Kenyan society through education and training" (Ministry of Education, Science and Technology, 2014, p. 3). Like the EDHC in Côte d'Ivoire, the curricula make no mention of the history of interethnic strive in Kenya, but incorporate topics related to citizenship education, diversity and conflict resolution. Because it is a non-examinable subject, peace education is often disregarded in the severe exam-oriented Kenyan system (Mendenhall & Chopra, 2016; Smith et al., 2016).

In-depth interviews ($N = 68$) as well as a survey research that we conducted among 925 secondary school teachers in Nairobi show that Kenyan teachers are generally very positive about ethnic diversity, value their pupils' background, and try to accommodate ethnic differences in the classroom. Teachers try, e.g., to use examples reflective of diverse ethnic groups, take mother tongue influence into account when helping pupils with the correct pronunciation of English, and are enthusiastic about extracurricular activities that celebrate ethnic diversity, such as music and theatre festivals. These are prototypical examples of multicultural teaching strategies that may contribute to a more socially cohesive Kenya in the future. Yet, teachers clearly prioritise unity over diversity. They believe that expressing ethnic identities through dress or language at school is divisive and detrimental to national unity. Promoting diversity does not exclude unity, however (Gay, 2013; Kymlicka, 2004). Many teachers themselves identify not only as a Kenyan, but also as a member of their ethnic group. Furthermore, while they value and foster cultural diversity, teachers refrain from discussing the highly sensitive issue of political ethnicity. What is more, our research has shown that many secondary school teachers in Kenya think stereotypically about ethnic groups – even though many say to be careful not to let their stereotypes influence their teaching practices (Kuppens & Langer, 2018b). Besides, many teachers express a significant in-group bias (Kuppens & Langer, 2018b), and one out of four teachers acknowledged that they had favoured a coethnic pupil – e.g., providing transport fares to coethnic students and helping them out after class hours (Kuppens, L., & Langer, A. 2018. *Ethnicity and Education in Kenya: Are Teachers Immune to Ethnic Favouritism?* Unpublished manuscript). Such attitudes and practices may actually contribute to solidifying the most common ethnic stereotypes and to perpetuating ethnic favouritism, whether directly or indirectly, consciously or unconsciously. Unmistakeably, the challenge in Kenya is to address ethnic politics and to eradicate ethnic favouritism and prejudice. The Kenyan peace curriculum and teachers could play a crucial role in this regard. By openly dealing with and critically examining issues of ethnicity, ethnic stereotyping and favouritism in the classroom, education could contribute to a change in mentality and contribute to building a more socially cohesive Kenya.

10.5 Conclusions

While education alone cannot fulfil the promise of a socially cohesive society, education in citizenship, multicultural education and peace education can help imparting the "rules of the game" in a democracy and contribute to developing a shared sense of national identity and citizenship. In this chapter, we have reviewed and analysed how Côte d'Ivoire and Kenya have attempted to use their education systems to rebuild and promote social cohesion in their countries. Both Côte d'Ivoire and Kenya incorporated notions of peace, respect of diversity and citizenship and identity into their educational curricula after the emergence of severe political tensions and violent conflicts. On the basis of extensive survey and in-depth research that the authors conducted in both countries, it emerged however that the actual contribution of these curricula towards promoting and strengthening social cohesion appears to have been quite limited. Indeed, democratic principles and notions of tolerance and peace are only addressed superficially and are not put to practice in the overall school environment; the violent past is silenced and therefore continues to linger on; teachers remain prejudiced, divided and traumatised; and diversity at times is suppressed in the name of unity.

What broader lessons can be learnt from Côte d'Ivoire and Kenya's experiences in dealing with the violent past in schools? And more generally how can education be effectively used to promote and advance social cohesion in multi-ethnic societies in Africa? A first lesson that emerges from these two cases is that a country needs to address its divisive and often painful past in order to build a more cohesive future (e.g., Cole, 2007; Davies, 2016; Emerson, 2012). Because of the extremely sensitive nature of issues of ethnicity, ethnic tensions and violent conflict, post-conflict and ethnically divided societies often shy away from addressing their countries' conflict histories and/or ethnic tensions and divisions in the school system. Indeed, particularly in post-conflict situations, countries often follow a "let sleeping dogs lie"-strategy (see also Davies, 2010; Freedman et al., 2008). Kenya and Côte d'Ivoire are cases in point. Yet, such a culture of silence risks reinforcing the social identities of previously opposing groups (Weinstein et al., 2007). Hence, in line with previous research (e.g., Cole, 2007; Emerson, 2012), we argue that constructive, open and honest reflections and engagement with a country's conflict history as well as with the prevalent ethnic and/or societal divisions and tensions, either connected or unconnected to a country's violent past, seems to be a more productive, effective and successful approach towards building social cohesion in the future. Promisingly, diverse textbook revisions and projects have already been set up to break down exclusive identities and address the root causes of conflict in diverse post-conflict contexts, including Germany and France, Israel-Palestine and the countries of the former Yugoslavia (see Korostelina & Lässig, 2013). Encouraging perspective taking is crucial in this regard: by familiarising pupils with a range of perspectives on and explanations for understanding their country's past and present, and by critically examining teachers' own views, education can foster mutual understanding and empathy among formerly conflicting groups (Emerson, 2012; Salomon, 2002). This, in turn, is likely to have a positive impact on societal reintegration and makes a common peaceful future conceivable again. The programme "Facing the Past" is a good example in this respect. By confronting teachers with multiple narratives on the violent past, it aims to break down stereotypes and rebuild trust between teachers. The programme has already showed positive results in South Africa and Northern Ireland (Murphy et al., 2016; Weldon, 2010).

Further, to advance social cohesion in ethnically divided societies, countries should not attempt to disregard or ignore ethnocultural diversity and differences in educational curricula, classrooms and schools but rather proactively attempt to increase mutual knowledge, respect and understanding among pupils and students regarding different ethnocultural traditions and groups (see, e.g., Banks, 1993; Banks & Banks, 2001). Without an explicit effort to recognise and familiarise pupils and students with the different ethnocultural traditions and groups present in a country, and alternatively treating intergroup differences as if they do not exist, there is a clear risk that curricula and the school system more generally may implicitly become a reflection of the language, worldview and/or values of the dominant group in society. This in turn may lead smaller ethnocultural groups to feel excluded and culturally marginalised. Further, while education reform and change in divided societies cannot *and* should not happen without broad-based political support, it is crucial that – as much as possible – politics is kept out of curriculum design/reform and content development.

A second broad lesson we can take from Côte d'Ivoire and Kenya's experiences is that teachers are a potentially important force for social cohesion building, but only if they are properly trained and challenge their own biases. In this respect, it was noteworthy that although most teachers in Côte d'Ivoire and Kenya agreed that schools had an important role play in educating pupils about the past, a substantial proportion of teachers was nonetheless reluctant to address their country's conflict history in their classrooms because many of them perceived themselves to lack the necessary intercultural knowledge, competences and skills to teach these sensitive issues. Further, as noted above, teachers are not necessarily "neutral" transmitters of a curriculum, and may have prejudiced, intolerant and exclusionary views and opinions, which run counter to social cohesion building. Thus, if teachers are to become agents of social cohesion building they need to be educated and properly trained (including stereotypes awareness training, culturally sensitive communication techniques) on how to deal with their country's violent past, the different conflict narratives that may be circulating in society, and issues of ethnocultural diversity and differences in a classroom setting.

A third important lesson that clearly has relevance beyond the cases of Côte d'Ivoire and Kenya is that multicultural or multi-ethnic societies always need to find a balance between recognising, explaining and celebrating group differences and maintaining and promoting unity in the face of these differences. If schools are to become places of social cohesion building it is crucial that young people are not only being taught about and familiarised with other ethnocultural groups' histories, traditions and customs. It is equally important to teach pupils and students about the history they share with other groups, the historical relations and interactions (both conflictual and cooperative) they have had with people and groups in their society, and the ties that have bound them together in the past and will bind them together in the future. Banks (2006, p. 208) aptly notes in this respect: "Multicultural societies are faced with the problem of constructing nation-states that reflect and incorporate the diversity of its citizens and yet have an overarching set of shared values, ideals, and goals to which all of its citizens are committed. Diversity and unity must be balanced in multicultural nation-states." Finding the right balance between unity and diversity is on-going process, which involves an extremely difficult balancing act. This balancing act is difficult in multicultural or multi-ethnic societies without a history of violence (e.g., Belgium and Canada), but it poses even bigger challenges for ethnically divided and/or post-conflict societies. Yet, if African countries are to strengthen the cohesiveness of their societies in the future, it is essential that they get this balancing act right, both in the education system and the society at large.

References

Ajulu, R. 2002. Politicised ethnicity, competitive politics and conflict in Kenya: A historical perspective. *African Studies.* 61(2): 251–268.

Akindès, F. 2017. "On ne mange pas les ponts et le goudron": Les sentiers sinueux d'une sortie de crise en Côte d'Ivoire. *Politique africaine.* 4(148): 5–26.

Akindès, F., Fofana, M. and Koné, G. 2010. Côte d'Ivoire: Insurrection et contre-insurrection. *Alternatives Sud.* 17(93): 93–97.

Almond, G. A., and Verba S. 1963) *Civic Culture: Political Attitudes and Democracy in Five Nations.* Thousand Oaks, CA: Sage.

Alwy, A., and Schech, S. 2004. Ethnic inequalities in education in Kenya. *International Education Journal.* 5(2): 266–274.

Amnesty International. 2013. *Côte d'Ivoire: The Victor's Law. The Human Rights Situation Two Years after the Post-Electoral Crisis.* London: Amnesty International Publications.

Amnesty International & Human Rights' Watch. 2017. *"Kill Those Criminals": Security Forces Violations in Kenya's August 2017 Elections.* New York: Amnesty International & HRW.

Amutabi, M. N. 2003. Political interference in the running of education in post-independence Kenya: A critical retrospection. *International Journal of Educational Development.* 23(2): 127–144.

Bajaj, M. 2008. *Encyclopedia of Peace Education.* North Carolina: Information Age Publishing.

Bajaj, M., and Hantzopoulos, M. 2016. *Peace Education: International Perspectives.* New York: Bloomsbury Academic.

Banks, J. A. 1993. Multicultural education: Historical development, dimensions and practices. *Review of Research in Education.* 19(1): 3–49.

Banks, J.A. 2006. Democracy, diversity and social justice: Educating citizens for the public interest in the global age. In Ladson-Billings, G. and Tate, W.F. (eds.), *Education Research in the Public Interest: Social Justice, Action, and Policy.* New York: Teachers College Press, pp. 141–157.

Banks, J. A., and Banks, C. A. (eds.). 2001. *Multicultural Education: Issues and Perspectives* 4th edn. New York: Wiley.

Bekerman, Z. 2016. Experimenting with integrated peace education: Critical perspectives in the Israeli context. In Bajaj, M., and Hantzopoulos, M. (eds.), *Peace Education: International Perspectives.* New York: Bloomsbury Academic, pp. 51–68.

Bennett, M. J. 2009. Defining, measuring, and facilitating intercultural learning: A conceptual introduction to the Intercultural Education double supplement. *Intercultural Education.* 20(Suppl. 1–2): 1–13.

Berman, B. J., Cottrell, J., and Ghai, Y. 2009. Patrons, clients, and constitutions: Ethnic politics and political reform in Kenya. *Canadian Journal of African Studies.* 43(3): 462–506.

Bouquet, C. 2011. *Côte d'Ivoire: Le désespoir de Kourouma.* Paris: Editions Colin.

Brown, G. K. 2011. The influence of education on violent conflict and peace: Inequality, opportunity and the management of diversity. *Prospects.* 41 (2): 191–204.

Burgess, R., Jedwab, R., Miguel, E., Morjaria, A., and Padró i Miquel, G. 2015. The value of democracy: Evidence from road building in Kenya. *American Economic Review.* 105(6): 1817–1851.

Bush, K. D., and Saltarelli, D. (eds.). 2000. *The Two Faces of Education in Ethnic Conflict.* Florence: UNICEF Innocenti Research Centre.

Campbell, D. E. 2012. Introduction. In Campbell, D. E., Levinson, M., and Hess, F. M. (eds.), *Making Civics Count: Citizenship Education for a New Generation.* Boston: Harvard Education Press, pp. 1–14.

Cole, E. A. 2007. Transitional justice and the reform of history education. *International Journal of Transitional Justice.* 1(1): 115–137.

Colenso, P. 2005. Education and social cohesion: Developing a framework for education sector reform in Sri Lanka. *Compare: A Journal of Comparative and International Education,* 35(4): 411–428.

Committee on Review of Form One Selection Guidelines (22.20.2015). Form One Selection and Admission Guidelines. Presentation at the Kenya Institute of Curriculum Development Stakeholders' forum. Retrieved from www.google.com/url?sa=t&rct=j&q=&esrc=s&source=web&cd= 9&ved=0ahUKEwi6lz8L7bAhXRJVAKHawgCYMQFghuMAg&url= http%3A%2F%2Fwww.mygov.go.ke%2Fwpcontent%2Fuploads% 2F2015%2F10%2FFORM-ONE-SELECTION-GUIDELINES2015.ppt &usg=AOvVaw2JOa2pOcNfPocrAe KqY0K0. Accessed 4 June 2016.

Dabalen, A. L., and Paul, S. 2014. Estimating the effects of conflict on education in Côte d'Ivoire. *Journal of Development Studies.* 50(12): 1631–1646.

Daily Nation. (03.01.2018). *Experts meet to determine fate of bold school reforms.* Retrieved from www.nation.co.ke/news/education/Experts-meet-to-determine-fate-of-bold-school-reforms/2643604-4249376-7r8i0u/ index.html. Accessed 4 January 2018.

Davies, L. 2004. *Education and Conflict: Complexity and Chaos.* London: Routledge Falmer.

——— 2010. The different faces of education in conflict. *Development.* 53(4): 491–497.

Davies, L. 2016. The politics of peace education in post-conflict countries. In Langer, A., & , Brown, G. K. (eds.), *Building Sustainable Peace: Timing and Sequencing of Post-Conflict Reconstruction and Peacebuilding.* Oxford: Oxford University Press, pp. 181–199.

Dercon, S., and Guitérrez-Romero, R. 2012. Triggers and characteristics of the 2007 Kenyan electoral violence. *World Development.* 40(4): 731–744.

Direction de la Planification. 2014. de l'Evaluation et des Statistiques du Ministère de l'Education Nationale et l'Enseignement Technique (DPES-MEN). *Rapport d'analyse Statistique 2013–2014.* Abidjan: MENET.

Dupuy, K. E. 2008. Education in peace agreements, 1989–2005. *Conflict Resolution Quarterly.* 26(2): 149–166.

Emerson, L. 2012. Conflict, transition and education for "political generosity": Learning from the experience of ex-combatants in Northern Ireland. *Journal of Peace Education.* 9(3): 277–295.

Freedman, S. W., Weinstein, H. M., Murphy, K., and Longman, T. 2008. Teaching history after identity-based conflicts: The Rwanda experience. *Comparative Education Review. 52*(4): 663–690.

Freire, P. 1970. *Pedagogy of the Oppressed.* New York: Continuum International Publishing Group Inc.

Gay, G. 2013. Teaching to and through cultural diversity. *Curriculum Inquiry.* 43(1): 48–70.

Giroux, H. A. 1983. *Theory and Resistance in Education: A Pedagogy for the Opposition.* Massachusetts: Bergin & Garvey Publishers, Inc.

Green, A., and Preston, J. 2001. Education and social cohesion: Recentering the debate. *Peabody Journal of Education.* 76(3–4): 247–284.

Harneit-Sievers, A., and Peters, R.-M. 2008. Kenya's 2007 General election and its aftershocks. *Africa Spectrum.* 43(1): 133–144.

Harris, I. M., and Morrison, M. L. 2003. *Peace Education.* 2nd edn. Jefferson, NC: McFarland & Company, Inc.

Heyneman, S. P. 2000. From the party/state to multiethnic democracy: Education and social cohesion in Europe and central Asia. *Educational Evaluation and Policy Analysis,* 22(2): 173–191.

2003. Education, Social cohesion, and the future role of international organizations. *Peabody Journal of Education.* 78(3): 25–38.

Hornsby, C. 2013. *Kenya: A History Since Independence.* London: I.B. Tauris.

Human Rights' Watch. 2008. *Ballots to Bullets: Organized Political Violence and Kenya's Crisis of Governance.* New York: HRW.

International Crisis Group. 2011. *A Critical Period for Ensuring Stability in Côte d'Ivoire (ICG Report n°176).* Brussels: ICG.

2018. *After Kenya's Leaders Reconcile, a Tough Path Ahead (Crisis Group Africa Briefing N°136).* Nairobi/Brussels: ICG.

King, E. 2015. *From Classrooms to Conflict in Rwanda.* New York: Cambridge University Press.

Korostelina, K. V., and Lässig, S. 2013. *History Education and Post-Conflict Reconciliation.* New York: Routledge.

Kuppens, L., and Langer, A. 2016. Divided we teach? Teachers' perceptions of conflict and peace in Côte d'Ivoire. *Peace and Conflict: Journal of Peace Psychology.* 22(4): 329–333.

2018a. Peut-on apprendre la paix à l'école? Une évaluation du cours de l'Education aux Droits de l'Homme et à la en Côte d'Ivoire. *International Review of Education.* 64(5): 1–18.

2018b. "A Teacher is no politician": Stereotypic attitudes of secondary school teachers in Kenya. *International Journal of Educational Development,* 62: 270–280.

Kuppens L., Ibrahim, S. and Langer A. 2019. Unity over diversity? Teachers' perceptions and practices of multicultural education in Kenya.

Compare: A Journal of Comparative and International Education. DOI: 10.1080/03057925.2018.1557037.

Kymlicka, W. 2004. Foreword. In Banks, J. A. (ed.), *Diversity and Citizenship Education: Global Perspectives.* San Francisco: Jossey-Bass.

Ladson-Billings, G. 1995. Toward a theory of culturally relevant pedagogy. *American Educational Research Journal.* 32(3): 465–491.

Langer, A. 2005. Horizontal inequalities and violent group mobilization in Côte d'Ivoire. *Oxford Development Studies.* 33(1): 25–45.

2010. *Côte d'Ivoire's Elusive Quest for Peace (Centre for Development Studies, University of Bath Working Paper No. 11).* Bath, UK,: CDS.

Langer, A., Stewart, F., Smedts, K. and Demarest, L. 2017. Conceptualising and measuring social cohesion in Africa: Towards a perceptions-based index. *Social Indicators Research.* 131(1): 321–343.

Lanoue, E. 2007. Éducation, violences et conflits en Afrique subsaharienne. Sources, données d'enquête (Côte d'Ivoire, Burkina Faso) et hypothèse. *International Journal on Violence and Schools.* 3, 94–111.

Lewin, K. M., Wasanga, P., Wanderi, E. and Somerset, A. 2011. *Participation and Performance in Education in Sub-Saharan Africa with Special Reference to Kenya: Improving Policy and Practice (Research Monograph No. 74).* Sussex: University of Sussex.

Li, J. 2018. Ethnic favoritism in primary education in Kenya: The effects of coethnicity with the president. *Education Economics,* 26(2): 194–212.

Loader, R., and Hughes, J. 2017. Balancing cultural diversity and social cohesion in education: The potential of shared education in divided contexts. *British Journal of Educational Studies.* 65(1): 3–25.

McGovern, M. 2011. *Making War in Côte d'Ivoire.* London: Hurst and Company.

Mendenhall, M., and Chopra, N. 2016. Educating for peace in Kenya: Insights and lessons learned from peace education initiatives across the country. In Bajaj, M. and Hantzopoulos, M. (eds.), *Peace Education: International Perspectives.* New York: Bloomsbury Academic, pp. 89–106.

Ministère de l'Education Nationale (MEN). 2012a. *Programmes Educatifs et guides d'Exécution. Education aux Droits de l'Homme et à la Citoyenneté (EDHC). Secondaire 5eme/6eme.* Abidjan: MEN.

2012b. *Programmes Educatifs et guides d'Exécution. Education aux Droits de l'Homme et à la Citoyenneté (EDHC). Secondaire 4eme/ 3eme.* Abidjan: MEN.

Ministry of Education, Science and Technology. 2014. *Education Sector Policy on Peace Education.* Nairobi: Ministry of Education, Science and Technology.

Murphy, K., Pettis, S., and Wray, D. 2016. Building peace: The opportunities and limitations of educational interventions in countries with identity-based conflicts. In Bajaj, M., and Hantzopoulos, M. (eds.), *Peace Education: International Perspectives*. New York: Bloomsbury Academic, pp. 35–50.

Mwaka, M., Kafwa, V. N., Musamas, J. K., and Wambura, B. 2013. The national goals of education in Kenya: Interrogating the achievement of national unity. *Journal of Education and Practice*. 4(4): 149–156.

Nieto, S. 1996. *Affirming Diversity: The Socio-Political Context of Multicultural Education*. 2nd edn. White Plains, NY: Longman.

Novelli, M., Lopes Cardozo, M. T. A., and Smith, A. 2017. The 4R's framework: Analyzing education's contribution to sustainable peacebuilding with social justice in conflict affected contexts. *Journal on Education in Emergencies*. 3(1): 14–43.

Nyatuka, B. O., and Bota, K. N. 2014. Equity in access to secondary education in Kenya: A historical perspective. *Journal of Education and Practice*. 5(2): 48–54.

Obura, A. P. 2002. *Peace Education Programme in Dadaab and Kakuma, Kenya: Evaluation Summary*. Nairobi: UNHCR.

Ole Katitia, D. M. 2015. Teacher education preparation programme for the 21st century. Which way forward for Kenya?' *Journal of Education and Practice*. 6(24): 57–63.

Osler, A., and Starkey, H. 2005. *Changing Citizenship: Democracy and Inclusion in Education*. Maidenhead. Open University Press.

2006. Education for democratic citizenship: A review of research, policy and practice 1995–2005. *Research Papers in Education*. 21(4): 433–466.

Piccolino, G. 2017. Rhétorique de la cohésion sociale et paradoxes de la "paix par le bas" en Côte d'Ivoire. *Politique africaine*. 4(148): 49–68.

Quaynor, L. 2012. Citizenship education in post-conflict contexts: A review of the literature. *Education, Citizenship, and Social Justice*. 7(1): 37–57.

Reardon, B. A. 1988. *Comprehensive Peace Eductation: Educating for Global Responsibility*. New York: Teachers College Press.

Russell, S. G., and Quaynor, L. 2017. Constructing citizenship in post-conflict contexts: The cases of Liberia and Rwanda. *Globalisation, Societies and Education*. 15(2): 248–270.

Salomon, G. 2002. The nature of peace education: Not all programmes are created equal. In Salomon, G., and Nevo, B. (eds.), *Peace Education: The Concept, Principles, and Practices around the World*. New York: Psychology Press, pp. 3–13.

Salomon, G., and Cairns, E. 2010. *Handbook on Peace Education*. New York: Psychology Press.

Sany, J. 2010. *Education and Conflict in Côte d'Ivoire*. Washington, DC: USIP.

Sayed, Y., Badroodien, A., Salmon, T., and McDonald, Z. 2016. Social cohesion and initial teacher education in South Africa. *Educational Research for Social Change (ERSC).* 5(1): 54–69.

Sinclair, M., Davies, L., Obura, A., and Tibbitts, F. 2008. *Learning to Live Together: Design, Monitoring and Evaluation of Education for Life Skills, Citizenship, Peace and Human Rights.* Eschborn: GTZ.

Sleeter, C. E. 2011. An agenda to strengthen culturally responsive pedagogy. *English Teaching: Practice and Critique.* 10(2): 7–23.

Smith, A., Marks, C., Novelli, M., Valiente, O., and Scandurra, R. 2016. *Exploring the Linkages between Education Sector Governance, Inequity, Conflict, and Peacebuilding in Kenya: Research Report Prepared for UNICEF Eastern and Southern Regional Office (ESARO).* Nairobi: UNICEF.

Stephan, W. G., and Stephan, C. W. 2001. *Improving Intergroup Relations.* Thousand Oaks, CA: Sage.

Tawil, S., and Harley, A. (eds.). 2004. *Education, Conflict and Social Cohesion.* UNESCO International Bureau of Education: Paris.

Tibbitts, F. 2002. Understanding what we do: Emerging models for human rights education. *International Review of Education,* 48(3–4): 159–171.

2008. Human rights education. In Bajaj, M. (ed.), *Encyclopedia of Peace Education.* Charlotte, NC: Information Age Publishing, Inc.

Torney-Purta, J. 2002. The school's role in developing civic engagement: A study of adolescents in twenty-eight countries. *Applied Developmental Science.* 6(4): 203–212.

UNICEF. 2011. *The Role of Education in Peacebuilding: A Literature Review.* New York: UNICEF.

United Nations. 1999. *United Nations Declaration and Programme of Action on a Culture of Peace, A/RES/53/243, Resolution Adopted by the General Assembly on 13 September 1999.* New York: ONU.

Weinstein, H. M., Freedman, S. W., and Hughson, H. 2007. School voices: Challenges facing education systems after identity-based conflicts. *Education, Citizenship and Social Justice.* 2(1): 41–71.

Weldon, G. 2010. Post-conflict teacher development: Facing the past in South Africa. *Journal of Moral Education.* 39(3): 353–364.

11 | Remaking Cape Town
Memory Politics, Land Restitution, and Social Cohesion in District Six

CIRAJ RASSOOL

This chapter demonstrates the complexities and contradictions involved in the policies or practices designed to bring inclusive development and social cohesion. It shows how complicated the implementation of social redress is when it comes up against community memory of previous experiences of exclusion and repression, and how such memory cannot easily be directed to new purposes. More specifically, this study is an account of the politics of urban social reconstruction and social cohesion in Cape Town in the two decades after the end of apartheid. It is about the contradictions and tensions arising from a variety of processes and projects through which the eastern edges of inner city Cape Town are being remade in material and symbolic ways after the ravages of apartheid urban planning. It is also an analysis of the contests that are unfolding over different imaginaries about Cape Town's pasts and futures. The study concerns the politics of memory as inscription in the landscape and as social practice. It is about the interface of urban gentrification, land restitution and housing provision, as well as civic activism, memory politics and historical representation.

There is a much wider study to be made about struggles and contests over housing provision in greater Cape Town – about housing backlogs and the growth of informal settlements in the aftermath of the demise of apartheid's coloured labour preference policies. Cape Town remains profoundly marked by race in ways that continue to give life to patterns of privilege, seclusion and exclusion that have substantial continuities with apartheid. "African" people continue to be excluded and marginalised in the city and these relations of marginality are reproduced further in townships, where immigrant and refugee communities experience the violence of social dislocation.

This account, however, focuses on Cape Town's District Six, which has been the site for imprinting new South African imaginaries onto real estate development, through new forms of compromise and accommodation. As attachments to inner city land have been asserted through land restitution or declarations of its historic significance, these claims have been contained through planning agendas that have prioritised mixed use development, speculation and gentrification. As the state tries to imprint a development framework fragmented between themed environments of land restitution, commerce and the business of property, civic forums have contested the field of memory, with new approaches to redefining citizenship in the post-apartheid city. These bodies have challenged the projects of urban regeneration, renewal and orderly citizenship that the state has inaugurated, demonstrating that social cohesion and urban reconstruction need to be based upon memory work, especially about the social experience of those whose material traces apartheid sought to destroy.

As District Six, site of long histories of removal and displacement from the 1901 expulsion of Africans to Uitvlugt to the removals and demolitions under apartheid's Group Areas Act, experiences sequences of renewed hope about the prospects for speeding up the settlement of land claims through redevelopment, the edges of downtown Cape Town have been undergoing rapid processes of urban gentrification. Through its memory work, the District Six Museum has sought to contest the priorities of urban redevelopment and gentrification in Cape Town as ways of imprinting new meanings on the landscape.

As a museum of process focusing on urban forced removals, the District Six Museum has tried to intervene in the field of cultural representation, and its forums have provided a model for exchanges and transactions between different genres of knowledge and political and cultural expression through notions of remembering influenced both by human rights discourses as well as noncollaborationist histories of political mobilisation. The museum is now challenged to extend these methodologies and introduce issues of memory into the redevelopment process as land restitution occurs in fits and starts, hampered by difficult technical and political challenges, and rendered more complex by how different imaginaries of claimant representative bodies have been legitimised by the state. The South African Heritage Resources Agency (SAHRA), seemingly unable to extend its work of declaration and conservation, based previously largely on architectural and archaeological value, to landscapes of complex history, has failed to create a heritage framework for a District Six redevelopment process that prioritises the sites of a wounded memory of forced displacement.

These contests unfolding on the edges of central Cape Town over the representation of underclass histories, forced removal and the politics of land restitution affect the character of the post-apartheid city as it is being shaped, planned and imagined within and outside the state. This chapter looks at these challenges and disputes, analyses the forums and networks involved, as well as the systems and relations of knowledge caught up in these unfolding contradictions, as a contribution to understanding the remaking of a city with a deep colonial and apartheid past that continues to haunt it.

11.1 Social Cohesion and Memory Work

Rather than thinking about social cohesion as a measurable condition reflecting a balance between national belonging and ethnic accommodation or as a development instrument (see OECD, 2011), this needs to be thought of as a field of cultural production and social imagination, in which identities are made and remade through the imaginative work of culture, creativity and memory. This is a contested terrain of the cultural politics of person and identity formation, in which national states intervene through national heritage institutions and projects of national culture formation and where local states seek to reinvent civic identities through urban regeneration, planning and governmentality. But it is also an arena of multiple contending forces of knowledge formation and memory activism, through which varied imaginaries of citizenship and nation are presented through cultural work of historical narration and site interpretation.

This contested field of social cohesion has emerged out of the immediate post-apartheid cultural work of reimagining the nation and "settling the past" through the discourse of reconciliation, as spearheaded by the Truth and Reconciliation Commission, and of the selected remapping of racial space through land restitution (Dhupelia-Mesthrie, 1999; James & Van de Vijver, 2001; Walker et al., 2011). The workings and findings of the Truth and Reconciliation Commission and the parameters and boundaries of land restitution have been challenged as inadequate and limited in their efforts to settle the past with too much historical continuity in the society's patterns of power and dispossession, a "diminished truth" (Mamdani, 2001) and a democratic settlement that remains "tenuously balanced between promiscuous peace and victor's justice" (Du Toit, 2013). As part of the events commemorating the centenary of the promulgation of the 1913 Land Act, the Department of Rural Development and Land Reform (DRDLR) announced that not only would the land claims programme be reopened, but also that claims relating to dispossession before 1913 would also be allowed (DRDLR, 2013a). Nevertheless, the ongoing projects of reconciliation and incomplete processes of land restitution continue to mark South African society and its field of social cohesion.

Reconciliation remains a vital discourse of the nation, requiring cultural and memory work as an aspect of the afterlife of the Truth and Reconciliation Commission, while land restitution continues to be reined in by inherited patterns of property and limitations on jurisdiction. These processes continue to affect the contested terrain of social cohesion, marked by cultural projects of "unity in diversity" (predominantly in the form of community consultations and national summits; Mashatile, 2013), forms of heritage planning and governmentality, and the work of building nonracial futures through the resources of memory and local capacity building. In District Six as in other places on the edges of downtown Cape Town, different imaginaries of urban renewal and social regeneration continue to unleash themselves, as the demands of land restitution, heritage inscription and memory work reflect contests of meaning over social cohesion and citizenship.

These contests even attach themselves to the naming of the land itself and to the determination of its boundaries, as planning for commercial zoning and business development seeks to contain and even displace land restitution. These processes of city-making are also made up of networks, interconnections and contestations of knowledge expressed through different models of hierarchy, communication and politics, as expertise is claimed and challenged, involving institutions of knowledge and research centres, as well as social movements as research spaces. These affect the very processes of social cohesion as ongoing projects of memory, imagination and knowledge formation.

11.2 Contests of Land Restitution in District Six

Cape Town is in many ways a wounded, ghostly city. It bears the marks of generations of forced removal from at least the beginning of the twentieth century. This was when African people were removed from areas of the city proximate to the dockland, when the spread of bubonic plague prompted city officials to use health legislation as a pretext to evict and relocate people to the farm Uitvlugt through what Maynard Swanson called the "sanitation syndrome". Social historians of Cape Town have narrated this removal – the making of the first African settlement in Cape Town at what became Ndabeni – as the beginning of a chain of dislocations that culminated in apartheid removals all across the city (Jeppie & Soudien, 1990; Maylam, 1995; Swanson, 1977).

And in this historiography, the most prominent example of Group Areas Act removals, sometimes overshadowing other experiences of displacement, was District Six, where removals occurred quite late, in the 1970s and 1980s, at a time when the alliances that constituted apartheid had already changed. This history of forced removals created a garrison city of far-flung segregated dormitory townships and an urban spatiality characterised by fragmentation, exclusion and segregation. District Six, on the edge of the centre of Cape Town, was left bare, largely undeveloped, like a ghostly scar, save for a white technical university (The Cape Technikon, now the post-apartheid Cape Peninsula University of Technology [CPUT]) whose architects, imported from other provinces, incorporated District Six material artefacts, such as kerbstones, into its design. As a white group area, District Six was renamed *Zonnebloem* ("sunflower"), after the historic eighteenth-century colonial farm on the edge of the city (Jeppie & Soudien, 1990).

The failure to develop a large area of the Zonnebloem as a white group area gave the vacant land on the city's edge its wounded character, made even more poignant by the visibility of its old mosques and churches, as seen on the journey to the city along the Nelson Mandela (formerly Eastern) Boulevard. This failure might have been caused by shifts in the nature of apartheid planning, but the idea of housing development in apartheid Zonnebloem also came up against a sequence of initiatives in the 1980s geared towards resisting any such move on "salted earth". Most significant in this sequence was the Hands Off District Six (HODS) alliance of civic and other organisations which united in 1987 to prevent the redevelopment of District Six without the removed former residents themselves. It was at the HODS conference held at the historic Zonnebloem College in 1988 that a resolution was passed calling for the initiation of a memory and museum project for District Six (Jeppie & Soudien, 1990; Rassool & Prosalendis, 2001, pp. 146–148).

After the ending of apartheid, a land restitution programme was implemented as one of the instruments of national recovery through the operations of the Commission on Restitution of Land Rights, conducted in accordance with the Restitution of Land Rights Act (Act 22 of 1994). However, this process has been slow and inconsistent in relation to District Six, with long experiences of disappointment marked by occasional bursts of increased momentum. The processing of District Six land claims, as pooled into a single development plan, has been subject to political contest among the national, the provincial and the local states, and has generally been marked by a lack of will on the part of the city and the province, unsure of the impact of the return of low-income residents to prime city real estate on economic development and modernist planning.

After a decade of the lodging and verification of District Six land claims, as well as the extension of the land claims period after the initial exclusion of mainly African former tenants from the process, the building of houses seemed to begin in earnest in 2004. The representatives of the former residents, the District Six Beneficiary and Redevelopment Trust (D6BRT) had high hopes for 4,000 homes to be built on the land as part of land restitution, despite many restitution claimants opting for financial compensation. After the return of former residents Dan Ndzabela and Ebrahim Murat and their families to their new homes on 11 February 2004, further land restitution homes were built and allocated by the D6BRT to the rest of the 24 oldest former rent-paying claimants, and handed over in a special ceremony in June 2005, dubbed "the return of the elders" (City of Cape Town Communication and Marketing Directorate, 2005; Nicholson, 2011d).

A celebratory homecoming ceremony addressed by Deputy President Thabo Mbeki on 20 November 2000 had entrusted the redevelopment of the land to the D6BRT. On this 40-hectare site, 20,000 people made up of 2,600 claimants and their families were to be accommodated in 4,000 two- or three-storey units. It was envisaged that the "rest of the development" would contain religious buildings, community and educational facilities, shops, offices and "limited light industry" (District Six Museum, 2005). Yet, by 2011 only sixty-eight houses had been built, with a "Second Homecoming" celebration held to hand-over keys to forty-four returning families on 11 February 2011, the forty-fifth anniversary of the Group Areas proclamation. In the presence of the national and provincial ministers as well as Cape Town's deputy mayor, in a remarkable show of co-operative government, the president, Jacob Zuma lay "his head on a block" over District Six, "guaranteeing that development in the area will be completed in the next three years" (Bamford, 2011).

While the D6BRT, formed in 1997 to co-ordinate and monitor the restitution process in consultation with claimants, had taken on the role of being the claimant representatives, by 2011 two other bodies had come into existence, the District Six Claimants Committee, formed 6 years before and representing about 200 claimants, and the District 6 Advocacy Committee, representing about 300 former home owners in District Six (*Cape Times,* 2011). In co-ordinating the claims of District Six claimants, the D6BRT managed to achieve consensus early on in the restitution process that the programme of return would involve an integrated development plan and prioritise the elderly as well as those who had been tenants rather than home owners, who made up about one-quarter of the claimants. The D6BRT also sought to prevent property speculation and "anti-social practices prevalent in the existing townships", including dealing in drugs and alcohol. It required successful claimants to commit themselves to occupy their homes for a minimum of five years, and to making a "moral community" through a "social compact" that also encouraged the fullest "integration" and the rejection of "separate 'ghettos' for poorer tenants and wealthier land owners" (Layne, 2008, p. 90).

The D6BRT was well aware that land restitution involving low-income returnees stood incongruously amid inner-city gentrification and rising land values could very quickly give way to market forces, with land restitution simply becoming another arm of urban housing development. Their concept of the reconstructed, returned District Six community involved a concept of citizenship rooted in the values of solidarity and the resources of resistance, and not any managerial notion of a new orderly, land owning, rate-paying client of the city, whose citizenship resided in rights to service delivery on the part of the state. Among the leaders of the D6BRT were those activists who had initiated the HODS campaign and the District Six Museum Foundation during the 1980s, suggesting substantial continuity in the leadership of the main organisations involved in addressing the scarred District Six landscape through agitation, restitution and memory work as processes of social intervention. In contrast, it seems as if the Advocacy Committee and the Claimants Committee represented the interests of former home owners, who were interested in being prioritised for return to freestanding houses on reclaimed, demarcated plots, and who claimed never to having been adequately consulted (Johns, 2011).

The renewed commitment to speeding up District Six restitution followed on from the creation of a new task team consisting of city and provincial officials as well as the land commission, with a commitment to drafting a new business plan for the design of housing units. A "special purpose vehicle" (SPV) would handle the "full-scale development" that would deliver 2,500 houses to land claimants. In addition, a further 2,500 units would be made available "on the open market, with a mixed-use component". Initial plans were to develop "lower density single-storey units" up the hill, with "increased densities" lower down, closer to the city centre (Mtyala, 2010). As representatives of the claimants, the D6BRT had seen themselves as development agents. Instead, the entire process was placed on a professional footing, driven by the state through a formal development framework, and the D6BRT seemingly turned into claimant representatives, who would encourage buy-in and participation, and decide on the order and sequence of eligible returnees to be allocated to houses as they were built.

By the beginning of December 2011, it was announced that, after 40 years, a "major breakthrough" had been achieved, with agreement from all tiers of government, and that the "plan for District Six" was ready. This would "restore" the "successful, vibrant and racially integrated space" to what it had been before apartheid demolitions had "laid it bare" (Nicholson, 2011a). Minister of Rural Development and Land Reform, Gugile Nkwinti said

This plan ensures that all the claimants can return to dignified homes, which reinvokes the vibrant non-racial character we strive for in society and which creates a strong, sustainable community through building an integrated and economically stable future, for all the people who will repopulate District 6. (Nicholson, 2011a)

The plan was made available for public inspection in the form of an exhibition of posters, storyboards and planning details, with a scaled model of how the area would look once development was complete. With architects and planners from the Task Team on hand during the week to answer questions, the minister encouraged "the widest possible participation" in this "exciting project" (Nicholson, 2011a).

The plan proposed rejecting the option of offering claimants houses at no cost and selling off District Six land to cover the costs of restitution. To do this would mean selling the area's "crown jewels", with claimants "los[ing] the area's legacy". Instead, with a proposed R250,000 that claimants would pay towards their homes, they would also acquire shares in the proposed special purpose vehicle (SPV) that would run the development. By becoming shareholders, all land would fall under the "control" of claimants, and revenue would also be created through the leasing of land and sale of additional homes. It was estimated that within 5 years, claimants would begin deriving dividends from their investments. As District Six restitution home-owners who had benefited from government grants, they would not be able to sell their houses for 10 years, while they would be encouraged to "hold on to their asset for at least 15 years" (Nicholson, 2011b, 2011c).

Those who had gathered at Trafalgar High School were certainly concerned about the progress of their claims. Many gathered "clutching their restitution documents" and "shared [their] memories of the area". And the planned "new inner city neighbourhood" would incorporate the old Zonnebloem Estate and Trafalgar Park of the old District Six, as well as the late 1970s and 1980s post-removal infrastructure such as the Good Hope Centre and the campus of the CPUT. Canterbury and Roeland Streets were planned as the border with the city centre. Significantly, it was envisaged that the old historic street grid would be reinstated in a grand disinterment, with Hanover Street reinstalled as the reborn area's retail and commercial spine. And as the claimants gazed longingly at the detailed elements of the scale model of the Reconstituted District Six, and touched and stroked the model's transparent cover, their hopes for the future met their resources of memory, as the new plan offered the opportunity for "complete restorative justice to undo the pain of forced removals" and held the tangible promise of reconstruction and recovery as the basis of social cohesion, with restitution framed as a "return home" (Nicholson, 2011d).

Yet as ex-residents of District Six sought a connection between their land claims in District Six and their memory of the area, and as the SPV option of investment was presented as a means of holding on to the area's "crown jewels", the design of the houses promised to be "sensitive to the history and memory of District Six". In addition, recognising that the 1,500 registered and verified claims represented only "a fraction" of those displaced from District Six, the opportunity presented itself to address "a wider imperative". The plan for District Six would "create a more integrated society" and "take on the challenge of restitution in its fullest sense". In gaining a share in the District Six "development vehicle", claimants would not get merely a house; they would gain a "valuable asset". They would be able to "own and rent out valuable residential and commercial property", in a development framework that contained "checks and balances to counter gentrification" (District Six Task Team, 2011).

Despite these strides, in September 2012, Minister Nkwinti called a workshop for registered claimants only, both tenants and land owners, on the development proposals at the Cape Town International Convention Centre, which he addressed personally. At this workshop, a Reference Group, described as "democratically elected" was established comprising two new committees, a "technical committee" which would study and explain the "contents and implications" of the business plan and SPV, and another to "deal with social integration" and report on "all social aspects" of restitution (South African Press Association, 2012; District Six Social Integration Team, 2013). Time was now of the essence and the minister seemingly took steps to "deal directly with all claimants" to ensure that the timeline for delivery would be able to meet the commitments made by the president. And it was clear from a subsequent meeting held by the Minister with the Social Integration Team on 7 December 2012 that the Department looked forward to "tangible results" and that it wanted the new process to "bring back credibility" to the complex restitution processes. It was suggested that 15 years of delays had made claimants "disillusioned", and that they had begun "to lose confidence" in the D6BRT, for "not acting transparently" and in allegedly having become "referee and player" in the development process of Phases 1 and 2 for District Six pilot housing (DLDLR, 2013a; District Six Reference Group, 2013, p. 5).

In January 2013, the two teams of the Reference Group completed their reports on their deliberations on the technical matters of restitution and issues of social integration respectively. The recommendations of the Technical Team proceeded from a critique of the 2011 Final Draft Development Framework deliberated on by the Task Team with claimants through public participation. This framework, the Technical Team suggested, supported a business plan "with a pre-meditated motive to place business interest before the restitution of land rights claimants" by "intending to erect high-rise density dwellings". The claimants, they said, rejected this framework which asked claimants "to return to a District Six that never existed". To try and give "a semblance" of District Six by building "a few facades at some strategic places" is "to totally ignore the deep emotional bonds" that claimants had for their birthplace and "the true and real heritage that they want the world to experience when D6 has been developed according to claimants' needs" (District Six Reference Group, 2013, pp. 8–9).

The Technical Team also challenged the economic argument of the D6BRT of emphasising the value of the land and that claimants would acquire an asset and not only a home, and for using the danger of gentrification "to inculcate fear and uncertainty in the hearts and minds of the claimants". It was as if there was a "Big Brother" who claimed to know best, they said, for the "smaller and less educated brothers", who needed to be protected from the "ruthlessness of the business moguls". The Technical Team also rejected any social compact which would unlawfully limit the full ownership rights of claimants, especially to sell their property and "unlock some value of their properties in their lifetime". Among the meetings held by the Reference Group between September and December 2012 was one with "the broad claimant community", which it marked as its "first success" in having its direction "endorsed", with one claimant suggesting that "the spirit of D6" had been "rekindled" in them. Another was with the D6BRT itself, to "foster more cordial relations", given the "vast institutional memory" its office bearers were recognised as having. It was hoped this "first engagement" could set "the scene for further more constructive engagements" (District Six Reference Group, 2013, pp. 8–15, p. 29).

In rejecting the economic model of the Final Draft Development Framework, the Technical Team recommended that claimant restitution land for residential purposes be separated from any land that may be earmarked for transfer to an SPV for commercial and business investment, and that any option to invest in an SPV be separated from claimant restitution. The team also recommended that given the "greatly reduced" available land for restitution, 2,800 single and/or duplex units be built for residential purposes in the final phases of redevelopment, on plots that should be at least 210 m², leaving flexibility for "future expansion". The restitution of claimants should not be linked in any way to the payment of contributions to the cost of their houses, with claimants encouraged to buy shares in the development with "down-stream" benefits, "as and when they have the financial means to do so" (District Six Reference Group, 2013, pp. 20–23).

The Technical Team called for a District Six land audit, especially of undeveloped and developed residential and commercial/retail land sold off after the date the area was declared one for restitution of its displaced people. They suggested that serious consideration be given to expropriation of land such as Bloemhof Flats, Drury Lane Flats, Stirling Flats and Eaton Place, to be used for claimants and other former District Six residents who did not claim before the 1998 closing date. Further, it was argued that the CPUT campus, built on the ruins of District Six, represented the "biggest blot on the landscape", should be given back and turned into a "multipurpose integrated community facility", with the educational provision relocated to other parts of the city. The site would be "an iconic symbol of restitution" with the "heart of District Six" given back to the people, and "pride and dignity" restored to the restitution process. As the "central buzz and hub of a new community", the CPUT site could become a hotel on Hanover Street, and be used as a conference centre, as well as for retail outlets, restaurants and franchises. With some "imagination and courage" it could be turned into an "iconic space" of "restitution excellence" and become a tourist attraction and "must experience" that can "rival the Waterfront". There might even be room for a hospital and perhaps even a major gym facility. And with the imagination of the Technical Team running riot, they even suggested that the District Six Museum could relocate to the CPUT campus and be expanded to include sports heritage (District Six Reference Group, 2013, pp. 29–31).

The handover of Phase Two homes by Minister Nkwinti to almost seventy mostly elderly District Six claimants in late August 2013 was an occasion for much celebration and at the same time revealed simmering "discontent" and lingering tensions in the land restitution process. As keys were handed over to former District Six tenants, some now described as "indigent", the Minister explained that claimants no longer had to pay the R250,000 as initially set out by the Task Team and the D6BRT. Two-bedroomed homes would be "free", but those "choosing bigger homes would have to contribute to the cost". Also included amongst the returnees now for the first time, were former landowners, who had felt sidelined by earlier processes. While the D6BRT participated in the handover, its leaders refused to share the platform with leaders of the provincial and city government, which were "lethargic" and "stalling the land restitution process". The city still needed to hand over 42 hectares of land to the trust to build further houses. As D6BRT leader Anwah Nagia put it: "We don't want the captains of the construction industry and other business to get their filthy paws on land earmarked for the community" (Kamaldien, 2013; Nicholson, 2013b).

The programme of events of the August handover had wanted the absent D6BRT chairperson to address the "finalisation" of Phase Two, but the opportunity was given to the representative of the District Six Reference Group to provide a "glimpse of the future of the development" (DRDLR, 2013d). It was the Reference Group that was called upon to speak for the future. To make matters more complex, the occasion was also graced by the presence of the new District Six Working Committee which had been formed in May 2013 to represent the interests of the "thousands of potential beneficiaries" who had missed the original 1998 deadline to register as claimants. The working committee wanted the minister to "disband" the reference group "so that the late claimants could be part of the process and be treated equally" (Nicholson, 2013a). In their different ways, the D6BRT and the Reference Group had been drawn into the stakeholder procedures and systems of governmentality, land restitution and development, as claimant representatives and brokers, but they chose different paths to seeking the symbolic rebirth of a committed District Six community. One did this through the "symbolic politics" of a social compact and a plan for claimants to invest in their control over all aspects of the area, and the other approached these entanglements in ways that might create a new District Six as a restitution themed environment, with new, unbridled forms of commerce and accumulation on its doorstep.

While land restitution and memory work have sometimes been directly connected in the long saga of District Six, they have often been formally separated from each other as social practices. This is particularly the case in the relationship between, yet different emphases of, the D6BRT and the District Six Museum, both of whose origins lie in the work of HODS, and which have had overlapping board memberships, and for the most part, an overt or implied alliance. Notwithstanding these relations of alliance and contestation, all these initiatives have produced imaginaries of the past and the future of District Six and have worked with notions of memory and memorial, just as the local state has sought to plan for the future of the landscape of District Six through dividing restitution land from land designated for other purposes. And it is increasingly becoming clear that the future of land restitution is not about housing; rather its success as social cohesion lies in the field of symbolic politics, in understanding District Six as a landscape of memory.

11.3 Memory and Heritage in District Six Land Restitution

While all developmental initiatives seeking to rebuild the landscape of District Six have proceeded from a framework of memory, perhaps the most significant memory work about the traumatised landscape and its people has been done by the District Six Museum. The museum opened as an exhibition and collection in a building in December 1994, but its genealogy can be traced to earlier points of generation, including civic and cultural formations in District Six in the 1930s and 1940s, and to the invocation of a District Six memory project as part of the work of HODS in 1989, styled as a District Six Museum Foundation (Rassool & Prosalendis, 2001).

A body of literature written by staff and trustees of the District Six Museum has emphasised the work of the museum as that of a museum of process and transactions of knowledge based on internal expertise in a range of fields of research and knowledge production within the museum itself, and has resisted attempts to place the museum's work as rooted simply in community as ordinary experience and the innocence and authenticity of the local. The District Six Museum's work has not merely been an engagement with the local social history of removals, restitution and memory in District Six. On the contrary, it has been an intervention in the production of history itself, in reorienting public history away from the notion of accessible representations of scholarship by experts for ordinary people. This has seen the emergence of an approach to social cohesion as contesting relations of expertise in the process of knowledge formation.

Central to the museum process has been "highly successful methodologies for community participation and ownership of heritage and development", drawing upon "the knowledge generated by communities in the process of remembrance", and a "conscious process of community knowledge creation" (District Six Museum, 2003). The spaces of the museum have been "filled with argumentation and debate about cultural expression, social history and political life in the District, about local history and national pasts", and "how best to reflect these" in the work of the museum. "Annunciation, conversation and debate formed the lifeblood" of the museum's "creative and curatorial process and memory politics". While the museum became "one of the only sites in the city with a sense of legitimacy to address the future of the city and its concept of citizenship", and to debate issues of urban renewal and cityness, at moments these debates concerned the very categories of "museum" and "exhibition" itself (Rassool, 2006, 2008).

These transactional, inscriptive and participatory methods have influenced the processes of collecting, the research for and design of exhibitions, as well as the social lives of the exhibitions themselves as they were constantly critiqued, interfered with and updated. They have also been sustained as the programmes of the District Six Museum transcended exhibition work as one of the key outcomes of its memory work to embrace antiracist, human rights education work on contemporary issues that connect with the District Six experience (Sanger, 2008). This processual and inscriptive methodology also influenced other collecting and design projects such as "Huis Kombuis", which worked with the practices of "culinary rituals" and other instances of home craft through which the "deep resonances and connections" with District Six were "maintained and reinforced" (Smith, 2008).

The work of memory and social cohesion of the District Six Museum may have taken place in relation to the scarred District Six landscape of removal and restitution since the mid-1990s, but it was only from the early 2000s that this work became a significant means of seeking directly to influence the future meanings of the land in the unfolding land restitution process. In 2003, the museum produced a plan for the framing of District Six as "cultural heritage precinct" that aimed to "provide leadership and direction" for the "interpretive and narrative reclamation and redevelopment" of the area. The museum sought to produce a "cohesive framework for the narration of the heritage of District Six and its wider significance", and to introduce new interpretive strategies by encouraging the "re-establishment" of the "alignments" of the old streets, with the retention and reclamation of remaining stone gutters, cobbles and curbstones as "tangible markers for narratives", and to provide the "narrative and voice" for the planning and development of a Memorial Park. By emphasising "pedestrian and vehicular routes", supporting the re-establishment of shops, markets and community facilities and promoting street corners and steps as places for "cultural expression" and "social interaction", the museum would contribute to the reconstruction of a "sense of place" of District Six, and encourage the "use of public spaces in the Precinct as spaces for the celebration of memory" (District Six Museum, 2003).

In this plan, the District Six Museum began to argue that land restitution in the area was not only about housing, but was fundamentally about landscape and memory. Indeed, with its work having started in the late 1980s on the platform of "hands off" the District Six "salted earth", this renewed focus signalled a switch to "hands on" District Six, and an event was held to announce plans for the establishment of the newly acquired Sacks Futeran Complex as a new cultural and "homecoming" centre for the new District Six, with plans to develop a memorial park and to turn the broader District Six site into a cultural heritage precinct.

By June 2006, the District Six Museum produced a draft Conservation Management Plan (CMP) for District Six and made a presentation to the final meeting of the second Council of the SAHRA in August 2006. In addition to defining the value and significance of District Six for national heritage, the draft plan focused on research approaches and methodologies as well as management strategies and conservation principles, providing samples of programmes and materials for site protection and interpretation, oral history and focus group transcripts, a description of the public process and guidelines for memorialisation of sites and routes. The ideas about conservation sought to transcend District Six merely being turned into "a thing that is named, mapped and listed", under the National Heritage Resources Act No 25 of 1999 and to work beyond the built environment and documented history, with "people's experiences, and their memories and interpretations of having lived in and used certain spaces", with "local knowledge" and the landscape's "layered history" and with "reconstruction through cultural activity" (District Six Museum, 2007).

While the museum understood the objectifying dangers of the discourse of heritage, the decision to develop the CMP and make the case for District Six's declaration was a strategic move to utilise the instruments of heritage preservation to protect the layered memory and social value of the landscape from infrastructure development that flew in the face of the history of the area. A national heritage site declaration also held the promise of creating a framework for development to be led by heritage interpretation. Persuaded that District Six was a site of national significance and by the importance of a CMP produced by a locally engaged heritage project rather than the usual heritage consultant, the SAHRA council decided at its final meeting held in Cape Town in September 2006 that District Six should be declared a national heritage site (District Six Museum, 2007, p. 61; SAHRA, 2007). Unfortunately, this decision was never carried out and, in the absence of a clear framework of heritage interpretation, the area became a site of balkanised and fragmented infrastructure development, characterised by a wavering and vacillating restitution programme that was increasingly segregated from commercial development, business and cultural planning.

As complaints were mounted about the failure by SAHRA to declare District Six, its leadership admitted that the heritage resources authority lacked the political will to follow these declarations through. One explanation blamed the failure on the lack of clarity over what the boundaries of District Six were, and that this had emerged as a problem in their consultations with the business leaders of the area. Or perhaps it was simply that SAHRA had become accustomed to operating under instruction by the Minister of Arts and Culture. There were however deeper epistemic issues that lay behind the failure to declare District Six as a national heritage site. The intention behind the creation of SAHRA as the democratic national heritage resources authority was to create a platform for a more inclusive approach to heritage preservation and to move away from the prior concentration on the built environment, architectural and archaeological heritage. This signalled some focus on sites and objects of history.

A large number of national heritage site declarations saw the addition of graves of struggle heroes added to the national estate, usually to coincide with national commemorative days. What seemed to fall through the cracks of heritage conservation were sites of complex histories, such as those like District Six that spoke of histories of removal and restitution, and of the defensive and reconstructive work of memory. Instead, SAHRA's interest in history took the form of an antiquarian concentration on heritage objects of national significance, such as stamps, guns and military technology, as well as objects and collections associated with mission stations (SAHRA, 2012, pp. 25–26). Other than the grave, SAHRA seemed incapable of declaring sites of history. The national heritage resources authority seemed unable or reluctant to assert the value of heritage over that of property, especially with property development and commerce in property given almost unfettered scope to trample over landscapes of history.

If SAHRA's failure to declare District Six was because of its inadequate approach to landscapes of complex histories, it is interesting that the approaches to the heritage of District Six on the part of the claimant representatives also had deficiencies and inconsistencies. The Reference Group claimed that the rebuilt District Six needed to be "innovative" yet "conceptually reflect the past". The past "street fabric" was desirable and spaces provided needed to "capture the wholesome experience that District Six was" so that "the shared heritage of the past can be expressed collectively through singing, poetry and so on". Redeveloping District Six was "like creating a living monument", and it, therefore, needed to "embrace the vibrancy that it had before". Also, the "style" of the new houses needed to be like "the original residential fabric" of District Six in size and scale. These dwellings should "reflect the true heritage and characteristics" of District Six houses, which claimants could "identify" with. Placing these desires for the real District Six alongside the Reference Group's ideas for the redemption of the CPUT site, it is clear that this was a concept of heritage that was about the built environment and space, as a setting for a restitution and heritage theme park, or even a cultural village (District Six Reference Group, 2013, pp. 16–20).

The Task Team's draft plan, in contrast, bore a resemblance to the D6BRT's approach to heritage, which was quite conventional. The historic street grid would be reinstated, and "historic sites" would be "protected" in an approach that would be "sensitive to the history and memory" of District Six. Moreover, its references to heritage lay in its desire to "counter gentrification" through "checks and balances". It recognised that the area was a "palimpsest", a "layering of different histories and memories". It called for "remaining community buildings" to be celebrated and conserved, and for archaeological sites to be preserved. But the major means by which a sense of heritage was connected to redevelopment was contained in the notions of the "spirit of the site" and the "idea of place", of "natural features" and "linkages to surroundings" as well as views and vistas that needed to be safeguarded (District Six Task Team, 2011; Le Grange Architects, 2008).

The Heritage Impact Assessment (HIA) that was produced in 2003 by founder member of HODS and the District Six Museum, architect Lucien le Grange, took an approach that prioritised the preservation of remaining architectural structures, fabric and spaces, and foregrounded the significance of archaeological research. Interestingly, the HIA's archaeological assessment was developed by historical archaeologist, Antonia Malan of the Contracts Office at the University of Cape Town (UCT), who had been involved in the District Six excavations through UCT's conventionally hierarchised historical archaeological research and "public" archaeology outreach work (Malan & Soudien, 2002; Rassool, 2006). As with Le Grange's earlier statements, the HIA also emphasised the objective to preserve the "idea of place". Consideration needed to be given, the HIA suggested, to the possible creation of "open site museums" at the sites of archaeological research at Horstley and Stukeris Streets, and the possibility that most of the area was "potentially an archaeological site" (le Grange, L, District Six: Heritage Impact Assessment. Draft Document. Unpublished manuscript; Lucien le Grange Architects and Planners; 2003).

The emphasis on "the spirit of the site" was to realise the prospect of a redeveloped District Six becoming a "living memorial", instead of staying a "dormant memory site". The "void" of the ruined landscape, as powerfully as it stood as a commemorative site, needed to be "filled" and "other forms of memorialisation" needed to be "imagined". And it was important to recognise that District Six could not be "recreated" and that to try any "artificial reconstruction" through a "scenographic" approach would be to "ridicule the process of restitution", and create "a semblance of a theme park or a Disney World". The only memorial alternative lay in identifying and utilising the "valuable and endearing historic urban design principles" of the original district for the purposes of development, and reinterpreting "the positive qualities of the old historic area". This included "keeping a fine grain on physical development" and developing "appropriately scaled land parcel sizes" with "large-scale" land parcels avoided. A "mix of land-uses and a range of building densities" needed to be considered while the "density and form" of development needed to be "varied and retain a human scale". The street pattern, ideally premised on the old grid, needed to be considered as outdoor pedestrian spaces and "designed as social spaces", while the "edges of urban blocks" could be "animated" and developed to permit "active frontages", create "positive street edges" and ensure "richness of the quality of streetscapes" (Le Grange, 2008, pp. 8–17).

One of the consistent threads through the memorial arguments of the D6BRT and the District Six Museum has been the establishment of a Memorial Park in the area around Horstley Street, a "steep, narrow cobbled street, remnants of which remain intact on a ghostly landscape" and the site of the earliest and last forced removals in District Six. As the site of 1901 "sanitation syndrome" removals and 1983 Groups Areas displacements, Horstley Street was also where "the best intact examples of urban fabric" were to be found "from an archaeological point of view" (Layne, 2008; Malan & Van Heyningen, 2001). It had been earmarked as early as 1993, following a proposal prepared by founding trustee and architect Lucien le Grange after being commissioned by the museum. As the chosen site for the future District Six memorial park, Horstley Street became the focus of attention by the District Six Museum as the "space of remembrance" to be set aside as the processes of redevelopment and return to District Six started in earnest, "as a monument to its own destruction" (Layne, 2008, pp. 86–88).

Lucien le Grange developed a graded scale model of what the Memorial Pak might look like, and archaeological research conducted by UCT's Martin Hall in conjunction with the District Six Museum Foundation uncovered aspects of social life such as that many buildings in Upper Horstley Street had been designed for "the poorest of tenants" (Malan & Soudien, 2002). The Museum turned Horstley Street into a site of memorial visiting, adding museum signage that explained the site's significance. Processes of earth removal for restitution housing saw truckloads of earth offloaded alongside Horstley Street, to be incorporated into the future memorial site, seen almost as an archaeological park. In some ways, the Memorial Park became the key focus of District Six heritage and memorial thinking and desire, as a historic site and importantly as a potentially rich site of archaeological research. It is possible that this emphasis contributed to an understanding of heritage as driven by archaeological interpretation, and as a process of mitigation of residential development, rather than a framework to determine the shape and form of development in the first place. And it might also be that memorial emphasis expressed through the desire for the memorial park contributed to the circumstances of nondeclaration of the full District Six landscape.

11.4 District Six as an "Undeclared" National Heritage Site

In the context of SAHRA's failure to provide a national heritage framework to regulate District Six land, property development and speculation have continued. CPUT constructed student halls of residence, which saw historic District Six images incorporated into the design of their exterior walls on the old Caledon Street. Located close to the historic Vernon Terrace, these macabre District Six architectural and design references seemed like a replay of the incorporation of old District Six kerbstones into the original architecture of the old white Technikon. And on the lower side of the Eastern Boulevard, the freeway that bisected District Six in 1967, and renamed Nelson Mandela Boulevard in 2011, a multistorey office park and shopping precinct, "The Boulevard", was built in the late 2000s and opened in 2009 in lower District Six.

Ironically spared from Group Areas removals by the building of the boulevard, itself an act of displacement, this lower area of historic District Six land had become administratively reincorporated into the adjacent grey (and later split coloured/white) group area of Wood-stock. This renaming also served in some way to protect lower District Six from any further threat of group areas displacement. Instead, in the period between removals and restitution, this lower area experienced a process of creeping business development, which encroached on pre-carious lives lived in the spaces of remaining District Six homes, schools and churches.

This lower area of District Six had been spared displacement by apartheid forced removals, but market-related property values, creep-ing gentrification and the slow development of a fashionable art gallery quarter after 2000 threatened to displace working class residents from the neighbourhood. With the area part of the wider District Six, caught between a stalled national heritage declaration procedure, a slow and difficult land restitution process, as well as the development of a patchwork of office block and middle class lifestyle residential pre-cincts, the city managers and business owners in the area perpetuated the old alibi of it being Woodstock, now seemingly permanently severed from its District Six history.

These instances of commercial development of District Six land for purposes other than land restitution, the remapping of the District Six landscape and the renaming of a section as "Woodstock" were part of the fragmentation of District Six so that land made available for restitution could be limited and that the meaning of the notion of "District Six" could be restricted. This balkanisation of District Six was geared towards freeing land for commercial development and to limit land for restitution as a means of creating order and stability through market principles.

The failure by SAHRA to carry out the decision by its council to protect the historic precinct of District Six by declaring it a national heritage site created the enabling environment for these instances of property and business development, and the fragmentation and balkanisation of District Six land. This has served to perpetuate an ahistorical remapping of the area, and to enhance apartheid's disfigurement of the area. It has generated a meaning of "District Six" to refer only to the land available for restitution, a themed environment contained within a more forward-looking commercial and educational environment still called by its apartheid name, "Zonnebloem", and with the area below the boulevard deemed to be part of Woodstock, the area into which it had been administratively absorbed after Zonnebloem's white declaration. This framing has also prevented restitution and commercial housing development from occurring with clear attention to an acknowledged public memory of forced removal of District Six's people and the demolition of its infrastructure. This was the fundamental historical experience that has marked the area and those who lived in it, and it is this history that should be the determining framework for its redevelopment, and for unifying and restoring the historic District Six landscape.

The fragmentation of District Six did not stop there. In 2010, Creative Cape Town, the strategic project of Cape Town Partnership, which planned and managed the Central City's culture-led development initiatives, produced a vision to transform the "East City" precinct into "The Fringe". This was a planning and branding initiative for one of the "twenty neighbourhoods" of the central city identified in 2008, and was conducted in partnership with the city and the province, with CPUT also listed as an initiating institution. Some of the founding circumstances were that the area was "close to a strong existing cluster of creative and knowledge industries" and already a "business centre" for a "creative economy", it had a "richly textured historical built environment", and it was an "area for networking" with cafes, restaurants, bars and clubs. Crucially, it was thought the returning District Six families would "regenerate" aspects of the central city and its economy (Cape Town Partnership, 2008; Creative Cape Town, The Fringe: Cape Town's Innovation District, unpublished PowerPoint presentation, 2010).

With the area seen as a "creative laboratory", and "next to a university", buy-in was sought from business, government and institutions of higher education for what would be a "creative industry hub" with a "design park innovation hub" and "incubator" creative businesses. Heritage was mentioned in the plan, but this seemed to be mainly a system of signage, place marking and "way-finding". And the Fringe would also be home to a future design museum, ensuring the creation of a "dynamic ecosystem for innovation". The Fringe seemed also to be a planning framework to "upgrade" public space and create opportunities for "development and property letting", with interest already shown by thirty-six firms (Creative Cape Town, The Fringe: Cape Town's Innovation District, unpublished PowerPoint presentation, 2010). This was indeed a grand plan for gentrification and dispossession in the name of creativity and culture-led development. Creative Cape Town's plan for the Fringe was part of its support given to Cape Town's World Design Capital bid, which was launched in 2010. The bid was seen as an opportunity for the city "to showcase its design assets and design savvy to the world" and to get design "into the public domain" and to "mobilise" around "using design for social change", especially "how it is using design to overcome the huge challenges caused by apartheid" (Creative Cape Town, The Fringe: Cape Town's Innovation District, unpublished PowerPoint presentation, 2010, pp. 4–26).

It became increasingly clear that the Fringe was a plan for property development through the promotion of a design industry, populated by entrepreneurs, and with links to the city and a technical university. It was located on land historically part of District Six, but thought of in the city's planning framework as the East City "fringe" between the district and downtown Cape Town. It was understood as "border[ing] onto the proposed District Six redevelopment", and having a "neglected edge relationship" with the central city. And by 2012, the plan had seemingly become real, and tourist maps started appearing naming this area "The Fringe" as if it had already been implemented. From as long ago as 2008, the city had begun to mark and map the "western edge" of District Six as the border of restitution development. It was clear that for the city, "District Six" referred to the land restitution area and not to the historic precinct. It seems that in the negotiations between the D6BRT and different arms of government, the agreement reached on the borders of land available for District Six restitution had been misunderstood as an agreement about the boundaries of District Six itself. Yet through planning and promotion by the city and the province, these new boundaries had seemingly been cast in stone, as if there had never been an enquiry into the heritage value of District Six as a potential national heritage site, with a clear understanding of the full extent of the map of the area. It was as if the District Six Museum and its deep engagements with the memory of that landscape did not exist.

Through the politics of land restitution, the resources of memory work and the economic imaginaries of urban planning, different District Sixes had come into existence. The District Six of memory was that of the 2006 CMP produced by the District Six Museum for SAHRA, of the area's full extent as lived environment of historical experience. For the city and the province, the boundaries of District Six extended no further than the land available for restitution. The District Six heritage map was premised on the idea of the resources of memory of a traumatised landscape as the basis for healing, restitution and a renewed sense of belonging, connectedness and social cohesion. The urban planning map reduced restitution to one contained element in a fragmented landscape, with the Fringe as a buffer between returnees and the city. The alteration of the built environment envisaged would mark an act of segregation and a displacement of memory. It would also conceal the "trauma" of culture-led urban development (Farouk, 2013). This was an approach to social cohesion based on orderly civic identities in a business environment, with the possibility of philanthropy towards the District Six poor.

With Cape Town having won the bid to be the World Design Capital in 2014, preparations for realising the Fringe began to intensify with internships, magazines, blogs and masterclasses, with World Design Capital events being hosted. The field became populated by young, hip entrepreneurs in formation, who networked in the new trendy coffee shops and bakeries in a part of District Six that had become their playground in the name of design. There they planned solutions for the area's problems of homelessness, and they had also taken it upon themselves to plan solutions for a new, developed District Six, with the Fringe district held up as District Six's "mirror", bringing "a new system of trolley paths, goods and services" to the district as a catalyst for urban growth (The Fringe website, N.D.). As opposition to the Fringe by the District Six Museum and urban activists grew, by 2014, the city seemed to take notice and stopped all use of the name, but not the planning for the installation of a creative precinct on a part of the old District (Cape Town Partnership, 2013).

To compound these acts of dispossession and re-dispossession, in 2014, CPUT began building a semi-privatised student residence on top of the spaces immediately adjacent to the last remaining portion of the old Hanover Street. This location had become a site of memorialisation over more than two decades, with regular meetings and commemorative events held at the site by ex-District Sixers and the District Six Museum resulting in the ongoing development of a memorial cairn. Without any consultation with the keepers of District Six memory and despite opposition from former residents, CPUT displayed its arrogance by completing the project, claiming to have conserved the fabric of the old street and the cairn. The cairn and the old street were now contained within the courtyard of a student residence and restrained by CPUT's memorial framework of monumentalisation, without any appreciation of the ideas of landscapes of memory as developed in the memory work of the District Six Museum (Jackman, 2014).

By 2015, it seemed like there was little chance of District Six being declared a national heritage site unless SAHRA was compelled by the Minister of Arts and Culture or by the intervention of parliament. While the dispossession caused by the Fringe may have been temporarily halted in the name of a more consultative process, this has not stopped the further balkanisation of the District Six landscape in the name of development and the restriction of the meaning of District Six to the limited land available for restitution. The time may be right, as some members of the District Six Museum's staff have proposed, to call for a "resalting" of the earth of District Six, and to assert the primacy of memory over land speculation and fragmentation.

In 2005, Indian theatre scholar Rustom Bharucha (2007) noted how remarkable it was that the museum "chose to embrace and exhibit the tender immediacies of home, a home away from home, everyone's home, instead of violence and destruction". He challenged the museum then to change its raison d'etre from "the desire to return", and to restrategise "its identity and creative struggle". Instead of "luxuriat [ing] in 'the lost home'", the museum needed to "re-insert the violence that had been strategically excised when the Museum first opened", to "open itself to the chill of history", and "to claim that all of District Six is District Six, not just the museum". The Museum needed to explore "new political strategies, practices, and interactions with the public", and to "re-politicise" its purpose through "new engagements with public space". In this vein, the time might be right for such a new curatorial framework of a "resalted earth" to focus on the ongoing violence and dispossession of culture-led development as gentrification and heritage as fragmentation and governmentality. The District Six Museum needs to reinscribe a more deliberate and assertive approach to social cohesion and memory politics as the only basis for an active and critical citizenship.

References

Bamford, H. 2011. Zuma promises District 6 action "in three years". *Weekend Argus*, 12 February 2011.

Bharucha, R. 2007. The politics of memory: Deconstructing the District Six Museum then and now. *Ziff Journal*, pp. 87–96.

Cape Times. 2011. Power struggles have delayed return. 13 September.

Cape Town Partnership. 2008. *Cape Town Central City into the Future: Central City Development Strategy (Workbook, Cape Town: Cape Town Partnership)*. Retrieved from www.capetownpartnership.co.za/trafalgar-the-park-of-possibilities/. Accessed 7 March 2013.

2013. Where to for the fringe? Retrieved from www.capetownpartnership.co.za/2013/12/where-to-for-the-fringe/. Accessed 8 April 2016.

City of Cape Town Communication and Marketing Directorate. 2005. Squatters on District Six land: Joint press statement by the City of Cape Town, the Regional Land Claims Commission and the District Six Beneficiary and Redevelopment Trust. *Media Release No 35*, 28 October 2005.

Department of Rural Development and Land Reform South Africa (DRDLR). 2013a. Minister Nkwinti urges all South Africans to come together and to pledge their commitment to help the rural poor. *Sunday Times*, 2 June 2013.

(DRDLR). 2013b. Programme for the Workshop on the Use of Archives, Oral History and Other Heritage Resources in Land Claims. *Cape Archives and Records Service*, 18–19 June 2013.

(DRDLR). 2013d. Programme of Ministerial Meeting with District Six Claimants: Hand-Over Ceremony of Houses of Pilot Phase 2. Cape Town: DRDLR.

Dhupelia-Mesthrie, U. 1999. The Truth and Reconciliation Commission and the Commission on Restitution of Land Rights: Some Comparative Thoughts. Conference on the Truth and Reconciliation Commission, University of the Witwatersrand, 11–14 June.

District Six Museum. 2003. *District Six Cultural Heritage Precinct: Summary Business and Implementation plan 2004–2008*. Cape Town: District Six Museum.

2005. *The Return*. Cape Town: District Six Museum.

2007. *Reflections on the Conference: Hands on District Six – Landscapes of Post-Colonial Memorialisation*. Cape Town: District Six Museum.

District Six Social Integration Team. 2013. *Draft Report: Version 3*. Cape Town: District Six Museum.

District Six Reference Group. 2013. *Technical Team Position Paper on Restitution and Related Matters (Part A)*. Cape Town: District Six Museum.

District Six Task Team. 2011. *District Six Draft Development Framework*. Cape Town: District Six Museum.

du Toit, F. 2013. Gaping hole in Project SA's fabric. *Cape Times*, 21 March.

Farouk, I. 2013. Conflicting rationalities: Post-apartheid spatial legacies and the creative city. *Public Discussion on "District Six on the Fringe: the absence of memory in design-led urban regeneration"*. African Centre for Cities and District Six Museum, 29 May.

Jackman, R. 2014. *CPUT Won't Stop Building in District 6*. Retrieved from www.iol.co.za/news/south-africa/western-cape/cput-wont-stop-building-in-district-6-1738742. Accessed 8 April 2016.

James, W., and van de Vijver, L. (eds.). 2001. *After the TRC: Reflections on Truth and Reconciliation in South Africa*. Athens: Ohio University Press.

Jeppie, S., and Soudien, C. (eds.). 1990. *The Struggle for District Six: Past and Present*. Cape Town: Buchu Books.

Johns, L. 2011. District 6 claimants protest over housing plans. *Cape Argus*, 9 September.

Kamaldien, Y. 2013. Grief Over District 6. *The New Age*, 26 August 2013.

Layne, V. 2008. "Sounds and voices, colours and landscapes": Aesthetics for a community site museum. In Bennett, B., Chrischené, J. and Soudien,

C. (eds.), *City Site Museum: Reviewing Memory Practices at the District Six Museum*. Cape Town: District Six Museum, pp. 76–93.

le Grange, L. 2008. Rebuilding District Six. In Bennett, B., Chrischené, J., and Soudien, C. (eds.), *City Site Museum: Reviewing memory practices at the District Six Museum*. Cape Town: District Six Museum.

Malan, A. and van Heyningen, E. 2001. Twice Removed: Horstley Street in Cape Town's District Six 1865–1982. In Mayne, A., and Murray, T. (eds.), *Archaeology in Urban Landscapes: Explorations in Slumland*. Cambridge: Cambridge University Press, pp. 39–56.

Malan, A., and Soudien, C. 2002. Managing heritage in District Six, Cape Town: Conflicts past and present. In Schofield, J. (ed.), *The Archaeology of Twentieth Century Conflict*. New York: Routledge, pp. 249–265.

Mamdani, M. 2001. A diminished truth. In James, W. and van de Vijver, L. (eds.), *After the TRC: Reflections on Truth and Reconciliation in South Africa*. Athens: Ohio University Press, pp. 58–61.

Mashatile, P. 2013. *Budget Vote Speech by the Minister of Arts and Culture at the National Assembly*. Retrieved from www.dac.gov.za/speeches/minister/2013/16-05-2013.html. Accessed 7 July 2013.

Maylam, P. 1995. Explaining the apartheid city: 20 years of South African urban historiography. *Journal of Southern African Studies*. 21 (1): 19–38.

Mtyala, Q. 2010. R6bn needed to develop District 6. *Cape Times*, 30 August.

Nicholson, Z. 2011a. After 40 years, plan for District Six is ready. *Cape Times*, 5 December.

2011b. Return to District Six. *Cape Times*, 6 December.

2011c. Range of homes offered in deal for District Six. *Cape Times*, 8 December.

2011d. District Six mission is for "total justice". *Cape Times*, 9 December.

2013a. District Six group to fight for inclusion. *Cape Times*, 6 May.

2013b. I'm so happy I lived to go back to my birthplace. *Cape Times*, 26 August.

OECD. 2011. *Perspectives on Global Development 2012: Social Cohesion in a Shifting World*. Paris: OECD Publishing. Retrieved from http://dx.doi.org/10.1787/persp.glob.dev-2012-en. Accessed 12 May 2013.

Rassool, C. 2006. Community museums, memory politics and social transformation in South Africa: Histories, possibilities and limits. In Karp, I., Kratz, C.A., Szwaja, L., Ybarra-Frausto, F., Buntinx, G., Kirshenblatt-Gimblett, B. and Rassool, C. (eds.), *Museum Frictions: Global Transformations/Public Cultures*. Durham, NC: Duke University Press, pp. 286–321.

2008. Contesting "museumness": Towards an understanding of the values and legacies of the District Six Museum. In Bennett, B., Chrischené, J. and Soudien, C. (eds.), *City Site Museum: Reviewing Memory Practices at the District Six Museum*. Cape Town: District Six Museum, pp. 68–75.

Rassool, C., and Prosalendis, S. (eds.). 2001. *Recalling Community in Cape Town: Creating and Curating the District Six Museum*. Cape Town: District Six Museum 2001.

Sanger, M. 2008. Education work in the District Six Museum: Layering in new voices and interpretations. In Bennett, B., Chrischené, J., and Soudien, C. (eds.), *City Site Museum: Reviewing Memory Practices at the District Six Museum*. Cape Town: District Six Museum, pp. 96–109.

Smith, T. 2008. Huis Kombuis and the senses of memory: A textile design project. In Bennett, B., Chrischené, J., and Soudien, C. (eds.), *City Site Museum: Reviewing Memory Practices at the District Six Museum*. Cape Town: District Six Museum, pp. 152–157.

South African Heritage Resources Agency (SAHRA). 2007. *Annual Report for 2006–2007*. Cape Town: SAHRA.

2012. *Annual Report for 2011–2012*. Cape Town: SAHRA.

South African Press Association (SAPA). 2012. *D6 Redevelopment Coming*. Retrieved from http://vocfm.co.za/index.php/news/district6/itemlist/tag/District%20Six?start=24. Accessed 21 May 2013.

Swanson, M. 1977. The sanitation syndrome: Bubonic plague and urban native policy in the Cape Colony, 1900–1909. *Journal of African History*. 18 (3): 387–410.

Walker, C., Bohlin, A., Hall, R., and Kepe, T. (eds.), *Land, Memory, Reconstruction and Justice: Perspectives on Land Claims in South Africa*. Scottsville, South Africa: University of Kwazulu-Natal Press.

12 Key Ingredients of Inclusive Politics

ABDUL RAUFU MUSTAPHA[1]

12.1 Introduction

Most countries in the world are multi-ethnic, a fact even more pronounced in African countries. How the state manages ethnic diversity remains an important challenge in most African states. The typical immediate post-independent African state put much store in "nation-building" and national unity. Within these states, "ethnicity was discouraged as an organising principle of statecraft" (Bangura, 2006, p. 6). Emphasis was put on the foreign language and secular values inherited from colonialism, and references to ethnicity and particularistic values were discouraged in public discourse, if not in the covert calculus of politicians. As the first President of Senegal, Leopold Senghor once asserted, the "tribe" was the enemy of the "fatherland". But this model of top-down nation-building ran counter to the everyday lived experiences of the majority of the population of these African states. In the first place, the colonial languages and their associated secular values were the preserve of a tiny minority of elites. And there was frequently an ethnic bias in the national distribution of these elites, making it possible for a relatively powerful section of the elite to substitute its own ethnic values for the "national values".

Second, as Kabeer (2002, p. iii) argues, in many developing countries, citizenship tended to operate at two levels: (a) membership of the imagined community of the nation-state; and (b) membership of various acknowledged and consequential subnational groupings. Within this context, "inclusion and exclusion are indeed ... two sides of the coin of citizenship" (Kabeer, 2002, p. 1). She argues that membership of subnational groupings "performs an allocative function" in the

---

[1] Sadly, Abdul Raufu Mustapha passed away before the completion of the book. To the extent possible, the reference list has been checked and completed by the editors.

distribution of scarce resources, social standing, and social recognition. She draws our attention to the phenomenon of "exclusions from within", through which individuals or groups suffer disadvantaged relationships to the nation-states to which they are formally right-bearing members. In many developing societies therefore, despite the rhetoric of "national unity":

relatively-defined statuses based on family, kinship, caste, ethnicity and so on continue to be seen as prior to the individual and constitutive of their entitlements and obligations: individuality as a way of social being "remains a precarious undertaking". (Kabeer, 2002, p. 14)

The resulting asymmetries between ethnic groups, to the extent that they become systemic, can translate into inequalities which "in turn feed on, and reproduce, asymmetries in social relationships" (Kabeer, 2002, p. 20). As a result of these dynamics, real or imagined threats to group interests remain a significant factor in the politics of the many multi-ethnic states in Africa.

Given this scenario, multi-ethnic countries with ethnicity-blind policies have a tendency to perpetuate the ethnic inequalities inherited from the past. In such contexts, ethnic entrepreneurs tend to easily find material or symbolic issues around which to agitate and mobilise. Where the state fails to regulate the relationship between ethnic groups, inequalities, competition, and even suspicion will tend to characterise the relationship between the groups. And in more recent years, African countries have undergone different degrees of democratisation, a process which also contributes to the increased politicisation of ethnicity (Bangura, 2006, p. 4; Eifert et al., 2010). Despite democratisation, however, increased presidentialism and dominant party control under Africa's hybrid regimes have tended to reinforce the zero-sum logic of electoral competition, as a result heightening the alienation of some ethnic communities from the state. Scholars of participation (Gaventa, 2002) have noted the growing crisis of legitimacy between citizens and state institutions across the world. This legitimacy deficit becomes worse in Africa in the face of the alienation of whole ethnic constituencies. Managing ethnic relations is therefore an important imperative for African states. It is far cheaper to manage diversity and thereby limit conflict, than to manage the violence and dislocations that may result from inattention to the challenges of diversity.

Yet, as Horowitz (2014, p. 8) argues, "[a] well-kept secret among proponents of various prescriptions for inter-ethnic accommodation is that they are rarely adopted", because the path to institutional reform is littered with hurdles. And even if states decide to get involved in the regulation of the relationship between ethnic groups, and between these groups and the state, it is far from clear what should constitute appropriate intervention measures. Some scholars see a distinction between policies aiming at integrating ethnic groups into the state through the redesigning of state institutions, and those that emphasise social mobilisation within civil society with the ultimate aim of gaining incorporation into existing state institutions. While the first set of scholars advocate measures of institutional redesign, the second advocate social mobilisation. Reflective of the second set of scholars, Dryzek (1996) argues against policies aimed at directly incorporating disadvantaged groups into the state. He argues that such incorporation must necessarily amount to tokenism without changing the fundamentals of exclusion, disadvantage, and inequality. Instead, he argues for incorporation into the wider polity through civil society. This rejection of direct inclusion of the disadvantaged into state institutions echoes the concerns of adverse incorporation theorists who highlight the fact that "the terms of inclusion can be problematic, disempowering or inequitable" (Hickey & du Toit, 2007, p. 3). The alternative path of inclusion through the wider polity – specifically through civil society – is seen as being capable of sustaining democratic pressure on the state from civil society, thereby making possible meaningful transformations of the state and the more substantive incorporation of the disadvantaged.

However, even amongst scholars who agree on the need for policies of direct institutional incorporation of the disadvantaged groups into the state, there are many fundamental differences in approach. For example, redistributive policies tend to vary across states. Some, like Malaysia, are premised on the assumption that the disadvantaged group will gain at the expense of the previously advantaged, while in other countries, redistributive policies do not single out gainers in such stark terms, emphasising instead, the principle of proportionality. In some countries, the public sector is the only target for redistributive policies, while in others, both the public and private sectors are targeted (Bangura, 2006, p. 16). Furthermore, while some countries use constitutional and institutional means to achieve redistribution, others tend to concentrate on informal extra-constitutional mechanisms. Finally, advocates of institutional redesign have been sharply divided between advocates of majoritarian reforms that encourage vote pooling, cross-ethnic institutions, moderation and adversarial politics, on the one hand, and advocates of power-sharing and consociation that takes ethnic groups as given, and encourages a risk-averse politics built around ethnic institutions sharing power, on the other. The choice of a majoritarian or power-sharing approach to nation building affects the party system, the electoral system, the nature of the cabinet, the territorial administrative division of the country, and the general tenor of governance (Bangura, 2006; Horowitz, 1985; Lewis, 1965; Lijphart, 1977).

Debates have raged over the relative merits and demerits of power-sharing and majoritarian approaches to managing ethnic diversity. While some support the view that "some kind of power-sharing has been a feature of government in all societies that have successfully overcome their internal divisions" (Spears, 2002, p. 123), others point out that some power-sharing experiences have tended to make the state hostage to ethnic elites with a vested interest in maintaining ethnic differences. They point out that power-sharing undermines vertical relationships of accountability, increases budgetary spending, and creates conditions for policy gridlock (LeVan, A. C., and Assenov, A. Africa's Cumbersome Cabinets: Citizen Preferences and Economic Performance since the 1970s. Unpublished paper; American University; 2009, p. 1). In the same vein, LeVan and Assenov (Africa's Cumbersome Cabinets: Citizen Preferences and Economic Performance since the 1970s. Unpublished paper; American University; 2009, p. 1) argue that data from forty-six African cabinets from 1972 suggest that multiparty cabinets are likely to collect less revenue, are more likely to run deficits, and generally have lower levels of economic growth.

How to intervene, and with what institutional model, are therefore burning questions in the management of ethnic diversity. Policy makers seeking to promote inclusive politics must necessarily take account of the political and economic consequences of the policies chosen. This chapter argues that this dilemma is not just about choosing technically appropriate institutions. Designing inclusive politics in the context of ethnic diversity is a political process shaped by the challenges of the ethnic structure of the society in question, the nature of inequalities between the groups, the historical pattern of the institutionalisation of power and the dominant culture of politics. These issues constitute the topic of the next section. This is then followed by a section looking at the possibilities for redesigning the institutions of African states to promote inclusive politics. Specific attention is paid to two of the most important targets of institutional redesign: the territorial division of the state and the rules governing political parties and electoral systems. The concluding section explores what the expected outcomes of institutional redesign might look like and draws our attention to the dilemmas and trade-offs implicit in the politics of inclusion.

12.2 Challenges to Inclusive Politics

Any design of inclusive institutions must be sensitive to the context of individual countries. While generalisations about principles such as majoritarianism may be valid, their practical implications will often be context specific. The ethnic context of individual African states differs in four important respects: (a) their ethnic structure; (b) the nature of inequalities between the groups; (c) the historical pattern of the institutionalisation of power and (d) the culture of politics.

The ethnic structure of a country is defined by the number of ethnic groups within the country, their sizes relative to each other and relative to the overall population. Related concepts include ethnic fractionalisation, which measures the probability that two randomly chosen individuals will not belong to the same ethnic group, and ethnic polarisation, which is high in countries with few large homogeneous groups and low in countries with many small groups. Bangura (2006, pp. 4–5) suggests that African countries can have any of four possible ethnic structures: (a) unipolar (e.g., Botswana), in which one ethnicity is overwhelmingly dominant; (b) tripolar (e.g., Nigeria), in which there are only three groups or three large groups surrounded by many smaller ones; (c) fragmented multipolar (e.g., Tanzania), in which there are many small ethnic groups; and (d) concentrated multipolar (e.g., Ghana and Kenya), in which fragmentation offers a few relatively larger groups the opportunity to organise selective coalitions. The politicisation of ethnicity will be different across ethnic structures. For example, in Nigeria, there are 360 ethnic groups, with the largest ethnic group constituting 30% of the population, the 2 largest groups constituting 50%, and the 3 largest groups constituting 67%.[2] In Tanzania, by contrast, there are 120 ethnic groups with the largest constituting a mere 13% of the population, the largest 2 constituting 17% and the largest 3, 21%. In Nigeria, ethnic mobilisation is prevalent in national politics because ethnic elites from each of the three dominant groups are fearful of an alliance of the other 2 against it. In Tanzania, on the other hand, ethnic loyalties and conflicts tend to be localised, while national politics is dominated by cross ethnic national parties.

The second important factor in the politics of ethnicity is the pattern of inequalities between the ethnic groups. Stewart (2008) highlights how the distribution of material and symbolic resources between ethnic groups in a country can have consequences for the wellbeing of individual members of such groups, and can also affect the predisposition towards conflict and violence by the groups. Horizontal inequalities between groups can manifest in four different spheres of society: (a) politics – political participation and the distribution of power and influence in various governmental institutions, including the bureaucracy; (b) economic resources and outcomes – defined in terms of access to assets, employment and incomes; (c) social –including access to vital services such as health, education, water and social networks in civil society and the professions and (d) cultural recognition – reflected in the distribution of symbolic value within the state and the differential treatment of religions, languages, dress codes and other ethnic customs. Where there are consistent and entrenched inequalities across these four fields between groups, then, all things being equal, there is the higher likelihood of conflict between the groups.

A third important factor in the impact of ethnicity on the politics of African states is the historical pattern of the institutionalisation of power in each state. Blanton et al. (2001) argue that post-colonial Anglophone states are more likely to suffer from inter-ethnic conflicts, compared with Francophone ones, because of the residual effects of the institutionalisation of colonial rule. Colonial Francophone states are

---

[2] Bangura's (2006) figures are consistent with those of the CIA's *World Factbook* which treats the composite Hausa-Fulani as a single ethnic group. However, the 1963 census figures for the largest ethnic group, the Hausa (without the Fulani) is 20.9%, the Yoruba, 20.3%, and the Igbo, 16.6%. The census gave the three groups 57.8% of the population.

said to be more autocratic in their relations to their African populations. Second, most ethnic groups in colonial Francophone states are said to have been treated badly when compared with the treatment meted out to the dominant ethnic group in the different colonies. Francophone colonial states therefore represented a ranked ethnic system of ethnic stratification in which relative privilege was concentrated in a few ethnic groups and competition between ethnic groups was forcefully discouraged. The authors argue that this pattern of institutional embedding of the Francophone African state was very different from the Anglophone pattern, where the system of Indirect Rule left intact ethnic mobilisation structures in a relatively unranked ethnic stratification system. In this Anglophone context, not only did disadvantaged ethnic groups have the incentives to challenge the colonial distribution of economic and political goods between ethnic groups, ethnic elites also had the ethnic mobilisation structures and strategies with which to give effect to their aspirations. Blanton et al. (2001) argue, therefore, that "ethnic conflict should be more frequent in former British colonies precisely because of the legacy of their colonial rule" (p. 481). French ex-colonies, on the other hand, "were left with a centralised bureaucratic power structure that impeded ethnic mobilisation and suppressed nonviolent ethnic challenges" (Blanton et al., 2001, p. 473). Furthermore, they suggest that statistical evidence on ethnic conflicts in post-colonial Africa supports the view that "inter-ethnic competition within the unranked Anglophone polities takes more extreme forms...." Thus the frequency of rebellious activity is greater in former British colonies" (Blanton et al., 2001, p. 486). They assert that "British colonial rule was positively and significantly related to civil war in Africa" (Blanton et al., 2001, p. 488).

However, a comparison of the institutionalisation of power in post-colonial Senegal and Côte d'Ivoire – both former French colonies – suggests that the colonial inheritance is not always the determining factor in explaining ethnic conflicts. A comparison of these countries raises the question of the connections between the degree of personalisation of state power and the potential for ethnic conflict. Dahou and Foucher (2009) argue that Senegal has an entrenched democratic culture centred on the lively urban culture of Dakar. Furthermore, in the Sufi Muslim Brotherhoods which dominate the spiritual life of the largely Muslim country – the Mourides and the two branches of the

Tijjaniyya – Senegal also has an effective mechanism for linking the rural peasantry to the urban political milieu. In exchange for agricultural services to the peasantry and selective patronage for the Sheikhs who control the Brotherhoods, the post-colonial Senegalese party-state could effectively mobilise support in the countryside. Senegal therefore had a stable mechanism of incorporation which linked the peasant-citizen to the party-state, and "urban elites, marabouts [sheikhs], and peasants constituted discreet parts of a functioning political system" (Dahou & Foucher, 2009, p. 13). Post-colonial Senegal was therefore a stable semidemocratic political system that was well-institutionalised through intricate formal and informal networks. This system was sufficiently robust and resilient that it could operate independent of the leader at the top. When the founding president, Senghor, left office in 1980, the system persisted, just as it did when two subsequent incumbent presidents were voted out of office.

The post-colonial settlement in Côte d'Ivoire could not be more different from that of Senegal. In contrast with Senegal, Côte d'Ivoire developed a more elitist, more ethnic, and more personalised political regime centred on the person of President Houphouet Boigny. As Akindes (2009) argues, the post-colonial Ivorian state was the manifestation of "the monopolistic creative vision of one man" (p. 31). For a long time, Boigny balanced ethnic interests within state institutions and distributed resources across regions to keep all ethnic elites onside. In all these manoeuvres, however, Boigny was the critical personal hub around which the wheel of the party and the state revolved. Boigny might have practiced ethnic balancing during his reign, but these were aimed at shoring up his power, not at building the institutional fabric of the state. Power was personalised to a much greater degree than in Senegal. When he died in 1990, the Houphouetist paradigm began to unravel, ultimately leading to protracted ethnic and regional conflicts and civil war. The degree of institutionalisation or personalisation of power is, therefore, one of the factors that will influence the potential for long-lasting inclusive politics. Even under democratisation, African states continue to exhibit very high levels of presidential discretionary powers because the institutions for checks and balances are frequently weak or absent. The inclusive tenor of the state can be affected by this tendency towards personalised presidentialism.

The culture of politics is a fourth important factor that can affect how inclusive politics is achieved in any given country. By culture of politics, I mean widely shared values, ideas and precepts within society about political life. Such ideas are sufficiently strong that they can structure the political preferences of significant sections of the population. In every country, the structural features of the state and the society such as the ethnic demographics and horizontal inequalities are not enough, on their own, to trigger conflict or violence. They have to be acted upon by ethnic elites or ethnic entrepreneurs, operating within shared cultures of politics with their constituents. Second, some political values have become very dominant within particular countries. In Nigeria, e.g., federalism is considered to be one of the few "givens" accepted by all, and must be respected in any political arrangement for the country. By contrast, the black majority in South Africa *reject* federalism because of its psychological association with the Bantustan policy of white racial domination. Recommending federalism as a tool of inclusive politics in either country must necessarily take account of both cultures of politics.

These four factors discussed above are important, first, to the extent that they highlight the uniqueness of the trajectories individual country must take in the search for inclusive politics. There is no all-encompassing formula that is applicable to every case. Second, the four challenges suggest that the quest for inclusive politics is as much about political calculations and statecraft, as it is about institution building and (re)design.

12.3 Designing Inclusive Politics

Given the above challenges to inclusive politics, the scope of the design effort is one important issue that should be settled from the very beginning. While some argue for inclusion only into civil society as the best strategy (Dryzek, 1996, p. 476), others argue for social, economic, and political inclusion in a "comprehensive and sustainable" way (Agrawal et al., 2012). The menu for possible institutional design is consequently quite broad, including the electoral system, party system, executive selection, territorial subdivision, fixed guarantees through quotas and affirmative action, veto powers, composition of the civil service, parliament, and special judicial protection. Indeed, "starting from nine dichotomous attributes of inclusion, Staffan Lindberg (2009 in LeVan, 2011, p. 7) counts at least 512 possibilities based on Lijphart's (1977) criteria on consociation (Lindberg, 2009 in LeVan, 2011, p. 7). However, in the context of most contemporary African countries, the two most important targets that must be addressed in every case are (a) the nature of administrative territorial subdivisions and political constituencies and (b) the electoral and party rules.

12.3.1 Territorial Subdivisions and Constituencies

Across Africa, ethnicity is increasingly linked to citizenship and place, and expressed in the language of autochthony. Even relatively mobile groups like pastoralists, where they have come under demographic pressure for grazing resources, are increasingly making claims to land by redefining themselves as "indigenous" peoples, and linking themselves to the wider global indigenous peoples' movement. Competing claims to territory and the question of who exercises what jurisdiction over any given territory are, therefore, important matters for inclusive politics. The key questions are how much self-rule a group can exercise and within what spatial parameters. These are addressed through the territorial subdivision of the state. In the African context, the approach to these questions has been through (a) federalism (Nigeria and Ethiopia); (b) regionalism (South Africa) and (c) decentralisation (Ghana).

Ethnic, regional and religious differences and repeated conflicts forced the governments of countries like Nigeria and Ethiopia to consider a federal solution to their political problems. Federal systems can have four critical elements: (a) elements of self-rule, (b) shared rule, (c) accommodation of difference and (d) integrationist tendencies (Iff, 2012, p. 229). Self-rule mechanisms include the demarcation of subnational boundaries, the recognition of specific group rights, and the nature of the division of responsibilities between the national level and the subnational units. Shared rule mechanisms include the nature of the electoral system, the party system, the design of the executive, parliament and the civil service. Accommodationist federal systems take the ethnic unit as given and build their institutions to accommodate ethnic, religious, linguistic and regional differences. Ethiopia's ethnic federalism is a prime example of this approach (Tegenu, 2006). Integrative federal systems, on the other hand, seek to incorporate ethnic identities within common national institutions and in the process, ethnic groups are crosscut by other identities. Nigeria and its majoritarian electoral rules and ethnic balancing affirmative action rules is a prime example.

In the accommodationist approach, the overall aim of the mechanisms of shared rule (electoral system, party system, executive, second chamber, public administration) is to enable the different ethnic groups to shape the political process at the federal level; in the integrationist approach it is to establish a common "national" identity (Iff, 2012, p. 238).

Despite its increasing popularity as a mechanism for managing national level ethnic conflicts, scholars are divided about the effectiveness of federalism. Summarising the literature, Iff (2012, p. 228) points to the fact that, for some scholars, the qualitative and quantitative evidence suggests that federalism has mixed results in dampening ethnoregional conflicts. On the other hand, others argue that federalism reduces the chances of rebellions. It has also been argued that federalism has a lower rate of breakdown of the state relative to unitary systems and that federations are better able to manage armed rebellion, minority discrimination and grievances. However, the existential fact that neither Nigeria nor Ethiopia has been able to overcome their ethnic and regional troubles reminds us of the fact that institutional and constitutional designs are no magic wands.

With the advent of democratisation after 1990, many African countries embraced the principle of decentralisation. Decentralisation is thus by far the most common form of territorial administration in Africa. Unlike federalism's emphasis on some measure of self-rule for subnational units, decentralisation is based on the principle of the delegation of some specific central powers to subnational units. Despite being "an earlier (and failed) fashion in development administration" (Crook, 1994, p. 339) there has been a renewed impetus in the adoption of decentralisation measures across Africa as a panacea for promoting democracy and development. Ghana's elaborate system of 110 District Assemblies (DAs) are characteristic of this renewed interest in decentralisation. Set up in 1989, the DAs have councillors elected on a nonparty basis, and a superintending secretary appointed from the centre. In theory, the DAs have tax-raising powers and are responsible for functions devolved to the local government. They also have oversight powers over the deconcentrated twenty-two line ministries of the central government. "The assemblies thus combine the prefectoral-style rule of government-appointed district secretaries with the democratic control, service provision and tax-raising powers of devolved local government" (Crook, 1994, p. 343).

However, a study of Ghana's decentralisation came to negative conclusions that are applicable to most other African countries. The developmental output of the DAs was only marginally better than the previous system of administration and remained inadequate. Worse still, the DAs "did not show any significantly closer responsiveness to popular needs" (Crook, 1994, p. 339). Local accountability was undermined by central control over staffing and finances. Agents of the central government, such as the secretaries, continued to control policy and its implementation. Responsibilities may be transferred downwards from the centre, but not always the powers and resources needed to address them effectively. However, despite their many imperfections, "ownership" of a district is an important political symbol for many subnational groups, and can go quite some distance to pacify them.

South Africa, with its history of deep racial and ethnic divisions is a particularly interesting field to observe the use of territorial adminis-tration as a tool for building national co-existence. In 1993, as the end of apartheid was being negotiated, different political groups advanced opposing views on the nature of territorial administration of the post-apartheid state. Extreme right-wing Boer Afrikaner groups demanded seven to eight ethnically defined territories, including an Afrikaner homeland or Volkstaat (Muthien & Khosa, 2007). On its part, the white minority ruling National Party demanded federalism and a Bill of Rights as a means of protecting the white population from a future black majority government. This demand was supported, and even extended, by the Inkata Freedom Party, which claimed to speak on behalf of the Zulu ethnicity and demanded "extreme federalism", amounting to a confederation in which the Zulu dominated KwaZulu-Natal Province would have the power to secede. The African National Congress (ANC), representing the majority of the black population, rejected any notion of federalism as a carry-over of the hated Bantustan policy and demanded instead, a unitary nonracial state.

To break the deadlock, the white-dominated Consultative Business Movement released a *Report to the Political Parties* in March

1993 and in it advanced a compromise premised on the adoption of regionalism. The report called for regional powers "that would provide additional checks and balances and that degree of security for different communities" (Simeon & Murray, 2001, p. 69). Subsequently, it was agreed to have subnational provinces under a strong central government. Constitutional Principle XIX, agreed on in 1993, gave both national and provincial governments both exclusive and concurrent powers, suggestive of a federal system, but provincial boundaries were not to follow racial or ethnic boundaries. South Africa explicitly rejected the notion of empowering distinct racial and ethnic groups with their own political institutions, though ethnic and provincial boundaries coincide in three of the nine provinces (Simeon & Murray, 2001, pp. 70–72).

South Africa's experiment ended up with nine provinces pitched half-way between federalism and decentralisation. The demarcation of provincial boundaries was presented as a technical exercise that was open to all stakeholders, but the result of that exercise was then subjected to backroom political negotiations through which the interests of the white minority and different African ethnic interests gained traction. More importantly, delineating provincial boundaries was separated from the question of determining the constitutional powers the provinces were to enjoy because of "considerable polarisation over a unitary versus a federal state form" (Muthien & Khosa, 2007, p. 305). The proposals to create a predominantly white Boer Afrikaner Volkstaat faced stiff opposition from the black population, with Nelson Mandela reportedly retorting that "as long as I live there will never be a Volkstaat in this country" and another influential ANC leader, the future president Cyril Ramaphosa, asking for Robben Island prison to be declared the Volkstaat! Many feared that such an entity "might easily have prefigured the beginnings of claims to independent statehood or secession" (Muthien & Khosa, 2007, 308–309).

The South African Constitution finally agreed in 1996 scrupulously avoided the use of the words "federalism" and "federation". However, it contained a number of important federalist elements, albeit of a highly centralised nature. The constitution explicitly recognised the national government, the provinces, and the municipal administrations. All tiers of government had the power to legislate. However, the constitution gave wide-ranging powers to the national government to set national standards and norms and "to override provincial legislations that threatens national unity or national standards" (Simeon & Murray, 2001, p. 72). Under these circumstances, "self-rule" at the provincial level is hostage to national legislation. Furthermore, though most critical matters were on the concurrent legislative list, in all these matters, national laws prevailed. Though a National Council of Provinces – a federalist second chamber – was created to give the provinces a say over national law, the single-party dominance of the political system by the ANC after 1994 and its control of seven of the nine provinces stunted the development of that body. The dominant position of the national government also extends into the financial sphere as it dominated all major revenue sources. The weak provinces and powerful national government makes South Africa at best, a "quasi federalism" (Simeon & Murray 2001, p. 66), in which many [local governance] "institutions with low levels of capacity are expected to meet huge demands despite little or inappropriate support being provided by the central government" (Koelble & Siddle 2014, p. 618).

The experiences of Nigeria, Ethiopia, Ghana and South Africa, summarised here, show that the design of the territorial administration is a critical ingredient in the development of inclusive politics in Africa. But there is no magic formula in this regard as each country must respond to its political, social and historical circumstances. As noted, while most Nigerians gravitate towards federalism as a tool for managing their "unity in diversity", most South Africans gravitate away from federalism because of its association with minority racial domination in the past. Even when federalism is seen as the best policy, it is still possible to have radically different versions of the principle; Ethiopia's accommodationist ethnic federalism is very different from Nigeria's integrationist territorial federalism. The important point therefore is to note the range of territorial tools available for political experimentation, and not to essentialise the virtues, or lack thereof, of any particular tool.

12.3.2 *Electoral, Party and Voting Systems*

If the pattern of territorial administration makes possible some measure of self-rule for ethnic and regional groups, the system of electoral and party competition influences their ability to participate in the central administration. How democracies manage ethnic political activity in multi-ethnic societies is a burning question that scholars and policy makers have grappled with for a long while (Cohen, 1997, p. 609). This is a particularly pertinent question in an Africa dominated by semidemocracies or hybrid regimes governed by dominant parties. It has been argued that while autocracies can repress dissident ethnic political activity, and democracies can accommodate them through the electoral process, semi-democracies often lack the institutional capacity either to repress or to accommodate dissent. "Therefore, semi-democracies are more likely to experience violent internal conflicts" (Blanton et al., 2001, fn. 12, p. 486). Electoral and party rules are therefore important elements in the management of ethnic diversity in Africa.

Multi-ethnic states in Africa have either of two ways to manage their electoral systems: (a) power sharing or proportional representation or (b) majoritarianism. Majoritarian systems reward moderation in party behaviour by encouraging vote pooling across different ethnic communities, while at the same time encouraging adversarial politics. Most African countries have one version or the other of the majoritarian system. Political parties in this system are multi-ethnic in composition, but might sometimes be alliances of different ethnic based parties or ethnic factions. They seek votes from diverse ethnic constituencies in an adversarial manner against similar parties. This is what Horowitz (1985) calls "integrative majoritarianism" (see also Bangura, 2006, p. 2; Bogaards, 2003, p. 61). Power-sharing systems, on the other hand, are often based on political parties representing distinct ethnic segments who are all accommodated in a consensus-based and non-adversarial power-sharing process. The power-sharing system takes ethnic parties as given, and promotes plurality, not at the party level, as is the case with the majoritarian system, but at the governmental level. South Africa between 1994 and 1996 was the nearest example to this system in Africa. While the majoritarian system provides incentives for political mobilisation and contestation that crosscut ethnic cleavages, the power-sharing system reinforces the relevance of the ethnic cleavage. These are therefore two ideal–typical electoral systems for the democratic management of ethnicity in plural societies: (a) least intensely competitive, most formally inclusive, based on ethnic proportionality and (b) most intensely competitive, least formally inclusive, based on aggregating ethnic factions into a dominant majority (Cohen, 1997, p. 609). The nature of the electoral system has an impact on the nature of the party system as the proportional representation system tends to produce many small independent parties, while the majoritarian system tends to gravitate towards two major parties (Bangura, 2006, p. 20).

There are many voting systems for achieving the proportionality desired in the power-sharing system and the majority desired by the majoritarian system. The Party List (PL) is often used for proportional representation. The entire nation is a single constituency and parties draw up lists of candidates to take the predetermined available seats in parliament. Starting from the top of the PL, each party gets assigned parliamentary seats commensurate with its percentage share of the votes. This is the current situation in South Africa. Under some PL systems, parties that get a certain percentage of votes not only get seats in parliament corresponding to their share of the votes, but are also invited to join the cabinet in a coalition government (Lewis, 1965; Lijphart, 1977). That was the situation in South Africa between 1994 and 1996. The PL voting system has however been criticised for giving too much power to party bosses and ethnic entrepreneurs who control who goes on the list and how high up the list they are. Parliamentarians elected under this system have no immediate constituents to whom they are accountable; instead, they are beholden to the party and ethnic leaders. This practice has been criticised for turning ethnic elites and party bosses into political gatekeepers who have a vested interest in maintaining the ethnic boundary in perpetuity, trapping the country in the politics of ethnicity.

The single transferable vote (STV) achieves proportional representation through the ranking of candidates in multiseat constituencies by the voter. Parties are incentivised to put forward a balanced team of candidates to contest for the available seats in a multiseat constituency. The voter has a single vote and he or she ranks all the competing candidates from "1" downwards according to his preference. Candidates do not need a majority of the votes cast to be elected; a candidate only requires an agreed minimum number of votes, the quota or threshold, to win one of the seats. All parties want to put up candidates who would get first or second order preferences and, therefore, stand a good chance of being elected. Any candidate who has reached or exceeded the quota is declared elected. If the candidate has more votes than the quota, the surplus votes are transferred to other candidates. Votes that would have gone to the winner go to the next preference indicated by the voter. If no one new meets the quota, the candidate with the fewest votes is eliminated and those votes are transferred according to the next preferences of the voters. This process is repeated until a winner is found for every seat.

The STV helps to achieve proportional representation but, unlike in the PL system, votes are cast for individual candidates, not principally for political parties. Second, parliamentarians are tied to specific constituencies and constituents to whom they are beholden. The close ties between the elected parliamentarian and the electors weaken the grip of the party and ethnic elites that we noted under the PL system. Accountability is from the parliamentarians towards their constituent electors, rather than towards the party apparatchiks and ethnic elites. The STV, therefore, empowers the candidates and the electors at the expense of ethnic and party gatekeepers that we saw under the PL system. The STV and its multimember constituencies generates incentives for parties to present a balanced team of candidates so as to maximise the number of higher preferences their candidates are likely to get. This benefits women and ethnic minority candidates. Because parties are broad coalitions, constituencies have multiple members, and candidates are dependent on their personal standing for winning, parliament is more reflective of a nation's views and more responsive to them (BBC, 2010; Electoral Reform Society, nd). Though the STV tilts the balance of power towards the candidates and the electors, political parties are still important in determining the list of candidates in the first place and they and ethnic elites continue to retain considerable influence.

Despite its touted virtues, there is no African country that uses the STV. Some observers have argued that the STV is impractical in African conditions because of the high levels of illiteracy and innumeracy. Voters unaccustomed to writing may find it hard going to adequately reflect their preferences on the STV ballot paper. Too many spoilt ballots may call the election result into question. Responding to these criticisms, an ANC member in South Africa advocated a modified version of STV for the country (Eisner, 2015). The modified STV is called the indirect single transferrable vote (ISTV). In this modified version, all *candidates* for the election must first publicly produce a ranked list of their fellow candidates to whom they would like their votes transferred, should (s)he fall by the wayside in the earlier stages of the vote counting process. In the actual elections, each voter votes for only one candidate. "Voters need not specify their second, third, and fourth choices. Instead, each candidate specifies his or her second, third, and fourth choices" (Eisner, 2015). When the candidates with the least votes in the election are eliminated, their votes are assigned according to the candidates they have listed in their ranked list. In the ISTV, it is the losing candidates who determine who amongst their fellow candidates will benefit from the transferred votes. But because each candidate's preferences were already known before the election, it can be argued that the voters had accepted their candidate's choice before voting for them. As Eisner (2015, p. 15) concedes, however, the ISTV "has the potential for corruption. One candidate could be bribed to list another as second choice". South Africa did not abandon the PL for the ISTV.

While the PL and the STV are associated with proportional representation systems, the first-past-the-post (FPTP) is a majoritarian method for aggregating votes in single member parliamentary constituencies. The candidates with the highest vote wins, even if their share of the vote is less than 50%. This is seen as wasteful of votes of the losing candidates, who collectively may have well over 50% of the votes. This system is not good for multi-ethnic constituencies, where elections can often turn into an ethnic census. Ethnic minorities will be at a permanent disadvantage, except in those few electoral niches where they constitute a majority. Another majoritarian voting system frequently recommended for multi-ethnic societies instead of the FPTP is the alternative vote (AV). The AV is used in single-member constituencies. Voters rank candidates in order of preference – as in the STV – and anyone getting more than 50% in the first round is elected. If that does not happen, the candidate with the fewest votes is eliminated and their ballots are reallocated according to the second choices expressed by the voters. This process continues until a winner emerges with 50% or more of the votes. The AV is seen as "voter-empowering as it allows the electorate to reward candidates who advance issues other than those of their core group or party" (Bangura, 2006, p. 19). Most African states use one form or the other of FPTP, partly because it is technically undemanding on the voter and the electoral body. AV, on the other hand, suffers the disadvantages concerning illiteracy and innumeracy.

One final approach to inclusive politics worth noting is another home-grown African initiative called constituency pooling. While most majoritarian voting systems seek to pool votes, constituency pooling seeks to pool constituencies. It is a single-member multiple-districts system in which the plurality principle is combined with multiple districts to decide a single winner amongst competing candidates. Under this system, each candidate must compete in multiple electoral districts spread across different ethnic and regional strongholds. The candidate with the most votes across the multiple constituencies – as in the FPTP system – wins. By having to compete in multiple districts spread across different ethnic strongholds, parties and candidates are forced to embrace moderation and cross-ethnic appeal (Bogaards, 2003). This system was promoted by Uganda's "Four Constituencies" 1971 Electoral Law, designed specifically to encourage ethnic moderation and inclusivity in the electoral system. The country was divided into four distinct regions, each covering a different cluster of ethnicities. Any candidate standing for parliament had to stand for election in four constituencies at the same time, one each from the four different regions. Their ancestral constituency was their "basic district". They also must compete in three other "national districts" strewn across the other three regions. And because candidates were fewer (two or three), compared with districts (four), "no candidate could expect to win on the basis of votes from his own district alone" (Bogaards, 2003, p. 66).

This plan sparked much debate at Makerere University. Critics of the plan argued that a situation might arise in which the parliamentarian for a "basic district" might be rejected at the polls in the district, only for him or her to emerge as winner owing to cumulative votes from the other three districts. In such an instance, the parliamentarian would be representing a constituency that had expressly rejected him or her. To counter this criticism, it was suggested that the winner must not only win the majority of votes across the four districts, but must also win the majority in his or her "basic district". President Milton Obote was overthrown by Idi Amin before the plan could actually be put into practice. The two home-grown ideas about electoral reforms – ISTV and single-

member multiple-districts – have never seen any practical application, suggesting the difficulties in transmitting reformist ideas into
practical policies.

For the designers of inclusive politics in Africa, the FPTP is a very
unattractive voting system because of the high possibility of making
ethnic minorities politically invisible. There is little agreement
between the majoritarian and power-sharing advocates, except their
shared rejection of the FPTP. Some supporters of power-sharing
like Lijphart (1977) recommend a PL system along with other con-
sociational elements – a grand coalition reflecting key sections of
society, proportional distribution of public sector jobs, territorial
autonomy and a minority veto. This is vehemently opposed by
supporters of majoritarian approaches such as Horowitz who criti-
cises power-sharing as capable of trapping a country in ethnic
politics in perpetuity. Instead, they recommend an integrative AV
voting system which they see as empowering the ordinary voter, not
ethnic elites, and incentivising politicians towards cross-ethnic moderation. From this majoritarian point of view, the PL is the worst
possible reform measure, the STV being only marginally better. The
single-member multiple-districts and ISTV have dropped out of
discussion. Meanwhile, the FPTP – in its various guises – continues
to be the most common voting system in Africa because of its ease
of application.

12.4 Conclusion: Designing Inclusive Politics

Scholars of participatory politics frequently note that regardless of the
many institutional innovations to promote participation, "there
remains a gap between the legal and technical apparatus that has been
created to institutionalise participation and the reality of the effective
exclusion of poorer and more marginalised citizens (Cornwall &
Coelho, 2007, p. 3). For example, in the Latin American countries of
Bolivia, Colombia, Ecuador and Guatemala, sizeable populations of
the Indigenous and Afro-descendant populations have for long been
marginalised from mainstream national life. Agrawal et al. (2012)
point out that while legal and constitutional reforms in these countries
have increased the numbers of Indigenous and Afro-descendant
members in the national legislature (descriptive representation), this
increase has yet to be translated into legislative or policy outcomes that

benefit these marginalised communities (substantive representation). This raises the question of how much inclusion, and what type of inclusion will be necessary to achieve substantive gains for the marginalised (Spears, 2002, p. 125).

The answer to such questions must necessarily be political and context specific. In general terms, however, what needs emphasis is that regardless of what formal and informal rules are adopted in any country, the over-riding principle should be the attainment of certain institutional and political ends which make for inclusive politics and harmonious inter-ethnic relations. First, the principle of subsidiarity should be affirmed. Subnational units should be left to handle matters they are in the best position to handle. Under whatever rubric – federalism, regionalism or decentralisation – subnational units, whether determined territorially or by ethnicity, must be able to exercise a measure of self-rule, so that they are not stifled by the national government. Enough responsibility and powers, including meaningful participation in the control over local resources, should be given to these subnational units. But at the same time, enough powers and resources should be retained at the national level for the protection and promotion of the commonwealth.

Second, there should be a clear definition of jurisdictions between the different units of governance, so that the rights and powers of different subnational agents are recognised and protected. Even where the rules are informal, such a clear definition is still desirable. In regulating their inter-ethnic relations, African countries should move away from personality-driven processes to a rules-based one. Third, the institutional framework must have explicit mechanisms for ironing out disagreements between different governmental levels. In short, the demands of inclusive politics are in essence the intensification of the democratisation process, especially as it relates to ethnic and regional contexts.

A social policy aimed at creating a common citizenry through shared rights and obligations is another tool of inclusive politics. As noted earlier, most African countries bear the scars of deep sociopolitical inequalities. These inequalities, in themselves, have the capacity to generate and fuel conflicts (Kyriacou, 2013). Addressing ethnic and regional inequalities is therefore an important foundation for other institutional innovations. Universal access to basic health and education are key components of this social policy. Affirmative action programmes, with specified sunset clauses, may also be needed to ensure balanced access to higher education and public sector jobs.

All these institutional and political ends, however, presuppose that reform processes that manipulate the territorial administration and electoral and party rules are designed and implemented with a clear idea of their expected outcomes. For instance, Cohen (1997) hypothesises that the implementation of federalism, a proportional representation voting system and multipartism would lower the threshold for political victory in a country, disperse the potential points of political victory and increase the opportunities for political victory for a greater number of groups within the country. He went on to analyse data on 233 ethnic groups in 100 countries over 5 years and concluded that federalism actually generates increases in the incidence of low-level ethnic conflicts, but stifles the development of high-level ethnic conflict. He also concluded that proportional representation stifles high-level ethnic conflict while not generating any increases in the incidence of low-level ethnic conflict (Cohen, 1997, pp. 612–626).

Political experimentation in Africa is often not backed by such precise expectations of outcomes. Most countries do not seem to respect the theoretical and normative divisions between the majoritarian and power-sharing schools of thought. Indeed, most African countries are heterodox in their choice of policy options. As Bangura (2006) argues, "although the pulls of majoritarianism and power-sharing are very strong, they do not always pull in opposite directions". He notes that while most multi-ethnic countries have opted for majoritarian solutions, "ethnic problems have forced some of them to incorporate power-sharing elements in their majoritarian institutions (Bangura, 2006, p. 22). In most African countries, therefore, what one is more likely to find is a policy potpourri that incorporates elements such as percentage thresholds of votes that must be won in elections before a party can be finally registered, ethnic quotas in the formation of the executive, the forced location of party headquarters in the capital, explicit banning of ethnic and regional parties and symbols, minimum territorial spread of votes even for winning candidates so as to avoid the concentration of support in ethnic enclaves, the adoption of regional quotas in the distribution of jobs and educational resources, the compulsory establishment of party offices in a minimum percentage of the regions and the enforcement of ethnic balance in the executives of the parties. In Francophone countries, majoritarian electoral systems are mixed with strong features of territorial decentralisation (Bangura, 2006, pp. 21–22).

On the whole, it seems a good thing that African countries feel sufficient ownership of these policies that they are willing to experiment creatively with different options. Yet the resulting admixtures of different types of policies make it difficult to isolate and calculate their outcomes. They compound the many other factors that render predicting institutional effects problematic: the multiple, unanticipated, and context-specific nature of institutional effects; the bounded nature of institutional designers' rationality; variation in short- and long-term institutional effects; and problems of environmental change and actor discontinuity (Pierson, 2004). Particularly in contexts where informal institutions mediate the impact of formal institutional reforms, as in most African polities, these factors render the effects of any institutional reforms highly uncertain.

While the principal objectives of inclusive politics and policies may thus be clear, it is therefore important that the "institutional designs for promoting equality and cohesion should not be seen as magic bullets" (Makandawire, 2006, p. xi), but as part of a wider process of social transformation with institutional, political, and social components. The design of institutions should not be reduced to an apolitical and technical process. Inclusion is a contested political process, not a set of institutions. We must therefore integrate institutional design into a process of political and social mobilisation, which keeps the achievement of substantive change always firmly on the agenda. The process will, therefore, be marked by dilemmas and political trade-offs, rather than the simple operationalisation of institutions.

References

Agrawal, N., André, R., Berger, R., and Escarfuller, W. 2012. Political representation, policy & inclusion. *Americas Quarterly*. Retrieved from http://www.americasquarterly.org/political-representation. Accessed 18 September 2018.

Akindes, F. 2009. Cote d'Ivoire since 1993: The risky reinvention of a nation. In Mustapha, A. R., and Whitfield, L. (eds.), *Turning Points in African Democracy*. Woodbridge, UK: James Currey, pp. 31–49.

Bangura, Y. (ed.). 2006. *Ethnic Inequalities and Public Sector Governance*. Basingstoke: Palgrave Macmillan.

BBC. 2010. Election 2010 Q&A: Electoral reform and proportional representation. Retrieved from http://news.bbc.co.uk/1/hi/uk_politics/election_2010/8644480.stm. Accessed 18 September 2018.

Blanton, R., Mason, T. D., and Athow, B. 2001. Colonial style and post-colonial ethnic conflict in Africa. *Journal of Peace Research.* 38(4): 473–491.

Bogaards, M. 2003. Electoral choices for divided societies: Multiethnic parties and constituency pooling in Africa. *Commonwealth & Comparative Politics.* 41(3): 59–80.

Cohen, F. S. 1997. Proportional versus majoritarian ethnic conflict management in democracies. *Comparative Political Studies.* 30(5): 607–630.

Cornwall, A., and Schattan Coelho, V. 2007. Spaces for change? The politics of participation in new democratic arenas. In Cornwall, A., and Schattan Coelho, V. (eds.), *Spaces for Change? The Politics of Participation in New Democratic Arenas.* London: Zed Books, pp. 1–31.

Crook, R. C. 1994. Four YEARS of the Ghana District Assemblies in operation: Decentralization, democratization and administrative performance. *Public Administration and Development.* 14(4): 339–364.

Dahou, T., and Foucher, V. 2009. Senegal since 2000: Rebuilding hegemony in a global age. In Mustapha, A. R., and Whitfield, L. (eds.), *Turning Points in African Democracy.* Woodbridge, UK: James Currey, pp. 13–20.

Dryzek, J. S. 1996. Political inclusion and the dynamics of democratization. *American Political Science Review.* 90(3): 475–487.

Eifert, B., Miguel, E., and Posner, D. N. 2010. Political competition and ethnic identification in Africa. *American Journal of Political Science.* 54(2): 494–510.

Eisner, J. 2015. 'Indirect STV Election: A Voting System for South Africa'. Unpublished paper; University of Cape Town.

Electoral Reform Society. N.D. Single transferable vote. Retrieved from www.electoral-reform.org.uk/voting-systems/types-of-voting-system/single-transferable-vote/. Accessed 18 September 2018.

Gaventa, J. 2002. Introduction: Exploring citizenship, participation and accountability. *IDS Bulletin.* 33(2): 3–6.

Hickey, S., and du Toit, A. 2007. *Adverse Incorporation, Social Exclusion and Chronic Poverty (CPRC Working Paper No. 81).* London: Chronic Poverty Research Centre.

Horowitz, D. L. 1985. *Ethnic Groups in Conflict.* Berkeley: University of California Press.

    2014. Ethnic power sharing: Three big problems. *Journal of Democracy.* 25(2): 5–20

Iff, A. 2012. Peace-promoting federalism: Making sense of India and Nigeria. *Publius: The Journal of Federalism.* 43(2): 227–250.

Kabeer, N. 2002. *Citizenship and the Boundaries of the Acknowledged Community: Identity, Affiliation and Exclusion (IDS Working Paper No. 171).* Sussex: Institute of Development Studies.

Koelble, T. A., and Siddle, A. 2014. Decentralization in post-apartheid South Africa. *Regional & Federal Studies.* 24(5): 607–623.

Kyriacou, A. P. 2013. Ethnic group inequalities and governance: Evidence from developing countries. *KYKLOS.* 66(1): 78–101.

LeVan, A. C. 2011. Power sharing and inclusive politics in Africa's uncertain democracies. *Governance: an International Journal of Policy, Administration, and Institutions.* 24(1): 31–53.

Lewis, A. W. 1965. *Politics in West Africa.* London: George Allen & Unwin.

Lijphart, A. 1977. *Democracy in Plural Societies: A Comparative Exploration.* New Haven, CT: Yale University Press.

Makandawire, T. 2006. Foreword. In Bangura, Y. (ed.), *Ethnic Inequalities and Public Sector Governance.* Basingstoke: Palgrave Macmillan.

Muthien, Y. G., and Khosa, M. M. 2007. The kingdom, the Volkstaat and the New South Africa: Drawing South Africa's new regional bound. *Journal of Southern African Studies.* 21(2): 303–322.

Pierson, P. 2004. *Politics in Time: History, Institutions, and Social Analysis.* Princeton, NJ: Princeton University Press.

Simeon, R., and Murray, C. 2001. Multi-sphere governance in South Africa: An interim assessment. *Publius.* 31(4): 65–92.

Spears, I. S. 2002. Africa: The limits of power-sharing. *Journal of Democracy.* 13(3): 123–136.

Stewart, F. (ed.). 2008. *Horizontal Inequalities and Conflict: Understanding Group Violence in Multiethnic Societies.* Basingstoke: Palgrave Macmillan.

Tegenu, T. 2006. *Evaluation of the Operation and Performance of Ethnic Decentralization System in Ethiopia: A Case Study of the Gurage People, 1992–2000.* Addis Ababa: University Press Addis.

PART III

Conclusions and Policy Recommendations

13 | National Cohesion in Africa
Beyond Ethnicity and Ethnic Communities

ERNEST ARYEETEY AND AMA
DE-GRAFT AIKINS

13.1 Introduction

National cohesion is a major concern for many African countries. Over the last six decades, since independence, many countries have experienced conflict, wars, political crises, economic crises, social displacement and poverty. These problems have varied in magnitude, intensity and sequence depending on national context. However, cumulatively and over time, they have been deeply implicated in the continent's underdevelopment. For a number of Africanist scholars and African leaders, these complex problems have been driven by the political economy of ethnicity on the continent. By extension, the idea of national development and cohesion has tended to privilege the dominant role of ethnicity and the development of national cohesion has been led by projects that seek to bond diverse ethnic communities. While these ideas and responses are influential, they have been subjected to increasing critique (cf. Hino et al., 2012).

In this chapter, we focus on the challenge of national cohesion in Africa and examine the role and limits of ethnicity and ethnic communities in this process. The chapter is structured in four section. In Section 13.2, we review the key definitions of ethnicity offered by Africanist scholars. We underscore the importance of anthropological and historical perspectives which define African ethnicities as complex, dynamic and situational, and as social categories that are made psychologically active by communities with multiple identities.

In Section 13.3, we synthesise the key arguments on the role of ethnicity and ethnic diversity in African development. We highlight the conceptual and methodological limitations in the thesis proposed by some economists and political scientists, which draws strong causal links between ethnic diversity and underdevelopment. We focus on the usefulness of the anthropological and historical perspectives, which leads to a thesis of examining social conflict and social cohesion as a function of political manipulation of human capital.

In Section 13.4, we review the evolution of national cohesion projects, starting from the postindependence strategies of national identity building to the current strategies of postconflict national identity restructuring. We focus on the communities that have been at the heart of these constructive processes and highlight the increasing role of nonstate actors in national cohesion projects. In Section 13.5, we discuss the importance and limits of nonstate actors in development projects, by presenting cases of civil society organisation (CSO) activities in three developmental areas: postconflict restructuring, the public health crisis of HIV/AIDS and the development of urban poor communities. Three insights emerge from the synthesis. First, bonding ethnic communities is not enough. Second, national cohesion projects have moved beyond bonding ethnic communities, to addressing crosscutting developmental issues that affect heterogeneous communities, including women, youth, and the disenfranchised urban poor. Third, nonstate actors have expanded beyond the visible and much studied group of development partners, international nongovernmental organisations (NGOs) and local NGOs. Diaspora communities, women's groups, religious organisations and youth groups are increasingly participating in reshaping development and democratic processes. We highlight a problematic lack of empirical study and theorisation of the role of these emerging groups. We conclude with a discussion of the implications of these conceptual and methodological absences and how these challenges may be addressed.

13.2 Definitions of African Ethnicities

"Ethnicity is a resilient paradigm in Africa", as Shaw (1986) has observed. The idea that the developmental fortunes of Africa are shaped by ethnicity is deeply rooted. However, the content and functions of ethnicity have nuanced features. The definition of ethnicity in Africa has evolved along three lines: primordial (or essentialist), constructivist and instrumentalist (for a detailed discussion on these three different perspectives on ethnicity, see Lentz, 1995; Lonsdale, 2012; Ranger, 1993). The primordial or essentialist approach views ethnicity as a natural entity shaped by distinct boundaries of geography, ancestry, kinship, religion, language and other cultural ideologies and practices. Members of primordial ethnic communities are perceived to share deep emotional, psychological and ideological bonds as a result of the (perceived) immutability of their ethnic identities (Lentz, 1995; Lonsdale, 2012). The constructionist perspective suggests that ethnicity is a social construct, "invented" or "imagined" by diverse social actors with complex intentions and interpretations of functional communities (Ranger, 1993). As such, ethnic communities are dynamic social organisations that are subject to change "in consciousness and composition" (Lonsdale, 2012, p. 22). The instrumentalist approach views ethnicity in terms of competitive social groups that emerge through the strategic manipulation of political elites who exploit imagined or invented kinship as a means to build and maintain political power (Lonsdale, 2012). A distinction is made between the change effected by instrumentalist ethnicity through elite strategies and the change effected by constructivist ethnicity based on evolving norms of a moral economy and a moral consciousness to which all social members, including elites, are subjected. Moral economies constitute "webs of trust and obligation that sustain social order and trustworthy, repeatable market transactions" (Lonsdale, 2012, p. 29), thereby ensuring the equitable distribution of symbolic (e.g., authority, power) and material (e.g., wealth, land) resources. A moral consciousness hinges on a shared collective commitment to principles of diversity, equality and justice (Chipkin & Ngqulunga, 2008; see also Chapter 1).

While the constructionist approach seems to be the dominant approach (Brown & Langer, 2012), some theorists have emphasised the usefulness of amalgamating the three interpretive approaches. Lonsdale (2012) argues that ethnicity is a "relational concept of social belonging that adjusts to changing situations" (p. 21) and African ethnicities are "'states of mind' as much as 'actual social organizations'" (p. 28). As a result the entity and functions of ethnicity take many different forms. He describes the complex social use of ethnicity thus:

Ethnic groups acquire internal cohesion and a sense of difference from – not always hostile to – "others" in countless negotiations of innovation and resistance that change their moral and social markers over time. This socially constructed cohesion is available for instrumental use by political or economic entrepreneurs whose (...) call to solidarity is that "we" are all one family, despite our inequalities and conflicts – and always have been. Readiness to form rival teams of common "blood" seems to be a primordial human instinct, against the common grain of history and often against our apparent self-interest (...) Yet (...) ethnic groups are also moral communities, potentially able to resist instrumental exploitation and to re-examine moral economy. (Lonsdale, 2012, p. 22–23)

An implicit central thread runs through this argument: the importance of the psychological dimension of ethnicity within the broader structure of social identity.[1] Young (2004, p. 7) notes: "ethnicity is defined by an active consciousness of collective selfhood. The group is invariably named, and its members hold a self-awareness of their collective affiliation." This self-identification process is akin to the primordial ethnicity process: here ethnic members possess intense emotional commitments and attitudes that mediate either inter-group cohesion or conflict. The concept of self-definition also introduces the process of self-identification across different social categories beyond ethnicity. Social psychological theorists propose that social identity is a fluid product of individual unique attributes and social attributes accrued over a lifetime through various group memberships and lived social experiences (Abrams & Hogg, 1990; Moscovici & Duveen, 2000; Turner & Oakes, 1986). Ethnic membership becomes part of a complex set of social memberships to which individuals self-identify. Within anthropology, theorists such as Elwert (1995), have referred to ethnic identity as "polytactic". Polytaxis or polytactic potential refers to the ability of individuals to "master different roles which [are] put in practice according to the situation" and the ability to "make consecutive use of several affiliations ... modes of belonging or identities" (Elwert, 1995, p. 5).

These ideas lead to at least three conclusions. First, we can argue that individuals will switch between functional ethnic categories (primordial, instrumentalist, constructionist). Second, individuals are likely to switch between ethnic categories, as well as between ethnic identities and other salient identities such as gender, class, generational status, religion and language groups. The switching processes at both levels will depend on the sociopolitical context and the particular needs of

---

[1] We have presented the following argument in a different form elsewhere (Aryeetey & de-Graft Aikins, 2013)

target individuals or groups in particular moments and across time. Finally, while ethnic and other social structures can exert a powerful force on individuals and social groups, individuals and groups can resist and challenge these structures. The mutual interaction and mutual constitution of social identities and sociocultural structures lead to the construction of new identities, social relations and social or political structures. These basic building blocks of the social psychology of societies apply to the African context. They are important for understanding the nature and functions of ethnic diversity in Africa.

13.3 Ethnic Diversity and African Development

The core arguments and controversies regarding the relationship between ethnicity and development hinge on the *ethnic diversity* of Africa. Two diverging lines of thought exist. On the one hand, ethnic diversity has been linked to Africa's underdevelopment. The basic hypothesis is that countries with high levels of ethnic diversity are likely to experience greater social polarisation arising from inequitable access to public goods like education, health care, employment and infrastructural development (Easterly & Levine, 1997). Social disagreements and struggles over the structure, components and functions of these public goods intensify ethnically based disparities in political power and social development. This view was made popular over a decade ago by some development economists and political scientists who used largely quantitative methods and standardised indices to propose strong causal links between ethnic diversity and developmental outcomes (Brown & Langer, 2012; Collier, 2007; Easterly & Levine, 1997).

On the other hand, the role of ethnic diversity on Africa's development is viewed as complex and unpredictable. Historians and anthropologists, employing largely qualitative – longitudinal and case study – forms of enquiry, have described the intricate relationships between ethnicity and other social categories, such as gender, generational status, class and religion and how this complex set of interacting social forces shapes development in Africa. Within this context, ethnicity is *only one* among several factors implicated in African underdevelopment (Berman, 2012; Brown & Langer, 2012; Lonsdale, 2012).

The evidence seems to bear out the second line of argument. The dominant methods used to make a case for the role of ethnic diversity and disparities in underdevelopment have noted flaws. Brown and Langer (2012) provide an accessible explanation of the limitations of ethnic fractionalisation, "the common and longest used 'pure' measure of ethnic diversity". Fractionalisation aims to capture, statistically, the degree to which a population is constituted by a large number of small groups. A statistical index, called the Ethnolinguistic Fractionalisation index, captures population homogeneity (a score of zero when the population constitutes one group) and population heterogeneity (a maximum score of 1 when the population constitutes infinite groups of one member). Brown and Langer (2012) observe that the reliability of the Ethnolinguistic Fractionalisation index has been criticised along three lines: (1) for focusing on linguistic categories, thus excluding multiple dimensions of ethnicity (e.g., religion); (2) for basing its measures on the *Atlas Naradov Mira*, an outdated worldwide survey of ethnic diversity conducted by a group of Soviet ethnologists in the early 1960s; and (3) suffering from coding inaccuracies. At a fundamental level, the validity of the fractionalisation measure is problematic "as it assumes that the political outcomes we are interested in vary with the level of fractionalisation rather than some other diversity measure" (Brown & Langer, 2012, p. 68).

These flaws have given rise to the construction of new measures. For example, a focus on demographic polarisation seeks to introduce another measure of diversity. Brown and Langer (2012) note: "while the fractionalization-conflict matrix rightly attributes a low chance of ethnic conflict to homogenous populations, highly fractionalised societies are also less likely to be conflictual as no group has the 'critical mass' necessary for conflict. Instead, they postulate that conflict is more likely the more a population is polarised into two large groups" (pp. 68–69).

Other theorists argue that it is not diversity that is the problem, but rather the type and intensity of diversity. Bangura (2006), e.g., synthesises the ideas of Geertz, Milne and Horowitz and develops a five-part typology that aims to illuminate the nature of diversity: unipolarity (societies with one dominant ethnic group), bipolarity (two roughly equal groups dominating), tripolarity (three large groups in a multi-ethnic setting), fragmented multipolarity (high levels of ethnic fragmentation) and concentrated multipolarity (a few large groups in a fragmented multi-ethnic context organise to access public goods). Berman and Takahashi (Chapter 5) outline the use of horizontal inequality indices that "track the changing relationship of ethnic groups with the development of the state and market and provide the essential basis for understanding the source of ethnic conflict and its anti-developmental consequences in particular contexts".

Ultimately, Brown and Langer (2012) summarise the fundamental problems in this subfield in two parts. First, researchers have created a gap between concept and measurement: while most researchers support the constructionist definition of ethnicity, their measurements employ census and survey data which are "dangerously close" to primordial definitions of ethnicity. This concept-measurement gap needs to be addressed. Secondly, it may be better to refer to ethnicity as an *"indicator* of social diversity and social distance", rather than as a cause. They suggest the need to blend the quantitative and qualitative traditions, observing the usefulness of iterative methods that "provide better insights into the particular mechanisms at work".

An interdisciplinary approach to ethnic diversity in Africa is welcome, but the conceptual focus must be socially relevant. The first problem – which Brown and Langer (2012) mention but do not interrogate fully – is that the social and economic outcomes of interest to economists and political scientists tend to be restricted to "violent group mobilisation, secessionist movements and economic growth differences" (p. 83). Other social and economic outcomes of concern to African citizens, which may or may not underpin tension or cohesion do not feature in these analyses. Neither does the process of self-identification in the use of ethnicity and other social categories.

Second, because of the absence of psychological meaningfulness in the economic models, the unpredictable functions of ethnic diversity are unlikely to be captured in the newer sophisticated measurements of fractionalisation and polarisation. Africa is not the only ethnically diverse continent: Asia and the Pacific share this feature. Within this global context, there are several ethnically diverse countries, including in Africa, that have experienced relative peace over a long historical period (Collier, 2007). Conversely there are ethnically pure countries, such as Somalia, with histories of intense social conflict (Collier, 2007).

The earlier discussion of social identity and polytaxis suggests that ethnicity and other social identities are deployed in complex ways. Lonsdale (2012), Berman (2012), Lentz (1995) and others have suggested that lay communities and political groups apply the three interpretive categories of ethnicity differently. At a fundamental level, citizens and political leaders draw on primordial and constructivist ethnicity. This combination approximates to a moral ethnicity, a term derived from moral economy which describes the webs of trust that sustain social order, trust, vigilance and reciprocity (Berman, 2012; Lonsdale, 2012) and drives a "politics of authenticity" (Bayart, 2005, cited by Berman & Takahashi, Chapter 5). However, elite leaders also use instrumental ethnicity to further political and economic interests, such as the manipulation of public goods like land (Rasool, Chapter 11; Amanor, Chapter 8) and education (Kramon & Posner, Chapter 9). These structural patterns of elite behaviour – termed political tribalism or neopatrimonialism – originated in the patrilineal African extended family system dominated by authoritarian older male heads, and transformed in the postindependence era into unfettered power exerted by "big men" in government and political institutions (Berman, 2012; Bratton, 1994). Bratton (1994) observes that

at the elite level neopatrimonialism is manifest in the overcentralisation of power ("one-man management"), arbitrary decision-making ("the rule of men") and the use of public resources for personal advancement ("corruption"). At the mass level, neopatrimonial culture reveals itself in obeisance and deference to political superiors ("respect"), in conformity in group behaviour ("government by consensus") and in economic dependence upon wealthy individuals ("patronage"). (p. 9)

The central argument is that it is not ethnic diversity *per se* that undermines development but the manipulation of ethnic diversity by powerful political actors (Berman, 2012; Lonsdale, 2012). It is the social and economic outcome of neopatrimonialism, some argue further, that is captured in econometric analysis of ethnic fractionalisation and polarisation. The complex negotiation of different categories of ethnicity by heterogeneous social actors within a broader moral economy is excluded. This thesis suggests that to understand the dynamics of sociopolitical tension or conflict, and its opposite – cohesion – the dynamic relationships between state actors ("political elites", "military elites", "big men") and ordinary citizens need to be understood. Kramon and Posner (Chapter 9), e.g., writing on education policy in Kenya make a case for how greater "citizen alertness" can contribute to the protection of public goods from ethnic politics. In the Nigerian context of regional divisions and conflicts, Raufu Mustapha (Chapter 2) demonstrates how neo-patrimonial structures can be unpredictably upturned by historically marginalised "northern" political actors.

13.4 National Cohesion in Africa: Beyond Ethnicity and Ethnic Communities

Nationalist projects in African countries have sought to superimpose national identities over ethnic affiliations. Bangura (2006) observes that in early independent Africa, "ethnicity was discouraged as an organizing principle of statecraft" (p. 304) and the evolving public sectors were shaped by the foreign languages and secular values of colonial authorities. Tanzania is offered as an example of this continental policy; references to ethnicity were discouraged in public discourse and a national language, KiSwahili, was developed to support the Tanzanian government's egalitarian policies. In Ghana, ethnic and religious affiliations were viewed as subordinate to national affiliation, as captured in Nkrumah's often-cited rallying cry: "seek ye first the political kingdom" (Biney, 2008). Nkrumah along with other national leaders (e.g., Sekou Toure of Guinea, Jomo Kenyatta of Kenya) also attempted to develop a supra-national identity through the Pan-African project and through the politically powerful and enduring ideology of the "African personality" (Lassiter, 2000). The level of acceptance of these nationalist projects varied across countries and depended on the internal structures of inter-ethnic relations. In Ethiopia, Nigeria and Uganda, e.g., leaders of major ethnic groups such as the Oromo (Ethiopia), Yoruba and Igbo (Nigeria) and Ganda (Uganda) spearheaded ethnonationalist projects to challenge the perceived threats of territorial nationalism. Democratisation and constitutional reform in these countries involved politically sensitive strategies aimed at accommodating and managing ethnic diversity (Berman, 2012).

Africa's lost decades of the 1980s and 1990s were characterised by bloody coup d'états, civil wars, conflicts and myriad political, economic and social upheavals that derailed nation building and social development (Bates et al., 2007; Mkandawire, 2002). Governments governed through development partners and their imposed policies (chiefly structural adjustment programmes) and ideologies (such as human rights and participatory citizenship; Brown, 2013; Mkandawire, 2002; Routley, 2011). These new political arrangements weakened state power politically, economically and culturally. State actors lost their ability to set relevant development agendas independently and to manipulate ethnicity and ethnic networks for private gain. This period also saw the re-emergence of CSOs as legitimate participants in governance. CSOs had always been present on the continent, mainly as traditional associational groups, and some groups had actively participated in the independence struggles of a number of countries (Bratton, 1994). Bratton (1994) observes that the associational life took different forms in different countries: "Christian churches in Kenya and Burundi, Islamic brotherhoods in Senegal and Sudan, lawyers' and journalists' associations in Ghana and Nigeria, farmer organisations in Zimbabwe and Kenya and mineworkers' unions in Zambia and South Africa" (p. 5). However, the scale and scope of CSO activities during the era of structural adjustment changed. Pre-existing networks of voluntary associations enlarged to encompass the World Bank's exhaustive list of CSOs: NGOs, labour unions, charitable organisations, faith-based organisations, professional associations, and foundations. These local organisations were joined by international versions. The Afrobarometer project which examined public perceptions of social, political and economic processes in twelve African countries – Botswana, Ghana, Lesotho, Malawi, Mali, Namibia, Nigeria, South Africa, Tanzania, Uganda, Zambia and Zimbabwe – reported that, by the early 2000s, almost 75% of survey respondents claimed membership of a voluntary association (Bratton et al., 2006).

These sociopolitical processes have persisted into the current era of debt relief, poverty reduction, the attainment of the Millennium Development Goals and Africa–China relations (Aryeetey & Ackah, 2011; Conceição et al., 2011; Mohan & Lampert, 2013). Countries emerging from long-term war and conflict are reconstructing nationhood and identity by managing ethnic diversity and tensions. In Cote d'Ivoire, e.g., the state sanctioned legal process of citizenship did not require disclosure of ancestral hometown. Being born in Cote d'Ivoire, even of parents of unknown origin, was enough to secure citizenship (Bah, 2010). The evidence suggests that state failures do not necessarily erase national attachment. While forms of resistance may exist their aim is not to destroy nationhood, but to regulate the moral economy. In Sierra Leone and Democratic Republic of Congo, where state failures led to impoverished and disenfranchised communities, individuals continue to express support for the national project (Young, 2004). In Rwanda, rural peasants, the most marginalised social group, seem to resist the state's ideological approach to national cohesion by using creative forms of everyday resistance. Yet these practices are not aimed at dismantling the national project; rather, they aim to fine tune democratic processes from the margins (Thomson, 2011).

Bratton (1994) observes that after independence, the priority given to state sovereignty and national security co-existed with a drive to bring about "de-participation". Ruling elites invested in the construction of one-party and military regimes and sought to discourage "autonomous organisations from taking root in civil society". Organisations were either incorporated into governing parties or were banned. But these strategies failed in most countries and the structural adjustment era saw the re-emergence and growing power of civil society. Now, nonstate actors play significant roles in governance and democratic processes in many countries and these roles are actively sought. Titeca and de Herdt (2011) argue that "failed states" have symbolic power; they survive and transform by leveraging their dwindling material power (e.g., the ability to develop infrastructure or collect and use tax revenues) into symbolic power through the support of and strategies of various nonstate actors who reify the idea and ideals of the state. Strong states also rely on nonstate actors, and may in fact derive their growing strength partly from participatory governance. Indeed, a key indicator of good governance, as espoused by the World Bank and other international development organisations, is civil society participation. The allure of CSOs is based partly on the perception that civil society, whatever its composition, is "the honest broker of the peoples' interest" (Kamat, 2004, p. 158). Civil society groups aim, ideally, to address the fragmentation of a state by focusing on and acting upon matters of the public good or the general welfare of a civic public (Kamat, 2004; Routley, 2011). The civic public transcends the "ethnic factionalism, communalism or tribalism" of neopatrimonial states. It aims to create and sustain a civic public realm by providing the space within which to hold the state to account while ensuring equity in the treatment of individuals (McNeil & Mumvuma, 2006; Routley, 2011).

Important socioeconomic transformations in Africa have implications for future development projects. Many African countries have exhibited steady economic growth over the past decade. The World

Bank lists six African countries among the top ten fastest growing economies: Sierra Leone, Mozambique, Ghana, Angola and Ethiopia. The nuanced effects of the lost decades have begun to be felt. The estimated 140 million Africans living outside the continent have become formidable providers of remittances to family and friends back home. Over the last decade studies have shown that remittances from the African diaspora exceed official development aid and are second only to foreign direct investment (Kayode-Anglade & Spio-Garbrah, 2012). Figures for 2010 show that the African diaspora remitted $51.8 billion (£34 billion) to the continent, while official development aid provided $43 billion (£28 billion) to Africa. These funds, termed "family aid", are estimated to be four times higher, because up to 75% of remittances are sent informally and cannot be tracked. They support the informal economies of many countries by enhancing family budgets and propping up small businesses.

Lonsdale (2012, p. 23) citing Skinner (1962), provides an interesting quote on the attitude of a West African man to the traditional African market 50 years ago: "when I get to the market I look for three persons: my girlfriend, my debtor, and my enemy...And when I go to the market and do not see them all, the market is not good". Lonsdale (2012) uses this quote to underscore the idea that markets are subjectively varied and may transform social relations vertically and horizontally. These subjective variations persist (men still juggle the tensions of love, debt and enmity), but the broader structures have changed. This situation has implications for the evolution of moral economies in Africa. The market is now physical, virtual and global. A young West African man is more likely to be urbanised and managing (or manipulating) the subjective variations of the market in a traditional stall, a shopping mall or on the Internet (Armstrong, 2011; Quayson, 2010). The urban market – specifically the vegetable stall of a young underemployed male college graduate, Muhammad Al Bouazizi – was the site for the protest that led to the toppling of the long-sitting Tunisian president, Zine El-Abidine Ben Ali. The ensuing "Arab Spring" has been fuelled by "youthquakes" aided by physical protests and virtual advocacy on the social media (African Development Bank, 2013a; Bratton, 2013). These changes are yet to be incorporated into the empirical study and concepts of development and national cohesion. We focus on CSO activities in three areas – postconflict restructuring, HIV/AIDS and urban settlements – to highlight the successes and limitations in national cohesion projects and the importance of incorporating these new socioeconomic transformations in future research.

13.5 Civil Society, Social Participation and National Cohesion

The Section 13.4 suggests two theoretically important shifts have occurred. First, the developmental focus has shifted from ethnic communities to heterogeneous communities with concrete needs and increasing voice – the rural and urban poor, women and youth. Second, the provider of public goods – both material and symbolic – has shifted from the state to a vast range of nonstate actors including the African diaspora. These shifts have evolved over at least two decades. Some theorists have argued that the shifts have implications for the conceptual approaches to African development and governance (Mkandawire, 2011). In particular, the dominant discourse on neopatrimonialism, which informs concepts and methods of ethnicity and development, needs major revisions. The case studies on CSO activities throw more light on the importance of these arguments.

Three key areas in which CSOs have played significant roles are in rebuilding peace and governance in postconflict societies (Brinkerhoff, 2005; Ekiyor, 2008; Jackson, 2005; De Medeiros, 2007), responding to the social crises of HIV/AIDS (Campbell, 2003; Ilife, 2006; Low-Beer & Stoneburner, 2003; Nguyen, 2010) and addressing the social inequalities arising from rapid urbanisation (Chipkin & Ngqulunga, 2008; UNFPA, 2011). In Sierra Leone and Liberia, CSOs turned the same factor associated with conflict – ethnic diversity – into a productive tool for postconflict peace building (Ekiyor, 2008; De Medeiros, 2007). Grassroots women's groups, e.g., were instrumental in applying cultural models of healing and social support to develop the solutions to the postconflict impact of gender-based violence (Ekiyor, 2008). In Burundi, CSOs are used to enhance development projects in agriculture and natural resource management (Vervisch & Titeca, 2010).

When the HIV/AIDS pandemic hit the continent, CSOs made significant contributions including the provision of institutional and home-based care, as well as advocating for opening access to life saving medicines and respecting the rights of infected individuals and affected families and communities. Faith-based organisations were particularly active, with Christian and Islamic leaders and organisations providing public health education and social support to their congregations and affected communities (Ilife, 2006). Trinitapoli and Weinreb (2012) report a recent study that examines the relationship between religion and AIDS in thirty African countries using secondary survey data. They show that the religious leaders and congregations continue to play an important role in HIV prevention and care in many countries. In the broader development discourse, the growing power of charismatic Pentecostal Christian leaders in national affairs has led to their crowning as the new "big men" (Gifford, 2004; McCauley, 2012).

Africa is the fastest urbanising region in the world (UNFPA, 2007, 2011). Across the continent there has been a rise of super-cities, like Lagos, and the transformation of small towns, like Ouagadougou, Douala, Kampala and Conakry, into major cities (Davis, 2006). This has had at least two consequences. First, the rise of major cities and super-cities create new urban environments of multi-ethnicity and multiculture. Second, rapid urbanisation within the context of limited growth has led to the creation and proliferation of large urban slums (UNFPA, 2011). The African Development Bank notes that Africa has the lowest proportion of the global urban population (32.8%), but the highest proportion of slum dwellers (65%) (African Development Bank, 2013b). Slum communities have severely restricted access to employment, goods and services and are confronted with health-disabling environments that increase their risk of complex diseases and premature death (Greif et al., 2011; Kyobutungi et al., 2008). Social relations in urban poor environments are often fragile. In South Africa urban spaces "of conviviality (bars, shebeens) are regular sites of bloodshed" and the family is a site of "profound contradiction", on the one hand a key institution that mediates the effects of unemployment and poverty, on the other a place of "ferocious gender violence" (Chipkin & Nqgulunga, 2008). A vast number of local and international CSOs have been established to address the multifaceted problems of urban poverty in countries like Kenya, Zimbabwe and Ghana. These CSOs aim to develop poor urban areas and communities, as well as seek to call the state and urban elites to order for poor urban policies and political inaction. As the group most likely to migrate to urban areas, youth groups are major actors in urban politics and their methods of advocacy include the use of social media. For example, as UN agencies and CSOs such as UH-HABITAT and Kibera-UK fight for the rights of slum residents of Kibera, Kenya's most prominent urban slum, slum residents themselves are using citizen journalism to shape public discourse about the challenges, needs and opportunities of life in the slums on their own terms (Patinkin, 2013).

Evaluations of CSO activities in these key areas emphasise the important role CSOs play in the developmental process as well as in fostering social cohesion (Bratton, 1994; Campbell, 2003; Ilife, 2006; Nguyen, 2010; Vervisch & Titeca, 2010). However, they also highlight a number of problems.

The first problem is one of quantity and fragmentation. Generally, countries with CSO presence suffer an overabundance of organisations. Ekiyor (2008) reports that 3,000 civil society organisations serve postconflict peace building interests in West Africa. Iliffe (2006, p. 98), discussing the role of NGOs and the evolution of HIV/AIDS care in Africa observes that "the scale and diversity of NGO action def[ies] summary":

In 1992, Uganda already had over 600 NGOs involved in AIDS work; by 2003 there were about 2000. Kisumu, the provincial capital of Kenya's heavily infected Nyanza province, had over 200 NGOs and community-based organizations combating Aids in 1999. Senegal was also rich in organisations, over 700 receiving public subsidies during 2004, the same number as those affiliated to Nigeria's Aids programme. South Africa had a vigorous NGO tradition, inherited especially from the anti-Apartheid movement, and counted over 700 bodies engaged in Aids work as early as 1993.

A second, ironic, problem is inequitable access. CSOs are reported to congregate in urban areas and political nerve centres of capital cities and to exclude remote rural areas (Handley et al., 2009). Thus, the most marginalised communities in many countries do not benefit from the developmental activities of CSOs. Iliffe (2006) highlights the way remote rural South African communities affected by HIV/AIDS were unable to access the care and advocacy activities of CSOs owing to the urban bias of CSO activities.

A third problem is the way social capital is conceptualised and deployed. The discourse on social capital within the African context has drawn largely on Putnam's definition: "features of social organization such as trust, norms and networks that can improve the efficiency of society by facilitating coordinated action" (Putnam et al., 2003, cited in Vervisch & Titeca, 2010). The conceptual offshoots of this definition are *bonding capital* (exclusive solidarity based on ethnicity, religion, cast or class), *bridging capital* (inclusive solidarity uniting people from different backgrounds) and *linking capital* (the capacity of the local population to leverage global modern or exogenous ideas information and resources from an external agent; Vervisch & Titeca, 2010, pp. 487, 489). The assumption when CSOs partner with international organisations on development projects is that local communities may already have bonding social capital. This capital is perceived as largely positive and without hierarchical tensions, particularly when target communities are selected based on ethnicity. The aim, therefore, is to enhance bridging capital by bringing different homogenous groups together and linking capital by offering external resources (e.g., knowledge, money) to these groups. Vervisch and Titeca (2010) highlight the danger of these assumptions in a case study of three CSO projects in Burundi that failed. The failures were attributed to a lack of understanding, on the part of the international donors, that the pre-existing social capital was hierarchical and double edged and that the chosen brokers of the development projects were not necessarily culturally influential or technically efficient. Grischow (2008), drawing on historical data on chieftaincy in Ghana, makes a similar point when he critiques the assumption that development projects that target traditional chiefs as partners will work because chiefs are the custodians of unproblematic social capital endowments. In Ghana, chiefs are courted by international donor agencies including the World Bank despite their historical role as shrewd self-interested manipulators of human and natural resources (see also Chapter 5).

Fourth, there are challenges regarding the politics of recognition. Some experts observe that CSOs are often narrowly defined as NGOs, thus excluding indigenous groups with a long history of social development, particularly in communities marginalised by the state. This extends to the current lack of information about diaspora groups and organisations on their role in providing family aid. Although family aid exceeds official development aid, 12% of the funds disappear in bank charges and countries seem to be reluctant to approve incentives, like diaspora bonds, that may enhance greater investments of diaspora funds in home countries (Kayode-Anglade & Spio-Garbrah, 2012).

A final problem is that the politics of developing a civic public may suffer the same ideological and relational challenges that plague dominant critiques of patrimonialism. The idea that CSOs are honest brokers of people's interests because they transcend the "ethnic factionalism, communalism or tribalism" of neopatrimonial states is not borne out in reality. Researchers assert that some NGOs get co-opted by the state (Ekiyor, 2008; Gyimah-Boadi, 1997; Routley, 2011). Routley (2011) presents a case study of the "grey practices" of national NGOs in Nigeria, which involve paternalistic perceptions of "the public" and morally ambiguous dealings with the state, that do not fall into neat categories of either developing a primordial public or a civic public. Ekiyor (2008) describes instances where CSOs working on postconflict peace building in Cote d'Ivoire, Guinea-Bissau, Liberia and Sierra Leone "align themselves with warring factions and assume political positions in the conflicts" (p. 28).

Fundamentally, as the state has shrunk, civil society has expanded. While state actors continue to be managed, monitored and evaluated by development partners, CSOs (including traditional rulers) have creative access to new forms of aid and development partnerships. Social cohesion circumscribed by moral consciousness lies at the heart of CSO structures, but the reality is more akin to the neopatrimonialism of traditional state actors. Conceptually, this has implications on the dominance of neopatrimonialism as the central divisive factor in ethnic and social relations. There still exists the manipulation of citizens for various political interests that merge with or diverge from nation building and development. However the identities of the manipulators have changed. The big men and political elite of old co-exist with big women, small boys and girls and poor people in a concrete, as well as metaphorical, sense. The life stories and motivations of these new political actors require as much critical study and analysis as their predecessors.

13.6 Conclusions

The central argument that has emerged from the interdisciplinary research on ethnic diversity and development is that it is not ethnic diversity per se that undermines development but the manipulation of ethnic diversity by powerful political actors through neopatrimonialism (Berman, 2012; Lonsdale, 2012). Historians and anthropologists assert that some of the economics and political science models are limited because they only focus on the social and economic outcomes of neopatrimonialism and they ignore the complex negotiation of different categories of ethnicity by heterogeneous social actors within a broader moral economy. In their view, the dynamics of social conflict and cohesion are better understood if systematic analysis is conducted on the dynamic relationships between state actors (political elites or big men) and ordinary citizens within broader evolving moral economies.

Our review of the evidence from these fields and external studies on African development has yielded three insights. First, ethnicity plays a role in national and social development, but it has limits for at least three reasons. Ethnicity is a complex, dynamic and situational social category that is made psychologically active by communities with multiple identities. Second, ethnicity or ethnic membership mediates social and political processes through co-existing social categories like gender, religion and socioeconomic status. We drew attention to social identity theories and the notion of polytaxis (Elwert, 1995), which highlight the role of psychological processes in the everyday use of ethnicity and other social identities, within and between groups. Third, ethnicity is restructured through broader sociocultural processes. In short, ethnicity and social development are mutually constitutive.

The second insight is that while social cohesion is crucial to national development, targeting ethnic communities as the primary recipients of cohesion projects is problematic. Cohesion in both traditional and contemporary formations can be a double-edged sword and must be understood as operating at different levels of social organisation and requiring careful management by disparate actors within and beyond the state. Social cohesion has been operationalised using Putnam's notion of social capital and its conceptual offshoots of bonding, bridging and linking capital. Bridging and linking capital are reported to be critical to the success of social cohesion projects and the ideological intent, technical process and legitimacy of the "social engineers" (Vervisch & Titeca, 2010) are key mediating factors.

The third insight is that meaning saturation may have been reached on theorising the role and limits of ethnicity in African development, as critics of the neopatrimonialism discourse suggest. Future research has to draw on, but move beyond, two current areas of consensus. First, as economists argue, a focus on ethnicity as an indicator of social diversity and social distance rather than the cause is likely to yield better insights into the mechanics between ethnicity, ethnic diversity and development. Second, as the historians and anthropologists argue it may not be ethnic diversity per se that undermines development but the manipulation of ethnic diversity by powerful political actors through neopatrimonialism. Both arguments incorporate the recognition that ethnicity, ethnic diversity and ethnic membership operate within a broader dynamic moral economy characterised by polytactic processes. For example, the argument that political actors manipulate ethnic diversity for private gains accommodates the possibility that political actors and citizens are subjected to the evolving norms of a moral economy operating within heterogeneous social structures. Crucially, as we argued, the mutual interaction and mutual constitution of social identities (including ethnic identities) and sociocultural structures lead to the construction of new identities, social relations and sociopolitical structures. We highlighted the changing features of political actors: women, youth, the urban poor and Africa's diaspora community have become major partners of development. We argued that what is required is a shift beyond the dominant conceptual and methodological focus on undifferentiated elites and big men and their manipulative vertical relationships with "primordial" ethnic communities. Future research has to be informed by in-depth nuanced study of dynamic communities that are shaping Africa's present and are likely to remain crucial to its future.

References

Abrams, D., and Hogg, M. A. (eds.). 1990. *Social Identity Theory: Constructive and Critical Advances*. New York: Springer-Verlag.

African Development Bank. 2013a. Inclusive growth. Retrieved from http://www.afdb.org/en/blogs/afdb-championing-inclusive-growth-across-africa/about-us/. Accessed 22 April 2013.

2013b. Urbanization in Africa. Retrieved from www.afdb.org/en/blogs/afdb-championing-inclusive-growth-across-africa/post/urbanization-in-africa-10143/. Accessed 22 April 2013.

Armstrong, A. 2011. *Sakawa' Rumours: Occult Internet Fraud and Ghanaian Identity (Working Paper No. 08/2011)*. London: University College London, Department of Anthropology.

Aryeetey, E., and Ackah, C. 2011. The global financial crisis and African economies: Impact and transmission channels. *African Development Review*. 23(4): 404–420.

Aryeetey, E., and de-Graft Aikins, A. 2013. Ethnicity, social development and wellbeing in sub-Saharan Africa: A conceptual review. In Agyemang, C., Airhenbuwa, C., and de-Graft Aikins, A. (eds.), *Ethnicity:*

Theories, International Perspectives and Challenges. New York: Nova Science Publishers, pp. 133–148.

Bah, A .B. 2010. Democracy and civil war: Citizenship and peacemaking in Cote d'Ivoire. *African Affairs*, 109(437): 597–615.

Bangura, Y. 2006. 'Ethnic inequalities in the public sector: A comparative analysis. *Development and Change*. 37(2): 299–328.

Bates, R. H., Coatsworth, J., and Williamson, J. 2007. Lost decades: Lessons from post-independence Latin America for post-independence Africa. *Journal of Economic History*. 67(4): 917–943.

Berman, B. J. 2012. Ethnic politics, economic reform and democratisation in Africa. In Hino, H., Londsale, J., Ranis., G., and Stewart, F. (eds.), *Ethnic Diversity and Economic Instability in Africa. Interdisciplinary Perspectives.* Cambridge: Cambridge University Press, pp. 169–201.

Biney, A. 2008. The legacy of Kwame Nkrumah in retrospect. *Journal of Pan African Studies.* 2(3): 129–159.

Bratton, M. 1994. Civil Society and political transition in Africa. *Institute for Development Research (IDR) Reports.* 11(6): 1–21.

2013. Briefing: Citizens and cell phones in Africa. *African Affairs.* 112 (447): 304–319.

Bratton, M., Mattes, R., and Gyimah-Boadi, E. 2006. *Public Opinion, Democracy and Market Reform in Africa.* Cambridge: Cambridge University Press.

Brinkerhoff, D. W. 2005. Rebuilding governance in failed states and post-conflict societies: Core concepts and cross-cutting themes. *Public Administration and Development: The International Journal of Management Research and Practice.* 25(1): 3–14.

Brown, W. 2013. Sovereignty matters: Africa, donors, and the aid relationship. *African Affairs.* 112(447): 262–282.

Brown, G. K., and Langer, A. 2012. The concept of ethnicity: strengths and limitations for quantitative analysis. In Hino, H., Londsale, J., Ranis., G., and Stewart, F. (eds.), *Ethnic Diversity and Economic Instability in Africa. Interdisciplinary Perspectives.* Cambridge: Cambridge University Press, pp. 56–90.

Campbell, C. 2003. *Letting Them Die: Why HIV/AIDS Intervention Programmes Fail.* Bloomington: Indiana University Press.

Chipkin, I., and Ngqulunga, B. 2008. Friends and family: social cohesion in South Africa. *Journal of South African Studies.* 34(1): 61–76.

Collier, P. 2007. *The Bottom Billion. Why the Poorest Countries Are Failing and What Can Be Done about It.* Oxford: Oxford University Press.

Conceição, P., Mukherjee, S., and Nayyar, S. 2011. Impacts of the economic crisis on human development and the MDGs in Africa. *African Development Review.* 23(4): 439–460.

Davis, M. 2006. *Planet of Slums*. London: Verso.

Easterly, W., and Levine, R. 1997. Africa's Growth Tragedy: Policies and Ethnic Divisions. *Quarterly Journal of Economics*. 112(4): 1203–1250.

Ekiyor, T. 2008. The role of civil society in conflict prevention: West African experiences. United Nations Institute for Disarmament Research (UNIDIR), *Disarmament Forum: The Complex Dynamics of Small Arms in West Africa*. 4, pp. 27–34.

Elwert, G. 1995. Boundaries, cohesion and switching. On we-groups in ethnic, national and religious forms. *Bulletin de l'APAD*. 10. Retrieved from http://apad.revues.org/1111. Accessed 27 June 2012.

Gifford, P. 2004. *Ghana's New Christianity: Pentecostalism in a Globalizing African Economy*. Bloomington: Indiana University Press.

Greif, M. J., Dodoo, F. N., and Jayaraman, A. 2011. Urbanisation, poverty and sexual behaviour: The tale of five African cities. *Urban Studies*. 48(5): 947–957.

Grischow, J. D. 2008. Rural "community", chiefs and social capital: The case of Southern Ghana. *Journal of Agrarian Change*. 8(1): 64–93.

Gyimah-Boadi, E. 1997. Civil society in Africa: The good, the bad, the ugly. *Civnet Journal*. 1(1).

Handley, G., Higgins, K., Sharma, B., Bird, K., and Cammack, D. 2009. *Poverty and Poverty Reduction in Sub-Saharan Africa: An Overview of the Issues (Overseas Development Institute Working Paper No. 299)*. London: ODI.

Hino, H., Londsale, J., Ranis. G., and Stewart, F. (eds.). 2012. *Ethnic Diversity and Economic Instability in Africa: Interdisciplinary Perspectives*. Cambridge: Cambridge University Press.

Iliffe, J. 2006. *A History of the African AIDS Epidemic*. Oxford: James Currey.

Jackson, P. 2005. Chiefs, money and politicians: Rebuilding local government in post-war Sierra Leone. *Public Administration and Development: The International Journal of Management Research and Practice*. 25(1): 49–58.

Kamat, S. 2004. The privatization of public interest: Theorizing NGO discourse in a neoliberal era. *Review of International Political Economy*. 11(1): 155–176.

Kayode-Anglade, S., and Nana Spio-Garbrah, N. 2012. Diaspora bonds: Some lessons for African countries. *AfDB Africa Economic Brief*. 3(13): 1–13.ief Economist Complex

Kyobutungi, C., Ziraba, A. K., Ezeh, A., and Ye, Y. 2008. The burden of disease profiles of residents in Nairobi slums: Results from a demographic surveillance system. *Population Health Metrics*. 6(1): 1–8.

Lassiter, J. E. 2000. African culture and personality: Bad social science, effective social activism, or a call to reinvent ethnology? *African Studies*

Quarterly. 3(1). Retrieved from www.africa.ufl.edu/asq/v3/v3i3a1.pdf. Accessed 24 April 2013.

Lentz, C. 1995. Tribalism' and ethnicity in Africa. A review of four decades of Anglophone research. *Cah. Sci. Hum.* 31(2): 303–328.

Lonsdale, J. 2012. Ethnic patriotism and markets in African history. In Hino, H., Londsale, J., Ranis., G., and Stewart, F. (eds.), *Ethnic Diversity and Economic Instability in Africa. Interdisciplinary Perspectives.* Cambridge: Cambridge University Press, pp. 19–55.

Low-Beer, D., and Stoneburner, R. L. 2003. Behaviour and communication change in reducing HIV: Is Uganda unique?' *African Journal of AIDS Research.* 2(1): 9–21.

McCauley, J. F. 2012. Africa's new big man rule? Pentecostalism and patronage in Ghana. *African Affairs.* 112(446): 1–21.

McNeil, M., and Mumvuma, T. 2006. Demanding Good Governance: A Stocktaking of Social Accountability Initiatives by Civil Society in Anglophone Africa (Report No. 38919, Community Empowerment and Social Inclusion Learning Programme*).* Washington, DC: World Bank Institute.

De Medeiros, L. S. 2007. Social movements and the experience of market-led agrarian reform in Brazil. *Third World Quarterly.* 28(8): 1501–1518.

Mkandawire, T. 2002. Incentives, governance, and capacity development in Africa. *African Issues.* 30(1): 15–20.

2011. Running while others walk: Knowledge and the challenge of Africa's development. *Africa Development.* 36(2): 1–36.

Mohan, G., and Lampert, B. 2013. Negotiating China: Reinserting African agency into China-Africa relations. *African Affairs.* 112(446): 92–110.

Moscovici, S., and Duveen, G. 2000. *Social Representations: Explorations in Social Psychology.* New York: New York University Press.

Nguyen, V. 2010. *The Republic of Therapy: Triage and Sovereignty in West Africa's Time of AIDS.* Durham, NC, and London: Duke University Press.

Patinkin, J. 2013. *The Rockefeller Foundation's Informal City Dialogues: The Illegal, Dangerous, Unreliable Electrical System That Everyone Supports.* Retrieved from http://nextcity.org/informalcity/entry/the-illegal-dangerousunreliable-electrical-system-that-everyone-supports. Accessed 18 September 2018.

Quayson, A. 2010. Kòbòlò Poetics: African urban scripts and Readerships. *New Literary History.* 41(1): 413–438.

Ranger, T. 1993. The Invention of tradition revisited: The case of colonial Africa. In Ranger, T., and Vaughan, O. (eds.), *Legitimacy and the State in Twentieth-Century Africa. St Antony's/Macmillan Series.* London: Palgrave Macmillan.

Routley, L. 2011. NGOs and the formation of the public: Grey practices and accountability. *African Affairs.* 111(442): 116 – 134.

Shaw, T. M. 1986. Ethnicity as the resilient paradigm for Africa: From the 1960s to the 1980s. *Development and Change.* 17(4): 587–605.

Thomson, S. 2011. Whispering truth to power: The everyday resistance of Rwandan peasants to post-genocide reconciliation. *African Affairs.* 110 (440): 439–456.

Titeca, K., and de Herdt, T. 2011. Real governance beyond the 'failed state': Negotiating education in the Democratic Republic of Congo. *African Affairs.* 110(439): 213–232.

Trinitapoli, J., and Weinreb, A. 2012. *Religion and AIDS in Africa.* Oxford: Oxford University Press.

Turner, J. C., and Oakes, P.J . 1986. The significance of the social identity concept for social psychology with reference to individualism, interactionism and social influence. *British Journal of Social Psychology.* 25(3): 237–252.

UNFPA. 2007. *State of the World Population, 2007. Unleashing the Potential of Urban Growth.* Retrieved from www.unfpa.org/swp/2007/eng lish/introduction.html. Accessed 14 July 2012.

2011. *State of World Population, 2011. People and Possibilities in a World of 7 Billion.* Retrieved from www.unfpa.org/publications/state-world-population-2011. Accessed 14 July 2012.

Vervisch, T., and Titeca, K. 2010. Bridging community associations in post-conflict Burundi: the difficult merging of social capital endowments and new "institutional settings". *Journal of Modern African Studies.* 48(3): 485–511.

Young, M. C. 2004. *Revisiting Nationalism and Ethnicity in Africa.* James S. Coleman Memorial Lecture Series, UCLA, 2004. Retrieved from http://escholarship.org/uc/item/28h0r4sr. Accessed 27 June 2012.

14 | From Divided Pasts to Cohesive Futures in Africa

Conclusions and Policy Recommendations

ARNIM LANGER AND JOHN LONSDALE

Most African countries have experienced rapid growth since the turn of the century, after a long period of stagnation, although growth has more recently slowed in all but a few. Much of this volatility is clearly due to changing global conditions. How far social conflict, caused by poverty and inequality, but also fanned by many of the continent's leaders in their manipulation of ethnic differences, is also responsible is a question that African citizens have long asked, as have scholars from Africa and elsewhere.

This book asks a different question. It is this: how far can governments in countries that continue to face the challenges of ethnic diversity, inequality and poverty pursue policies and their citizens adopt practices that encourage greater social cohesion, with all its expected benefits of peace, trust and well-being?

In offering possible answers to this question, this book differs from others in several important ways:

1. We do not propose the mere management of ethnic (and other) differences but something more: the achievement of greater social cohesion by social policies and institutional practices that foster popular trust in a common citizenship.
2. In this, therefore we go further than such classic studies of how to manage ethnic and other forms of diversity as were offered by Arend Lijphart (1977) or Donald Rothchild (1997).
   - These analyses assumed that social identities, ethnic membership especially, tended to be exclusive and perennial. We, in contrast, are more conscious of their historical volatility and how they may be (re)imagined in the present day, especially when facing the need, or opportunity, to redefine relations with state power.
   - Rothchild (1997) and Lijphart (1977) concentrated on the limits of negotiation between rather rigid corporate elites. We suggest,

instead, how new relations within and between different institutional and legal structures – with respect to land tenure, education, government devolution, economic redistribution and so on – might soften the corporate identities that Lijphart (1977) and Rothchild (1997) thought could not be changed and could therefore only be managed. Moreover, we believe that social cohesion requires social inclusion, which means bringing everyone, not just their elites, into the project of imagining and then creating a cohesive society.

– In summary, the management of a divided status quo is fundamentally different from our tentative prescriptions for diluting division, in search of a more commonly shared sense of citizenship.

3. We also disagree with classic Afro-pessimists like Robert Kaplan (2000) or Paul Collier (2007, 2009). These writers focus on clearly failed cases – on countries suffering chronic civil war such as South Sudan or the Democratic Republic of Congo, or on land-locked small states like Niger and Chad, or on those countries supposedly cursed by their wealth in oil or rare minerals, more than usually subject to the temptations of rent-seeking and corrupt deals. Kaplan (2000) regards cultural difference as immutable, while Collier (2007; 2009) sees local politicians as fundamentally self-seeking and as unlikely to change except under international pressure. Neither has faith in the reform potential of internal pressure to make a regime conscious of the need for a wider legitimacy. But these local circumstances can indeed, as the case studies in Part I of our book somewhat hesitantly show, encourage policies and practices that, by reducing regional and social inequality, and possibly by devolving state power, may soften the ethnic differences that are so often sharpened by fear of exclusion from that power.

4. We are closer, therefore, to Will Kymlicka's (2001) multicultural approach: we share his optimism that societies can become cohesive without necessarily losing their several group identities, but we add an economic dimension to his essentially political project.

Moreover, this book is empirically grounded. Our case studies in Part I examine the complexity of particular situations and the broader relevance of this close situational analysis. We are fully conscious of the difficulties Africans will encounter in pursuing any of the policies that we here tentatively suggest. Our analyses of recent history tell us the obvious: there are no simple solutions.

We picture social cohesion as a triangle of social relationships. Trust between strangers, we argue, is encouraged by their sense of a shared identity within a society that is not intolerably unequal and that respects the different situational identities that people experience in the changing contexts of their lives. This positive triangle of trust, identity and equality is no abstract concept; it can only be the product of a historical process of argument and adjustment. In many African countries, its absence is more marked than its presence, thanks to histories that have deepened rather than diminished horizontal inter-ethnic inequalities and vertical intra-ethnic, social, inequality. These divisive pasts inevitably erode trust between and within ethnic groups, so weakening a sense of belonging in a larger society and hardening exclusive, often fearful, ethnic identities. It is nonetheless possible to imagine policies and processes that encourage the emergence of trust, common identity and greater equality that, so we argue, foster social cohesion. Ethnic conflict is not a given.

We illustrate this key argument in the case studies contained in Part I of our book. Chapters 1 and 2, by Lonsdale and Mustapha, on Kenya and Nigeria respectively, analyse processes that have hindered social cohesion in the past and may just possibly begin to give greater political trust in the future. Chapters 3 and 4, on Tanzania and South Africa – each contributed, as if symbolically, by a collective of multicultural authors – show how a cohesive citizenry may indeed be constructed in the first case, and deep historical divides at least mitigated in the second. Chapter 5, by Berman and Takahashi, puts these difficult but not disheartening African findings into a global perspective.

We then go on to study the obstacles to be overcome in building future social cohesion. Policies will matter, naturally, but also, perhaps less obviously, so too will the behaviour of governing institutions that, to encourage public trust, must accept that they are subject to a rule of law. To retain clarity of focus, we concentrate on a select range of subjects: the distribution of public goods and decentralisation of power, on reforms in land tenure and education, and on the always difficult politics of both group memory and institutional change. On the basis of our analysis, we conclude the following:

a) There is no inherent conflict between income equality and growth. More equal distributions, to the contrary, tend to lead to improved education, health and political outcomes 걔. Chapter 6 (Stewart) provides examples of countries associated with improved distributions as well as others with greater inequalities, both social and regional, vertical and horizontal.

b) The dispersion and decentralisation of power can, as intended, contribute to inclusive development in divided societies. Chapter 7 (Ranis) compares the case of Indonesia with examples from East Africa.

c) Land tenure reform is perhaps the most sensitive problem in sub-Saharan Africa, since it is as crucial for local identity and family subsistence as for national economic growth. Chapter 8 (Amanor) shows the possible range of policy alternatives and makes the case for customary land ownership.

d) Enduring access to good quality education, particularly for the poor and for disadvantaged ethnic and regional groups, is vital. Chapter 9 (Kramon & Posner) argues, like Chapter 7, that dispersion of power is one means to secure greater educational equality across ethnic groups and regions, with quantitative evidence from Kenya, while Chapter 10 (Kuppens and Langer) argues that what is taught by way of civic education is at least as important for cohesion as equal access to schooling.

e) Improvements in material distribution are not enough: human beings are emotional beings. Any attempt to restore the social trust of those who feel wronged must respect their memory and value their culture, particularly where past injustices are still raw, as Chapter 11 (Rassool) shows for South Africa's Cape Town.

f) None of our suggested recommendations will be easy to implement. Vested interests and institutional inertia stand in the way of political inclusion and social cohesion. Chapter 12 (Mustapha) examines the political conflicts that must be expected.

g) Our authors are optimistic that policies designed to help create trust, greater equality, and a sense of national identity, will nonetheless become more feasible as the growth of mega-cities, Pentecostalism and the influence of returnees from overseas diaspora may make the elite manipulation of ethnic belonging more difficult. Chapter 13 (Aryeety and Aikins) argues this by lifting the analysis beyond issues of ethnicity to focus on the often more pressing cross-cutting, situational, but also nationwide identities that disadvantage women, the youth, and the poor, in particular.

What help, if any, comparative history from other continents has to offer Africa is a question we asked in our Introduction. More cohesive societies, with more social and political trust, do exist elsewhere – although recent history in Europe and America suggests that their comparative advantage is by no means assured. And any longer global history also suggests there is no obvious model of social cohesion for African politicians to study. Lessons from outside Africa are therefore tentative. One would not, for instance, wish a future for Africa that mirrored the centuries of dynastic warfare that dug the social and institutional foundations for Europe's nation-states, nor their international wars that rained blood and destruction across the world, not least on Africa. Nor, to recall other histories of large-scale polity-making, does sub-Saharan Africa have its own long history of state-building that can compare with the successive Chinese dynasties, the Mughals in India, or the Muslim caliphates of West Asia (the Middle East not seen from Europe) and Mediterranean Africa.

Even if one forgets the European wars of the twentieth century (and before), one should remember that European nation-building policies were often seen as remedies for the social conflicts caused by industrialisation and urbanisation. Africa has experienced mass urbanisation but not the industrialisation that might create a national economy and class structure with the cohesively disputatious potential that was the European experience. African statesmen and women will have to act to promote cohesion, unprompted by the historical processes that have forced remedial action on governments elsewhere.

If Africa lacks the cohesive asset of national economies, most of its states being largely primary producers with few upstream or downstream connections, then, equally, industrialising Europe did not have to contend with what Africa has experienced, the most rapid population growth that the world has ever known, perhaps the greatest challenge to social cohesion anywhere. Population growth that was almost as rapid in nineteenth-century China, after all, brought down the last imperial dynasty, the Qing, before Western powers tried to pick up the most attractive pieces. This reinforces the argument of Chapter 13, that governments must focus increasingly on the needs of the poor and of women, but perhaps especially on the socioeconomic integration of the young, whose energies otherwise have such potential for disruption.

Because sub-Saharan Africa lacks many of Europe or Asia's historic assets in the construction of polity and economy, we conclude by offering our recommendations with a due sense of their difficulty. Africa knows historical, economic and demographic conditions not found anywhere else in the world. Let nobody suppose that its leaders face anything other than a most daunting task. Any improvement in social cohesion can enlarge freedoms and self-respect only by allowing sufficient room for the multi-ethnic traditions of civility inherited from the past. Cohesion otherwise means oppression, not the expansion of the trust that appears to be so often lacking in Africa. Decentralised state powers that reduce the fear of exclusion from presidential favour may well be part of the answer. But how far devolved governments will or can agree to a greater equality of regional opportunity is clearly a question. Contradictions of self-interest and identity abound. We do not doubt that any increase in trust, in social cohesion, in equality of citizenship, in creative national patriotism, will be hard won.

References

Collier, P. 2007. *The Bottom Billion: Why the Poorest Countries Are Failing and What Can Be Done about It*. Oxford: Oxford University Press.

2009. *Wars, Guns, and Votes: Democracy in Dangerous Places*. New York: Harper Collins.

Kaplan, R. D. 2000. *The Coming Anarchy: Shattering the Dreams of the Post-Cold War*. New York: Random House.

Kymlicka, W. 2001. *Politics in the Vernacular: Nationalism, Multiculturalism and Citizenship*. Oxford: Oxford University Press.

Lijphart, A. 1977. *Democracy in Plural Societies: A Comparative Exploration*. New Haven, CT: Yale University Press.

Rothchild, D. 1997. *Managing Ethnic Conflict in Africa: Pressures and Incentives for Co-operation*. Washington, DC: Brookings Institution Press.

Index